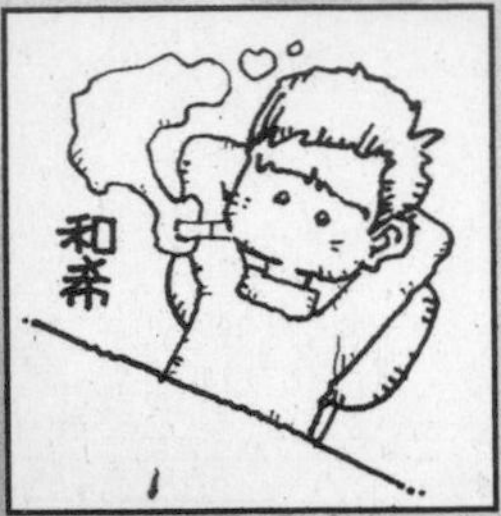
和希

KAZUKI TAKAHASHI

LATELY I'VE BEEN LEARNING HOW TO DRAW PICTURES WITH A COMPUTER. I'VE NEVER HAD A HEAD FOR DIGITAL THINGS, SO I'VE BEEN HAVING LOTS OF TROUBLE, BUT IT'S STILL FUN. IF YOU GET THE CHANCE TO TAKE A LOOK AT THEM, PLEASE DO!

Artist/author Kazuki Takahashi first tried to break into the manga business in 1982, but success eluded him until *Yu-Gi-Oh!* debuted in the Japanese *Weekly Shonen Jump* magazine in 1996. *Yu-Gi-Oh!*'s themes of friendship and fighting, together with Takahashi's weird and imaginative monsters, soon became enormously successful, spawning a real-world card game, video games and four anime series (two Japanese *Yu-Gi-Oh!* series, *Yu-Gi-Oh! GX* and *Yu-Gi-Oh! 5D's*). A lifelong gamer, Takahashi enjoys shogi (Japanese chess), mahjong, card games and tabletop RPGs, among other games.

AKIRA ITO

JUST A LITTLE WHILE INTO THE NEW YEAR, I GOT SICK AND WAS HOSPITALIZED FOR ABOUT THREE WEEKS. I CAUSED A LOT OF TROUBLE AND WORRY FOR THE READERS, MR. TAKAHASHI AND EVERYBODY INVOLVED IN THIS PROJECT. I NEVER THOUGHT I'D BE RESPONSIBLE FOR A "SERIES SUSPENDED DUE TO CREATOR'S SUDDEN ILLNESS" NOTICE. THAT WAS A SHOCK.

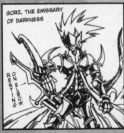

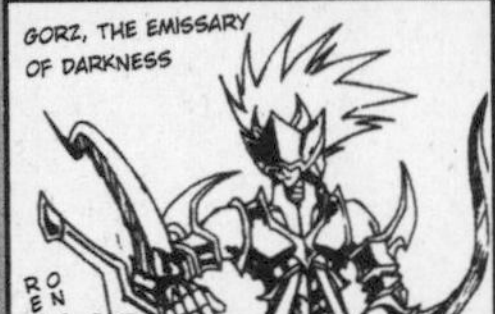
GORZ, THE EMISSARY OF DARKNESS
RESTING ON ELBOW

Akira Ito worked on the original *Yu-Gi-Oh!* manga as an assistant to Kazuki Takahashi. He also assisted in the creation of *Yu-Gi-Oh! GX*. *Yu-Gi-Oh! R* is his first work as lead creator.

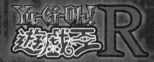

Volume 3
SHONEN JUMP Manga Edition

Original Concept/Supervised by **KAZUKI TAKAHASHI**
Story and Art by **AKIRA ITO**

Translation & English Adaptation **KINAMI WATABE & IAN REID, HC LANGUAGE SOLUTIONS**
Touch-up Art & Lettering **ERIC ERBES**
Cover Design **CAROLINA UGALDE**
Interior Design **DANIEL PORTER**
Editor **JASON THOMPSON**

VP, Production **ALVIN LU**
VP, Sales & Product Marketing **GONZALO FERREYRA**
VP, Creative **LINDA ESPINOSA**
Publisher **HYOE NARITA**

Printed in the U.S.A.

Published by VIZ Media, LLC
P.O. Box 77010
San Francisco, CA 94107

10 9 8 7 6 5 4 3 2 1
First printing, February 2010

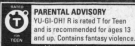

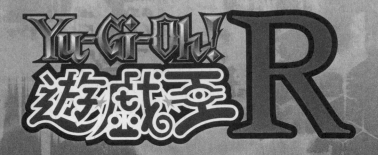

VOLUME 3
THE PERFECT DUEL!!

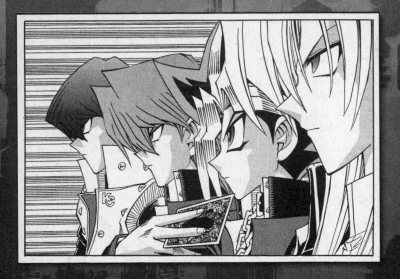

Original Concept/Supervised by **KAZUKI TAKAHASHI**

CAST & STORY

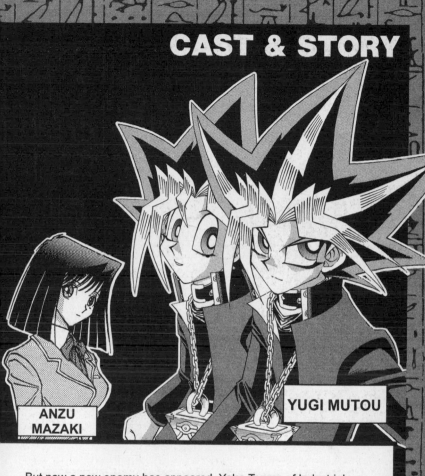

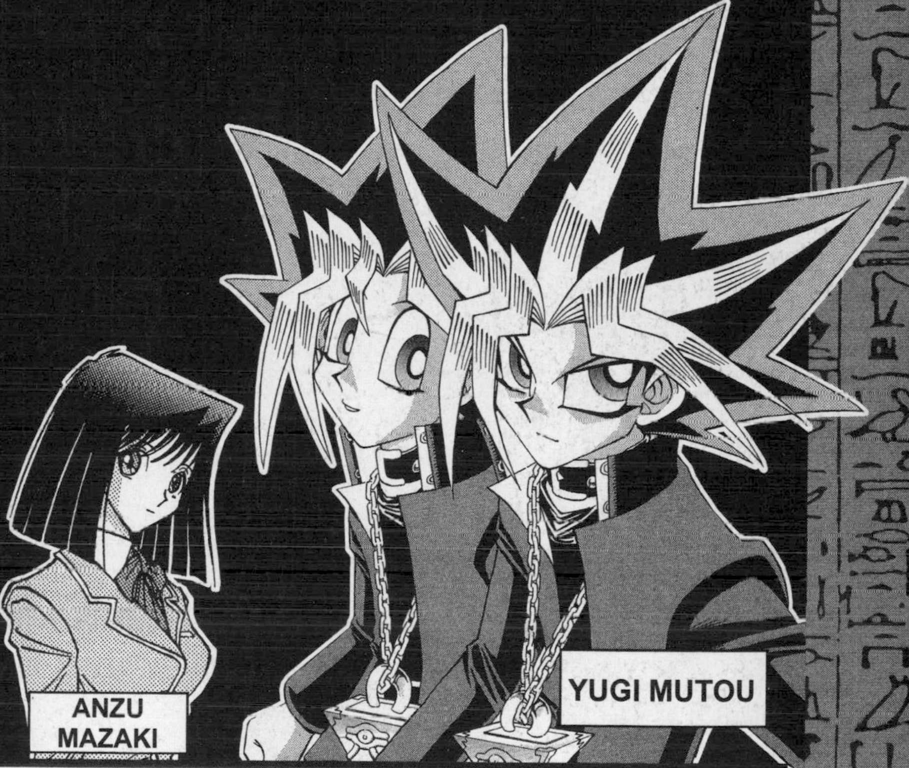
YUGI MUTOU
ANZU MAZAKI

But now a new enemy has appeared. Yako Tenma of Industrial Illusions, Pegasus's company, has made a hostile takeover of Kaiba Corporation and challenged Yugi to a duel. To ensure Yugi's participation, he has kidnapped Yugi's friend Anzu, intending to use her for the diabolical R.A. Project…resurrecting Pegasus's spirit in Anzu's body! To rescue their friend, Yugi and his friends rush to the Kaiba Corporation skyscraper. Inside, they are attacked by the "Card Professors," Tenma's duelist henchmen. But Gekko Tenma, Yako's brother, has joined forces with Yugi to stop his brother's madness…

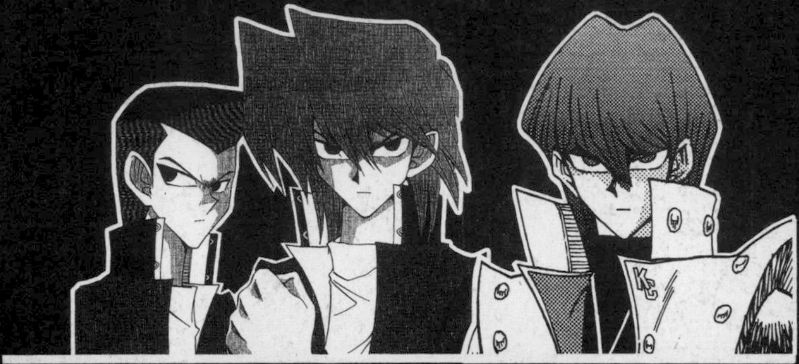

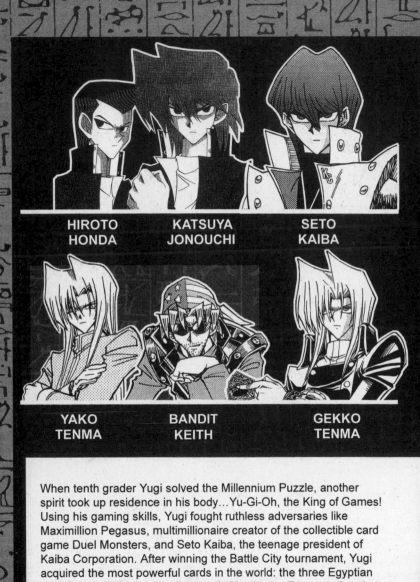

HIROTO HONDA

KATSUYA JONOUCHI

SETO KAIBA

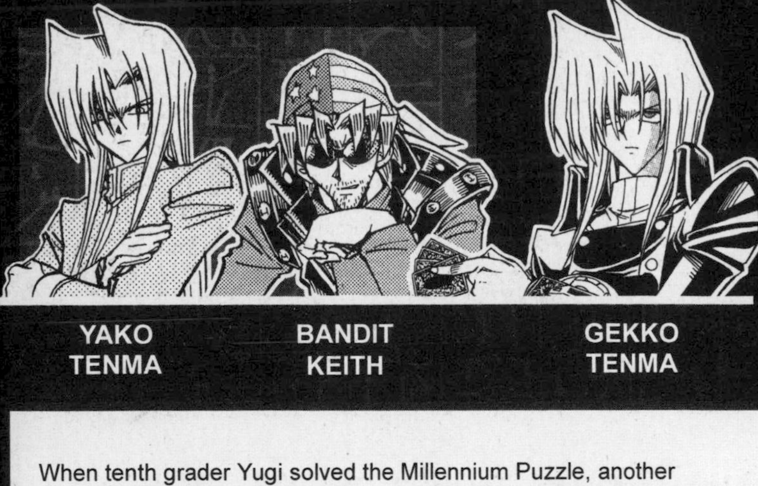

YAKO TENMA

BANDIT KEITH

GEKKO TENMA

When tenth grader Yugi solved the Millennium Puzzle, another spirit took up residence in his body…Yu-Gi-Oh, the King of Games! Using his gaming skills, Yugi fought ruthless adversaries like Maximillion Pegasus, multimillionaire creator of the collectible card game Duel Monsters, and Seto Kaiba, the teenage president of Kaiba Corporation. After winning the Battle City tournament, Yugi acquired the most powerful cards in the world: the three Egyptian God Cards "Slifer the Sky Dragon," "Obelisk the Tormentor" and "The Winged Dragon of Ra", which were created by Pegasus based on a mysterious ancient Egyptian card game.

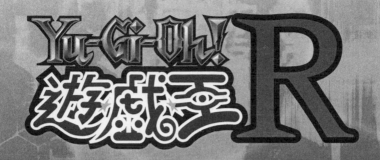

VOLUME 3
THE PERFECT DUEL!!

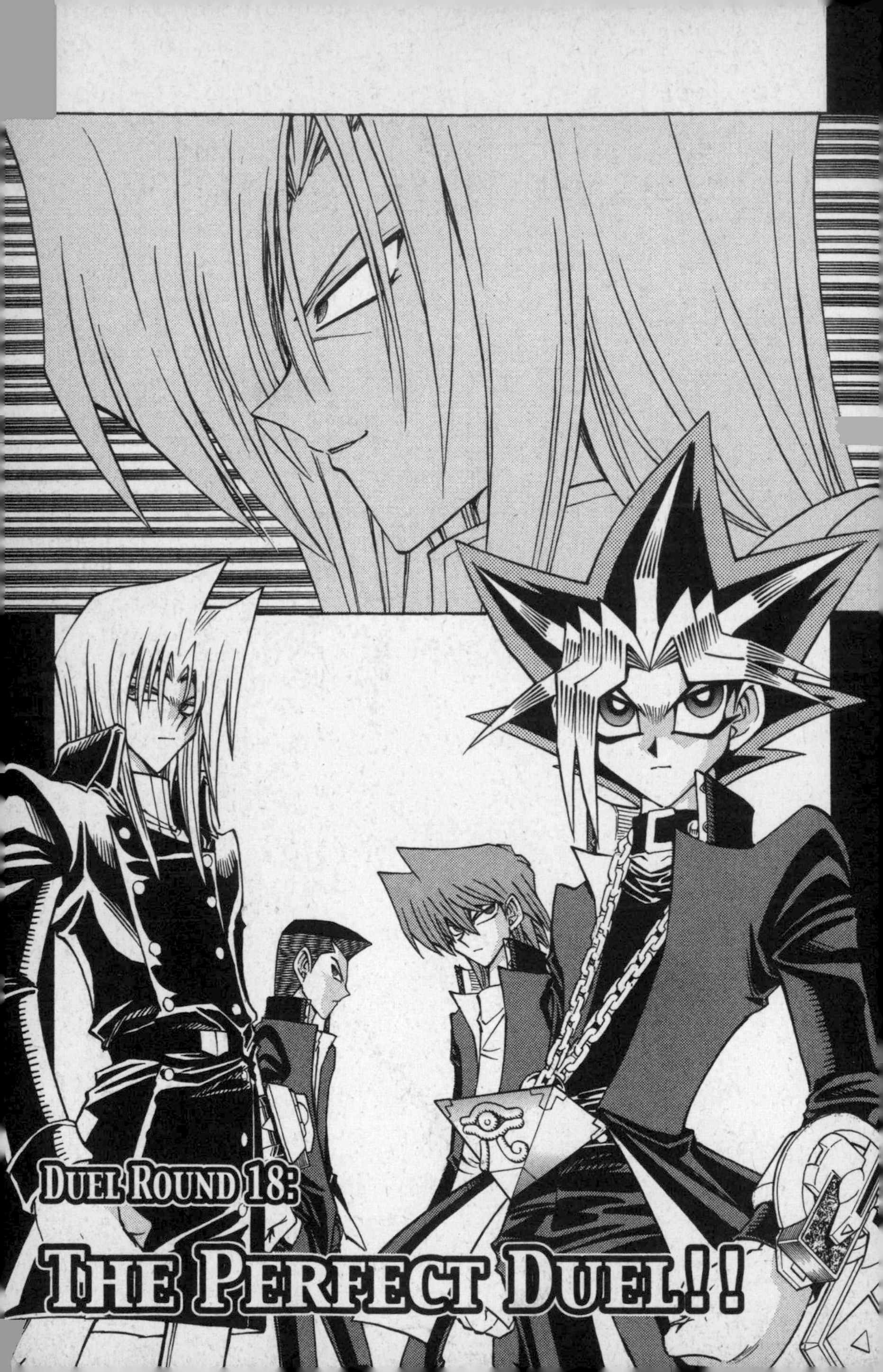
DUEL ROUND 18:
THE PERFECT DUEL!!

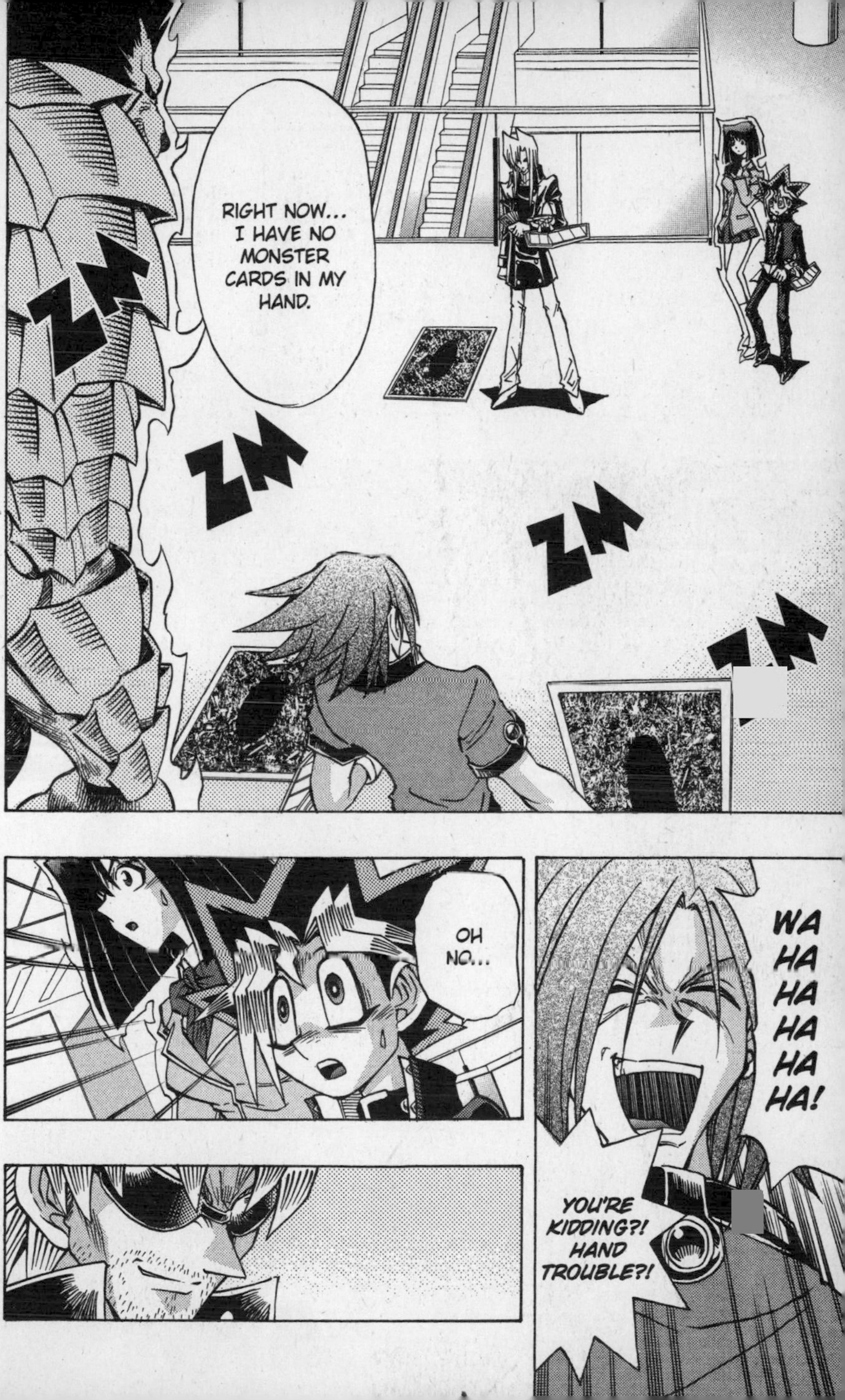
RIGHT NOW... I HAVE NO MONSTER CARDS IN MY HAND.
ZM
ZM
ZM
ZM
WA HA HA HA HA HA!
YOU'RE KIDDING?! HAND TROUBLE?!
OH NO...

READ THIS WAY

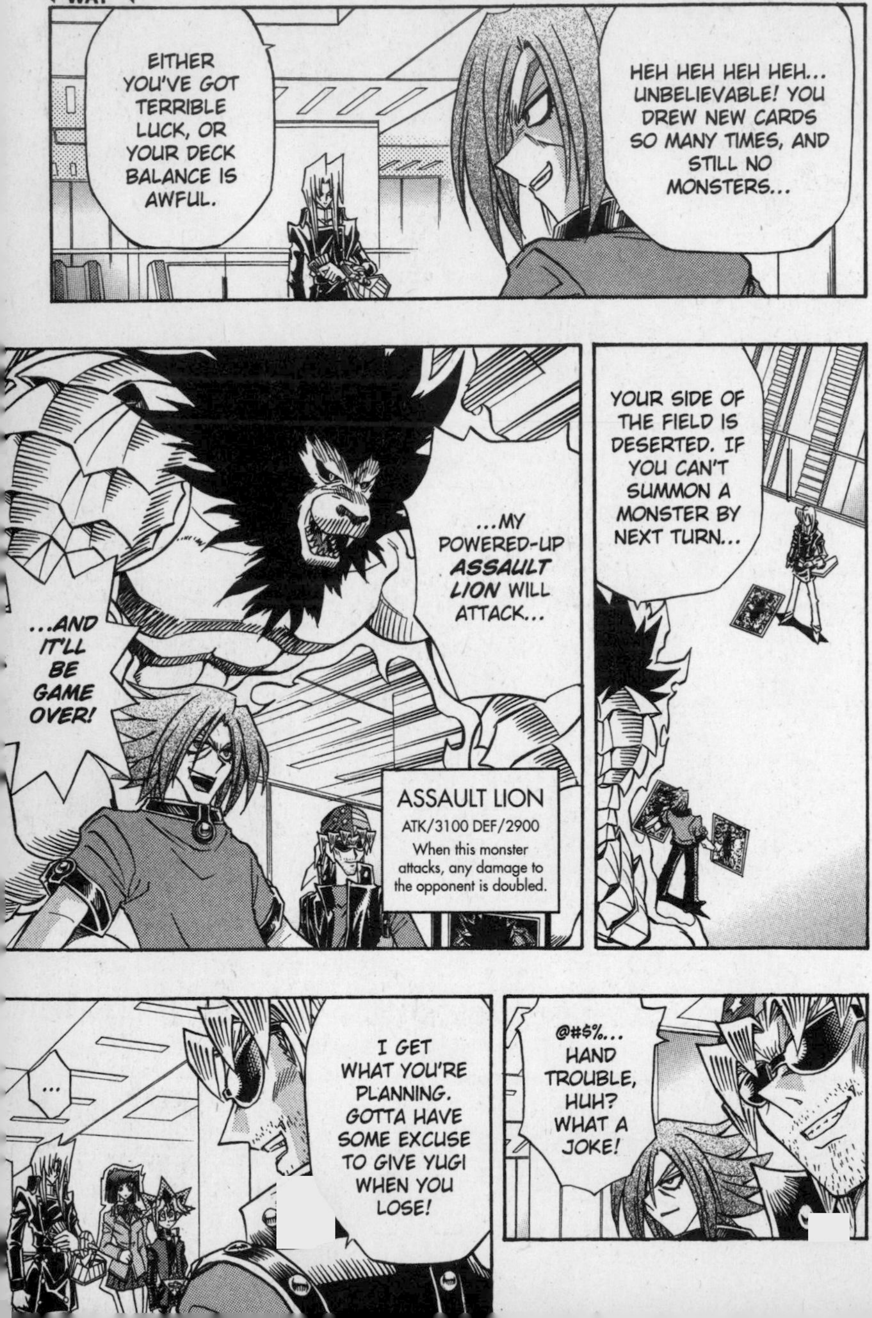
HEH HEH HEH HEH... UNBELIEVABLE! YOU DREW NEW CARDS SO MANY TIMES, AND STILL NO MONSTERS...
EITHER YOU'VE GOT TERRIBLE LUCK, OR YOUR DECK BALANCE IS AWFUL.
YOUR SIDE OF THE FIELD IS DESERTED. IF YOU CAN'T SUMMON A MONSTER BY NEXT TURN...
...MY POWERED-UP ASSAULT LION WILL ATTACK...
...AND IT'LL BE GAME OVER!
ASSAULT LION
ATK/3100 DEF/2900
When this monster attacks, any damage to the opponent is doubled.
@#$%... HAND TROUBLE, HUH? WHAT A JOKE!
I GET WHAT YOU'RE PLANNING. GOTTA HAVE SOME EXCUSE TO GIVE YUGI WHEN YOU LOSE!
...

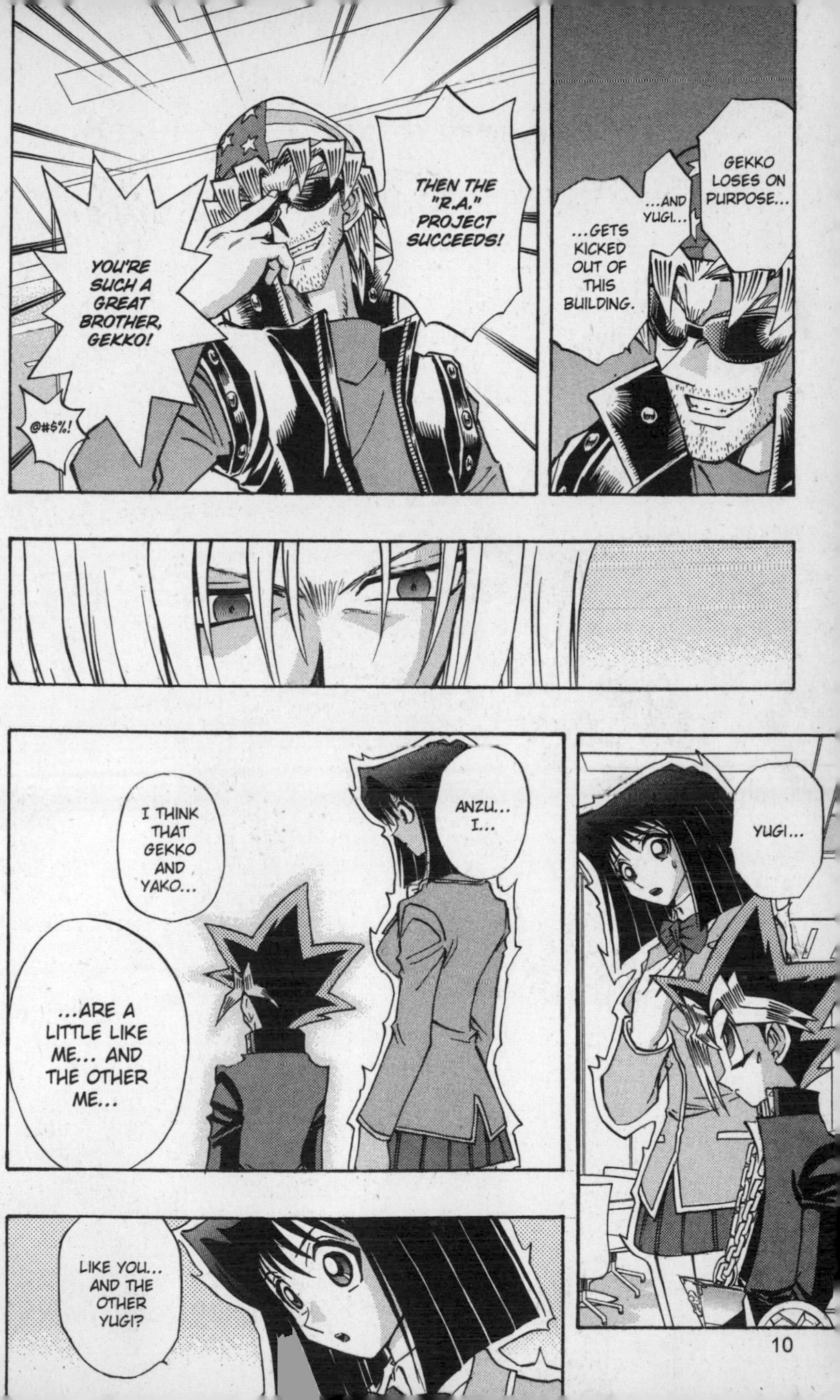
GEKKO LOSES ON PURPOSE...
...AND YUGI...
...GETS KICKED OUT OF THIS BUILDING.
THEN THE "R.A." PROJECT SUCCEEDS!
YOU'RE SUCH A GREAT BROTHER, GEKKO!
@#$%!
YUGI...
ANZU... I...
I THINK THAT GEKKO AND YAKO...
...ARE A LITTLE LIKE ME... AND THE OTHER ME...
LIKE YOU... AND THE OTHER YUGI?

READ THIS WAY

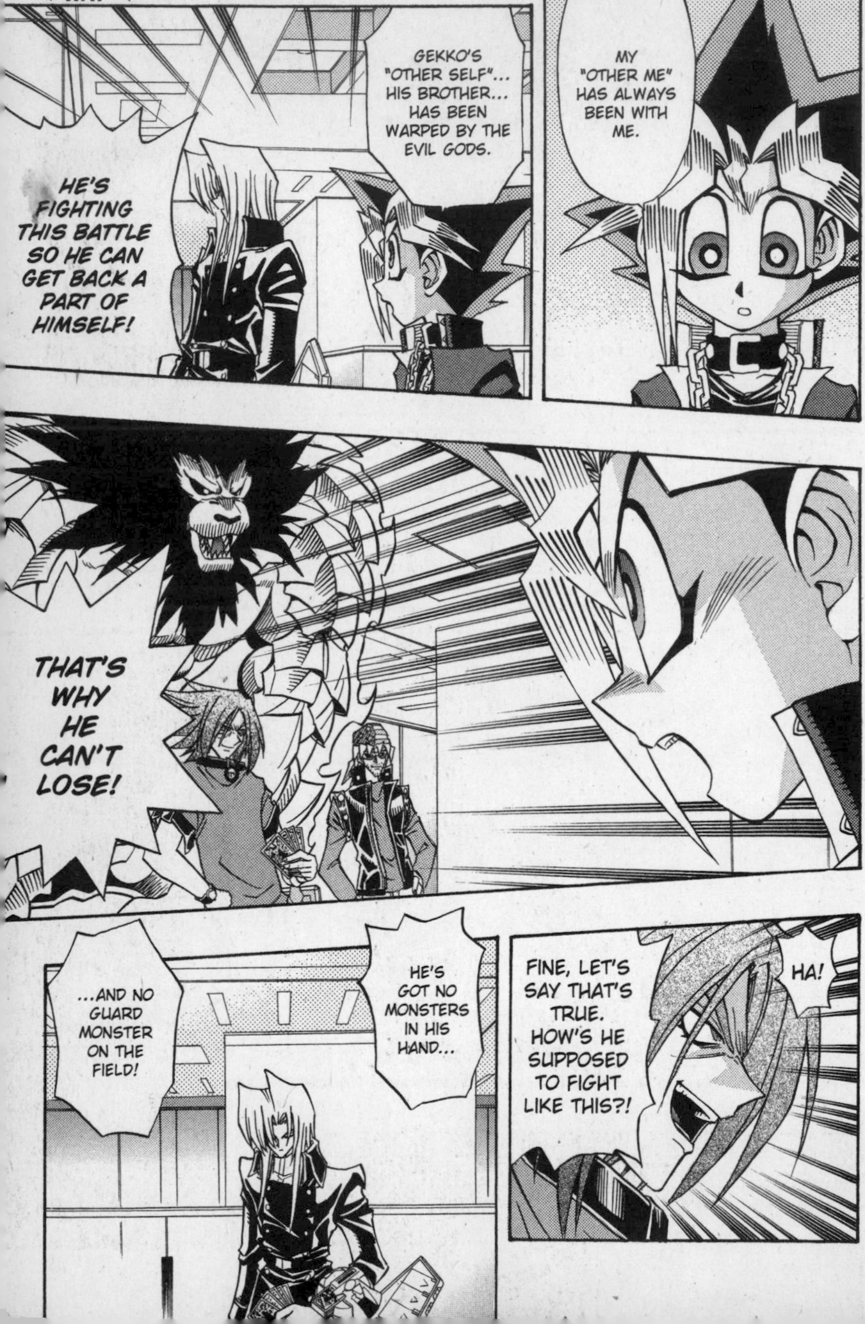
MY "OTHER ME" HAS ALWAYS BEEN WITH ME.
GEKKO'S "OTHER SELF"... HIS BROTHER... HAS BEEN WARPED BY THE EVIL GODS.
HE'S FIGHTING THIS BATTLE SO HE CAN GET BACK A PART OF HIMSELF!
THAT'S WHY HE CAN'T LOSE!
HA!
FINE, LET'S SAY THAT'S TRUE. HOW'S HE SUPPOSED TO FIGHT LIKE THIS?!
HE'S GOT NO MONSTERS IN HIS HAND...
...AND NO GUARD MONSTER ON THE FIELD!

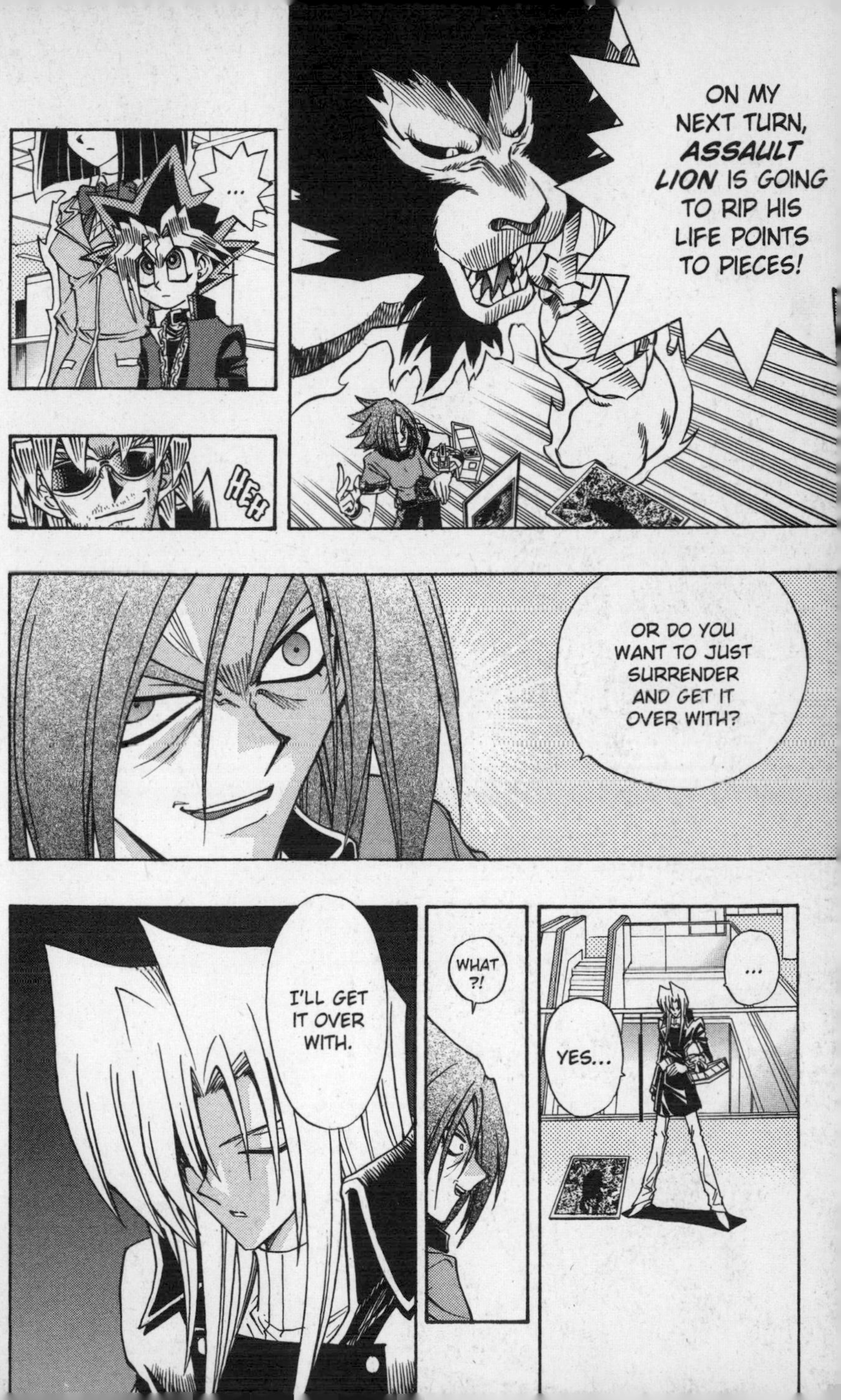
ON MY NEXT TURN, ASSAULT LION IS GOING TO RIP HIS LIFE POINTS TO PIECES!
...
HEH
OR DO YOU WANT TO JUST SURRENDER AND GET IT OVER WITH?
...
YES...
WHAT ?!
I'LL GET IT OVER WITH.

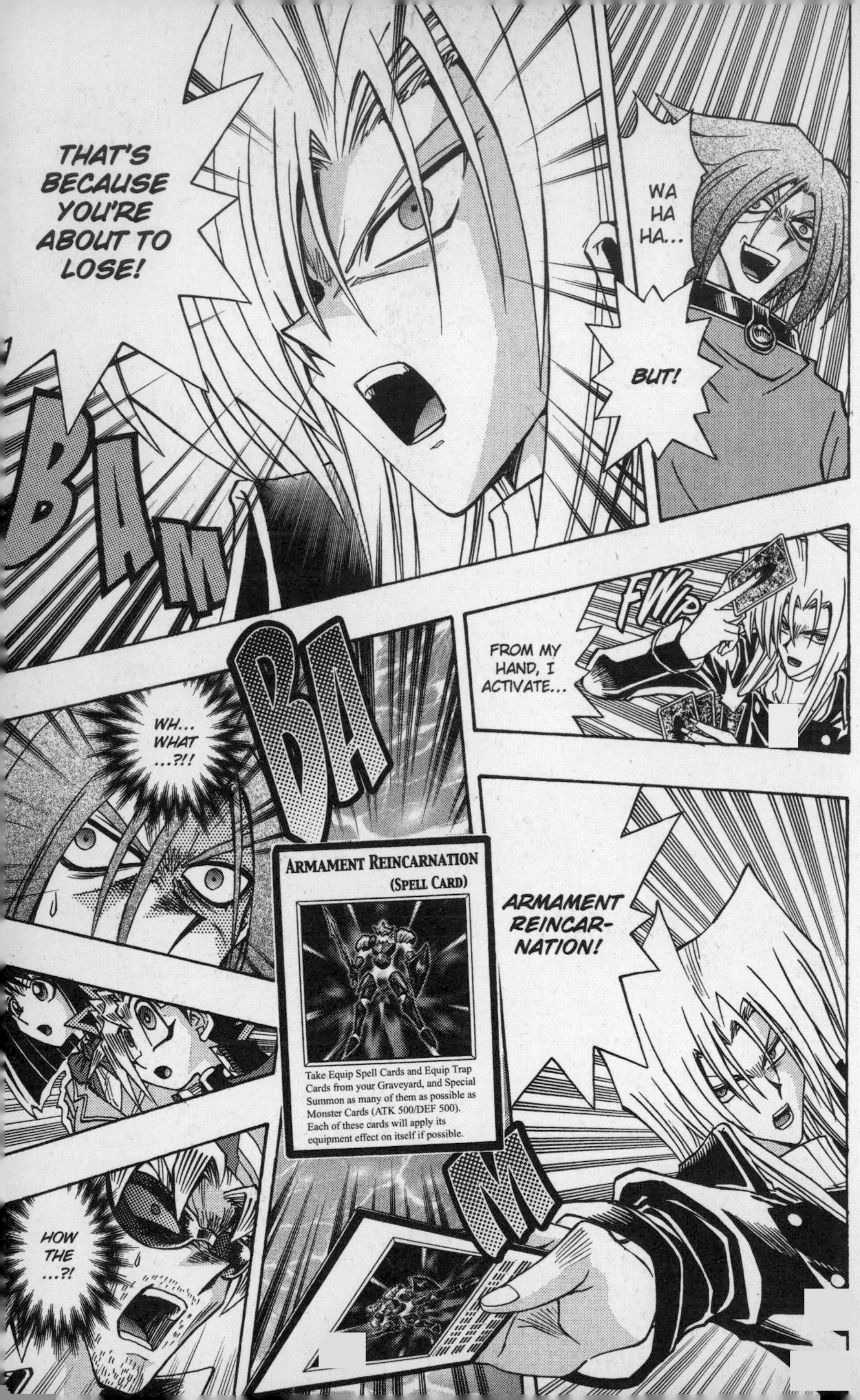

WA HA HA...
BUT!
THAT'S BECAUSE YOU'RE ABOUT TO LOSE!
BAM
FWIP
FROM MY HAND, I ACTIVATE...
ARMAMENT REINCARNATION!
ARMAMENT REINCARNATION
(SPELL CARD)
Take Equip Spell Cards and Equip Trap Cards from your Graveyard, and Special Summon as many of them as possible as Monster Cards (ATK 500/DEF 500). Each of these cards will apply its equipment effect on itself if possible.
BAM
WH... WHAT ...?!!
HOW THE ...?!

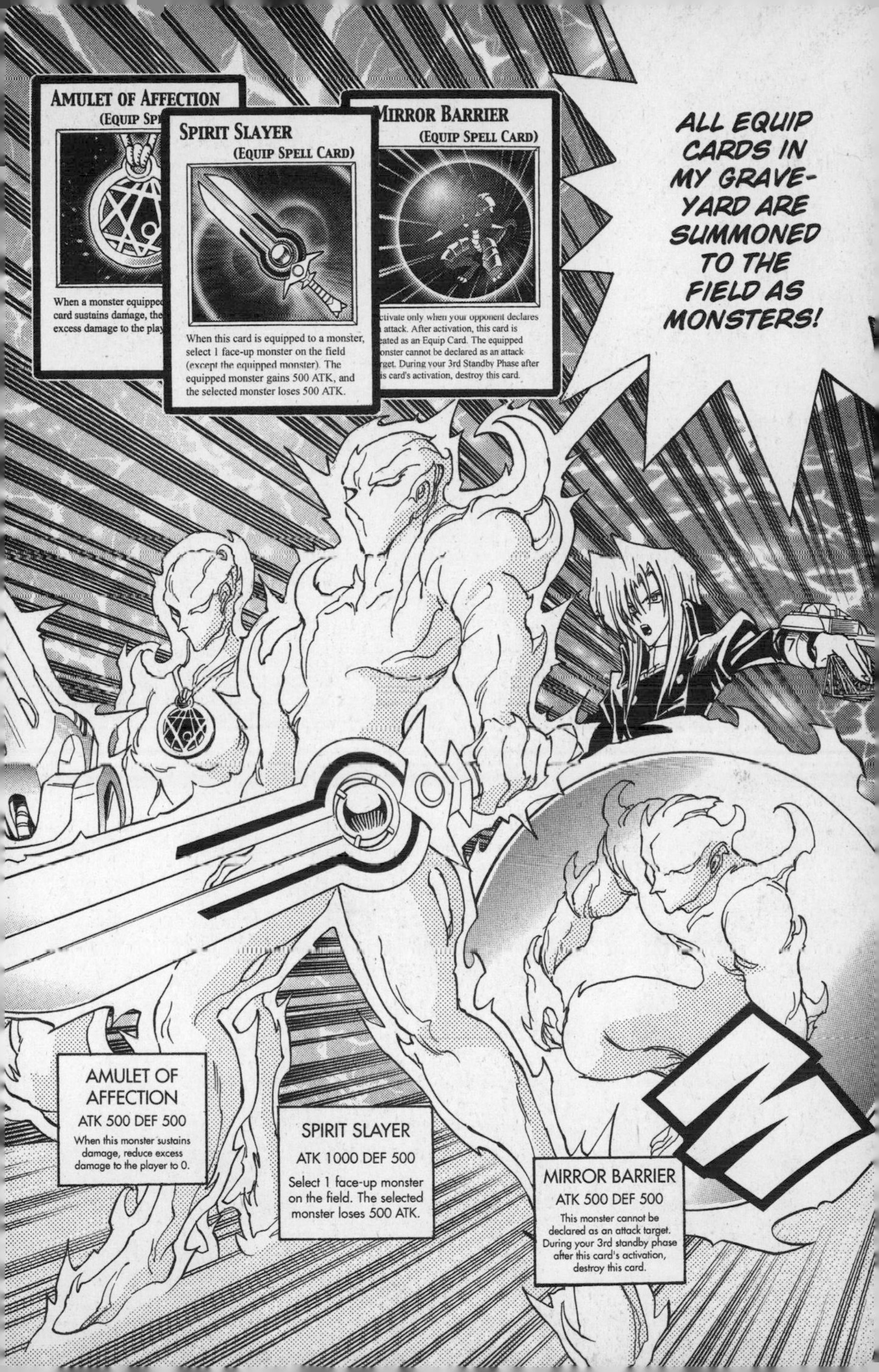

ALL EQUIP CARDS IN MY GRAVE-YARD ARE SUMMONED TO THE FIELD AS MONSTERS!
MIRROR BARRIER
(EQUIP SPELL CARD)
ctivate only when your opponent declares n attack. After activation, this card is eated as an Equip Card. The equipped onster cannot be declared as an attack rget. During your 3rd Standby Phase after is card's activation, destroy this card.
SPIRIT SLAYER
(EQUIP SPELL CARD)
When this card is equipped to a monster, select 1 face-up monster on the field (except the equipped monster). The equipped monster gains 500 ATK, and the selected monster loses 500 ATK.
AMULET OF AFFECTION
(EQUIP SP
When a monster equipped card sustains damage, the excess damage to the play
MIRROR BARRIER
ATK 500 DEF 500
This monster cannot be declared as an attack target. During your 3rd standby phase after this card's activation, destroy this card.
SPIRIT SLAYER
ATK 1000 DEF 500
Select 1 face-up monster on the field. The selected monster loses 500 ATK.
AMULET OF AFFECTION
ATK 500 DEF 500
When this monster sustains damage, reduce excess damage to the player to 0.

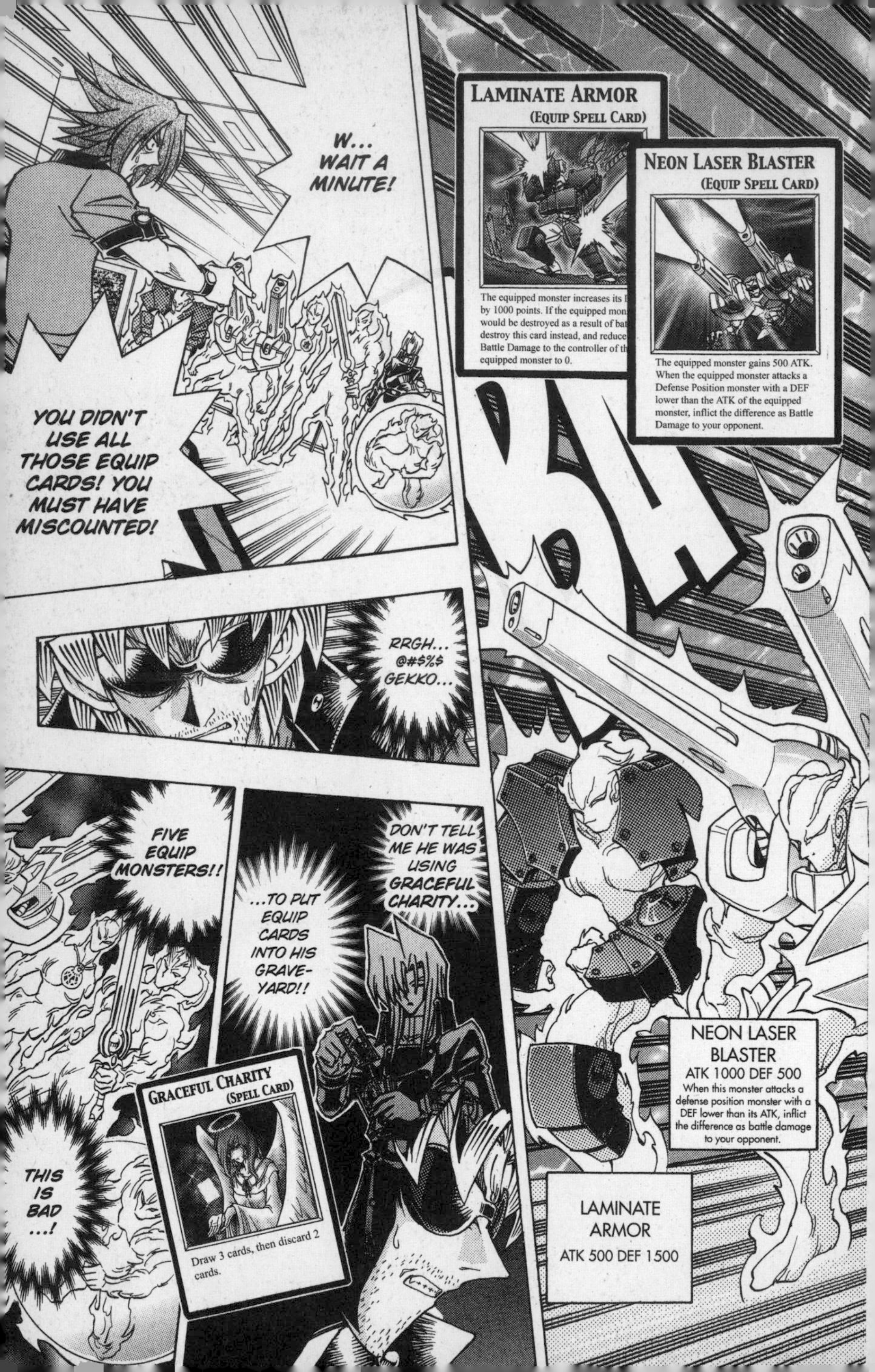
LAMINATE ARMOR
(EQUIP SPELL CARD)
The equipped monster increases its I
by 1000 points. If the equipped mons
would be destroyed as a result of bat
destroy this card instead, and reduce
Battle Damage to the controller of th
equipped monster to 0.
NEON LASER BLASTER
(EQUIP SPELL CARD)
The equipped monster gains 500 ATK. When the equipped monster attacks a Defense Position monster with a DEF lower than the ATK of the equipped monster, inflict the difference as Battle Damage to your opponent.
NEON LASER BLASTER
ATK 1000 DEF 500
When this monster attacks a defense position monster with a DEF lower than its ATK, inflict the difference as battle damage to your opponent.
LAMINATE ARMOR
ATK 500 DEF 1500
W... WAIT A MINUTE!
YOU DIDN'T USE ALL THOSE EQUIP CARDS! YOU MUST HAVE MISCOUNTED!
RRGH... @#$%$ GEKKO...
DON'T TELL ME HE WAS USING GRACEFUL CHARITY...
...TO PUT EQUIP CARDS INTO HIS GRAVE-YARD!!
GRACEFUL CHARITY
(SPELL CARD)
Draw 3 cards, then discard 2 cards.
FIVE EQUIP MONSTERS!!
THIS IS BAD ...!

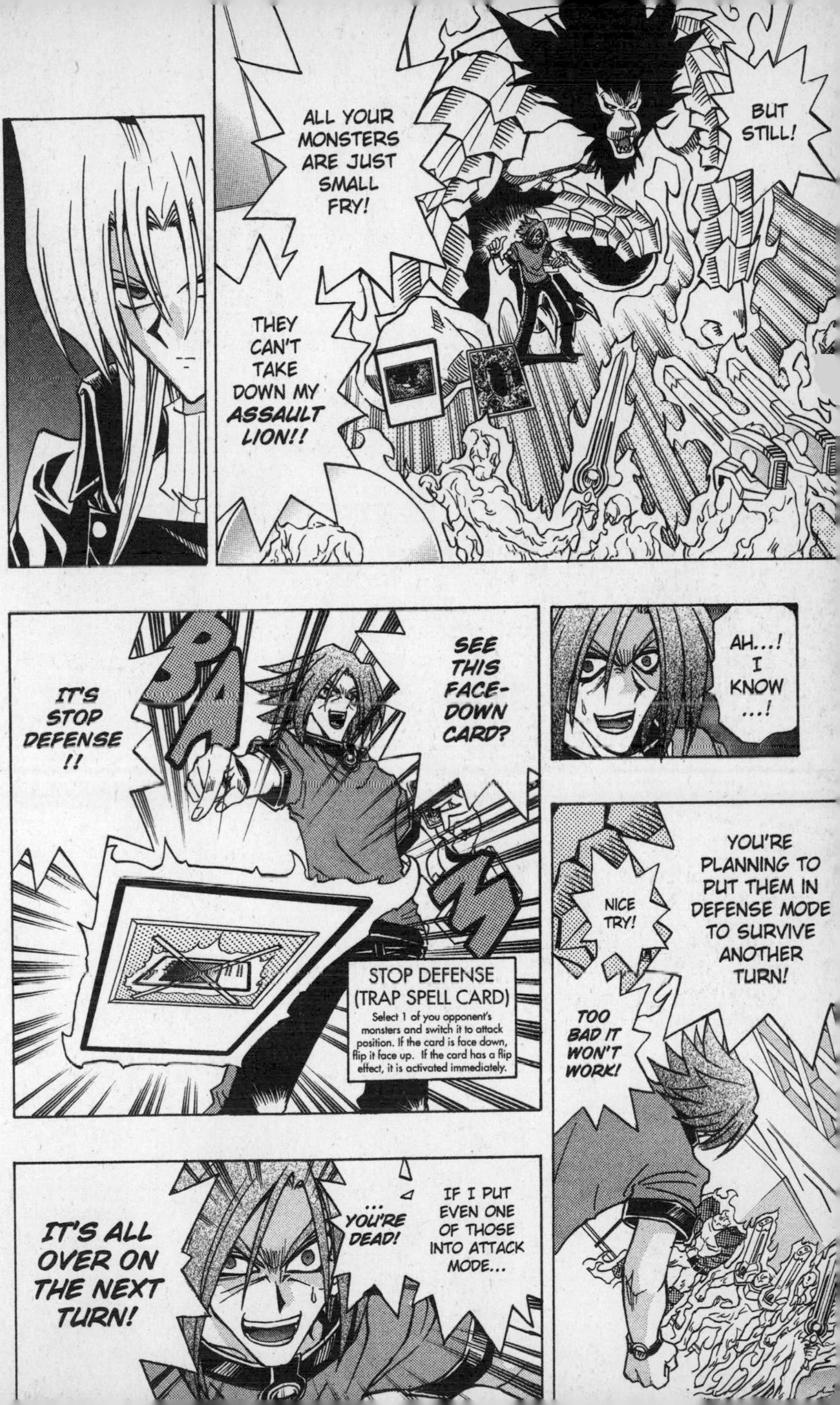
BUT STILL!
ALL YOUR MONSTERS ARE JUST SMALL FRY!
THEY CAN'T TAKE DOWN MY *ASSAULT LION!!*
AH...! I KNOW ...!
YOU'RE PLANNING TO PUT THEM IN DEFENSE MODE TO SURVIVE ANOTHER TURN!
NICE TRY!
TOO BAD IT WON'T WORK!
SEE THIS FACE-DOWN CARD?
IT'S STOP DEFENSE !!
STOP DEFENSE
(TRAP SPELL CARD)
Select 1 of you opponent's monsters and switch it to attack position. If the card is face down, flip it face up. If the card has a flip effect, it is activated immediately.
IF I PUT EVEN ONE OF THOSE INTO ATTACK MODE...
... YOU'RE DEAD!
IT'S ALL OVER ON THE NEXT TURN!

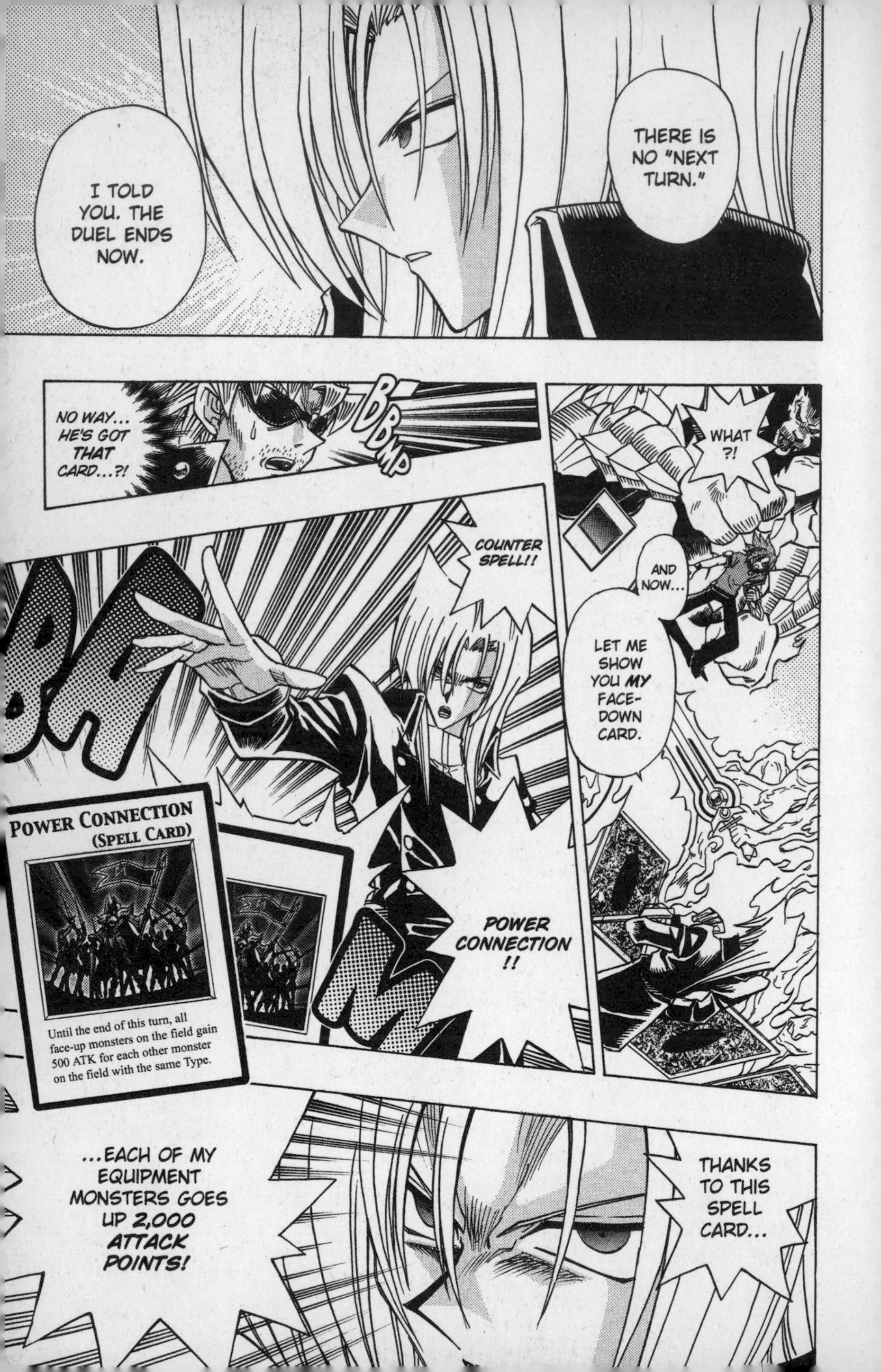
THERE IS NO "NEXT TURN."
I TOLD YOU. THE DUEL ENDS NOW.
WHAT?!
AND NOW...
LET ME SHOW YOU MY FACE-DOWN CARD.
BBMP
NO WAY... HE'S GOT THAT CARD...?!
COUNTER SPELL!!
POWER CONNECTION!!
POWER CONNECTION
(SPELL CARD)
Until the end of this turn, all face-up monsters on the field gain 500 ATK for each other monster on the field with the same Type.
THANKS TO THIS SPELL CARD...
...EACH OF MY EQUIPMENT MONSTERS GOES UP 2,000 ATTACK POINTS!

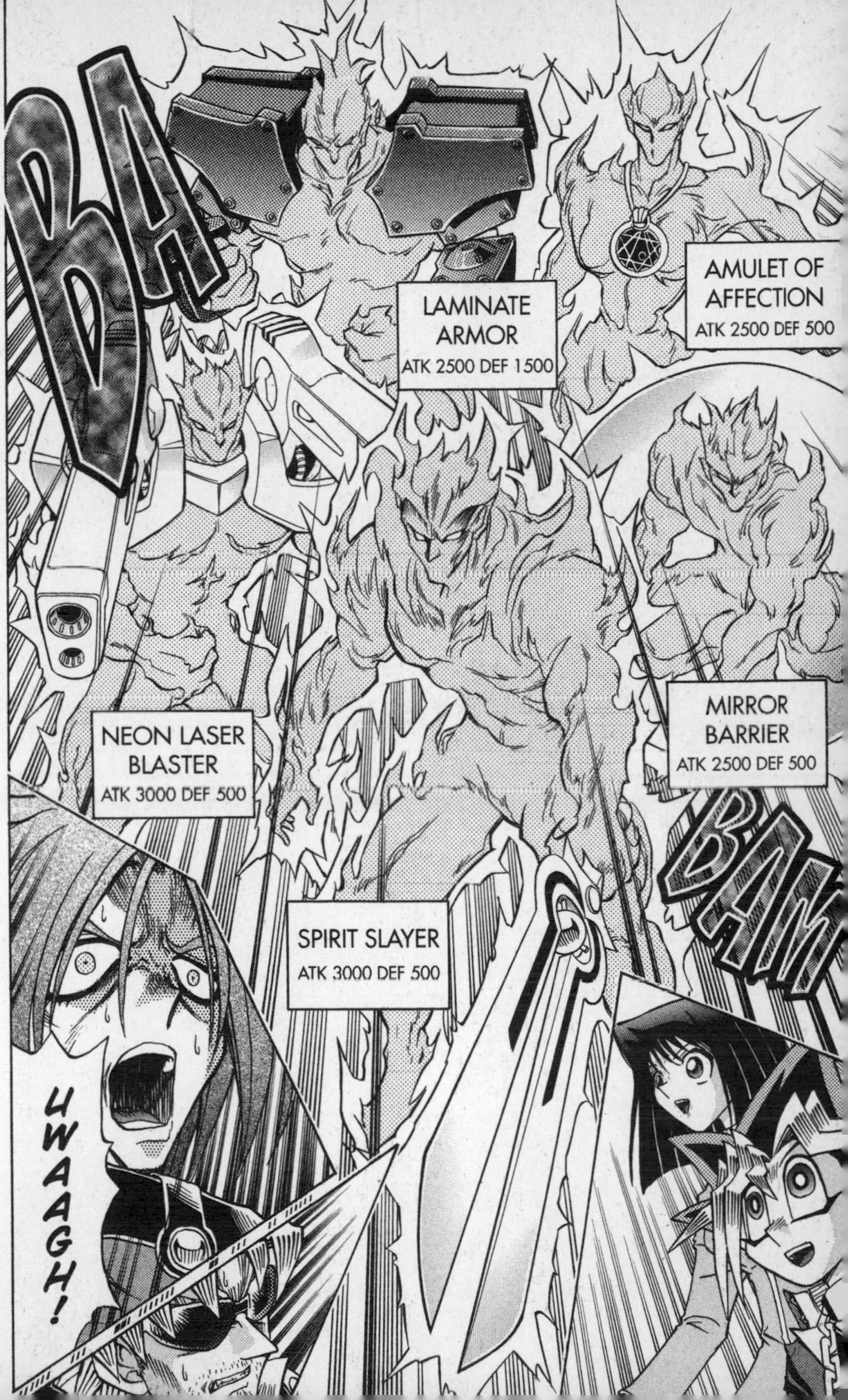
AMULET OF AFFECTION
ATK 2500 DEF 500
LAMINATE ARMOR
ATK 2500 DEF 1500
BA
MIRROR BARRIER
ATK 2500 DEF 500
NEON LASER BLASTER
ATK 3000 DEF 500
BAM
SPIRIT SLAYER
ATK 3000 DEF 500
UWAAGH!

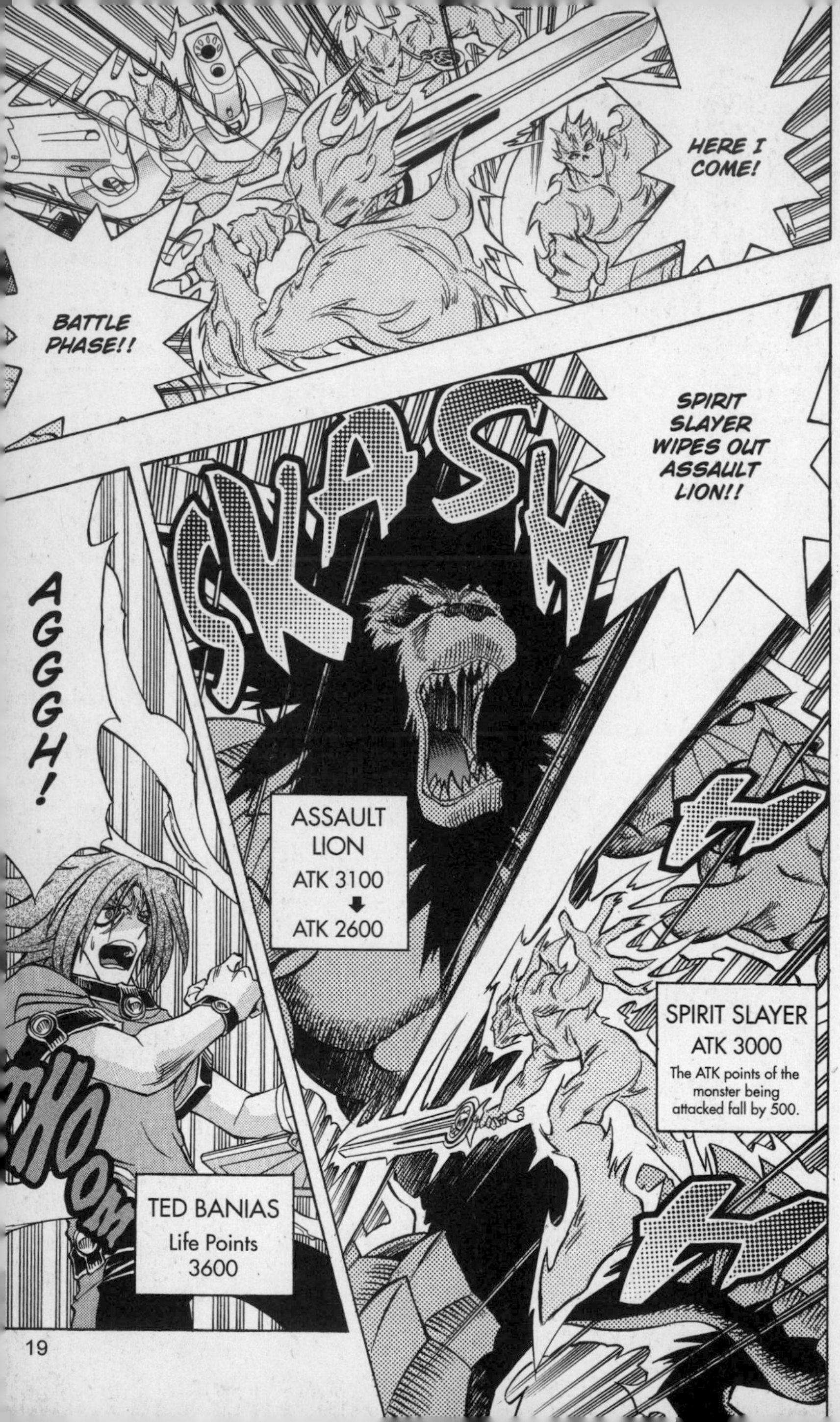
HERE I COME!
BATTLE PHASE!!
SPIRIT SLAYER WIPES OUT ASSAULT LION!!
SLASH
AGGGH!
SPIRIT SLAYER
ATK 3000
The ATK points of the monster being attacked fall by 500.
ASSAULT LION
ATK 3100
ATK 2600
THOOM
TED BANIAS
Life Points
3600

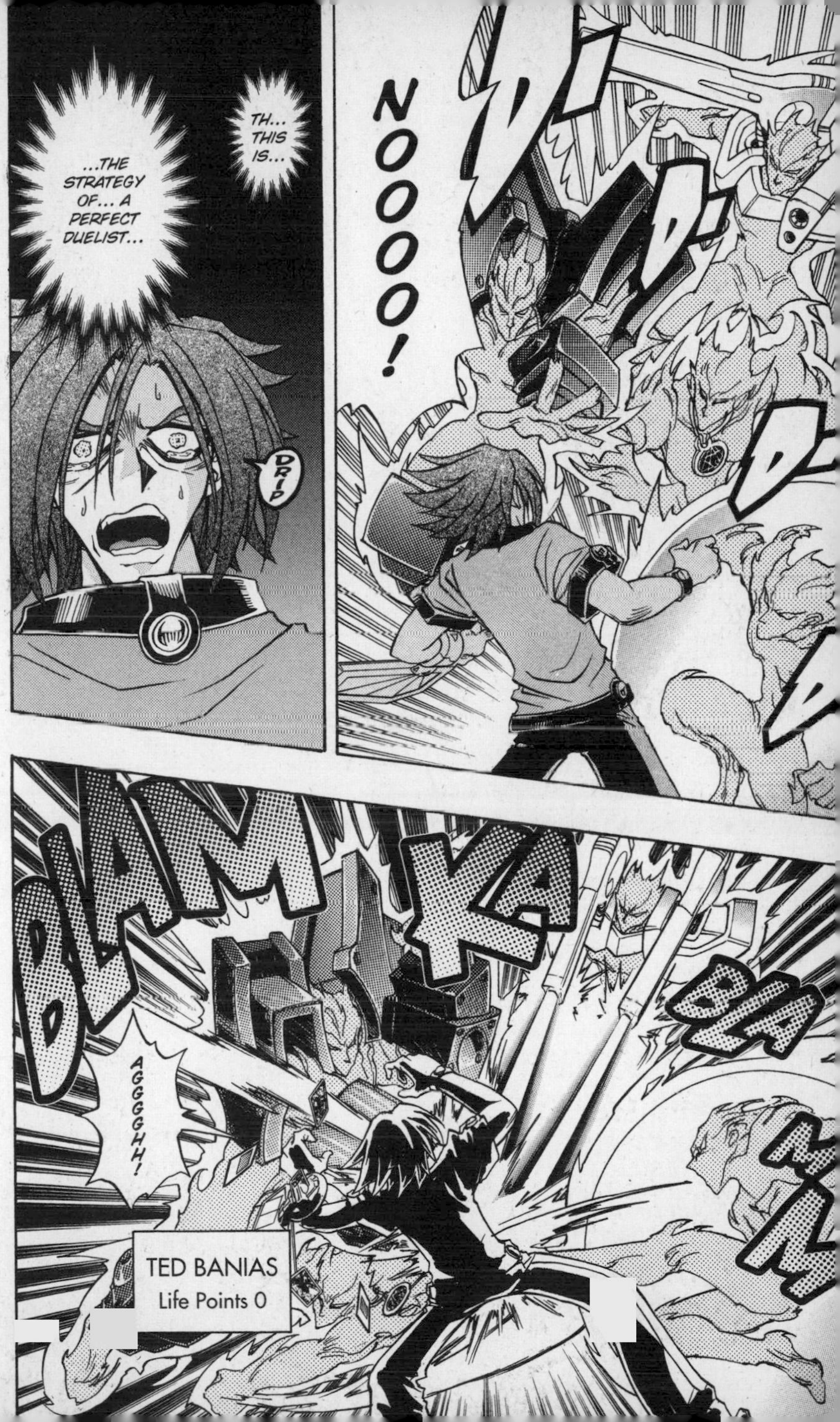
NOOOOO!
TH... THIS IS...
...THE STRATEGY OF... A PERFECT DUELIST...
DRIP
BLAM
AGGGGH!
TED BANIAS
Life Points 0

READ THIS WAY

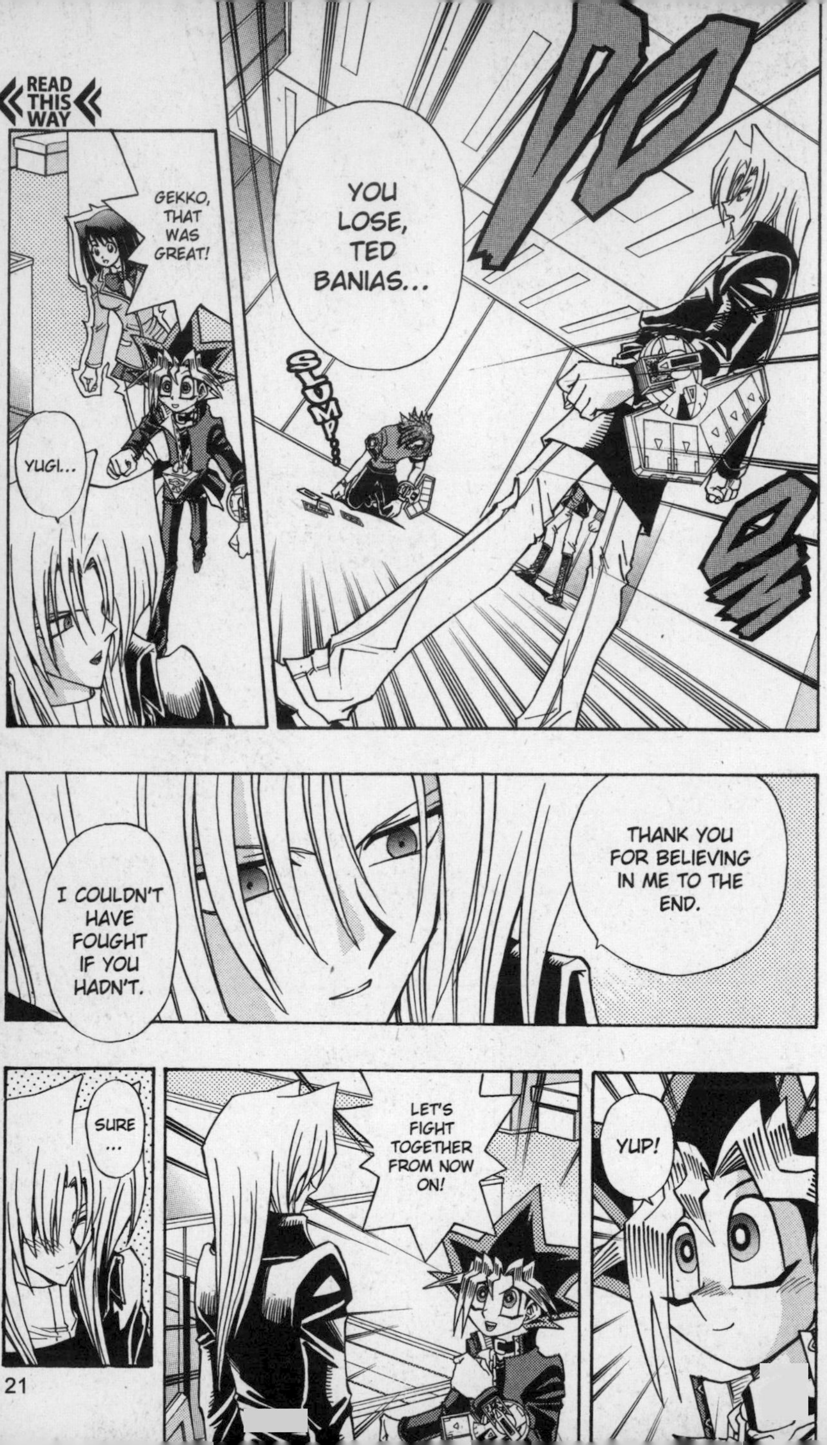
YOU LOSE, TED BANIAS...
SLUMP...
GEKKO, THAT WAS GREAT!
YUGI...
THANK YOU FOR BELIEVING IN ME TO THE END.
I COULDN'T HAVE FOUGHT IF YOU HADN'T.
YUP!
LET'S FIGHT TOGETHER FROM NOW ON!
SURE ...

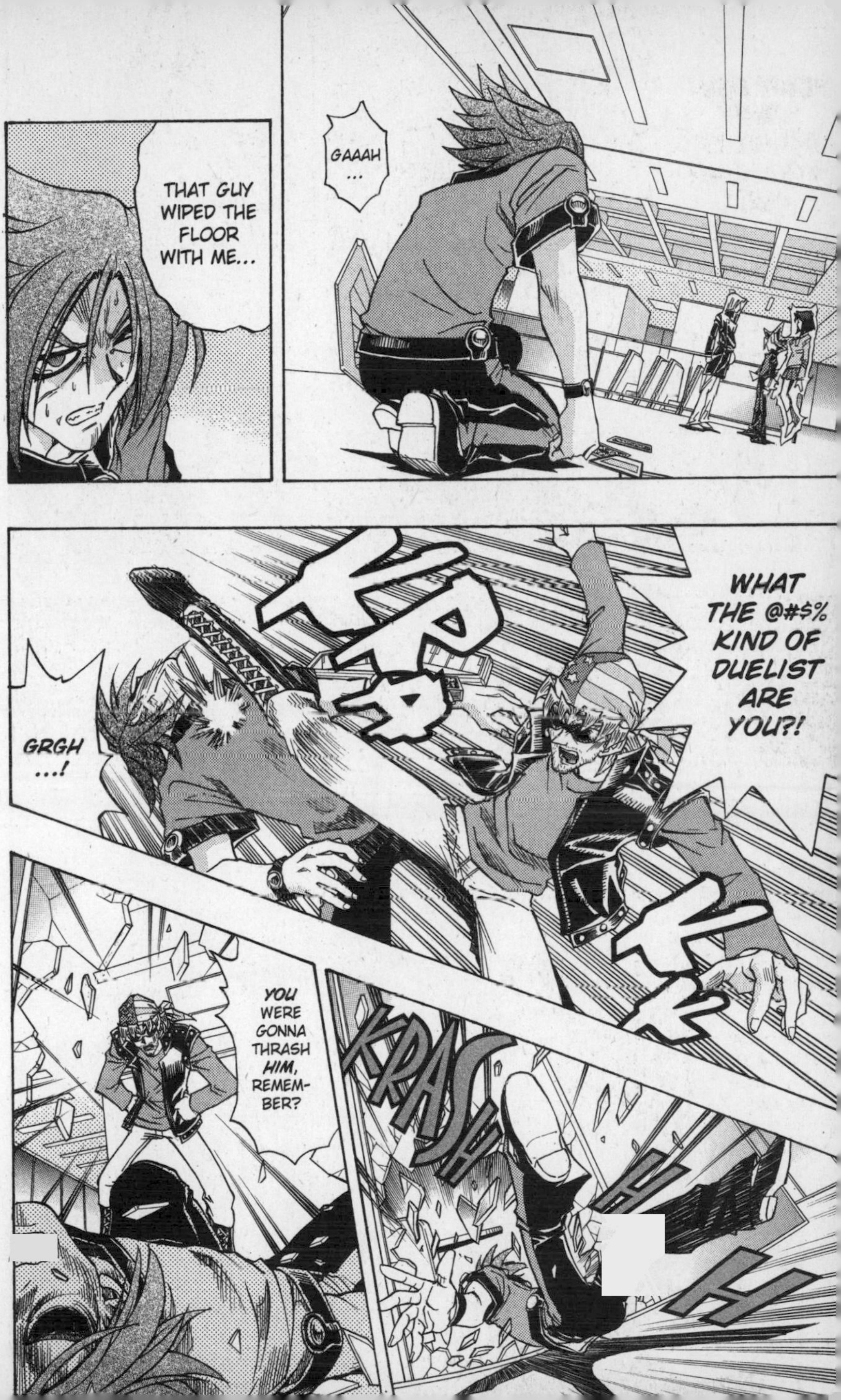
GAAAH ...
THAT GUY WIPED THE FLOOR WITH ME...
WHAT THE @#$% KIND OF DUELIST ARE YOU?!
GRGH ...!
KRASH
YOU WERE GONNA THRASH *HIM*, REMEMBER?

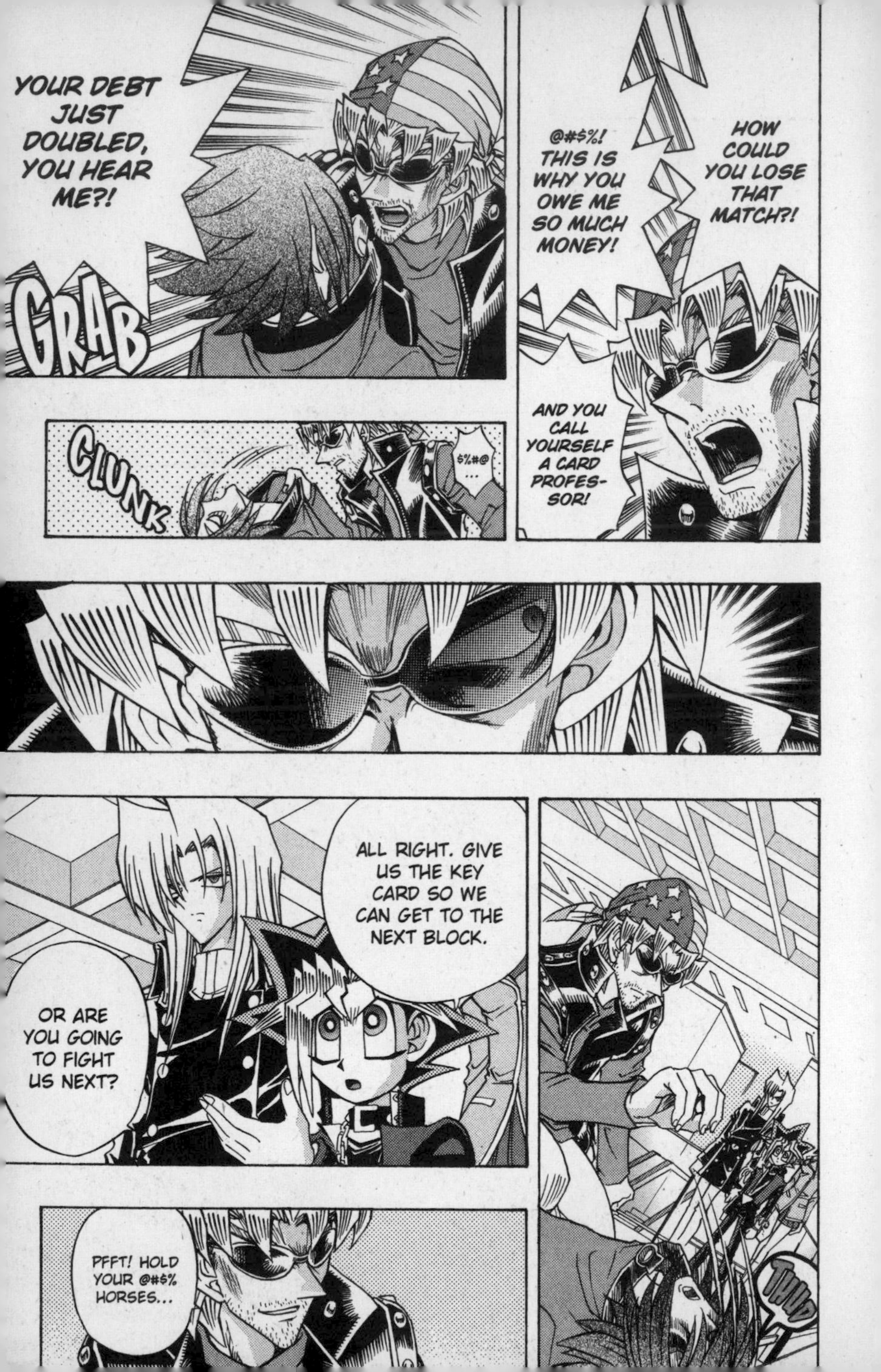
HOW COULD YOU LOSE THAT MATCH?!
@#$%! THIS IS WHY YOU OWE ME SO MUCH MONEY!
AND YOU CALL YOURSELF A CARD PROFESSOR!
YOUR DEBT JUST DOUBLED, YOU HEAR ME?!
GRAB
CLUNK
$%#@ ...
THUD
ALL RIGHT. GIVE US THE KEY CARD SO WE CAN GET TO THE NEXT BLOCK.
OR ARE YOU GOING TO FIGHT US NEXT?
PFFT! HOLD YOUR @#$% HORSES...

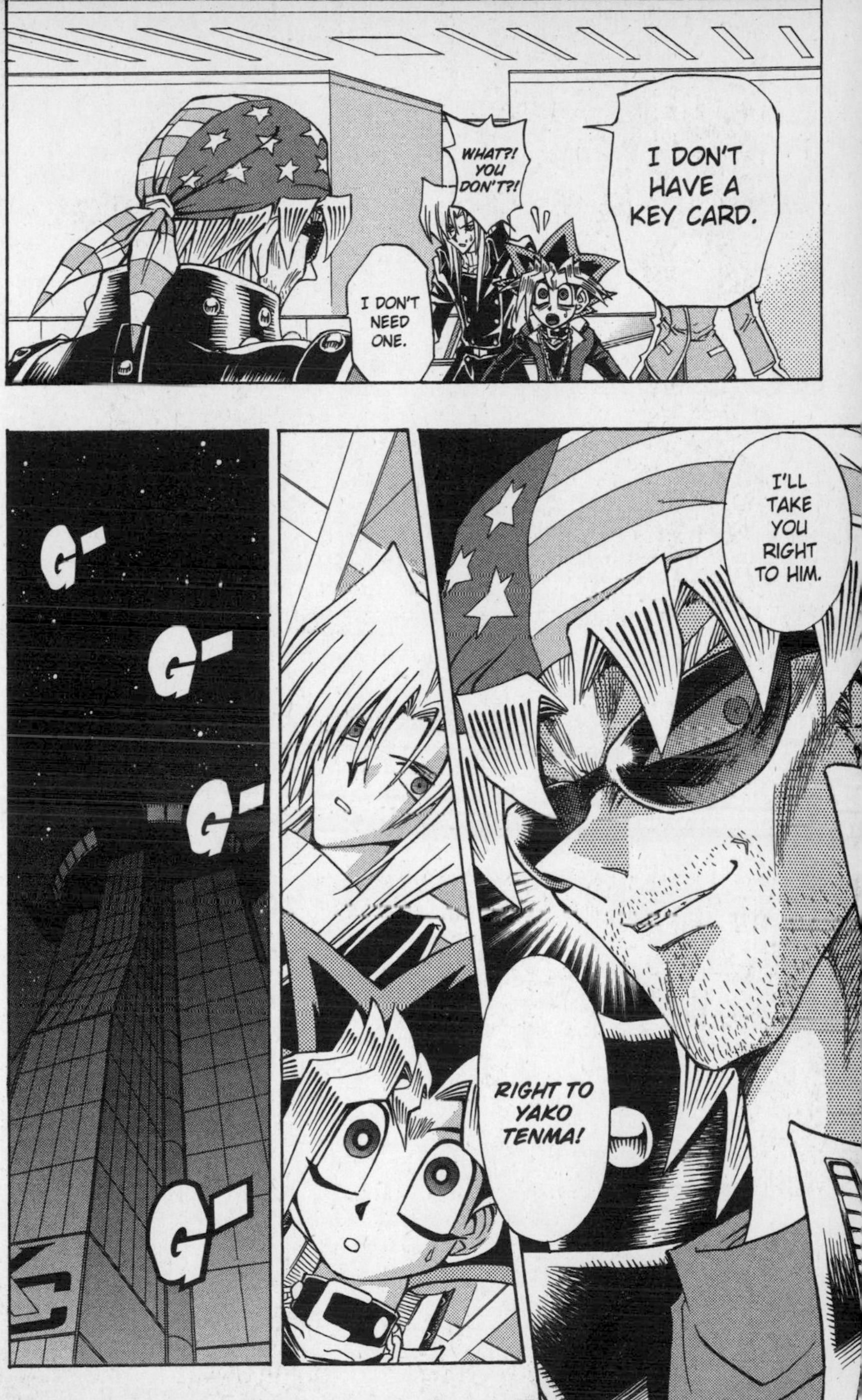
I DON'T HAVE A KEY CARD.
WHAT?! YOU DON'T?!
I DON'T NEED ONE.
I'LL TAKE YOU RIGHT TO HIM.
RIGHT TO YAKO TENMA!
G-
G-
G-
G-

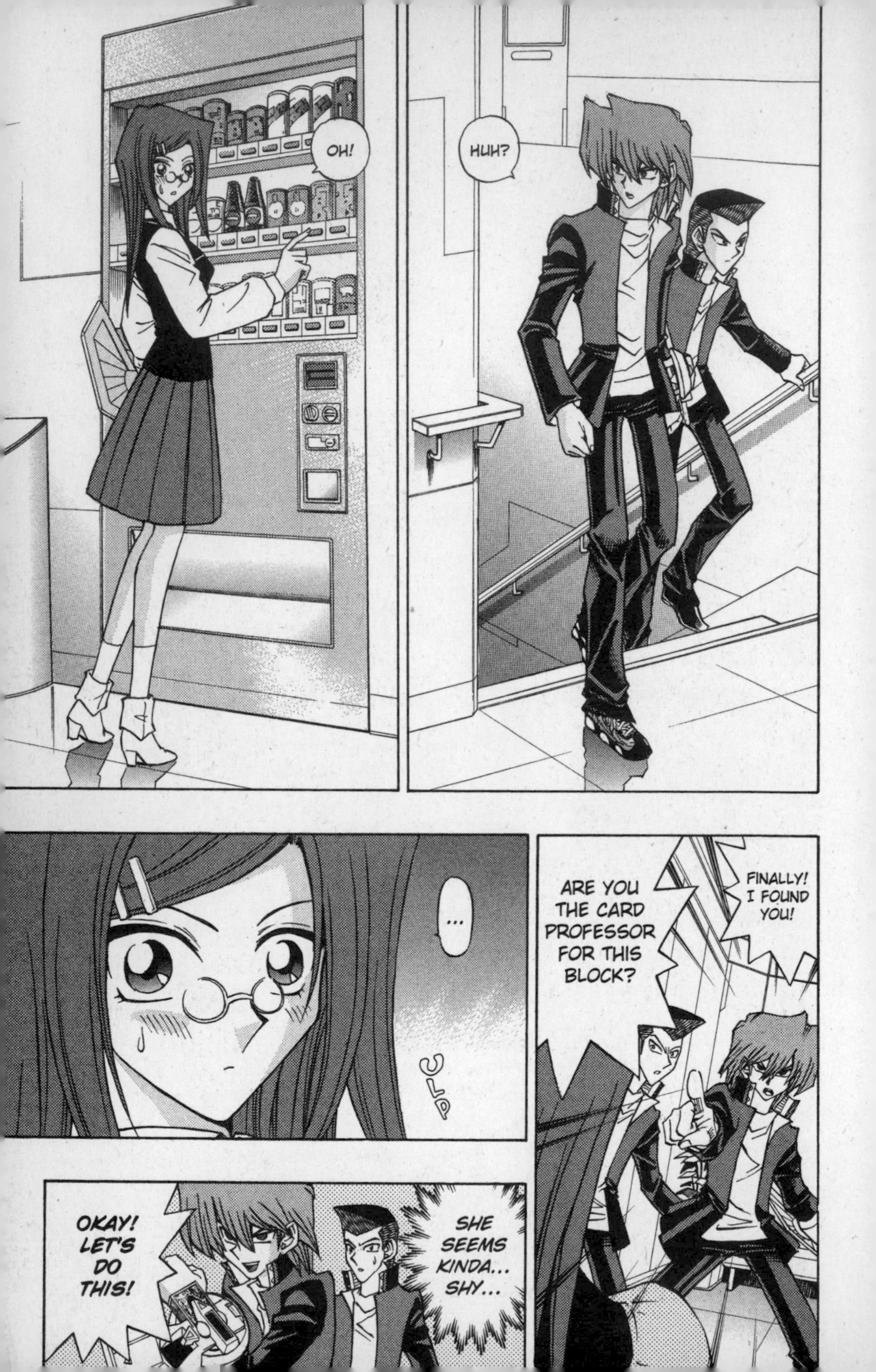
HUH?
OH!
FINALLY! I FOUND YOU!
ARE YOU THE CARD PROFESSOR FOR THIS BLOCK?
...
ULP
SHE SEEMS KINDA... SHY...
OKAY! LET'S DO THIS!

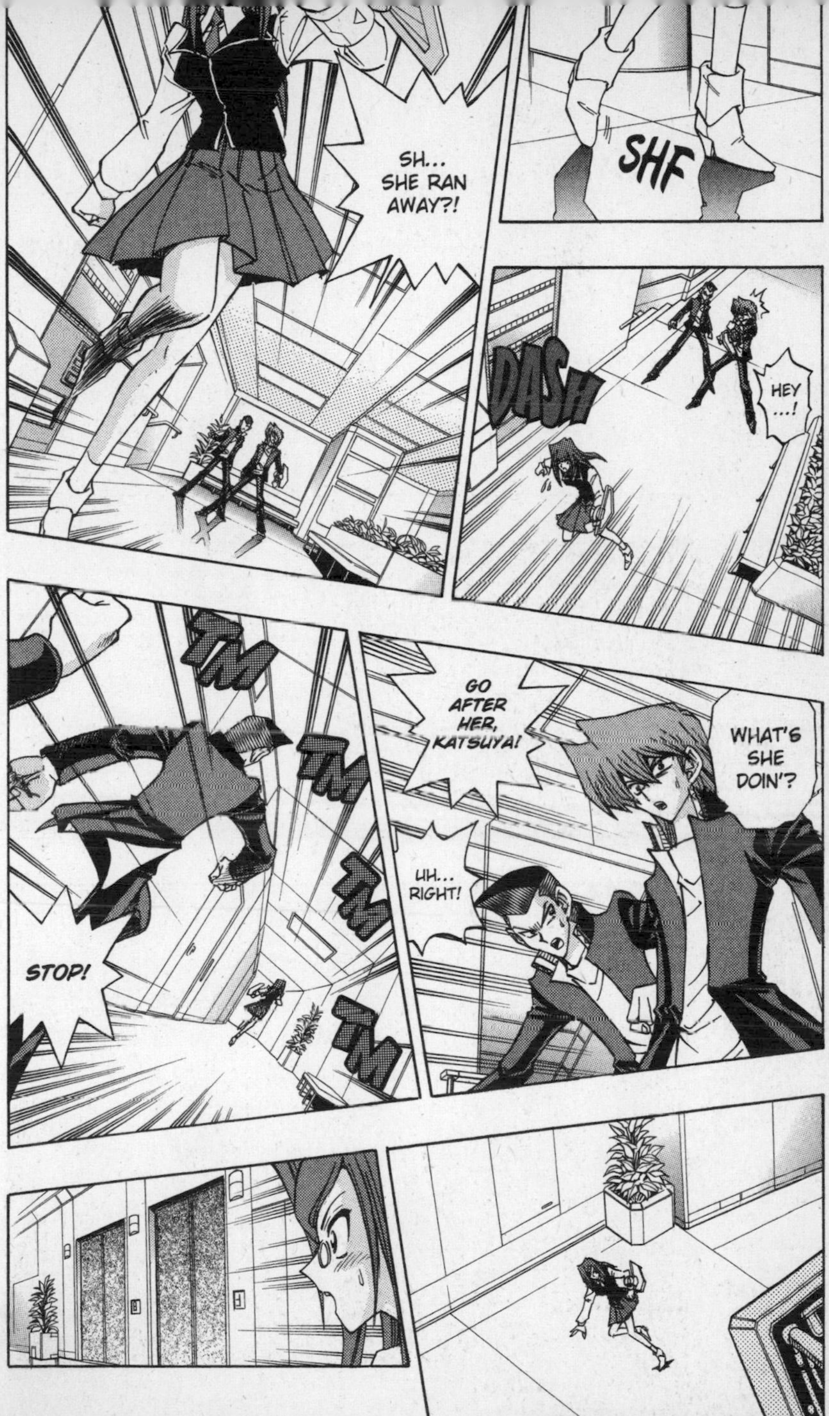
SHF
DASH
HEY ...!
SH... SHE RAN AWAY?!
WHAT'S SHE DOIN'?
GO AFTER HER, KATSUYA!
UH... RIGHT!
TM
TM
TM
TM
STOP!

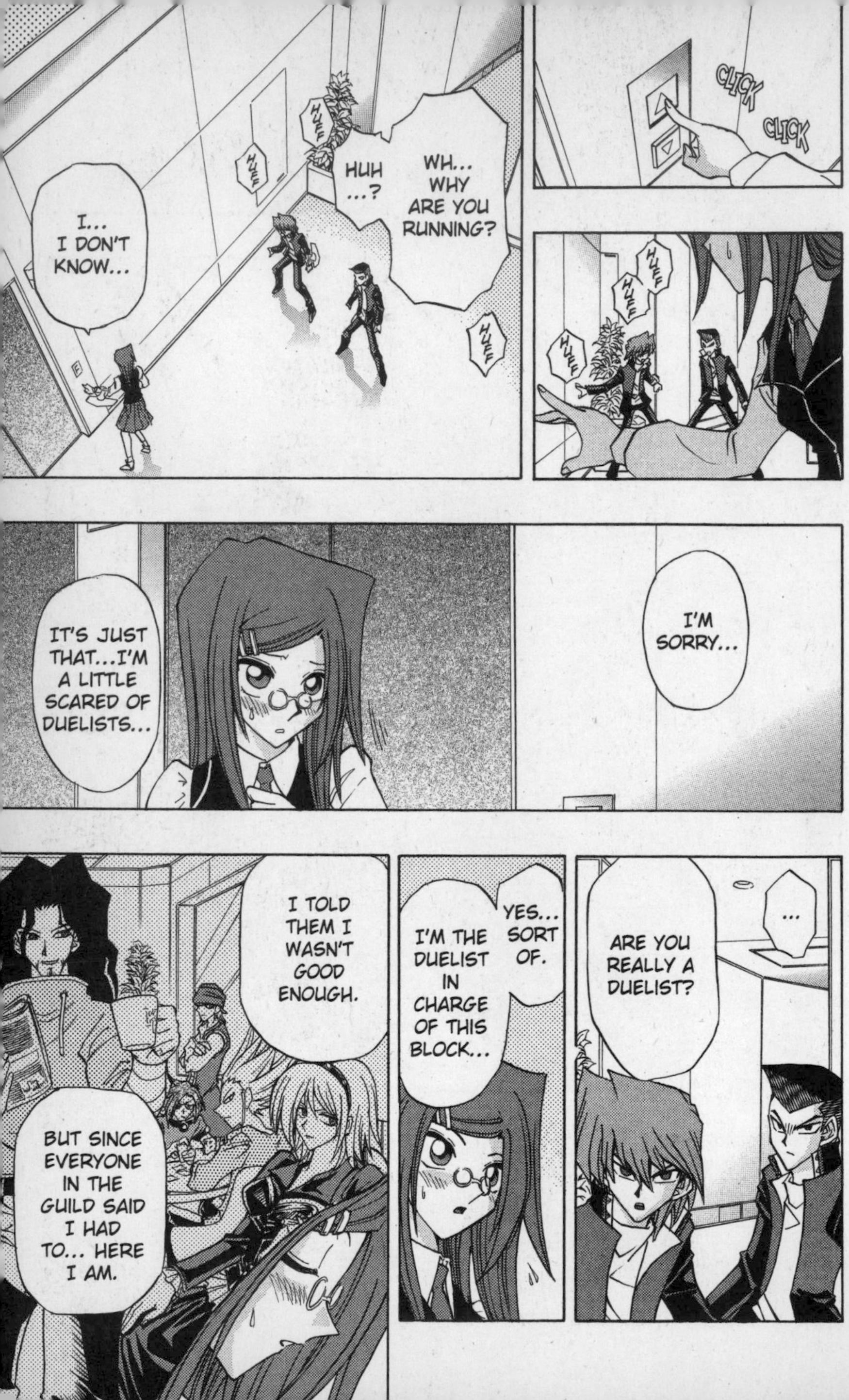
CLICK
CLICK
HUFF
HUFF
HUFF
WH... WHY ARE YOU RUNNING?
HUH ...?
HUFF
HUFF
HUFF
I... I DON'T KNOW...
I'M SORRY...
IT'S JUST THAT...I'M A LITTLE SCARED OF DUELISTS...
...
ARE YOU REALLY A DUELIST?
YES... SORT OF.
I'M THE DUELIST IN CHARGE OF THIS BLOCK...
I TOLD THEM I WASN'T GOOD ENOUGH.
BUT SINCE EVERYONE IN THE GUILD SAID I HAD TO... HERE I AM.

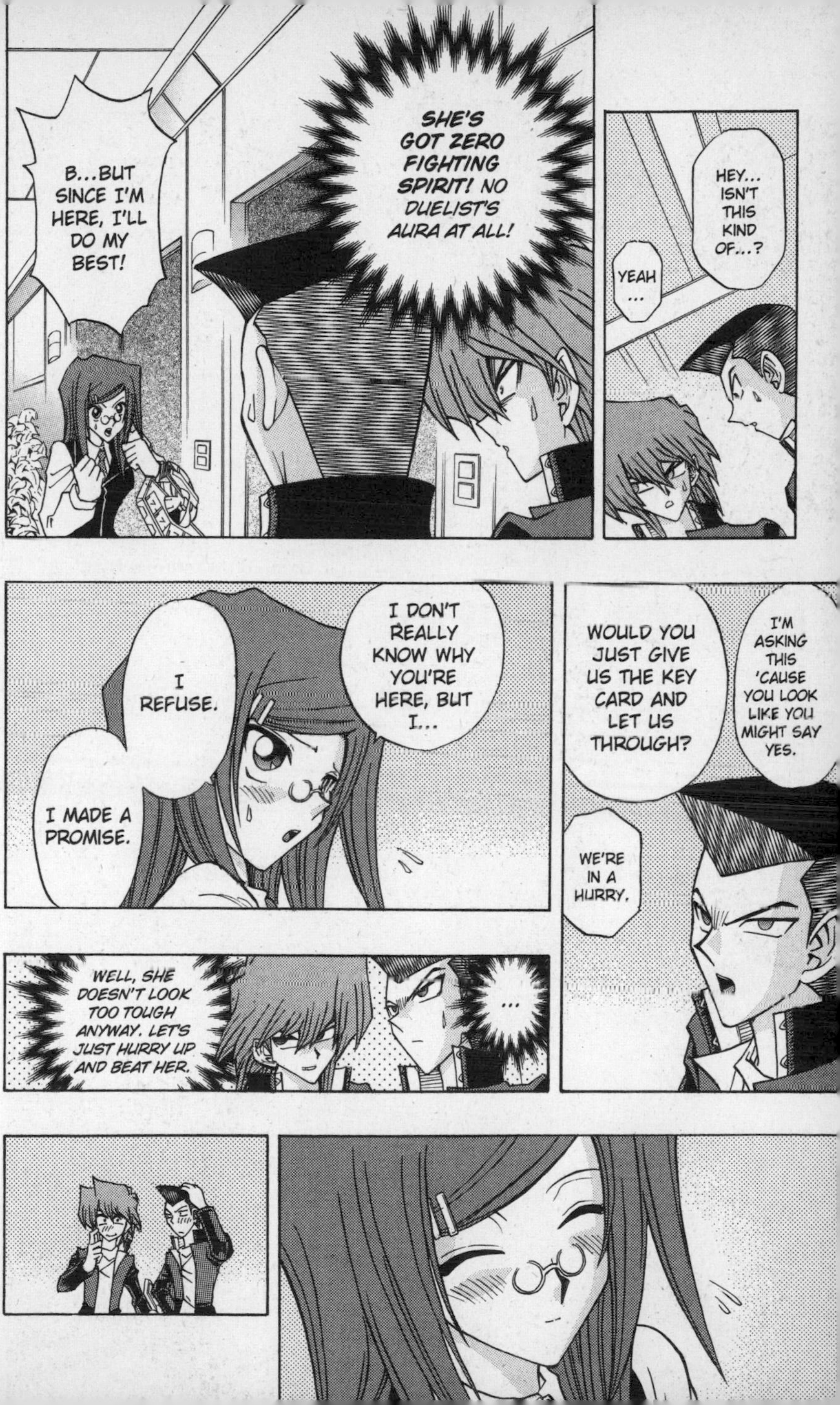
HEY... ISN'T THIS KIND OF...?
YEAH...
SHE'S GOT ZERO FIGHTING SPIRIT! NO DUELIST'S AURA AT ALL!
B...BUT SINCE I'M HERE, I'LL DO MY BEST!
I'M ASKING THIS 'CAUSE YOU LOOK LIKE YOU MIGHT SAY YES.
WOULD YOU JUST GIVE US THE KEY CARD AND LET US THROUGH?
WE'RE IN A HURRY.
I DON'T REALLY KNOW WHY YOU'RE HERE, BUT I...
I REFUSE.
I MADE A PROMISE.
...
WELL, SHE DOESN'T LOOK TOO TOUGH ANYWAY. LET'S JUST HURRY UP AND BEAT HER.

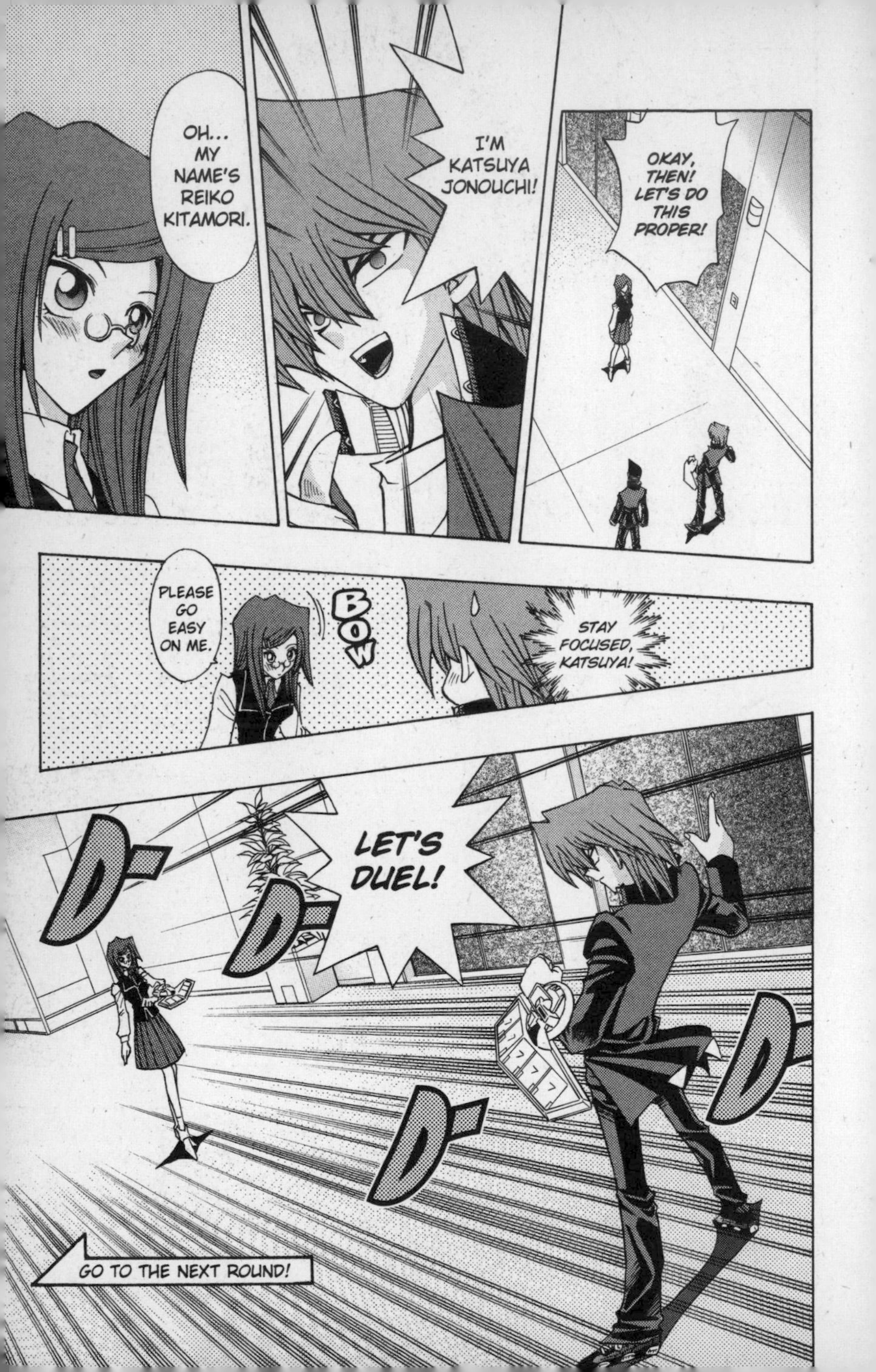
OKAY, THEN! LET'S DO THIS PROPER!
I'M KATSUYA JONOUCHI!
OH... MY NAME'S REIKO KITAMORI.
STAY FOCUSED, KATSUYA!
BOW
PLEASE GO EASY ON ME.
LET'S DUEL!
GO TO THE NEXT ROUND!

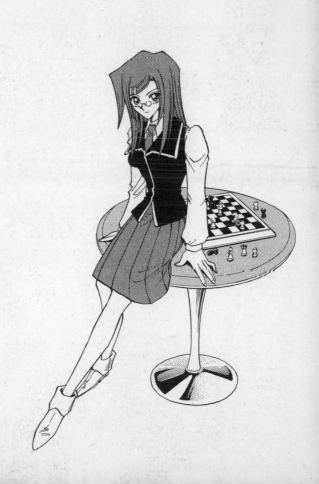

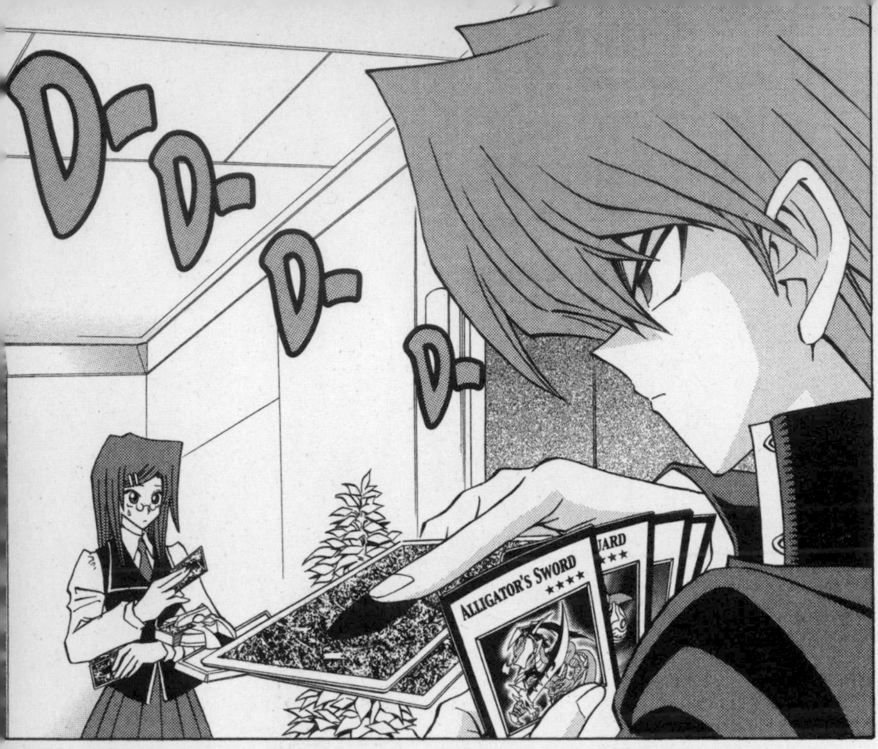
D-D-D-D-
ALLIGATOR'S SWORD

Duel Round 19: Jonouchi... Helpless?!

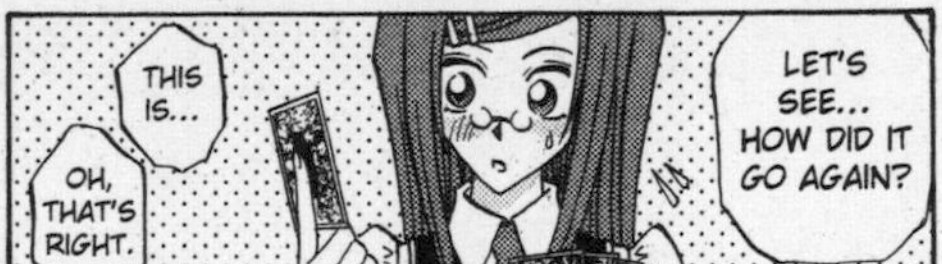
LET'S SEE... HOW DID IT GO AGAIN?
THIS IS...
OH, THAT'S RIGHT.

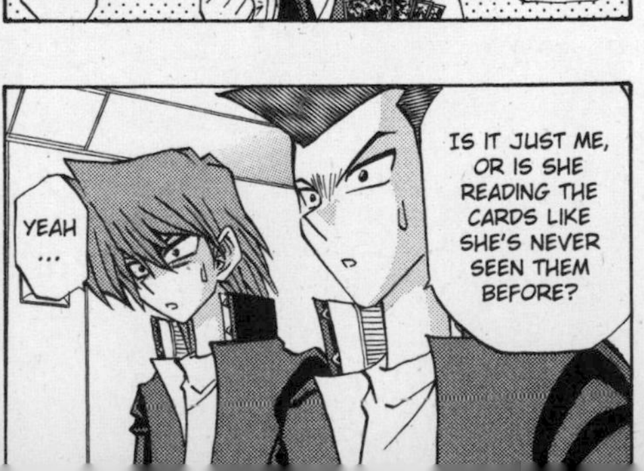
IS IT JUST ME, OR IS SHE READING THE CARDS LIKE SHE'S NEVER SEEN THEM BEFORE?
YEAH ...

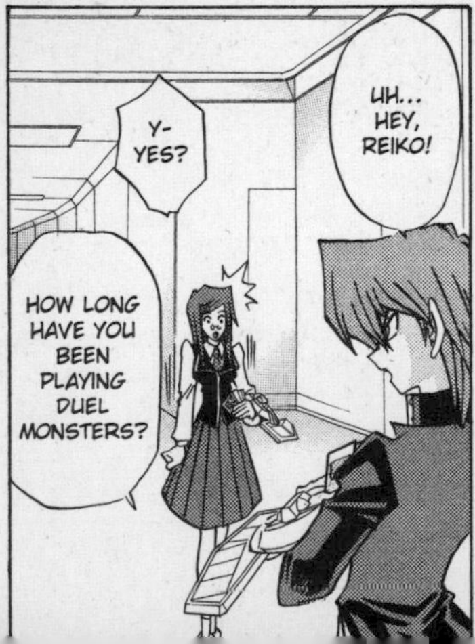
UH... HEY, REIKO!
Y-YES?
HOW LONG HAVE YOU BEEN PLAYING DUEL MONSTERS?

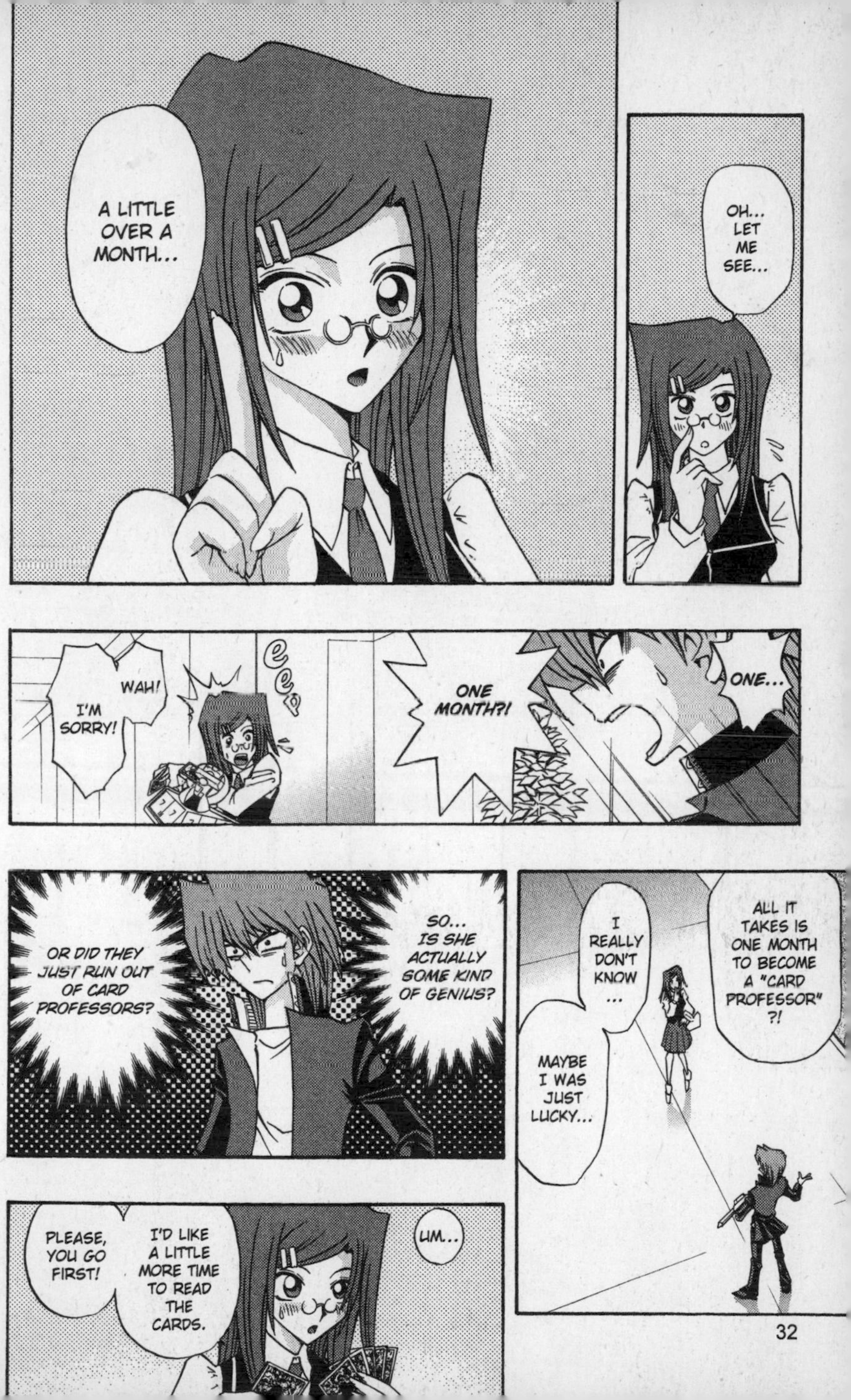
OH... LET ME SEE...
A LITTLE OVER A MONTH...
ONE...
ONE MONTH?!
eep
WAH!
I'M SORRY!
ALL IT TAKES IS ONE MONTH TO BECOME A "CARD PROFESSOR"?!
I REALLY DON'T KNOW...
MAYBE I WAS JUST LUCKY...
SO... IS SHE ACTUALLY SOME KIND OF GENIUS?
OR DID THEY JUST RUN OUT OF CARD PROFESSORS?
UM...
I'D LIKE A LITTLE MORE TIME TO READ THE CARDS.
PLEASE, YOU GO FIRST!

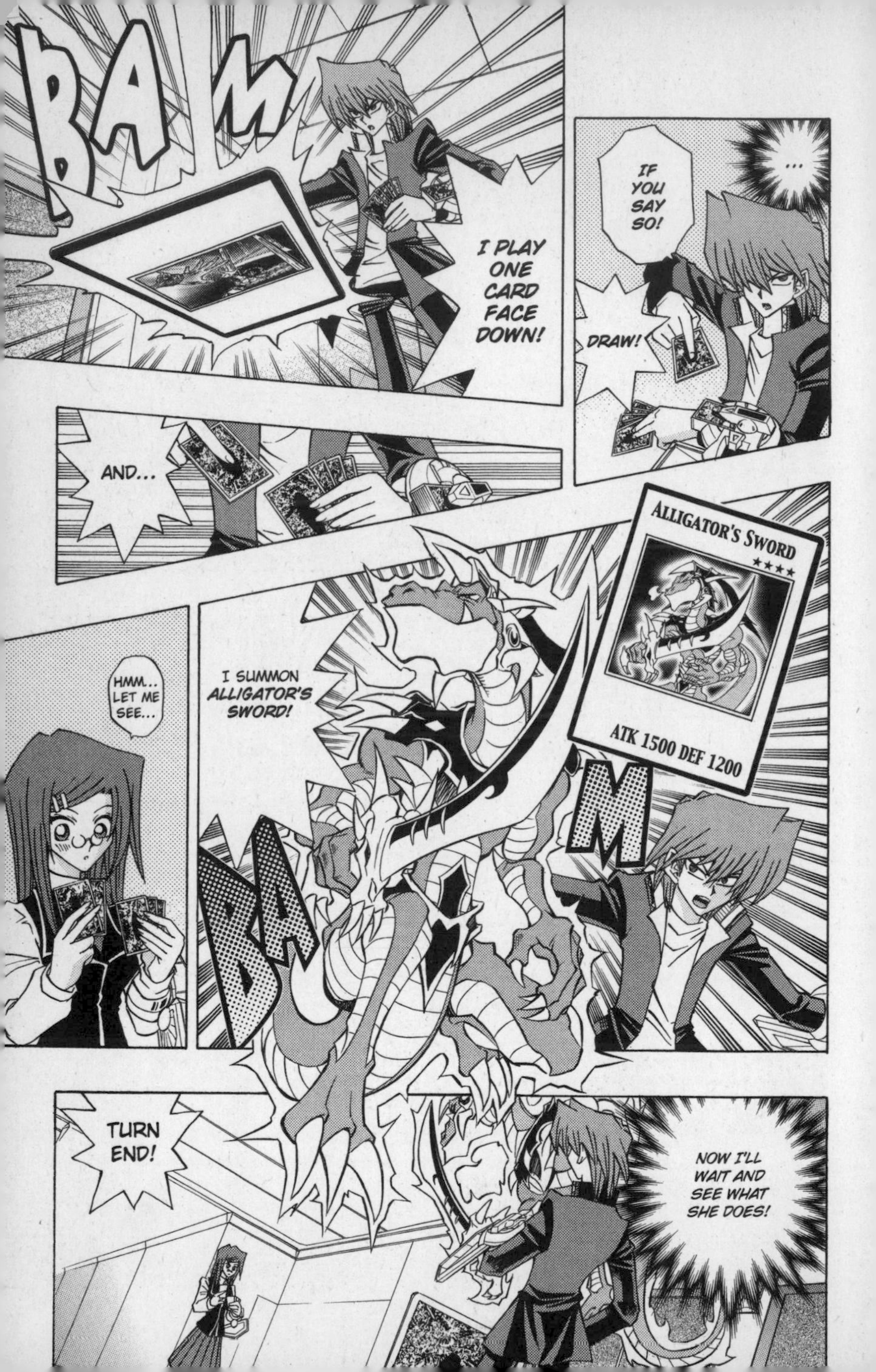
...
IF YOU SAY SO!
DRAW!
BAM
I PLAY ONE CARD FACE DOWN!
AND...
ALLIGATOR'S SWORD
ATK 1500 DEF 1200
BAM
I SUMMON ALLIGATOR'S SWORD!
HMM... LET ME SEE...
TURN END!
NOW I'LL WAIT AND SEE WHAT SHE DOES!

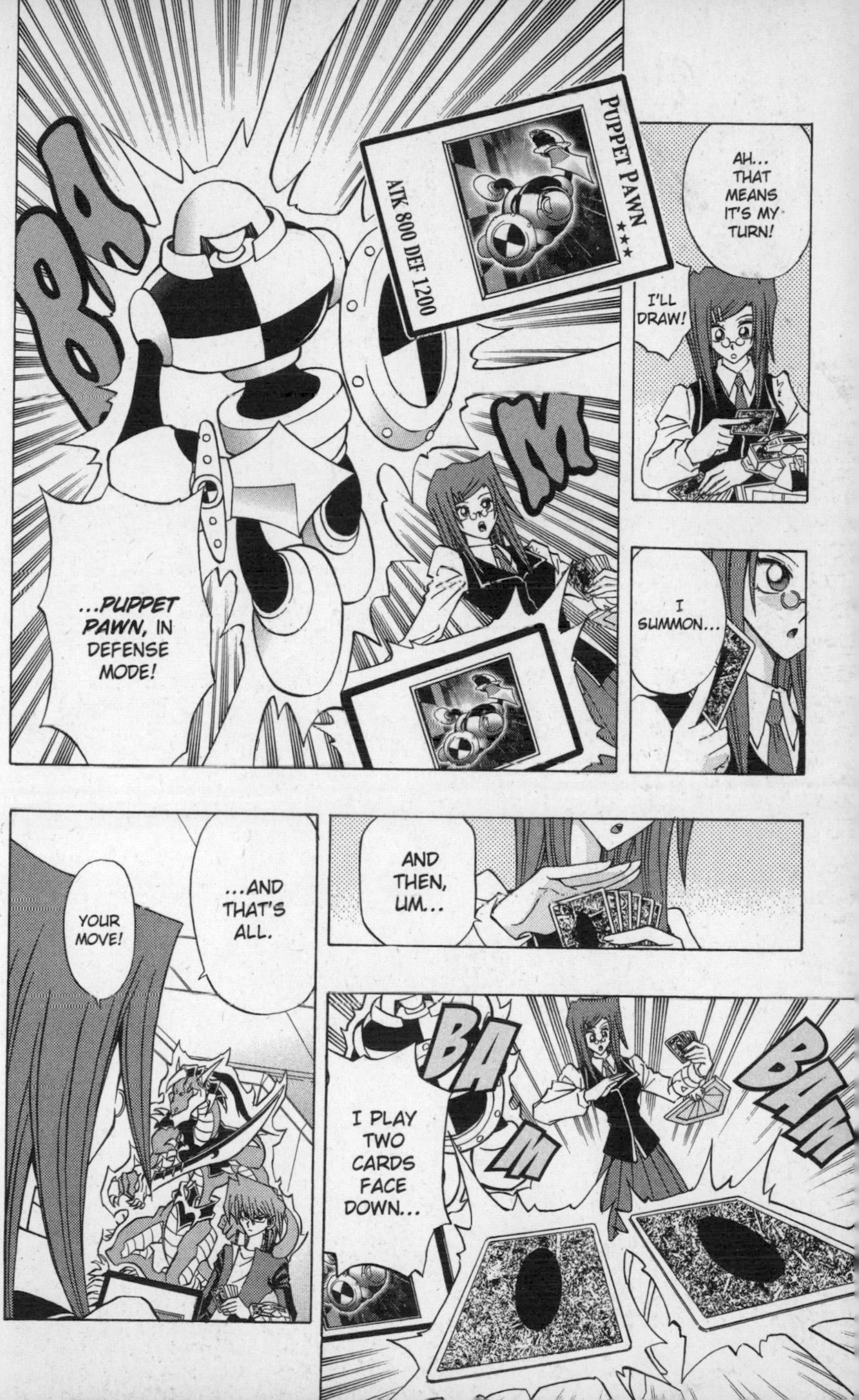

AH... THAT MEANS IT'S MY TURN!
I'LL DRAW!
I SUMMON...
BAM
PUPPET PAWN
ATK 800 DEF 1200
...PUPPET PAWN, IN DEFENSE MODE!
AND THEN, UM...
BAM
BAM
I PLAY TWO CARDS FACE DOWN...
...AND THAT'S ALL.
YOUR MOVE!

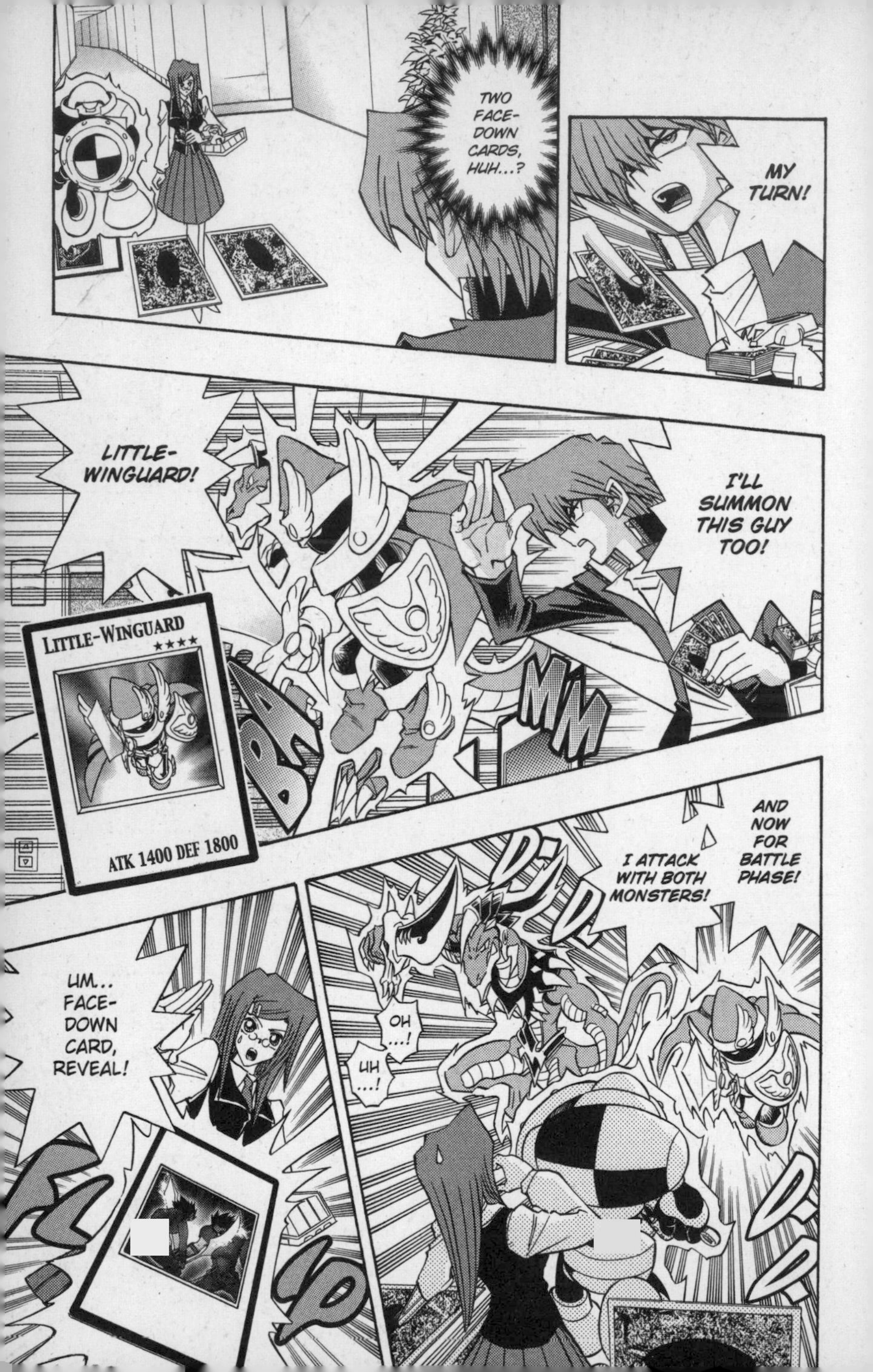
MY TURN!
TWO FACE-DOWN CARDS, HUH...?
I'LL SUMMON THIS GUY TOO!
LITTLE-WINGUARD!
LITTLE-WINGUARD ★★★★
ATK 1400 DEF 1800
AND NOW FOR BATTLE PHASE!
I ATTACK WITH BOTH MONSTERS!
OH ...!
UH ...!
UM.. FACE-DOWN CARD, REVEAL!

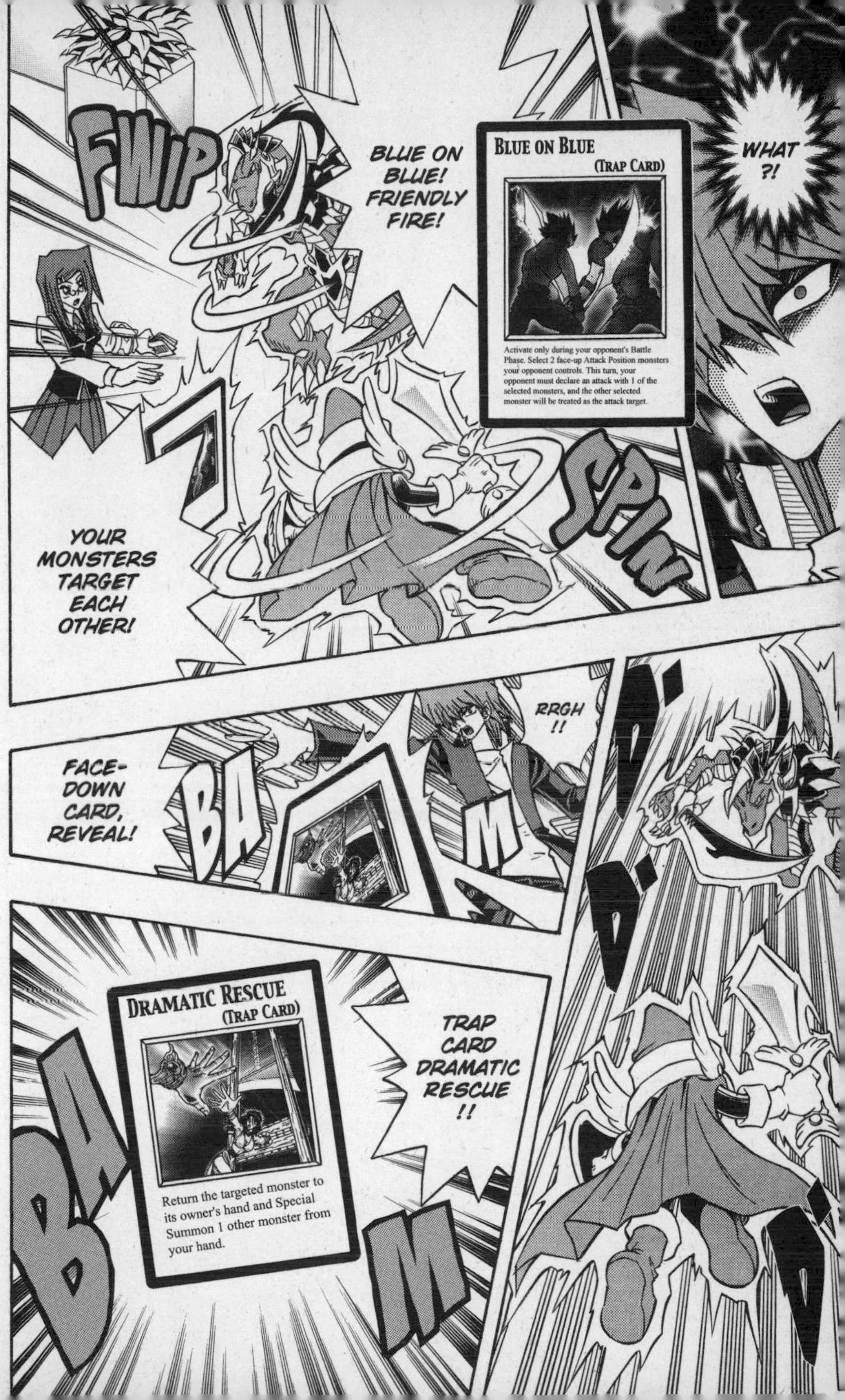
WHAT ?!
FWIP
BLUE ON BLUE! FRIENDLY FIRE!
BLUE ON BLUE
(TRAP CARD)
Activate only during your opponent's Battle Phase. Select 2 face-up Attack Position monsters your opponent controls. This turn, your opponent must declare an attack with 1 of the selected monsters, and the other selected monster will be treated as the attack target.
SPIN
YOUR MONSTERS TARGET EACH OTHER!
D D D D
RRGH !!
FACE-DOWN CARD, REVEAL!
BAM
TRAP CARD DRAMATIC RESCUE !!
DRAMATIC RESCUE
(TRAP CARD)
Return the targeted monster to its owner's hand and Special Summon 1 other monster from your hand.
BAM

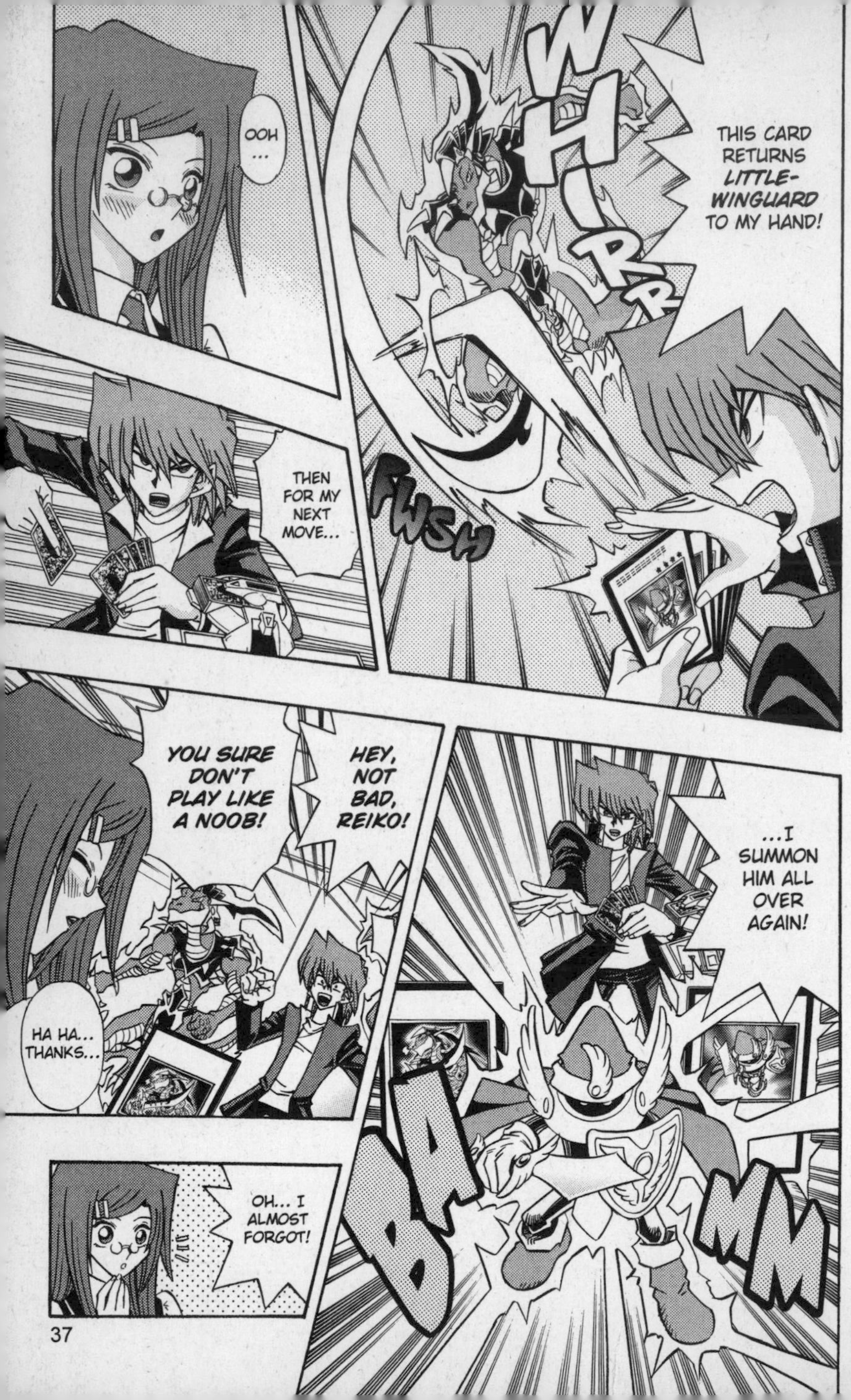
WHIRR
THIS CARD RETURNS LITTLE-WINGUARD TO MY HAND!
FWSH
OOH ...
THEN FOR MY NEXT MOVE...
...I SUMMON HIM ALL OVER AGAIN!
BAMM
HEY, NOT BAD, REIKO!
YOU SURE DON'T PLAY LIKE A NOOB!
HA HA... THANKS...
OH... I ALMOST FORGOT!

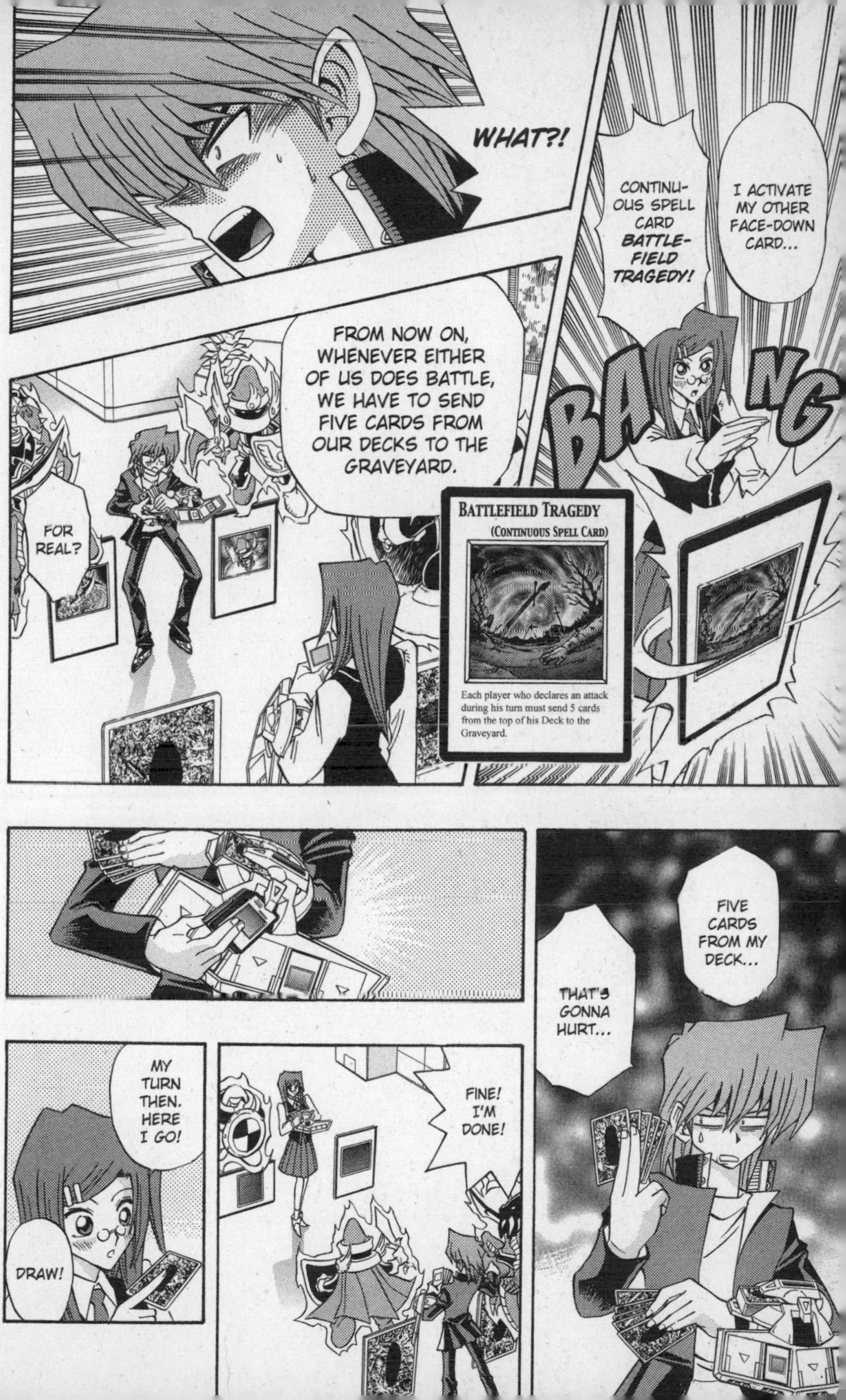
I ACTIVATE MY OTHER FACE-DOWN CARD...
CONTINU-OUS SPELL CARD BATTLE-FIELD TRAGEDY!
BANG
WHAT?!
FROM NOW ON, WHENEVER EITHER OF US DOES BATTLE, WE HAVE TO SEND FIVE CARDS FROM OUR DECKS TO THE GRAVEYARD.
FOR REAL?
BATTLEFIELD TRAGEDY
(CONTINUOUS SPELL CARD)
Each player who declares an attack during his turn must send 5 cards from the top of his Deck to the Graveyard.
FIVE CARDS FROM MY DECK...
THAT'S GONNA HURT...
FINE! I'M DONE!
MY TURN THEN. HERE I GO!
DRAW!

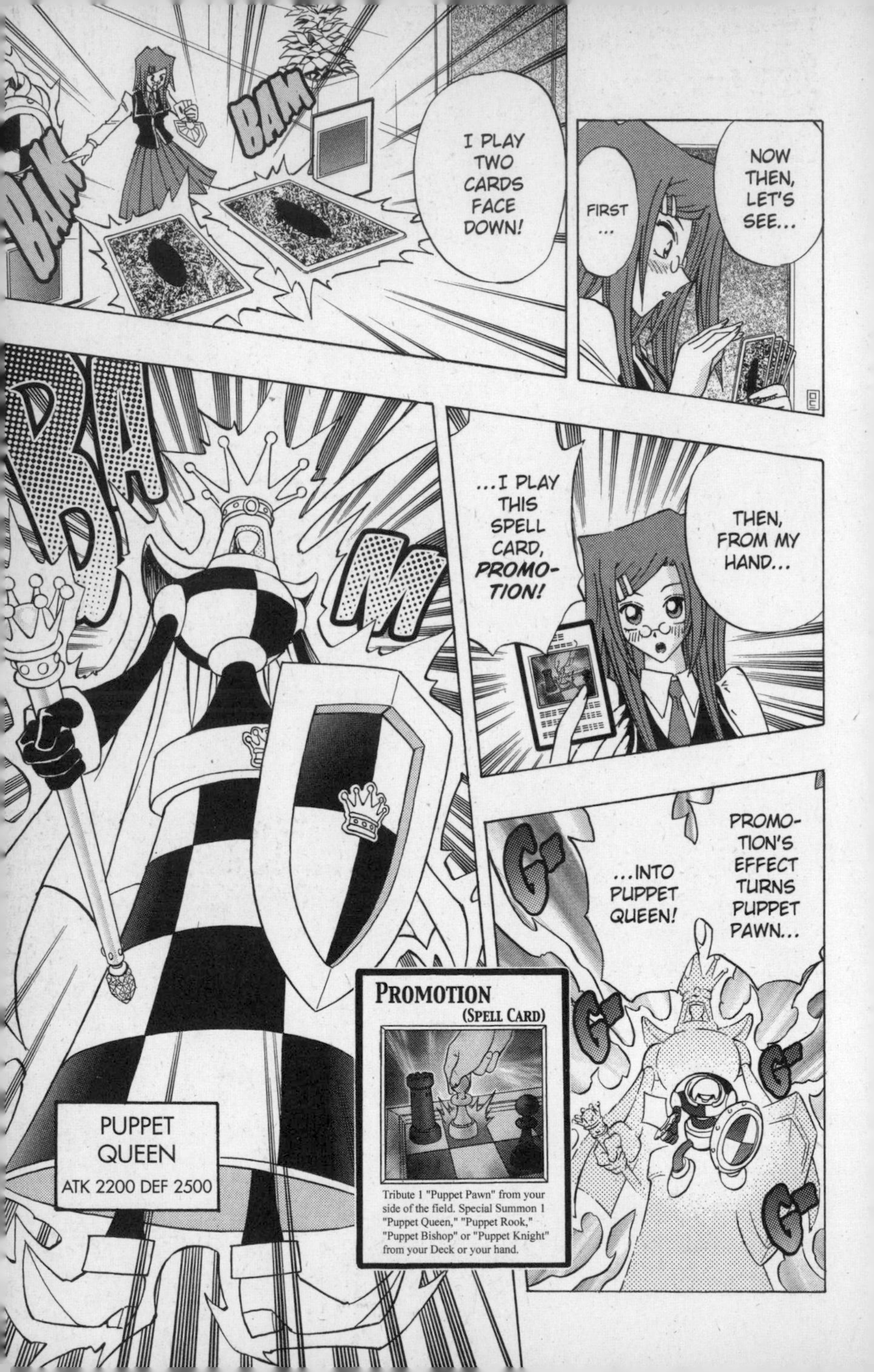
NOW THEN, LET'S SEE...
FIRST ...
I PLAY TWO CARDS FACE DOWN!
BAM
THEN, FROM MY HAND...
...I PLAY THIS SPELL CARD, PROMOTION!
PROMOTION'S EFFECT TURNS PUPPET PAWN...
...INTO PUPPET QUEEN!
PUPPET QUEEN
ATK 2200 DEF 2500
PROMOTION
(SPELL CARD)
Tribute 1 "Puppet Pawn" from your side of the field. Special Summon 1 "Puppet Queen," "Puppet Rook," "Puppet Bishop" or "Puppet Knight" from your Deck or your hand.

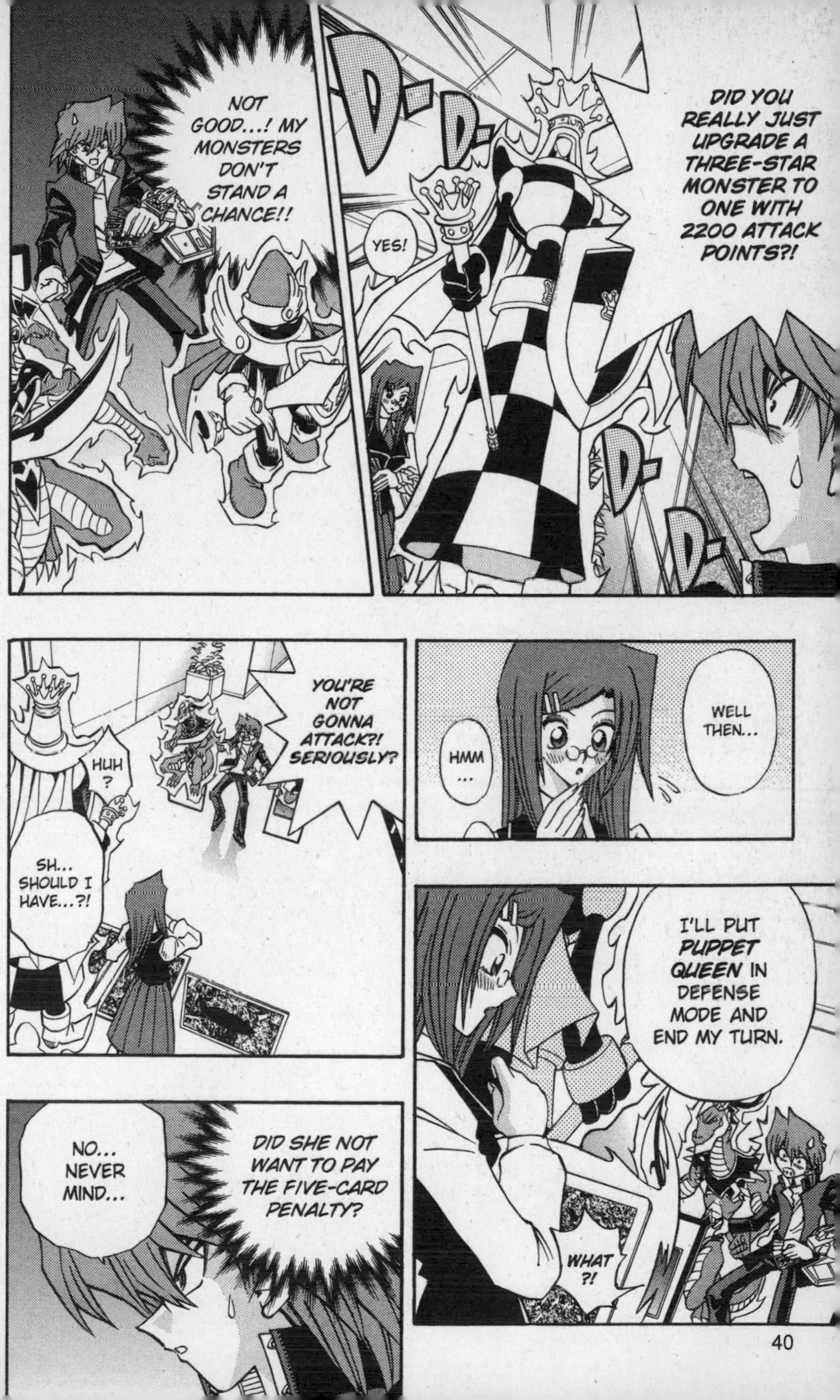
DID YOU REALLY JUST UPGRADE A THREE-STAR MONSTER TO ONE WITH 2200 ATTACK POINTS?!
D-
D-
YES!
D-
D-
NOT GOOD...! MY MONSTERS DON'T STAND A CHANCE!!
WELL THEN...
HMM ...
YOU'RE NOT GONNA ATTACK?! SERIOUSLY?
HUH ?
SH... SHOULD I HAVE...?!
I'LL PUT PUPPET QUEEN IN DEFENSE MODE AND END MY TURN.
WHAT ?!
DID SHE NOT WANT TO PAY THE FIVE-CARD PENALTY?
NO... NEVER MIND...

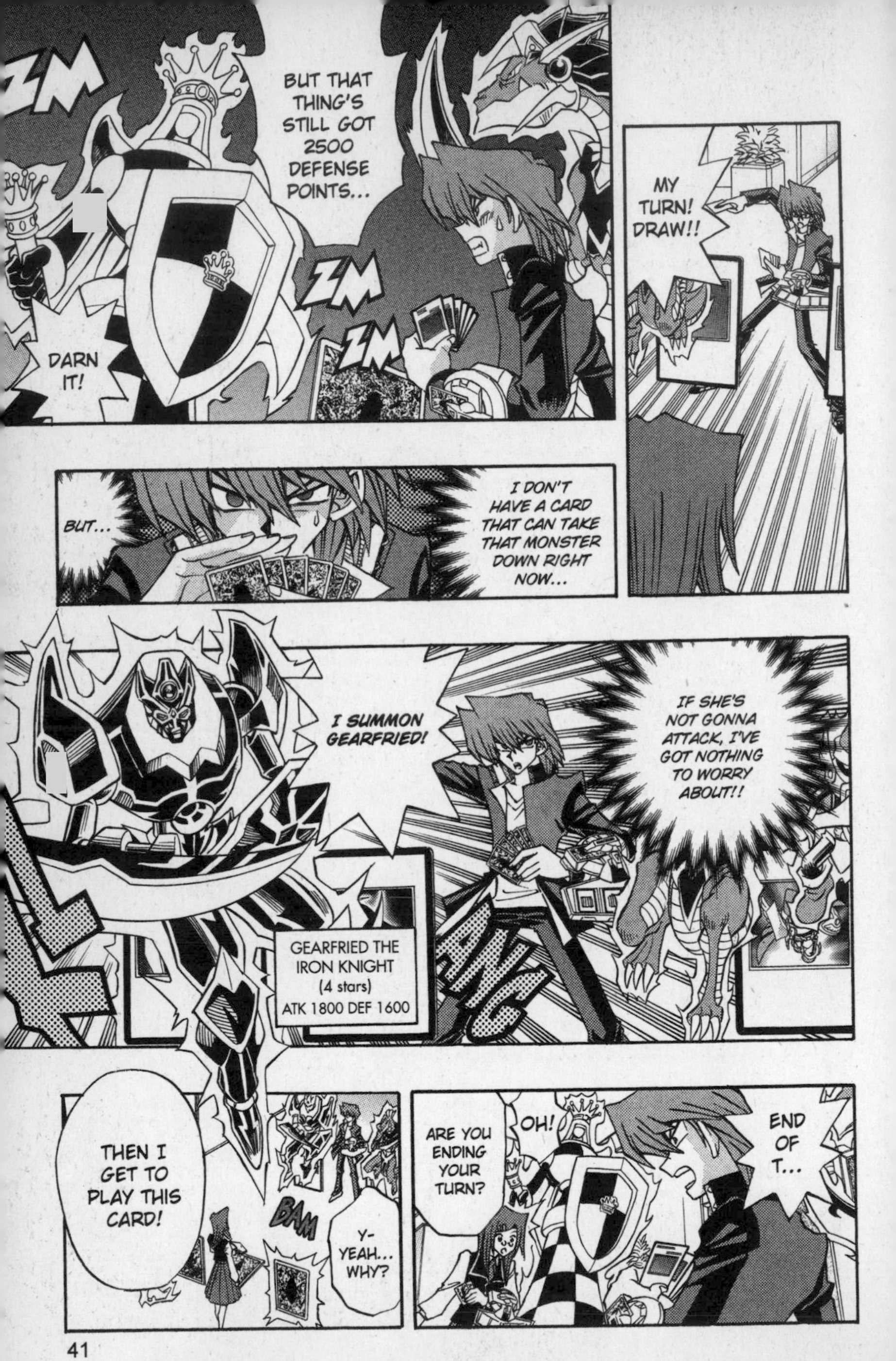
MY TURN! DRAW!!
BUT THAT THING'S STILL GOT 2500 DEFENSE POINTS...
ZM
ZM
ZM
ZM
DARN IT!
I DON'T HAVE A CARD THAT CAN TAKE THAT MONSTER DOWN RIGHT NOW...
BUT...
IF SHE'S NOT GONNA ATTACK, I'VE GOT NOTHING TO WORRY ABOUT!!
I SUMMON GEARFRIED!
GEARFRIED THE IRON KNIGHT
(4 stars)
ATK 1800 DEF 1600
END OF T...
OH!
ARE YOU ENDING YOUR TURN?
Y- YEAH... WHY?
BAM
THEN I GET TO PLAY THIS CARD!

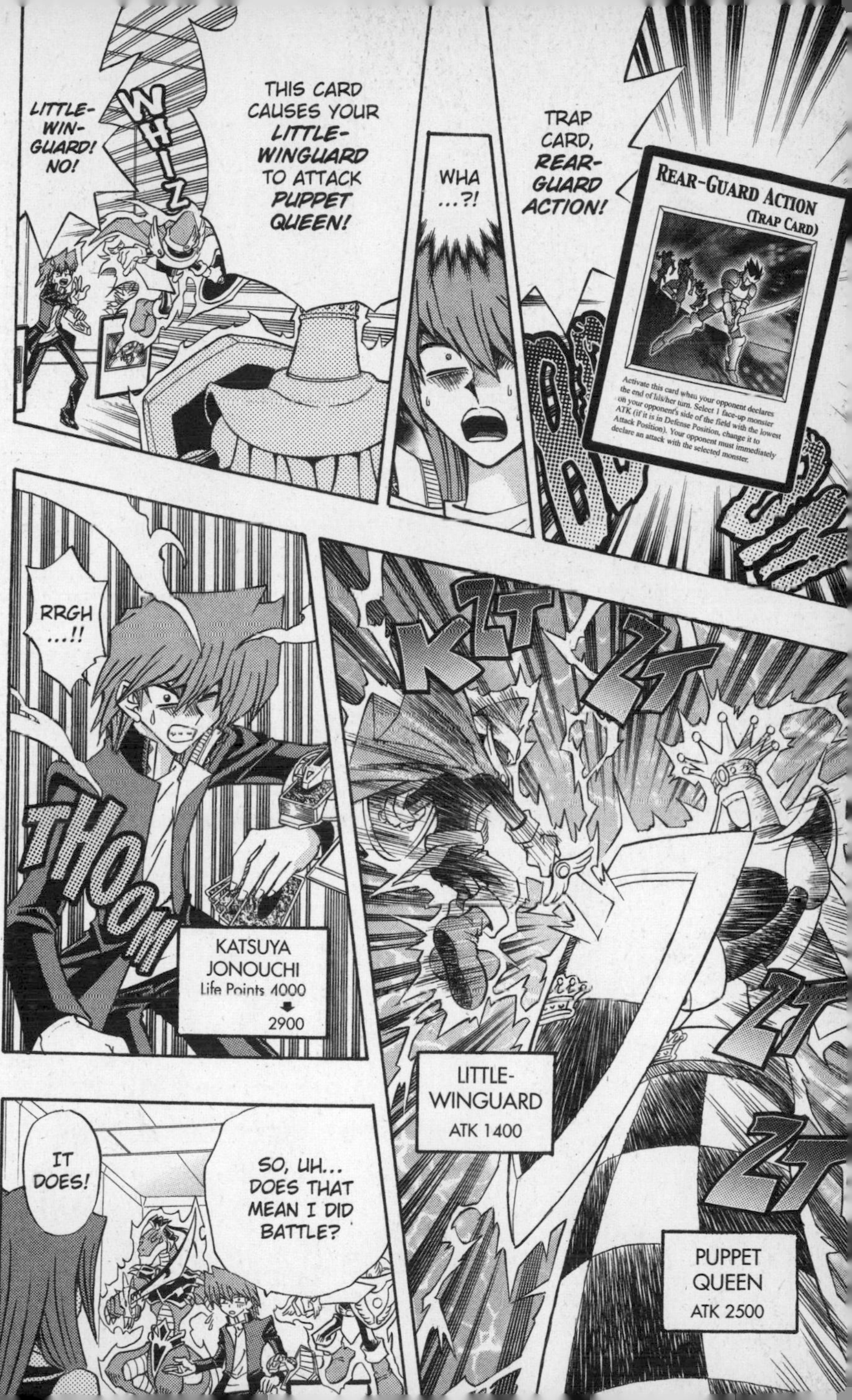
TRAP CARD, REAR-GUARD ACTION!
REAR-GUARD ACTION
(TRAP CARD)
Activate this card when your opponent declares the end of his/her turn. Select 1 face-up monster on your opponent's side of the field with the lowest ATK (if it is in Defense Position, change it to Attack Position). Your opponent must immediately declare an attack with the selected monster.
WHA ...?!
THIS CARD CAUSES YOUR LITTLE-WINGUARD TO ATTACK PUPPET QUEEN!
WHIZ
LITTLE-WIN-GUARD! NO!
KZZT
ZZT
LITTLE-WINGUARD
ATK 1400
ZZT
ZZT
PUPPET QUEEN
ATK 2500
RRGH ...!!
THOOM
KATSUYA JONOUCHI
Life Points 4000
2900
SO, UH... DOES THAT MEAN I DID BATTLE?
IT DOES!

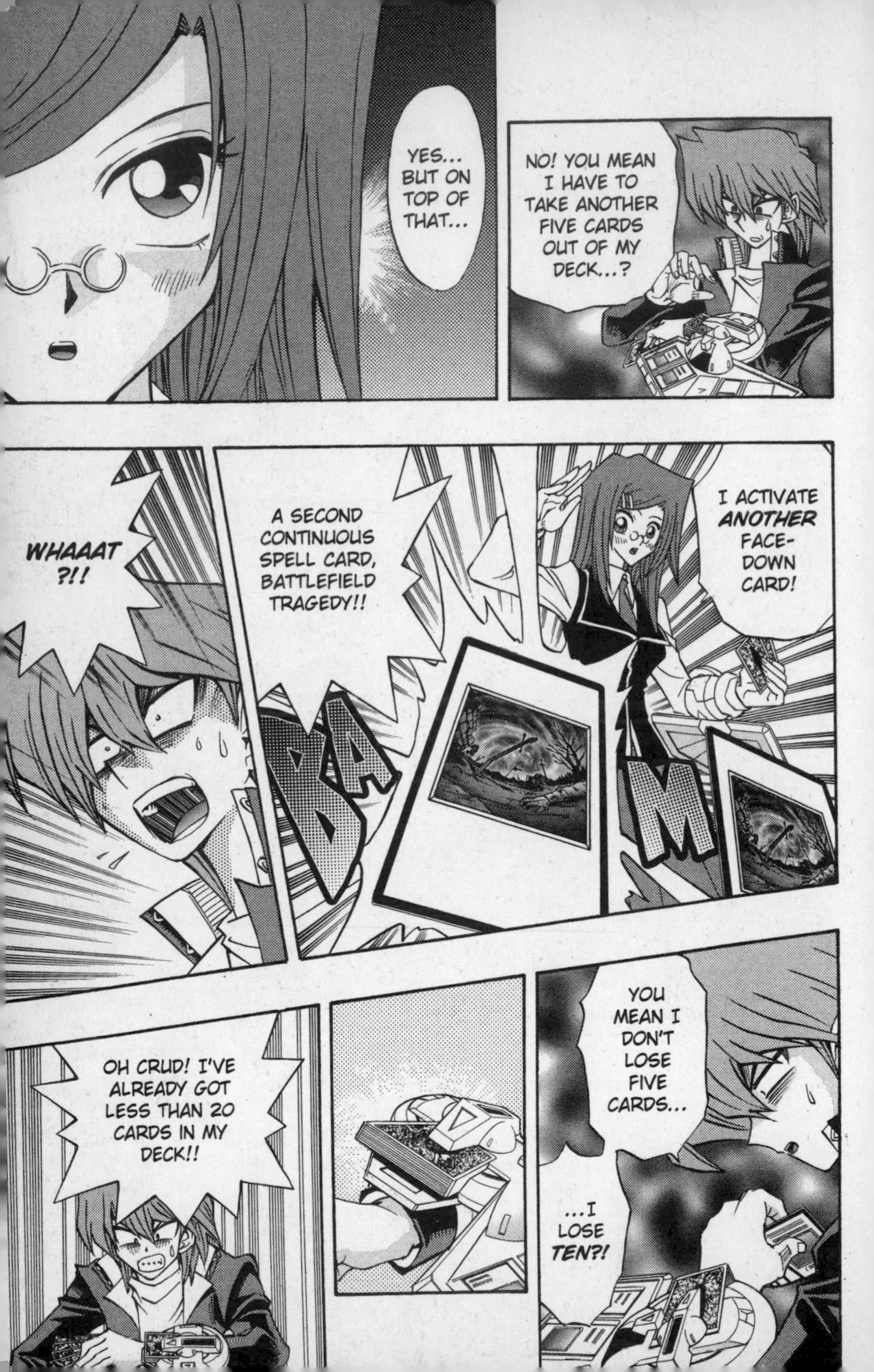
NO! YOU MEAN I HAVE TO TAKE ANOTHER FIVE CARDS OUT OF MY DECK...?
YES... BUT ON TOP OF THAT...
I ACTIVATE ANOTHER FACE-DOWN CARD!
A SECOND CONTINUOUS SPELL CARD, BATTLEFIELD TRAGEDY!!
BAM
WHAAAT?!!
YOU MEAN I DON'T LOSE FIVE CARDS...
...I LOSE TEN?!
OH CRUD! I'VE ALREADY GOT LESS THAN 20 CARDS IN MY DECK!!

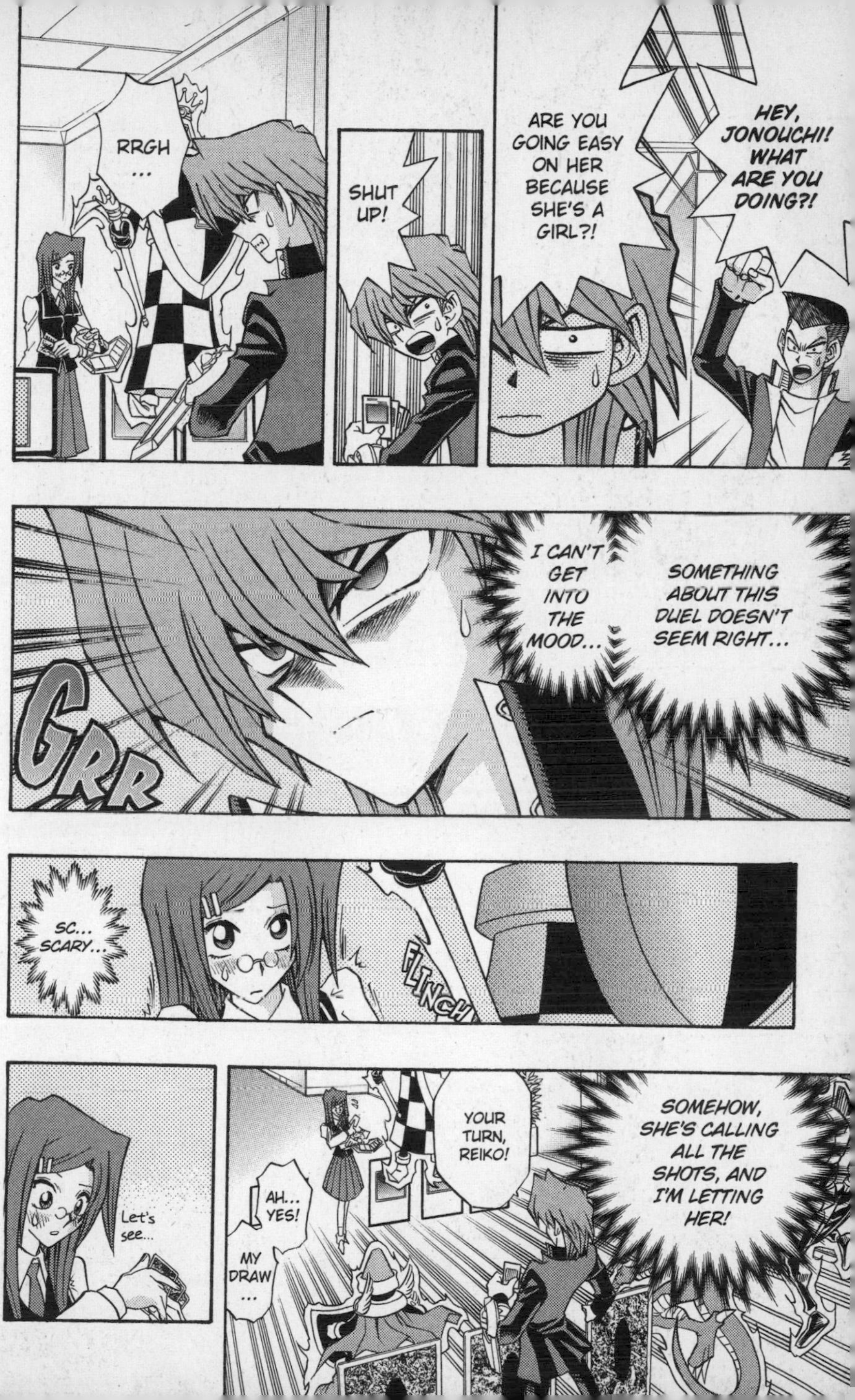
HEY, JONOUCHI! WHAT ARE YOU DOING?!
ARE YOU GOING EASY ON HER BECAUSE SHE'S A GIRL?!
SHUT UP!
RRGH ...
SOMETHING ABOUT THIS DUEL DOESN'T SEEM RIGHT...
I CAN'T GET INTO THE MOOD...
GRR
FLINCH
SC... SCARY...
SOMEHOW, SHE'S CALLING ALL THE SHOTS, AND I'M LETTING HER!
YOUR TURN, REIKO!
AH... YES!
MY DRAW ...
Let's see...

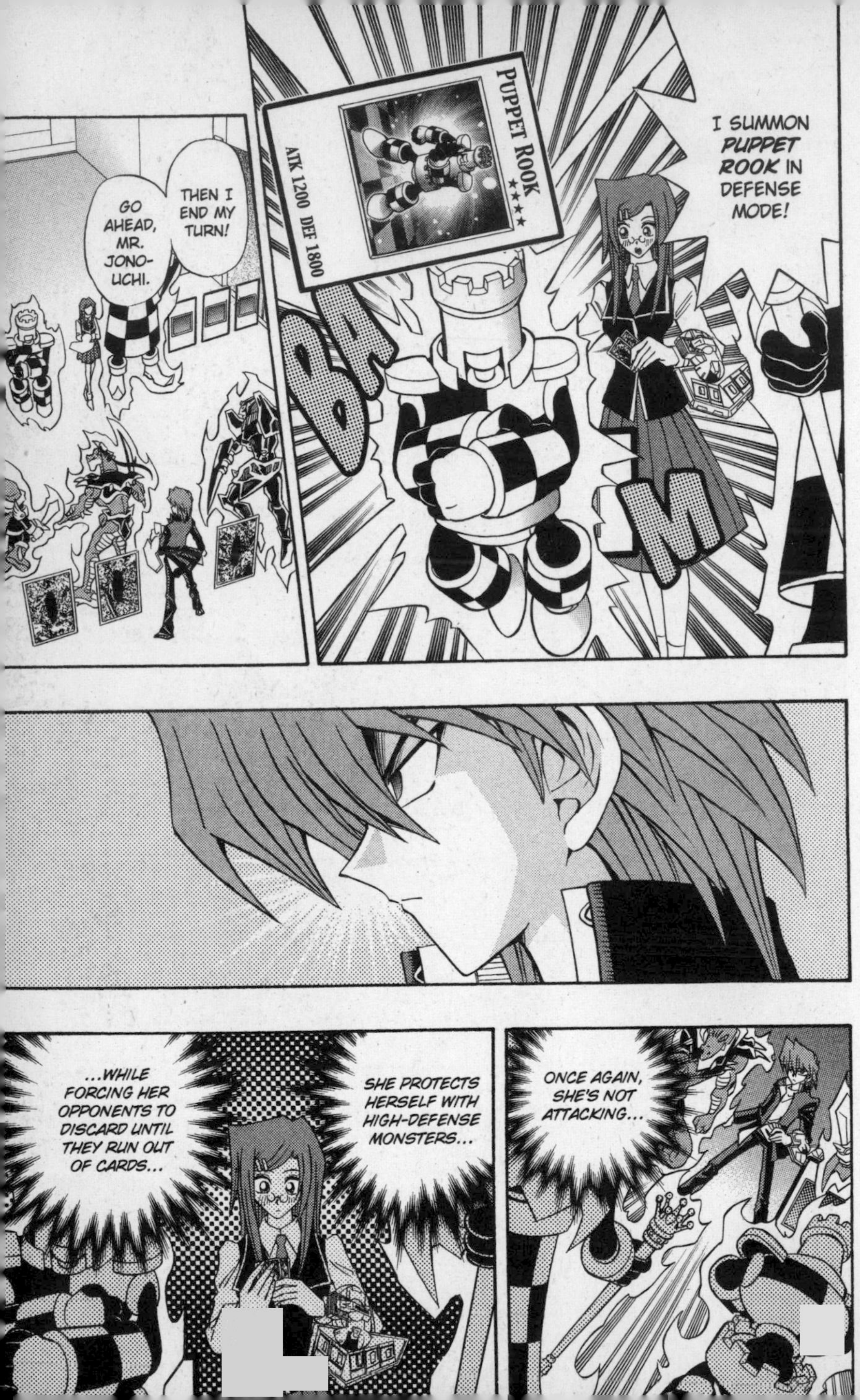
I SUMMON PUPPET ROOK IN DEFENSE MODE!
PUPPET ROOK
ATK 1200 DEF 1800
BAM
THEN I END MY TURN!
GO AHEAD, MR. JONOUCHI.
ONCE AGAIN, SHE'S NOT ATTACKING...
SHE PROTECTS HERSELF WITH HIGH-DEFENSE MONSTERS...
...WHILE FORCING HER OPPONENTS TO DISCARD UNTIL THEY RUN OUT OF CARDS...

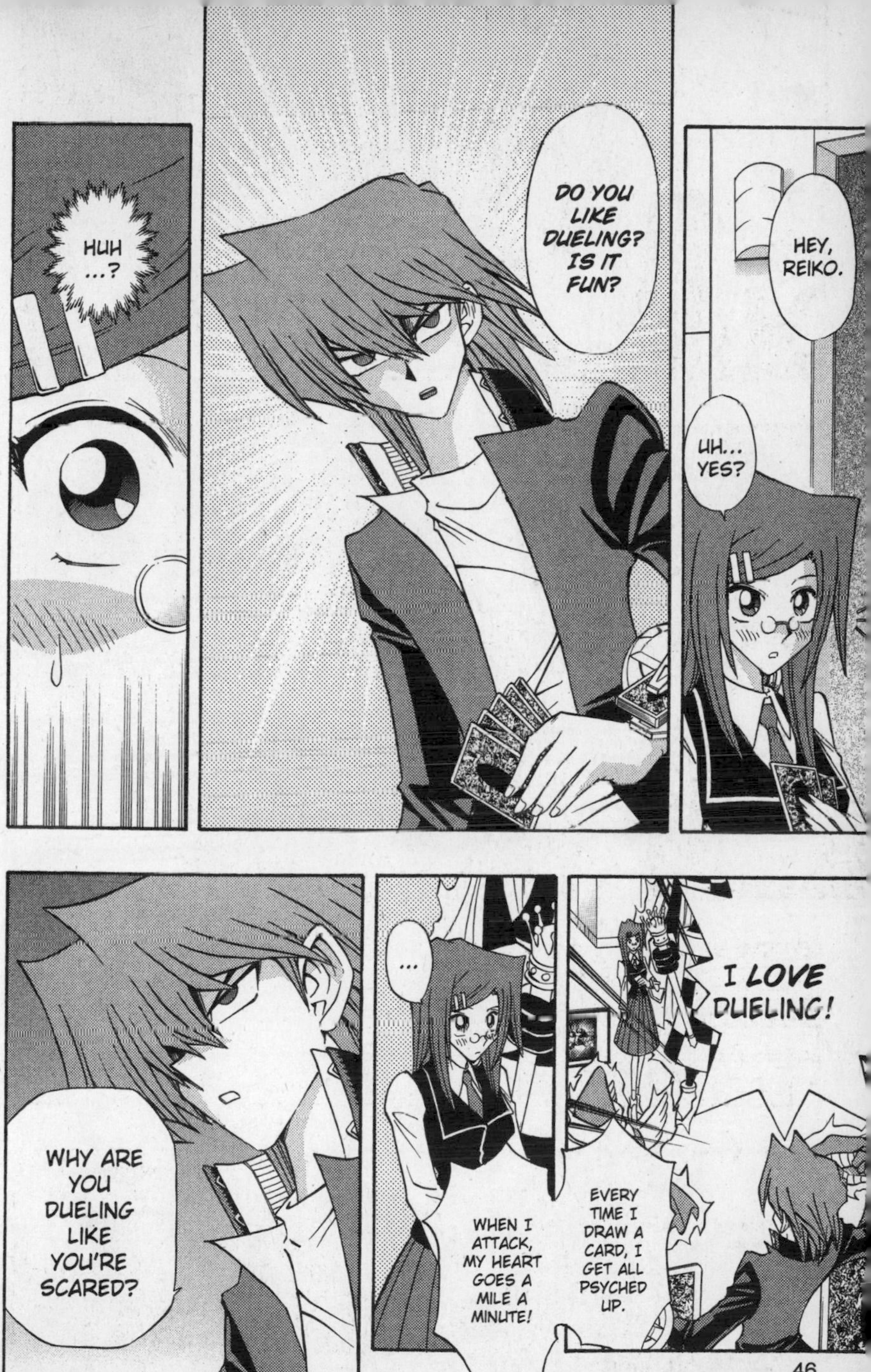
HEY, REIKO.
UH... YES?
DO YOU LIKE DUELING? IS IT FUN?
HUH ...?
I LOVE DUELING!
EVERY TIME I DRAW A CARD, I GET ALL PSYCHED UP.
WHEN I ATTACK, MY HEART GOES A MILE A MINUTE!
...
WHY ARE YOU DUELING LIKE YOU'RE SCARED?

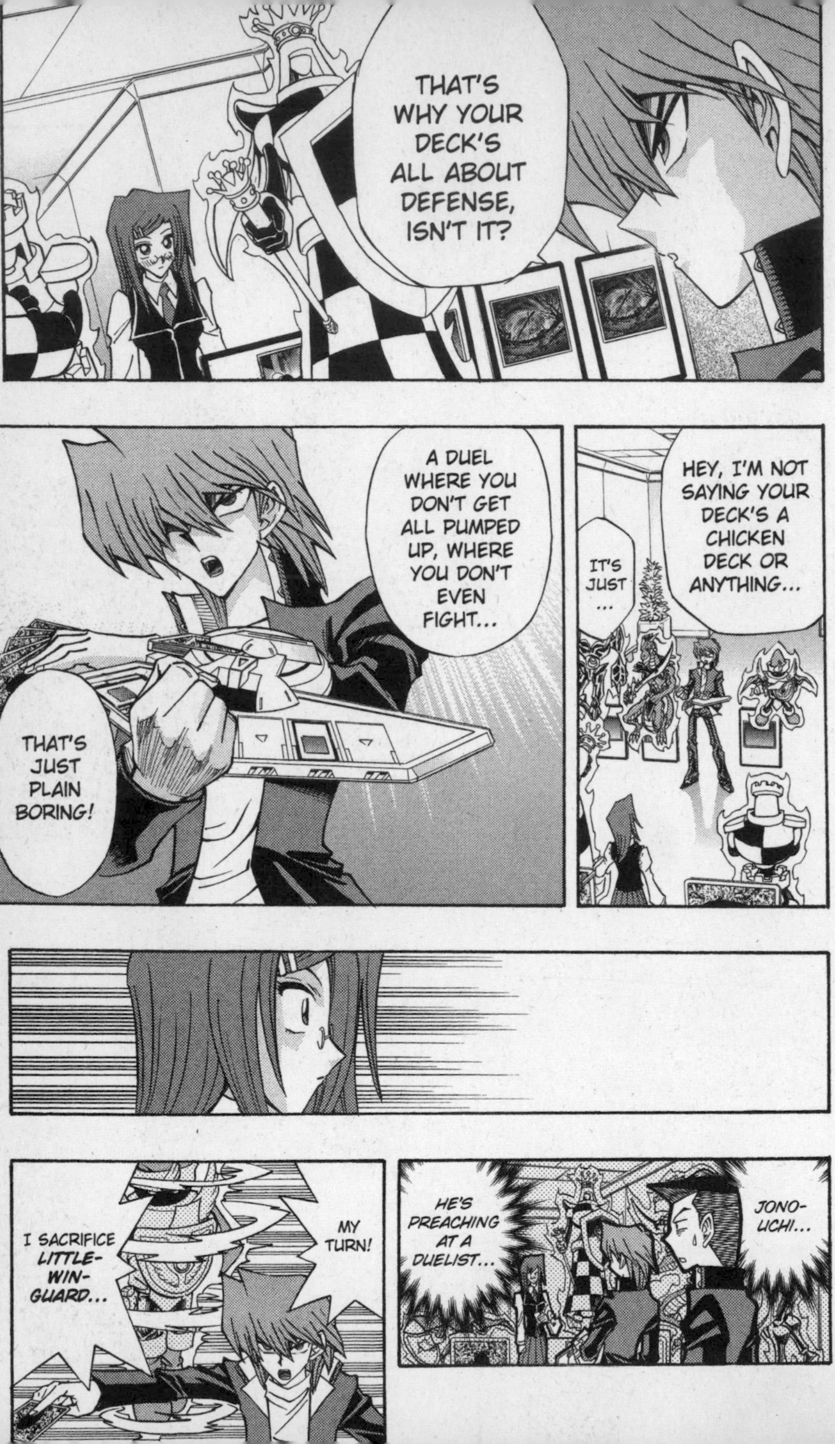
THAT'S WHY YOUR DECK'S ALL ABOUT DEFENSE, ISN'T IT?
HEY, I'M NOT SAYING YOUR DECK'S A CHICKEN DECK OR ANYTHING...
IT'S JUST ...
A DUEL WHERE YOU DON'T GET ALL PUMPED UP, WHERE YOU DON'T EVEN FIGHT...
THAT'S JUST PLAIN BORING!
JONO-UCHI...
HE'S PREACHING AT A DUELIST...
MY TURN!
I SACRIFICE *LITTLE-WINGUARD*...

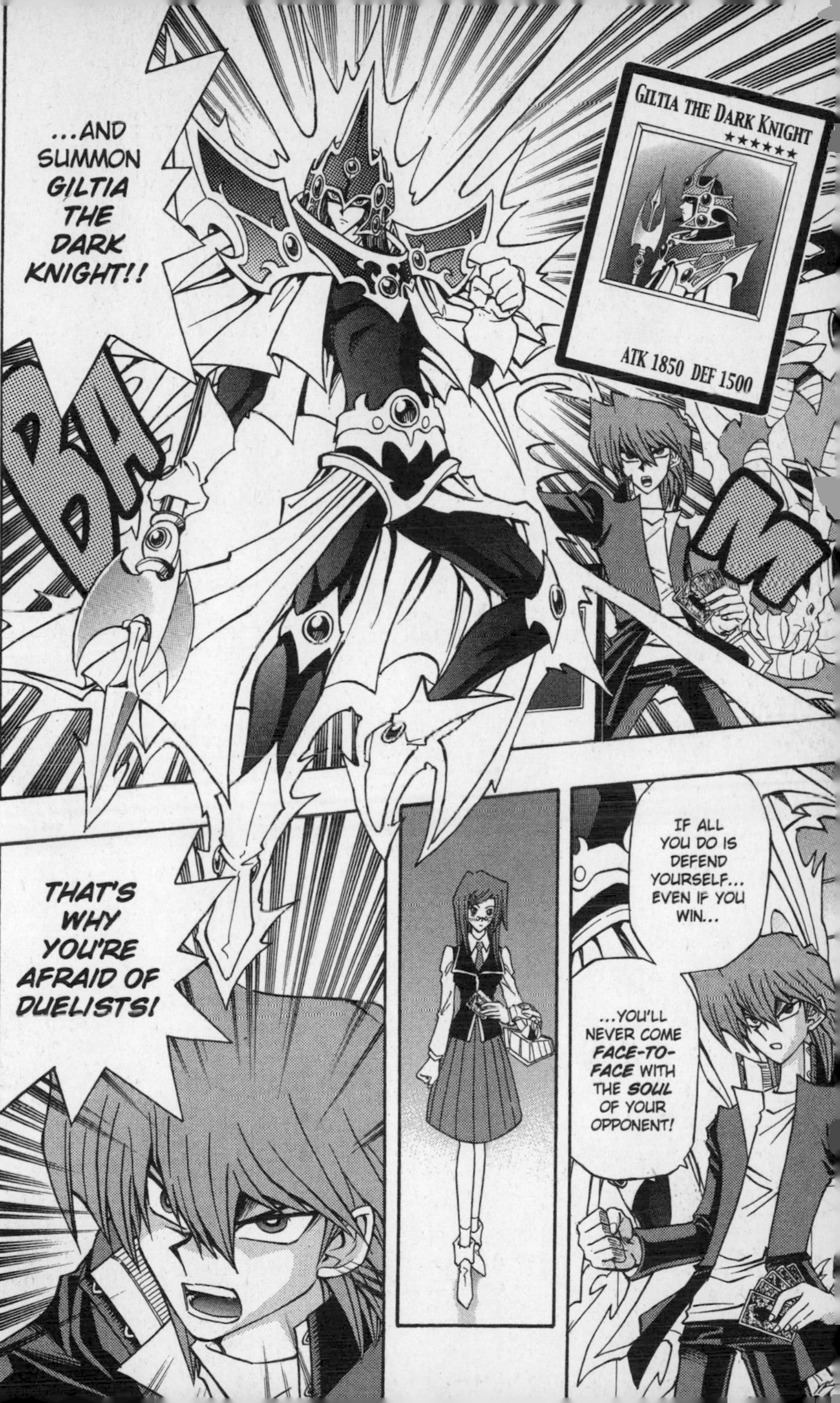

GILTIA THE DARK KNIGHT
ATK 1850 DEF 1500
...AND SUMMON GILTIA THE DARK KNIGHT!!
BA
M
IF ALL YOU DO IS DEFEND YOURSELF... EVEN IF YOU WIN...
...YOU'LL NEVER COME FACE-TO-FACE WITH THE SOUL OF YOUR OPPONENT!
THAT'S WHY YOU'RE AFRAID OF DUELISTS!

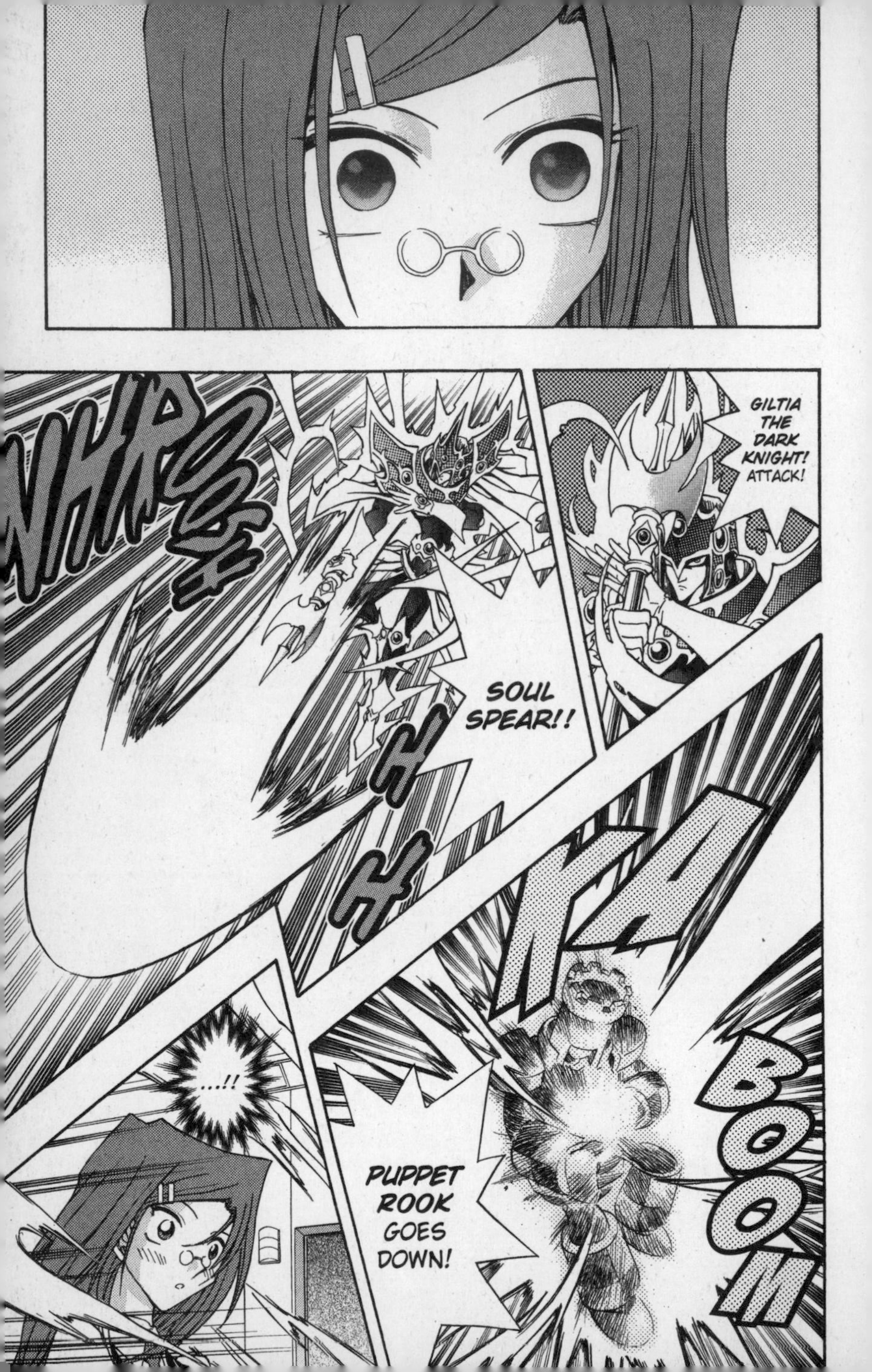
GILTIA THE DARK KNIGHT! ATTACK!
WHOOSH
SOUL SPEAR!!
KA
BOOOM
PUPPET ROOK GOES DOWN!
...!!

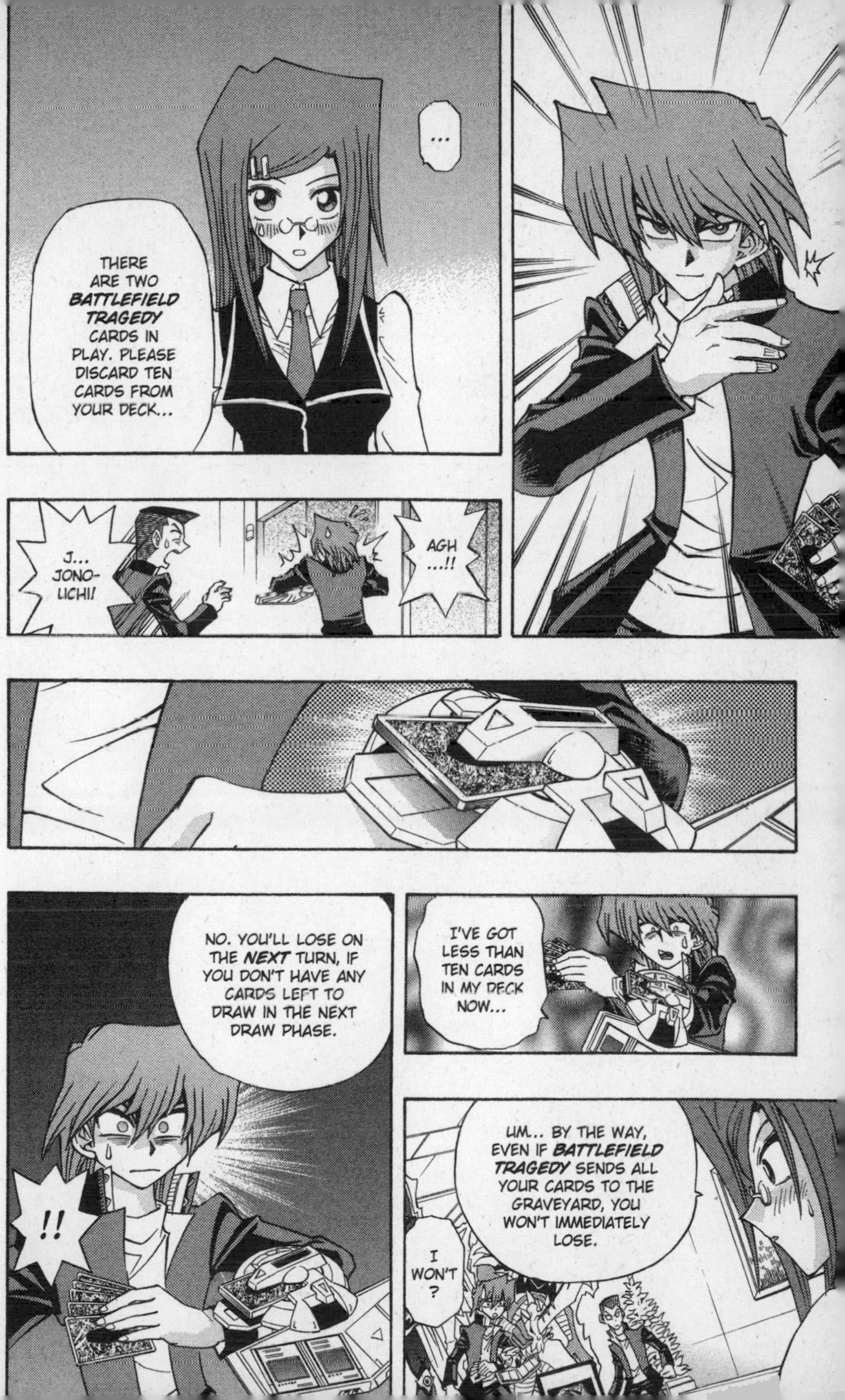
...
THERE ARE TWO BATTLEFIELD TRAGEDY CARDS IN PLAY. PLEASE DISCARD TEN CARDS FROM YOUR DECK...
AGH ...!!
J... JONO-UCHI!
I'VE GOT LESS THAN TEN CARDS IN MY DECK NOW...
UM... BY THE WAY, EVEN IF BATTLEFIELD TRAGEDY SENDS ALL YOUR CARDS TO THE GRAVEYARD, YOU WON'T IMMEDIATELY LOSE.
I WON'T ?
NO. YOU'LL LOSE ON THE NEXT TURN, IF YOU DON'T HAVE ANY CARDS LEFT TO DRAW IN THE NEXT DRAW PHASE.
!!

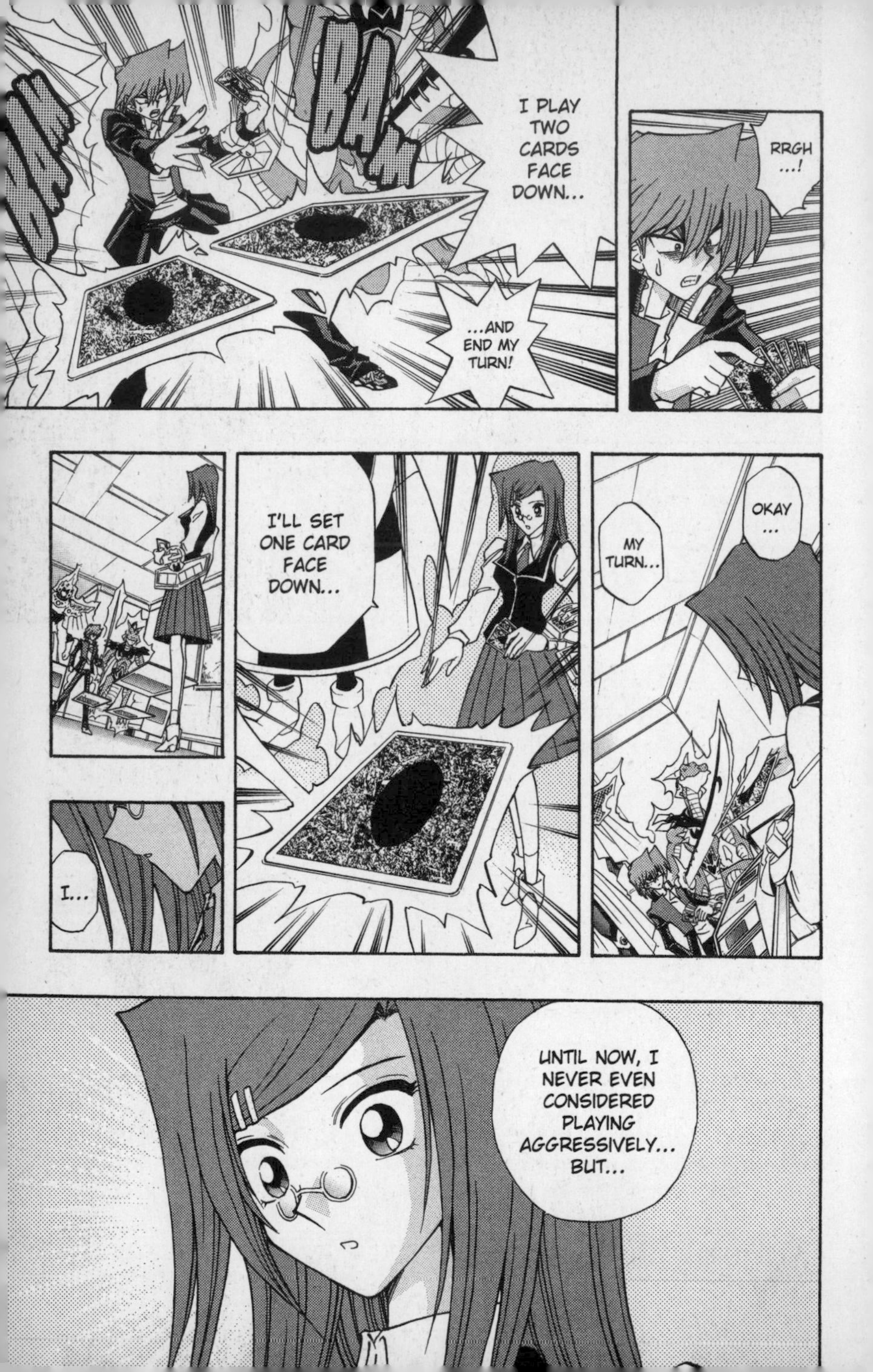
RRGH ...!
I PLAY TWO CARDS FACE DOWN...
...AND END MY TURN!
OKAY ...
MY TURN...
I'LL SET ONE CARD FACE DOWN...
I...
UNTIL NOW, I NEVER EVEN CONSIDERED PLAYING AGGRESSIVELY... BUT...

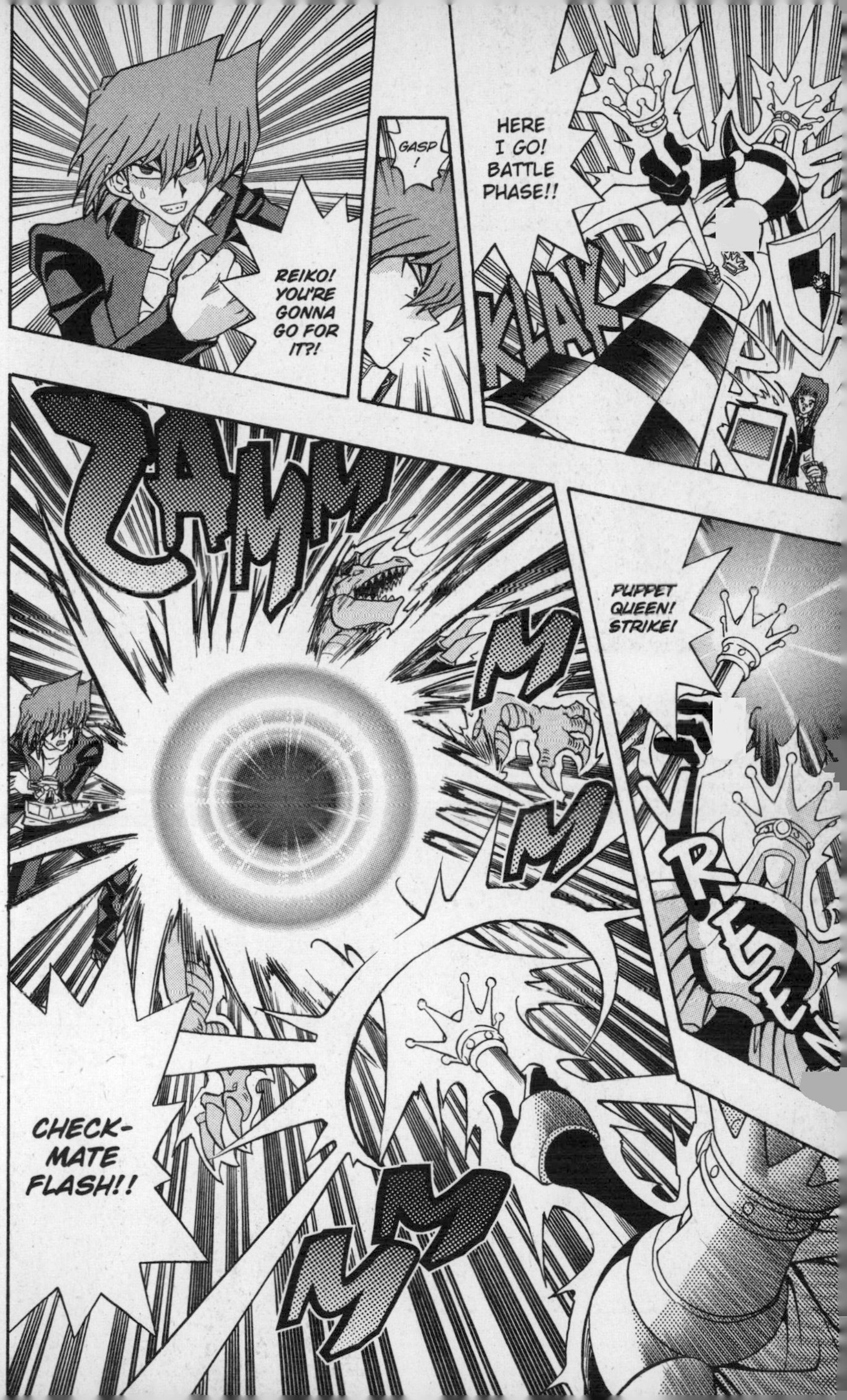
HERE I GO! BATTLE PHASE!!
KLAK
GASP!
REIKO! YOU'RE GONNA GO FOR IT?!
PUPPET QUEEN! STRIKE!
ZAMM
CHECK-MATE FLASH!!

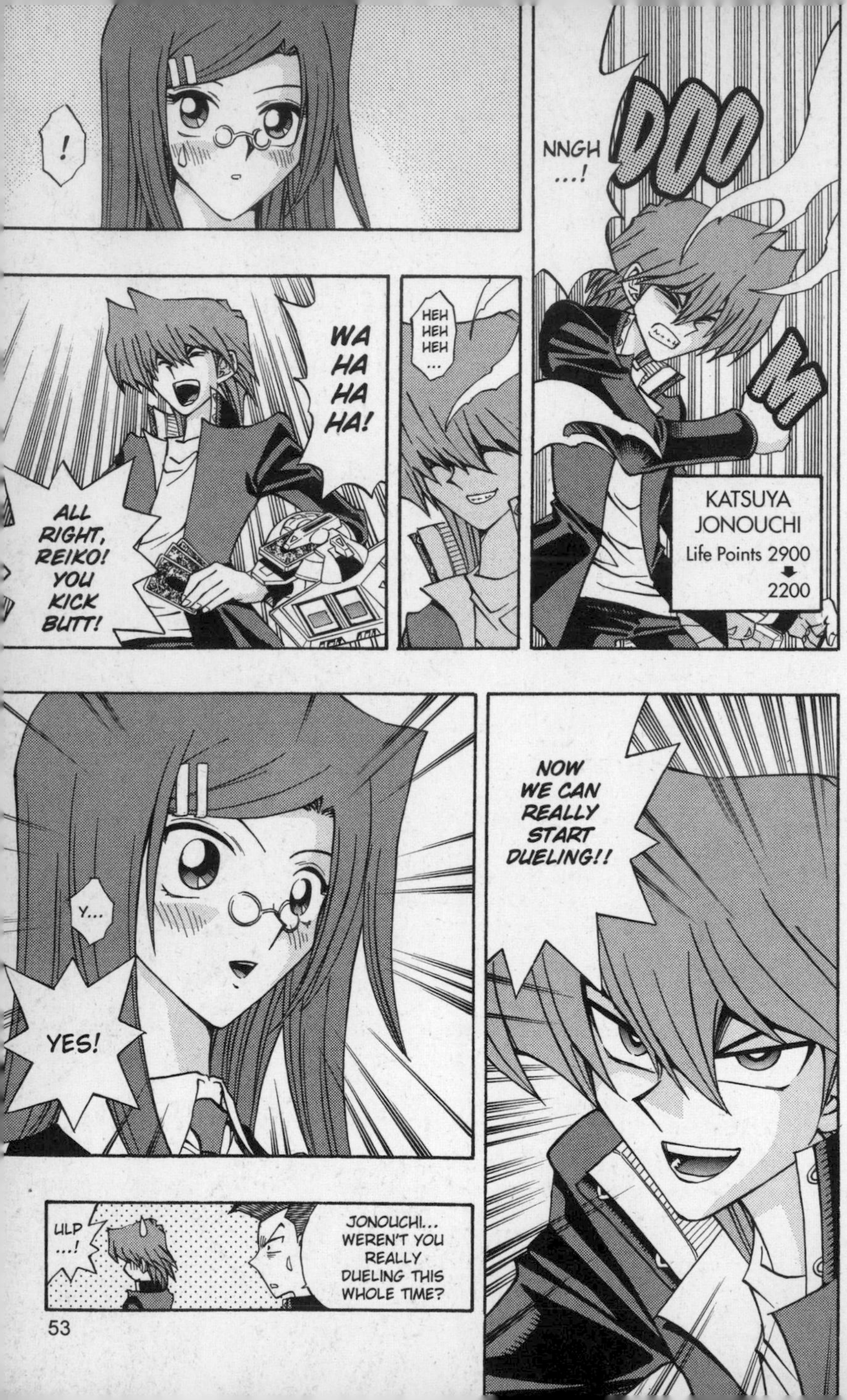
NNGH ...!
DOOM
KATSUYA JONOUCHI
Life Points 2900 ➡ 2200
!
HEH HEH HEH ...
WA HA HA HA!
ALL RIGHT, REIKO! YOU KICK BUTT!
NOW WE CAN REALLY START DUELING!!
Y...
YES!
JONOUCHI... WEREN'T YOU REALLY DUELING THIS WHOLE TIME?
ULP ...!

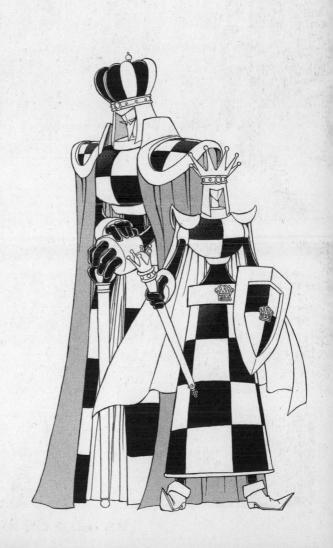

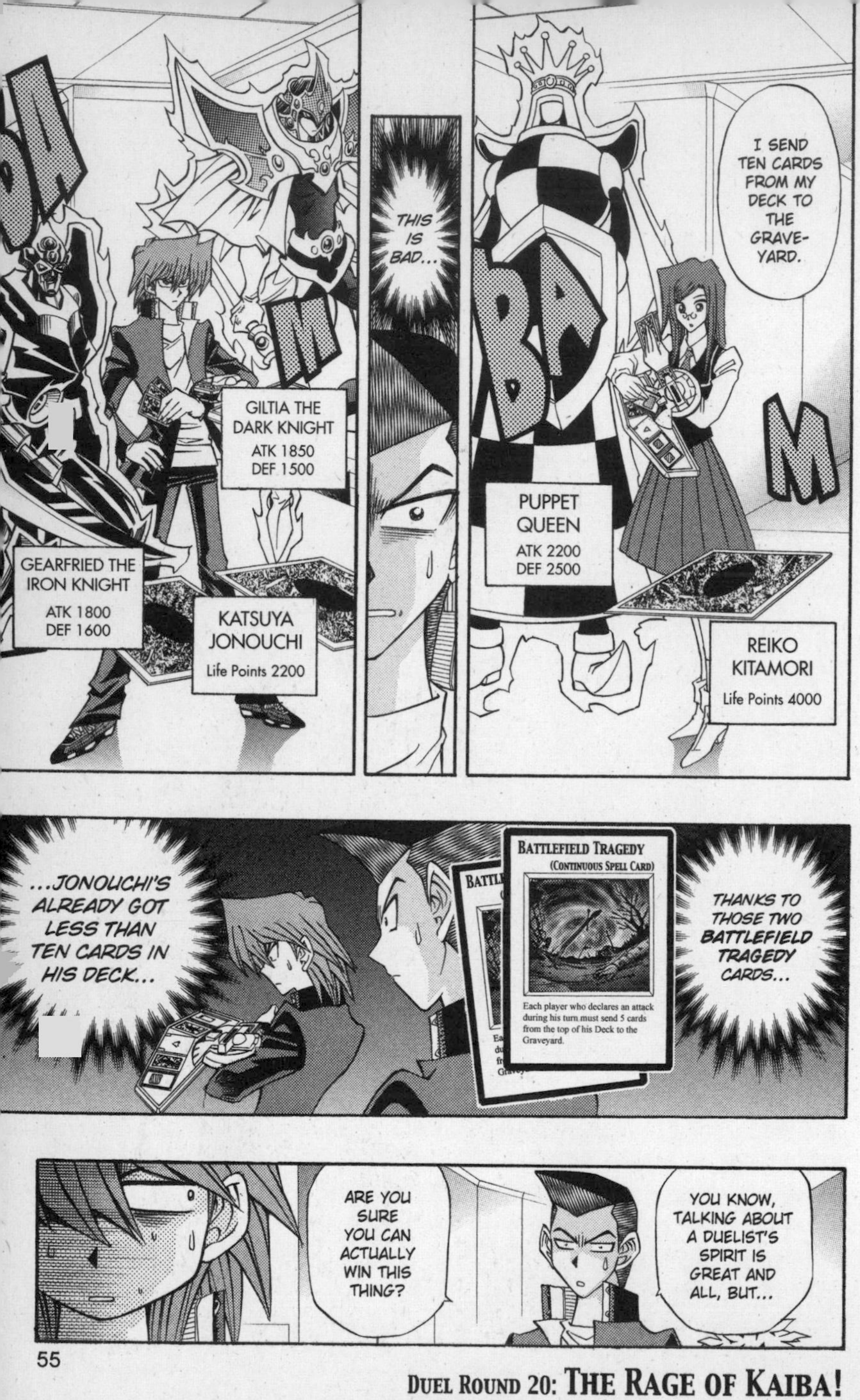
I SEND TEN CARDS FROM MY DECK TO THE GRAVEYARD.
BA
M
PUPPET QUEEN ATK 2200 DEF 2500
REIKO KITAMORI Life Points 4000
THIS IS BAD...
DA
M
GILTIA THE DARK KNIGHT ATK 1850 DEF 1500
GEARFRIED THE IRON KNIGHT ATK 1800 DEF 1600
KATSUYA JONOUCHI Life Points 2200
THANKS TO THOSE TWO BATTLEFIELD TRAGEDY CARDS...
BATTLEFIELD TRAGEDY (CONTINUOUS SPELL CARD)
Each player who declares an attack during his turn must send 5 cards from the top of his Deck to the Graveyard.
...JONOUCHI'S ALREADY GOT LESS THAN TEN CARDS IN HIS DECK...
YOU KNOW, TALKING ABOUT A DUELIST'S SPIRIT IS GREAT AND ALL, BUT...
ARE YOU SURE YOU CAN ACTUALLY WIN THIS THING?

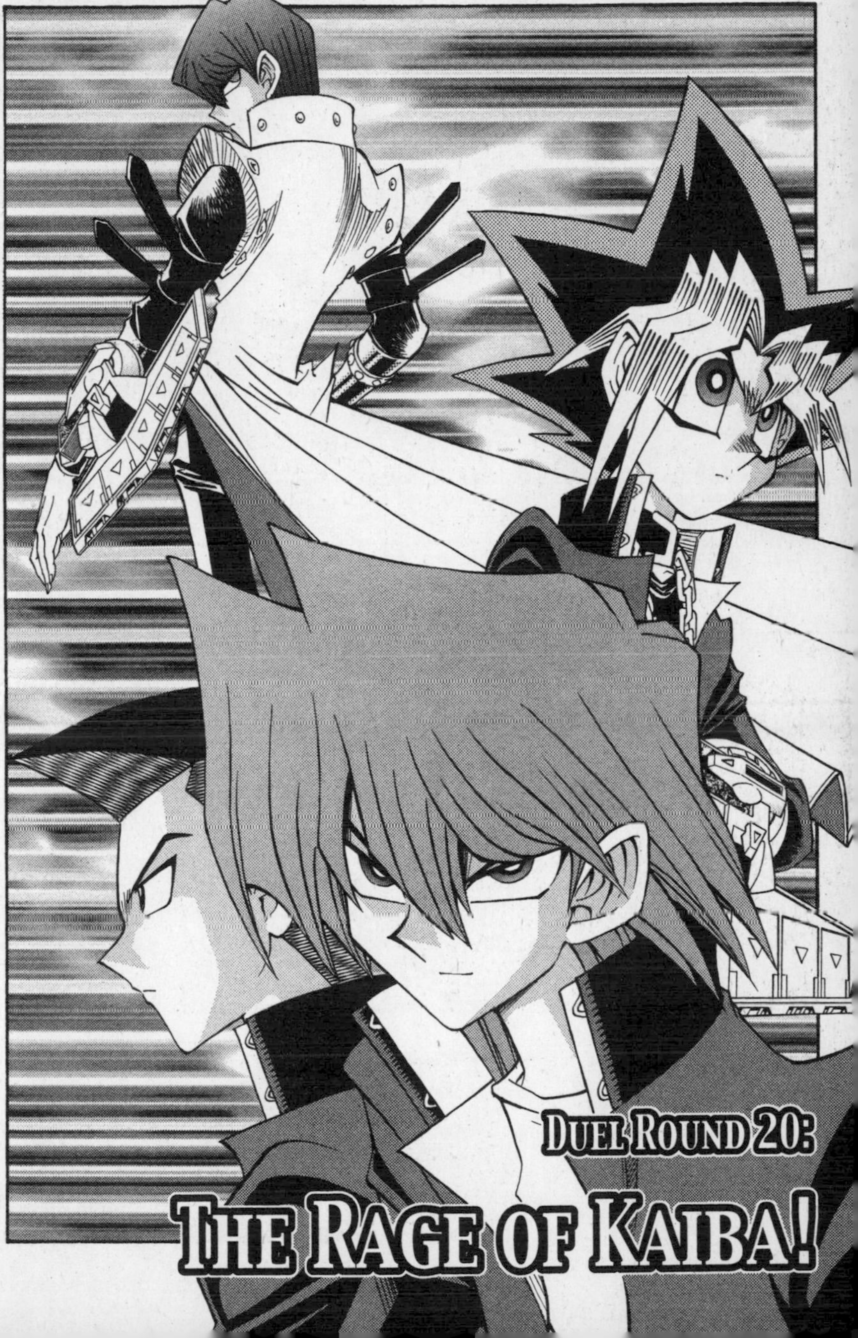
DUEL ROUND 20:
THE RAGE OF KAIBA!

READ THIS WAY

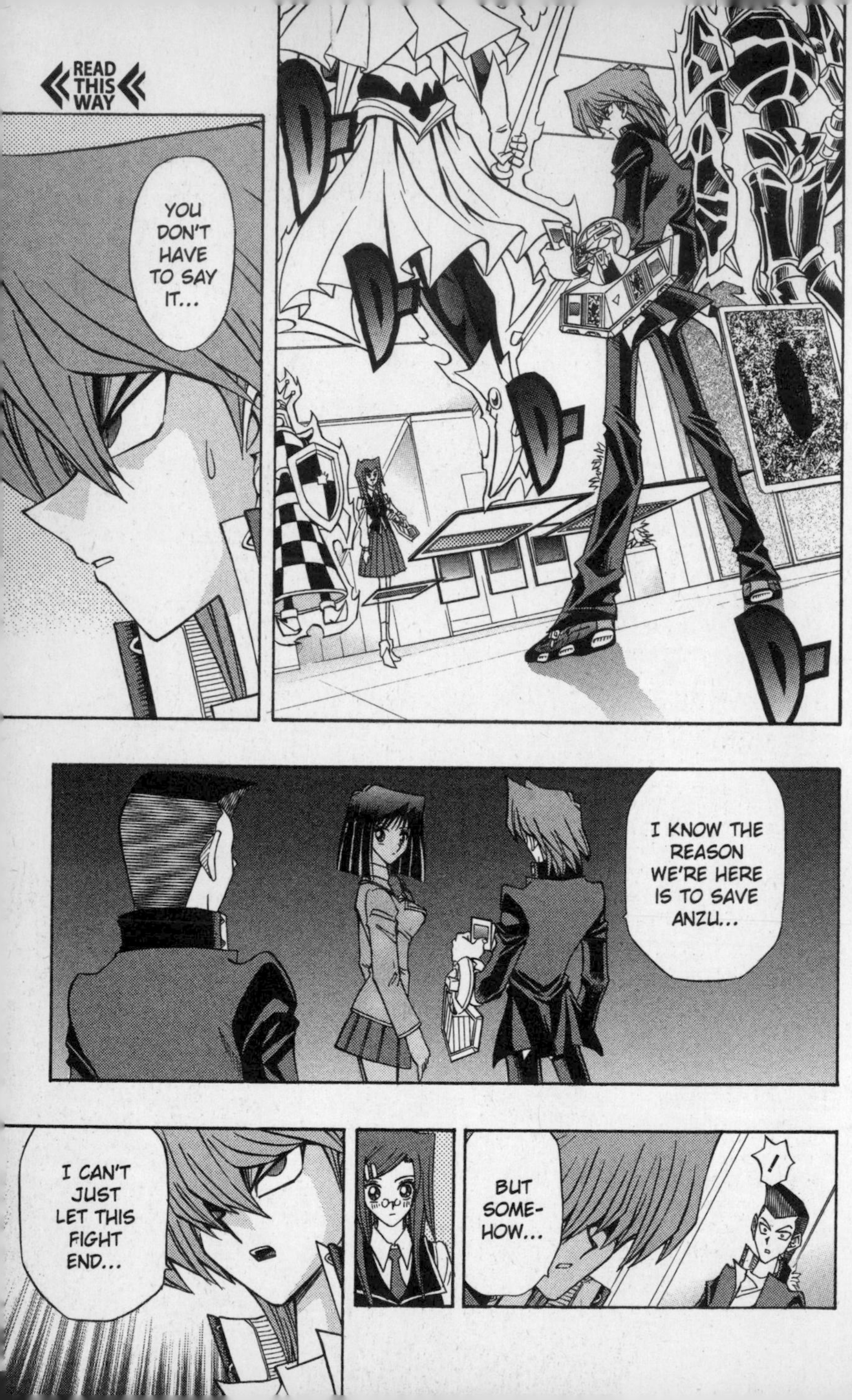
YOU DON'T HAVE TO SAY IT...
I KNOW THE REASON WE'RE HERE IS TO SAVE ANZU...
!
BUT SOME-HOW...
I CAN'T JUST LET THIS FIGHT END...

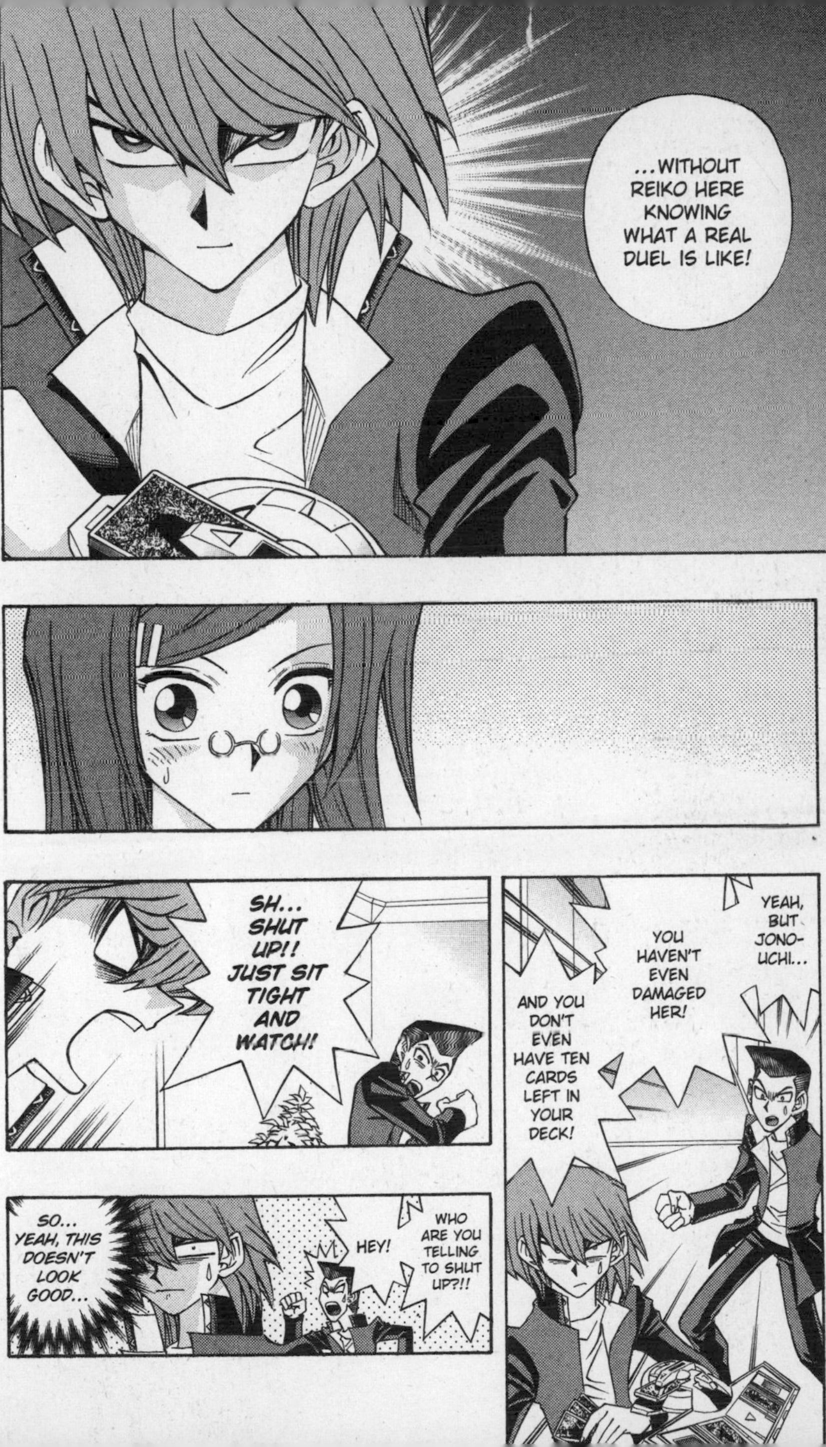
...WITHOUT REIKO HERE KNOWING WHAT A REAL DUEL IS LIKE!
YEAH, BUT JONO-UCHI...
YOU HAVEN'T EVEN DAMAGED HER!
AND YOU DON'T EVEN HAVE TEN CARDS LEFT IN YOUR DECK!
SH... SHUT UP!! JUST SIT TIGHT AND WATCH!
WHO ARE YOU TELLING TO SHUT UP?!!
HEY!
SO... YEAH, THIS DOESN'T LOOK GOOD...

READ THIS WAY

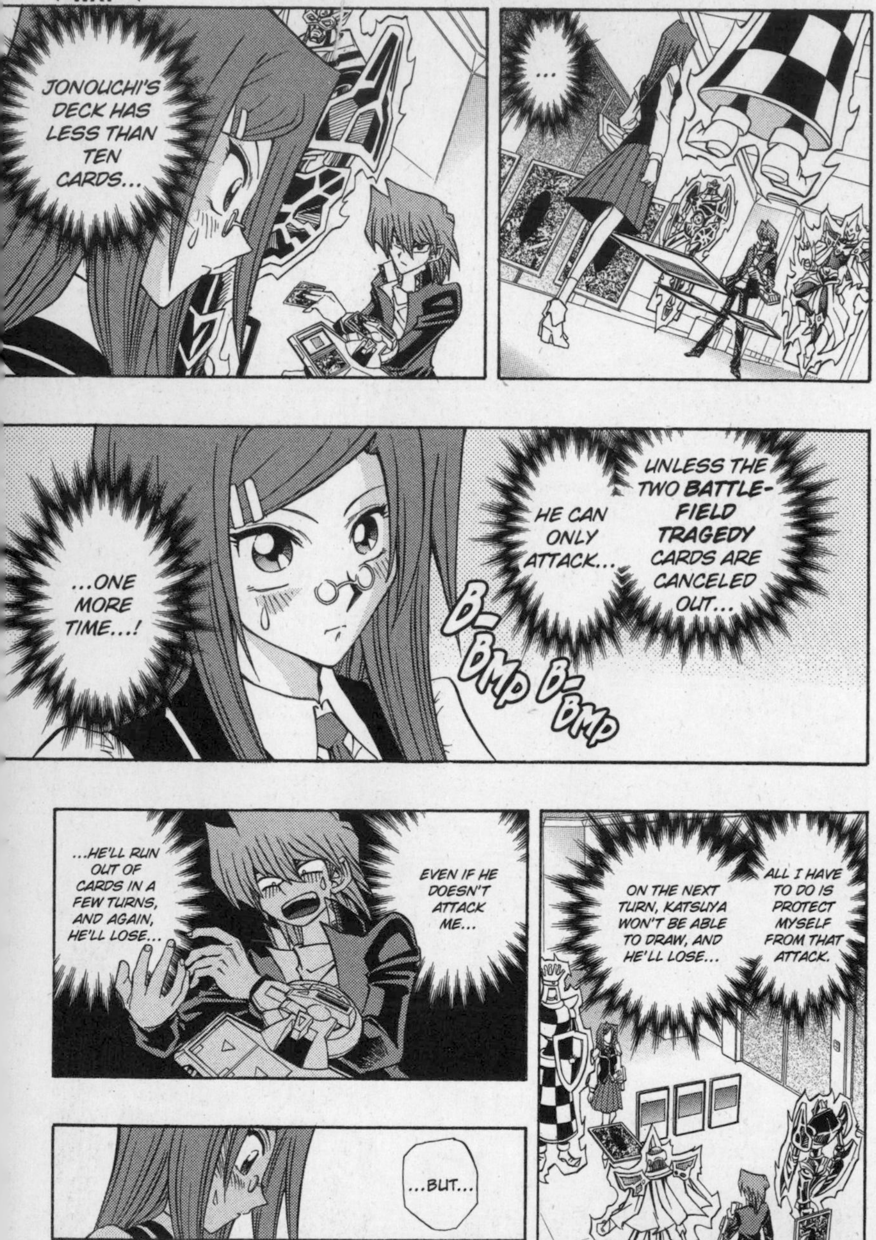
...
JONOUCHI'S DECK HAS LESS THAN TEN CARDS...
UNLESS THE TWO BATTLE-FIELD TRAGEDY CARDS ARE CANCELED OUT...
HE CAN ONLY ATTACK...
...ONE MORE TIME...!
B-BMP B-BMP
ALL I HAVE TO DO IS PROTECT MYSELF FROM THAT ATTACK.
ON THE NEXT TURN, KATSUYA WON'T BE ABLE TO DRAW, AND HE'LL LOSE...
EVEN IF HE DOESN'T ATTACK ME...
...HE'LL RUN OUT OF CARDS IN A FEW TURNS, AND AGAIN, HE'LL LOSE...
...BUT...

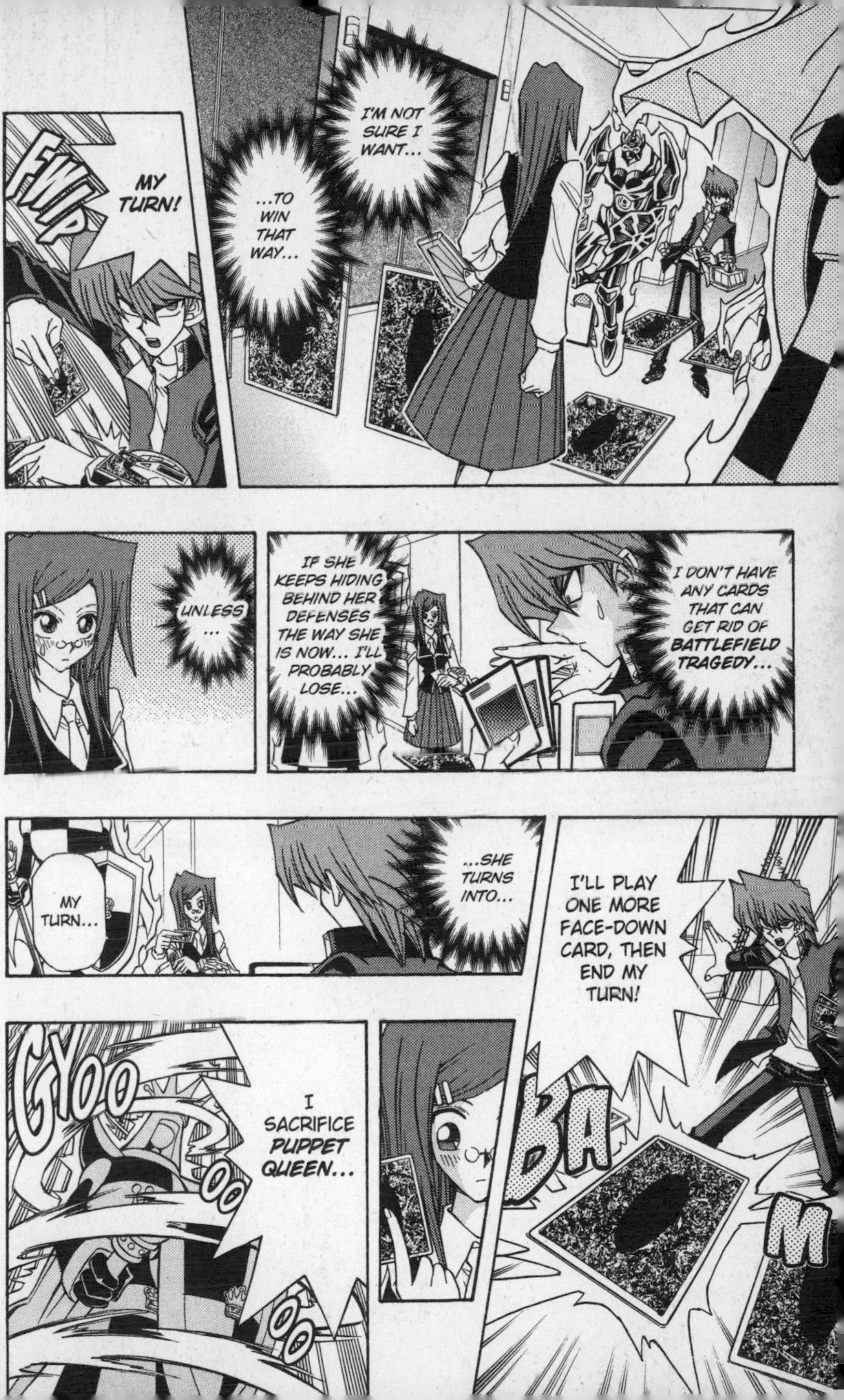
I'M NOT SURE I WANT...
...TO WIN THAT WAY...
FWIP
MY TURN!
I DON'T HAVE ANY CARDS THAT CAN GET RID OF BATTLEFIELD TRAGEDY...
IF SHE KEEPS HIDING BEHIND HER DEFENSES THE WAY SHE IS NOW... I'LL PROBABLY LOSE...
UNLESS ...
I'LL PLAY ONE MORE FACE-DOWN CARD, THEN END MY TURN!
...SHE TURNS INTO...
MY TURN...
BA
M
GYOOOOO
I SACRIFICE PUPPET QUEEN...

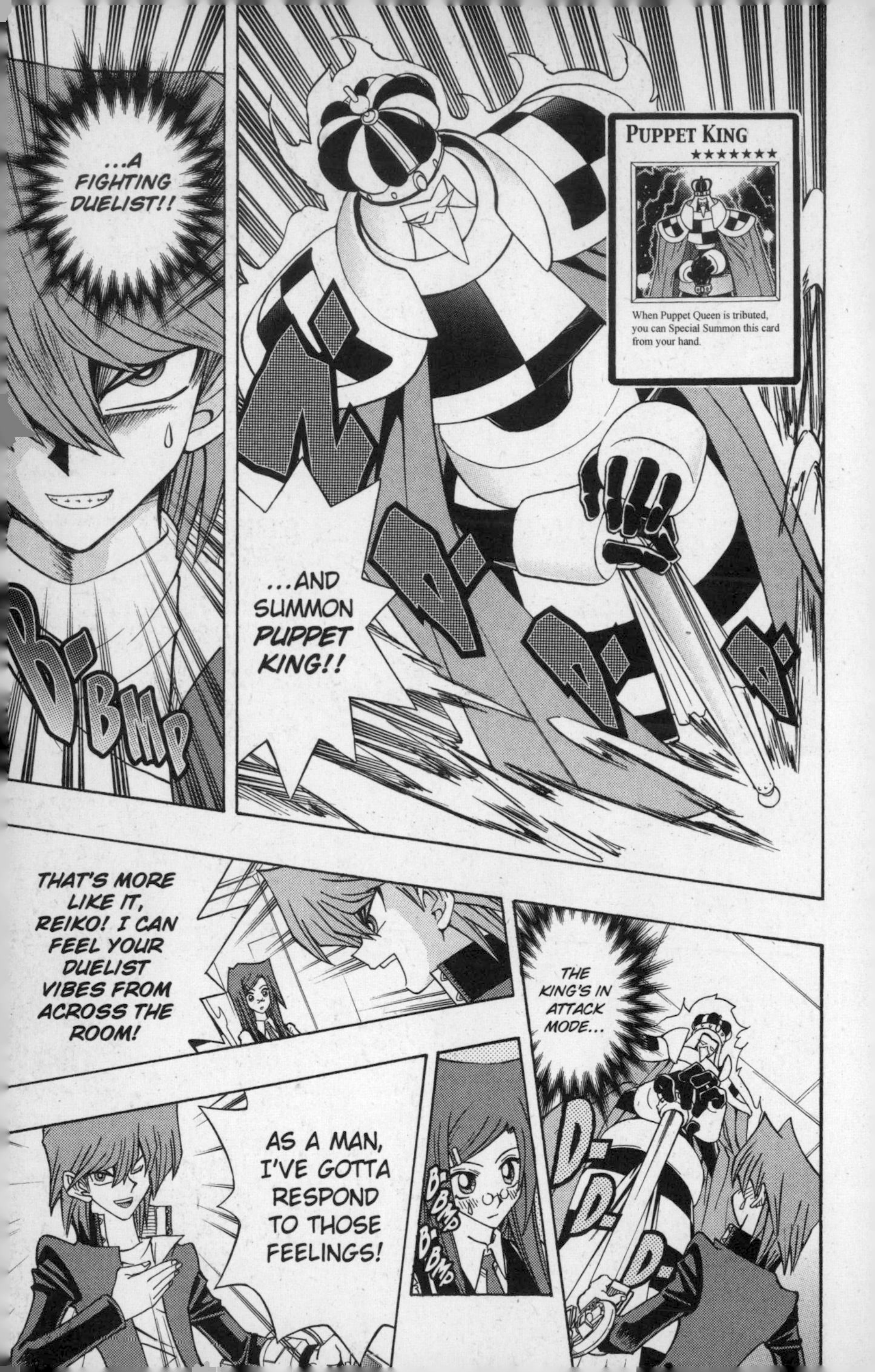
PUPPET KING
When Puppet Queen is tributed, you can Special Summon this card from your hand.
...AND SUMMON PUPPET KING!!
...A FIGHTING DUELIST!!
B-BMP
THE KING'S IN ATTACK MODE...
THAT'S MORE LIKE IT, REIKO! I CAN FEEL YOUR DUELIST VIBES FROM ACROSS THE ROOM!
B-BMP B-BMP
AS A MAN, I'VE GOTTA RESPOND TO THOSE FEELINGS!

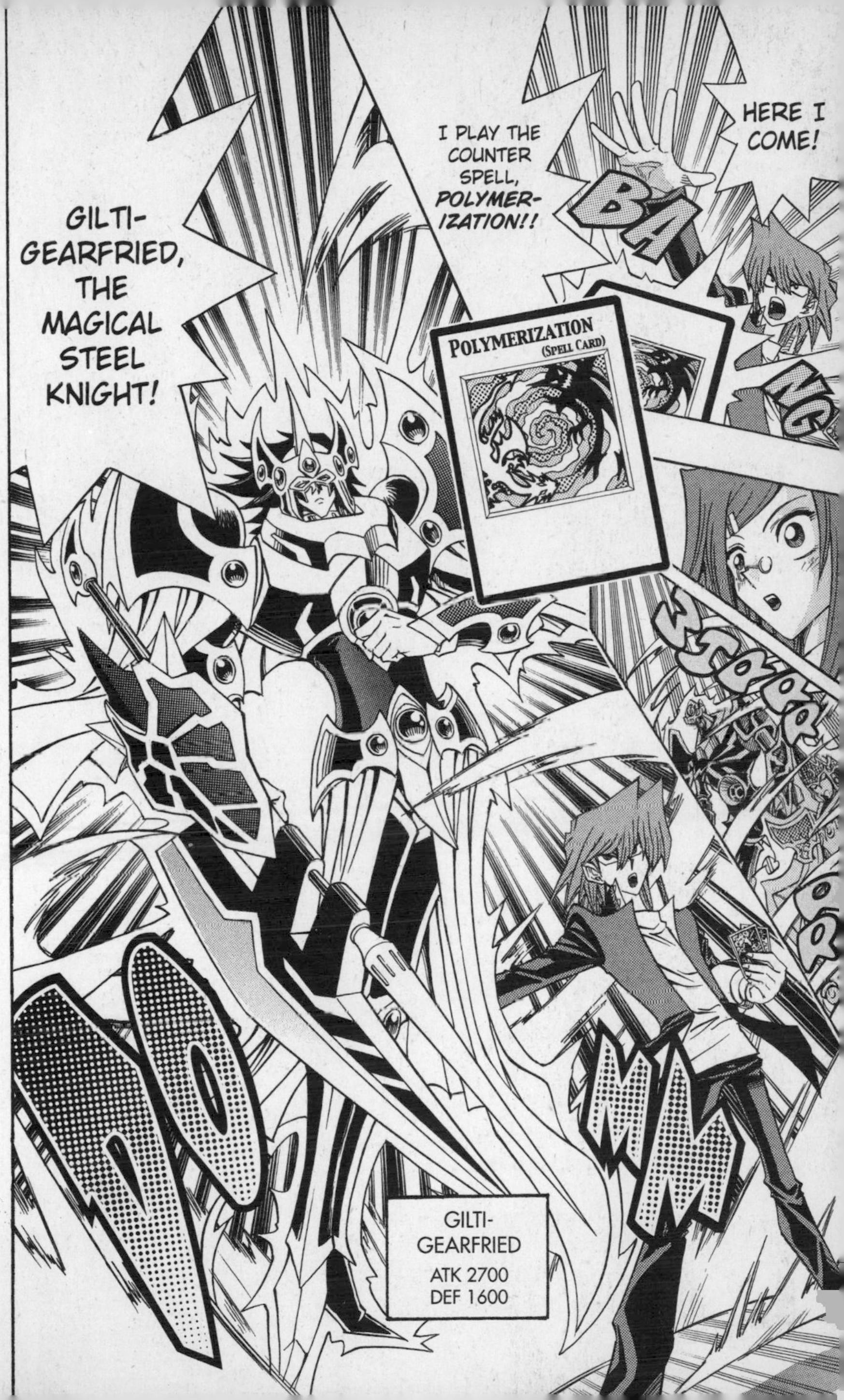
HERE I COME!
BA
I PLAY THE COUNTER SPELL, POLYMERIZATION!!
POLYMERIZATION
(SPELL CARD)
NG
GILTI-GEARFRIED, THE MAGICAL STEEL KNIGHT!
GILTI-GEARFRIED
ATK 2700
DEF 1600

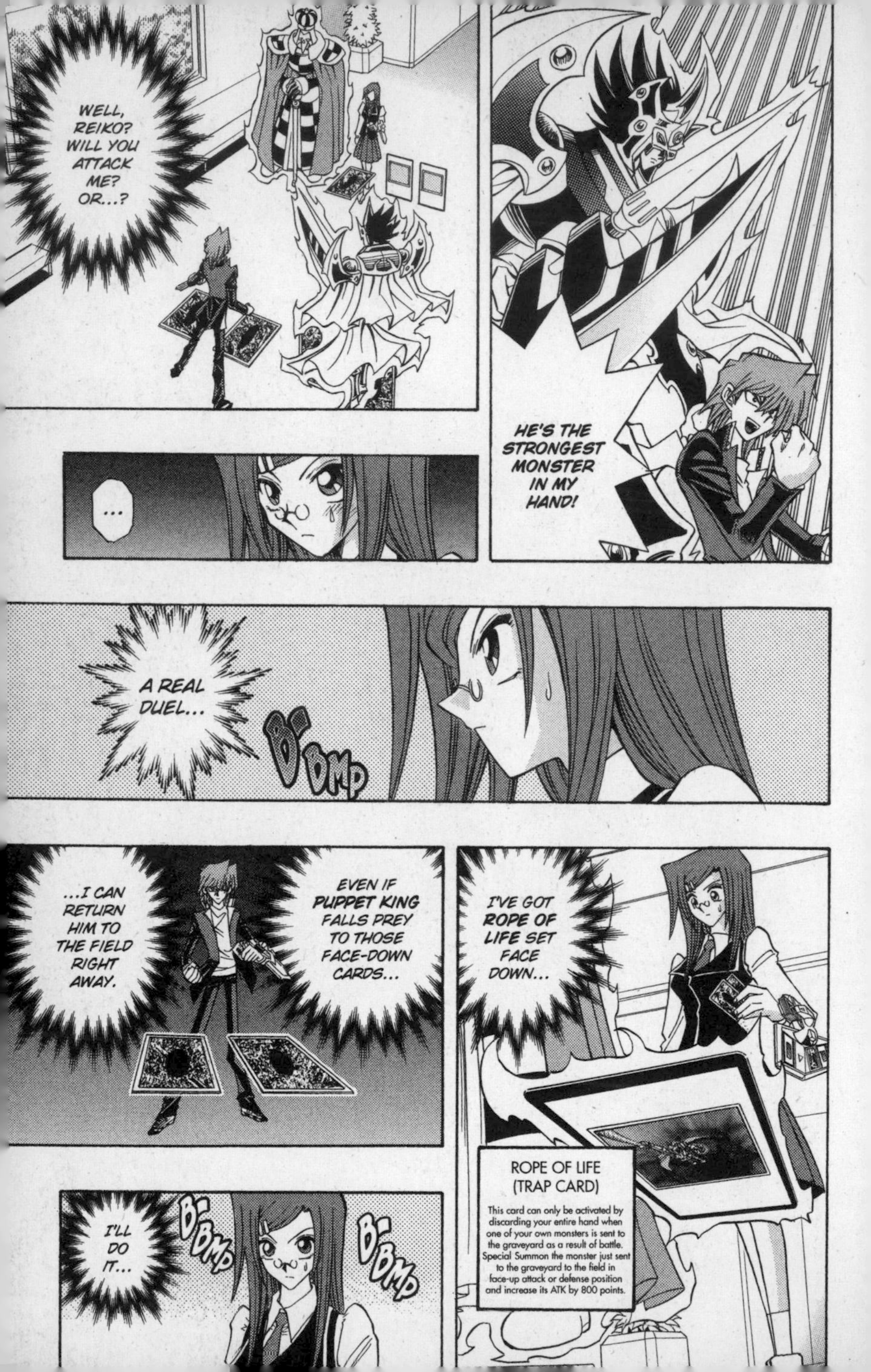
HE'S THE STRONGEST MONSTER IN MY HAND!
WELL, REIKO? WILL YOU ATTACK ME? OR...?
...
A REAL DUEL...
I'VE GOT ROPE OF LIFE SET FACE DOWN...
ROPE OF LIFE (TRAP CARD)
This card can only be activated by discarding your entire hand when one of your own monsters is sent to the graveyard as a result of battle. Special Summon the monster just sent to the graveyard to the field in face-up attack or defense position and increase its ATK by 800 points.
EVEN IF PUPPET KING FALLS PREY TO THOSE FACE-DOWN CARDS...
...I CAN RETURN HIM TO THE FIELD RIGHT AWAY.
B-BMP
I'LL DO IT...
B-BMP

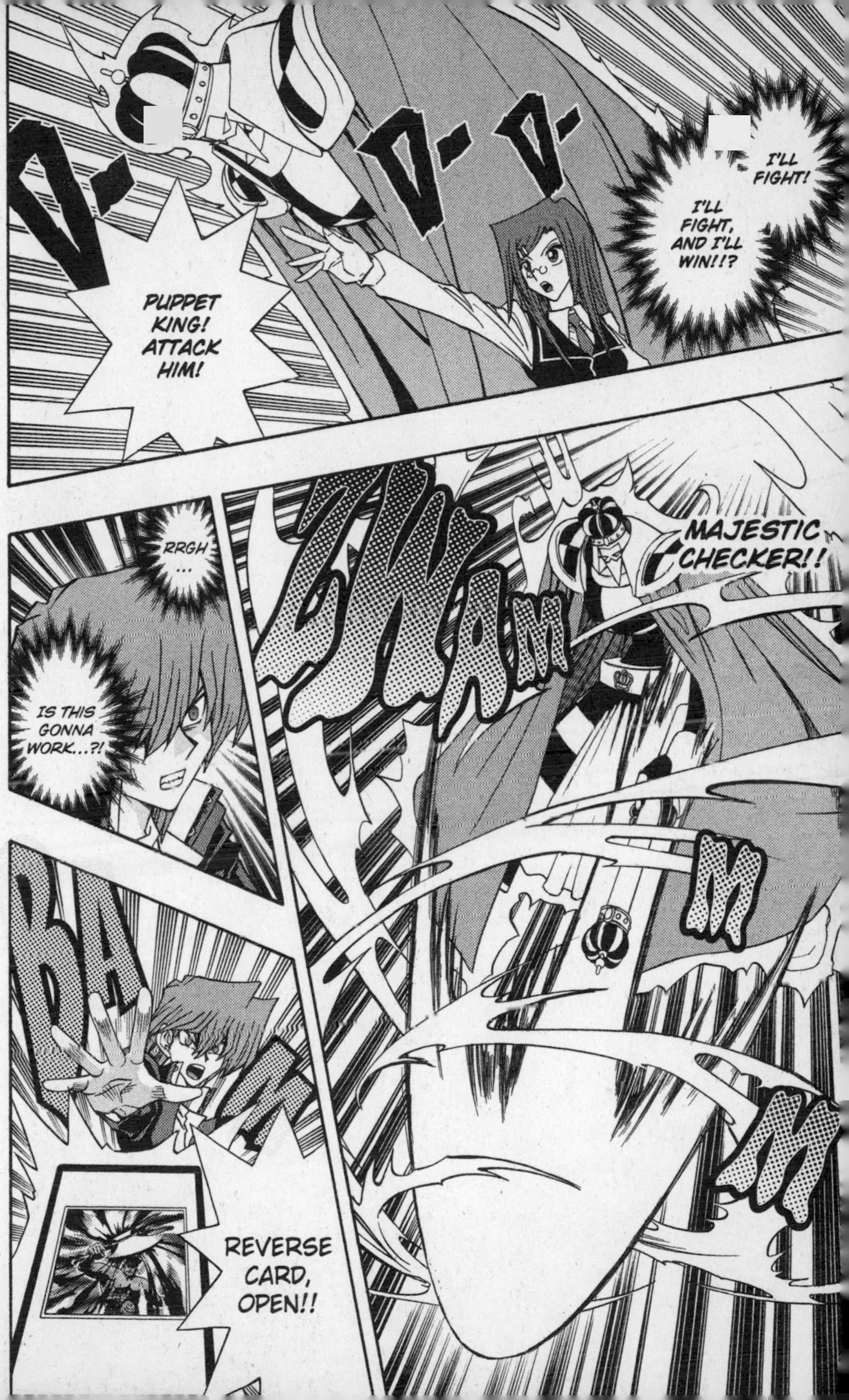

I'LL FIGHT!
I'LL FIGHT, AND I'LL WIN!!?
D- D- D- D-
PUPPET KING! ATTACK HIM!
ZWAM
MAJESTIC CHECKER!!
M
M
RRGH...
IS THIS GONNA WORK...?!
BAM
REVERSE CARD, OPEN!!

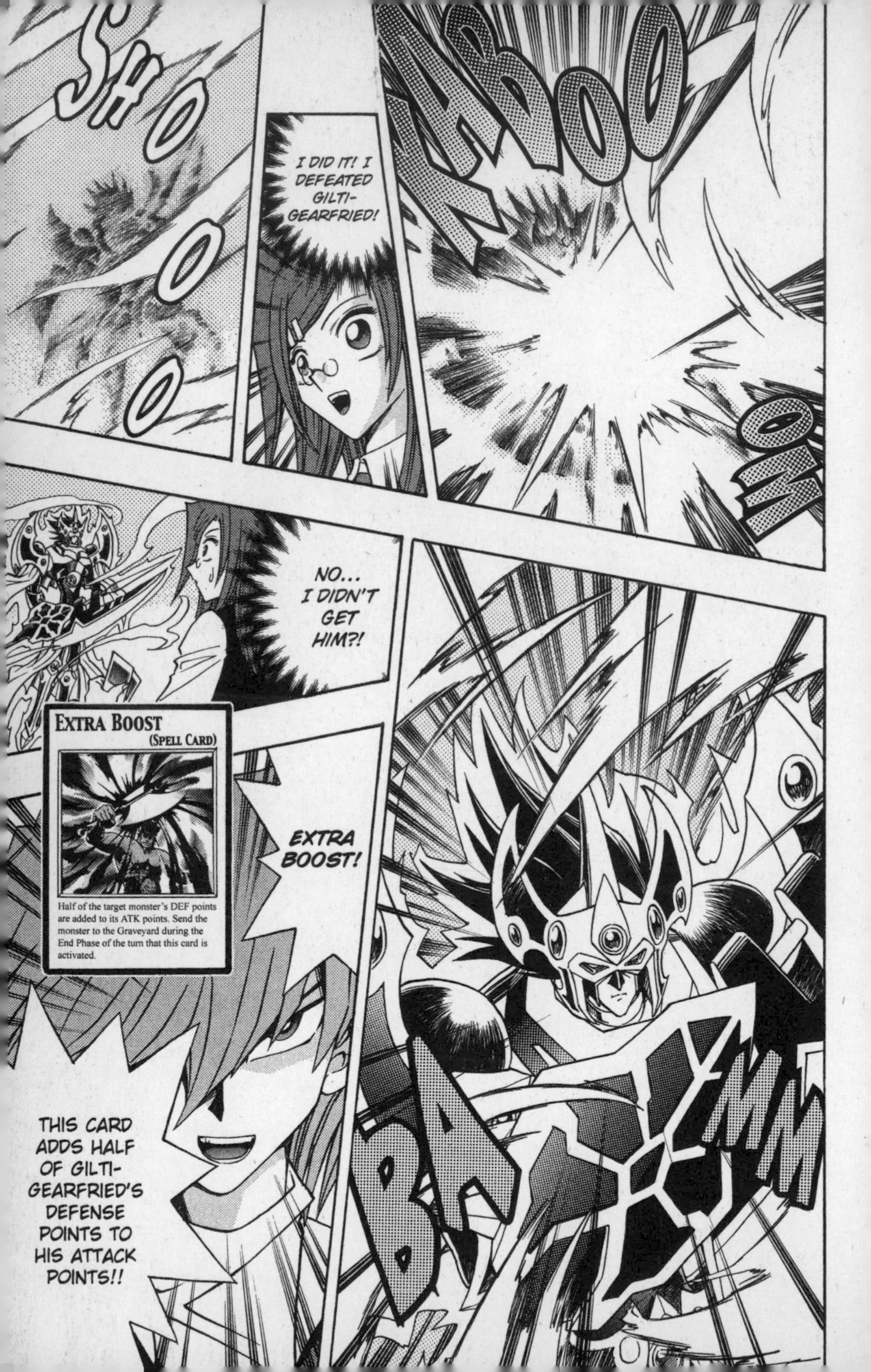
I DID IT! I DEFEATED GILTI-GEARFRIED!
SHOOOO
NO... I DIDN'T GET HIM?!
EXTRA BOOST
(SPELL CARD)
Half of the target monster's DEF points are added to its ATK points. Send the monster to the Graveyard during the End Phase of the turn that this card is activated.
EXTRA BOOST!
THIS CARD ADDS HALF OF GILTI-GEARFRIED'S DEFENSE POINTS TO HIS ATTACK POINTS!!

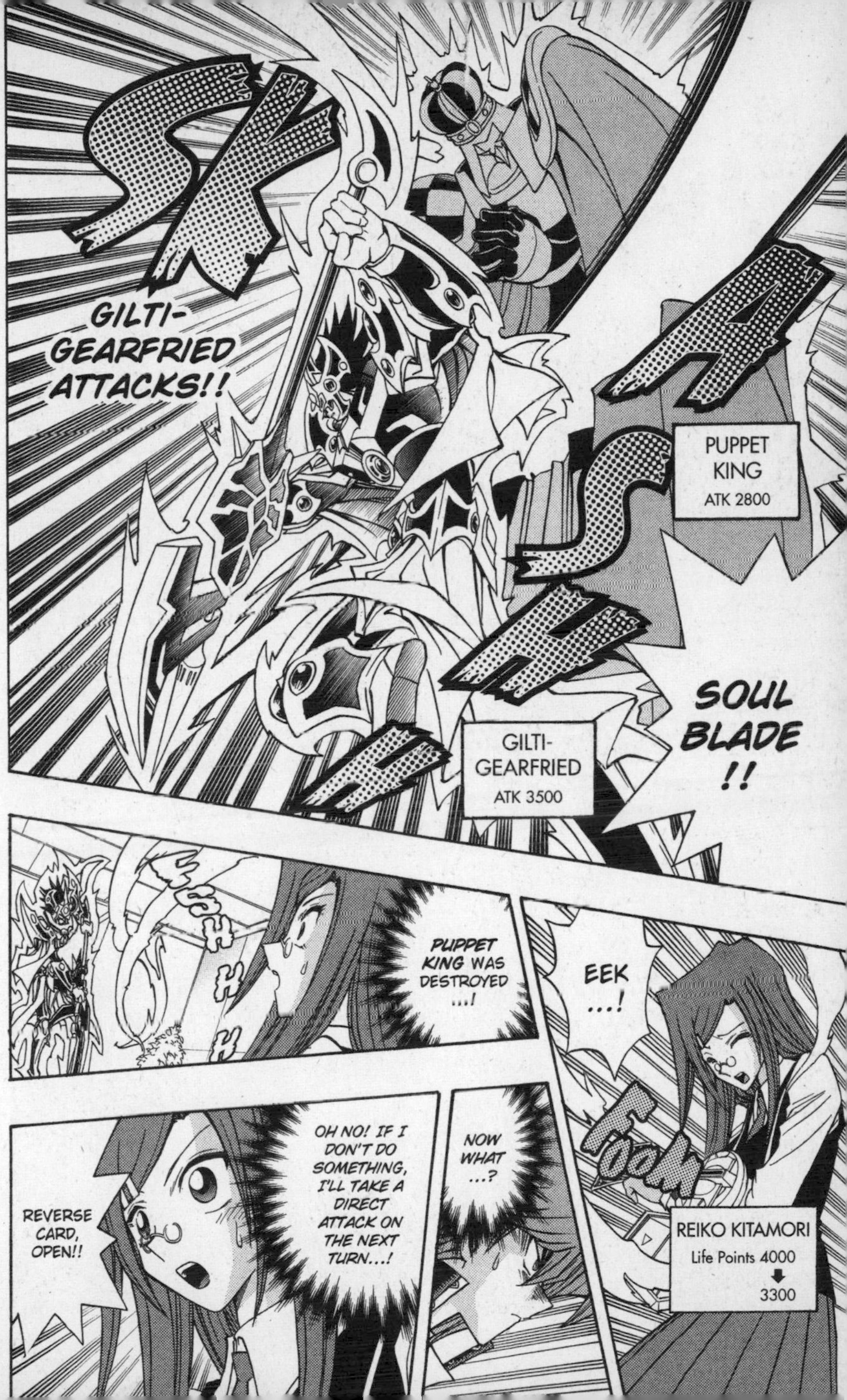
PUPPET KING
ATK 2800
GILTI-GEARFRIED ATTACKS!!
SOUL BLADE!!
GILTI-GEARFRIED
ATK 3500
EEK...!
REIKO KITAMORI
Life Points 4000
3300
PUPPET KING WAS DESTROYED...!
NOW WHAT...?
OH NO! IF I DON'T DO SOMETHING, I'LL TAKE A DIRECT ATTACK ON THE NEXT TURN...!
REVERSE CARD, OPEN!!

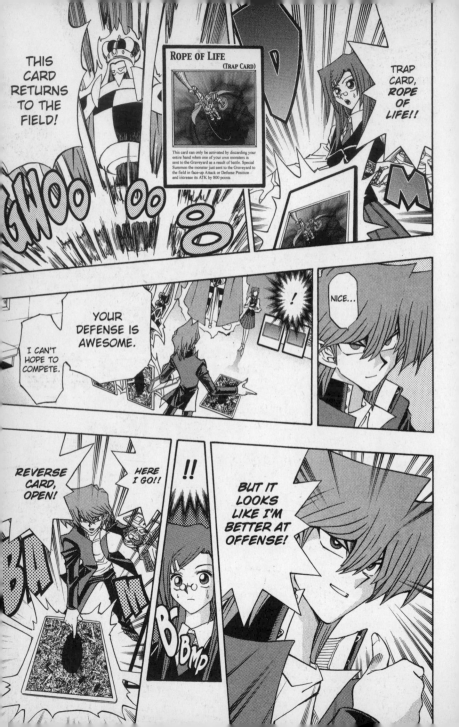

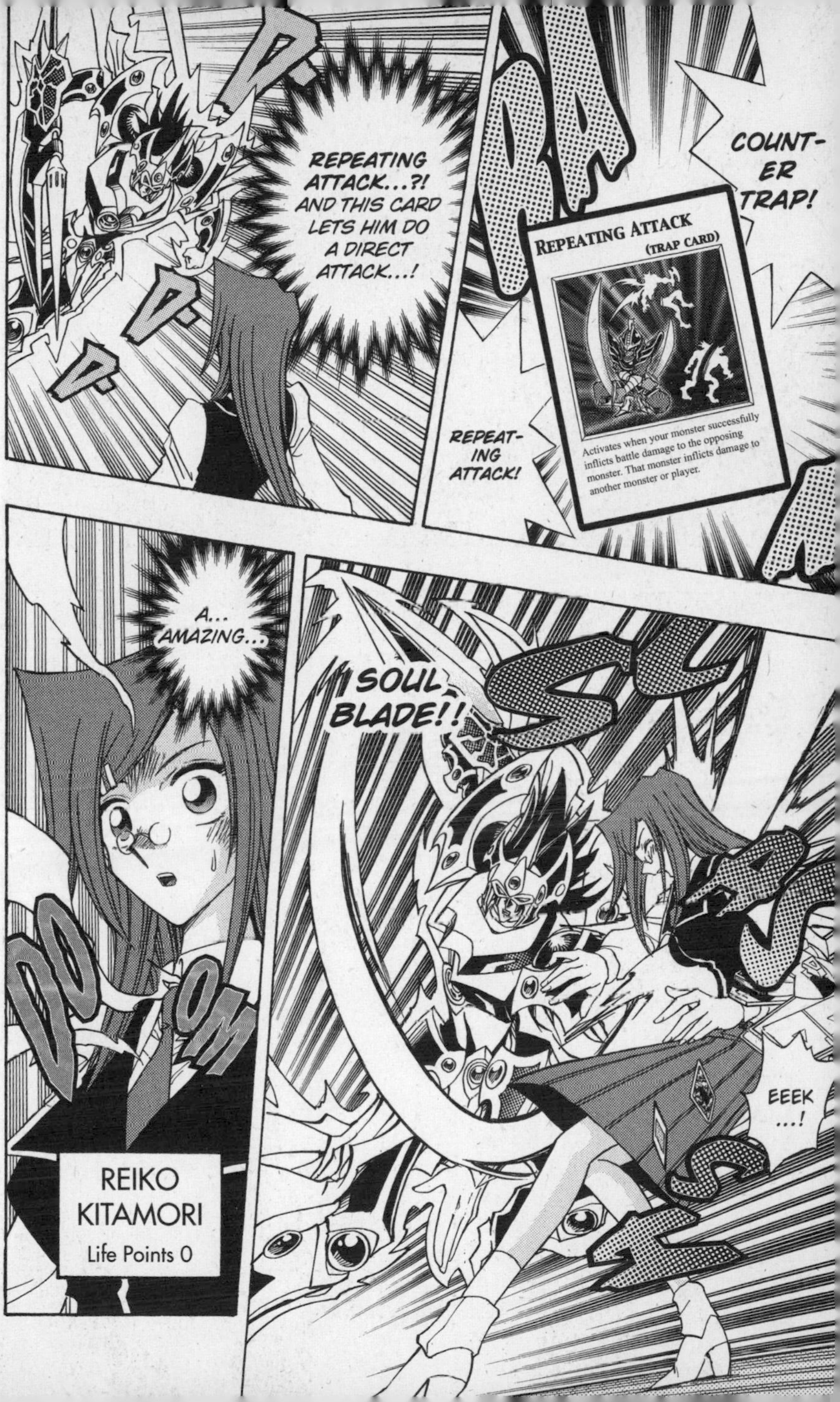
COUNTER-TRAP!
REPEATING ATTACK (TRAP CARD)
Activates when your monster successfully inflicts battle damage to the opposing monster. That monster inflicts damage to another monster or player.
REPEATING ATTACK!
REPEATING ATTACK...?! AND THIS CARD LETS HIM DO A DIRECT ATTACK...!
SOUL BLADE!!
EEEK...!
A... AMAZING...
DOOM
REIKO KITAMORI
Life Points 0

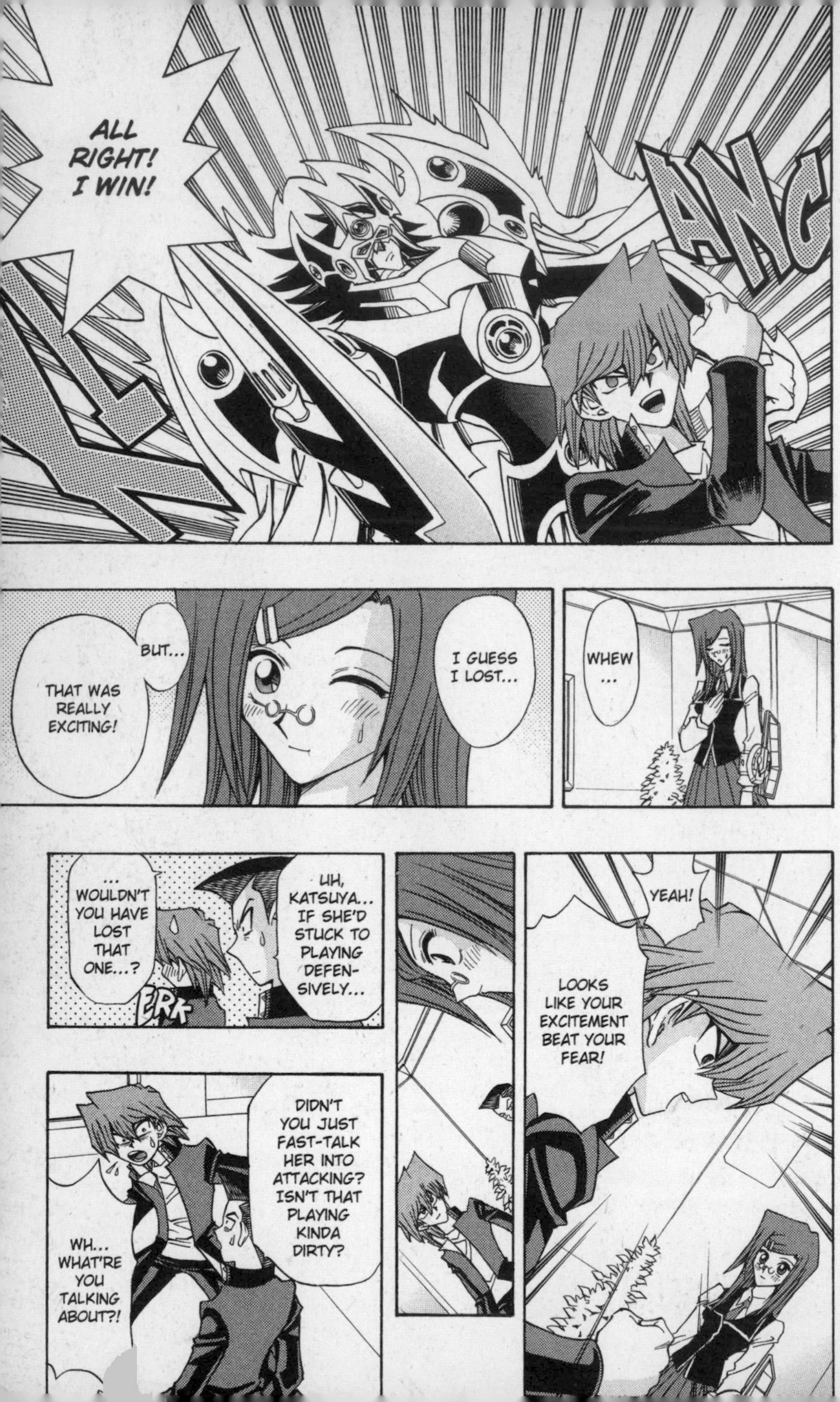
ANG
ALL RIGHT! I WIN!
WHEW ...
I GUESS I LOST...
BUT...
THAT WAS REALLY EXCITING!
YEAH!
LOOKS LIKE YOUR EXCITEMENT BEAT YOUR FEAR!
UH, KATSUYA... IF SHE'D STUCK TO PLAYING DEFENSIVELY...
... WOULDN'T YOU HAVE LOST THAT ONE...?
ERK
DIDN'T YOU JUST FAST-TALK HER INTO ATTACKING? ISN'T THAT PLAYING KINDA DIRTY?
WH... WHAT'RE YOU TALKING ABOUT?!

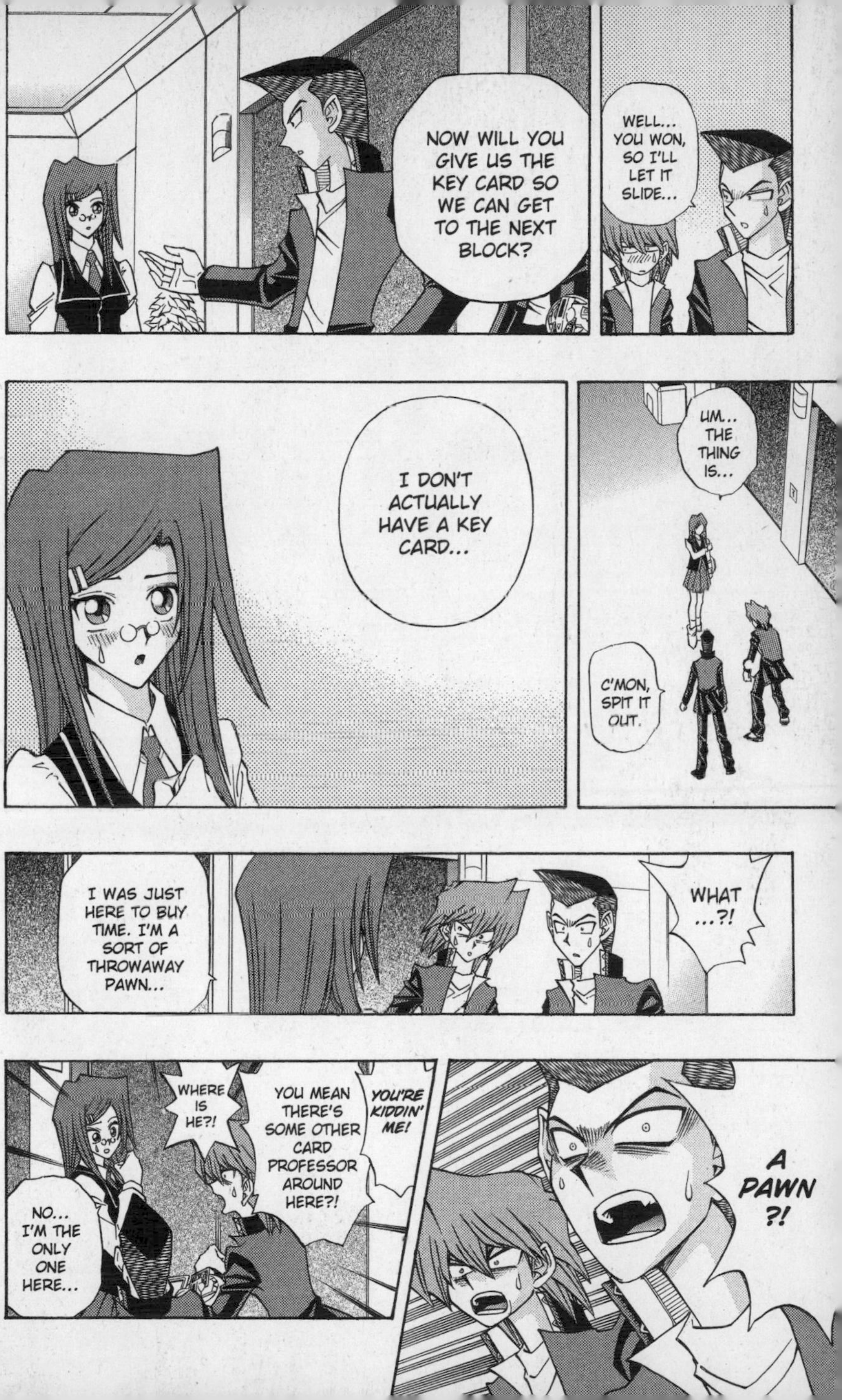
WELL... YOU WON, SO I'LL LET IT SLIDE...
NOW WILL YOU GIVE US THE KEY CARD SO WE CAN GET TO THE NEXT BLOCK?
UM.. THE THING IS...
C'MON, SPIT IT OUT.
I DON'T ACTUALLY HAVE A KEY CARD...
WHAT ...?!
I WAS JUST HERE TO BUY TIME. I'M A SORT OF THROWAWAY PAWN...
A PAWN ?!
YOU'RE KIDDIN' ME!
YOU MEAN THERE'S SOME OTHER CARD PROFESSOR AROUND HERE?!
WHERE IS HE?!
NO... I'M THE ONLY ONE HERE...

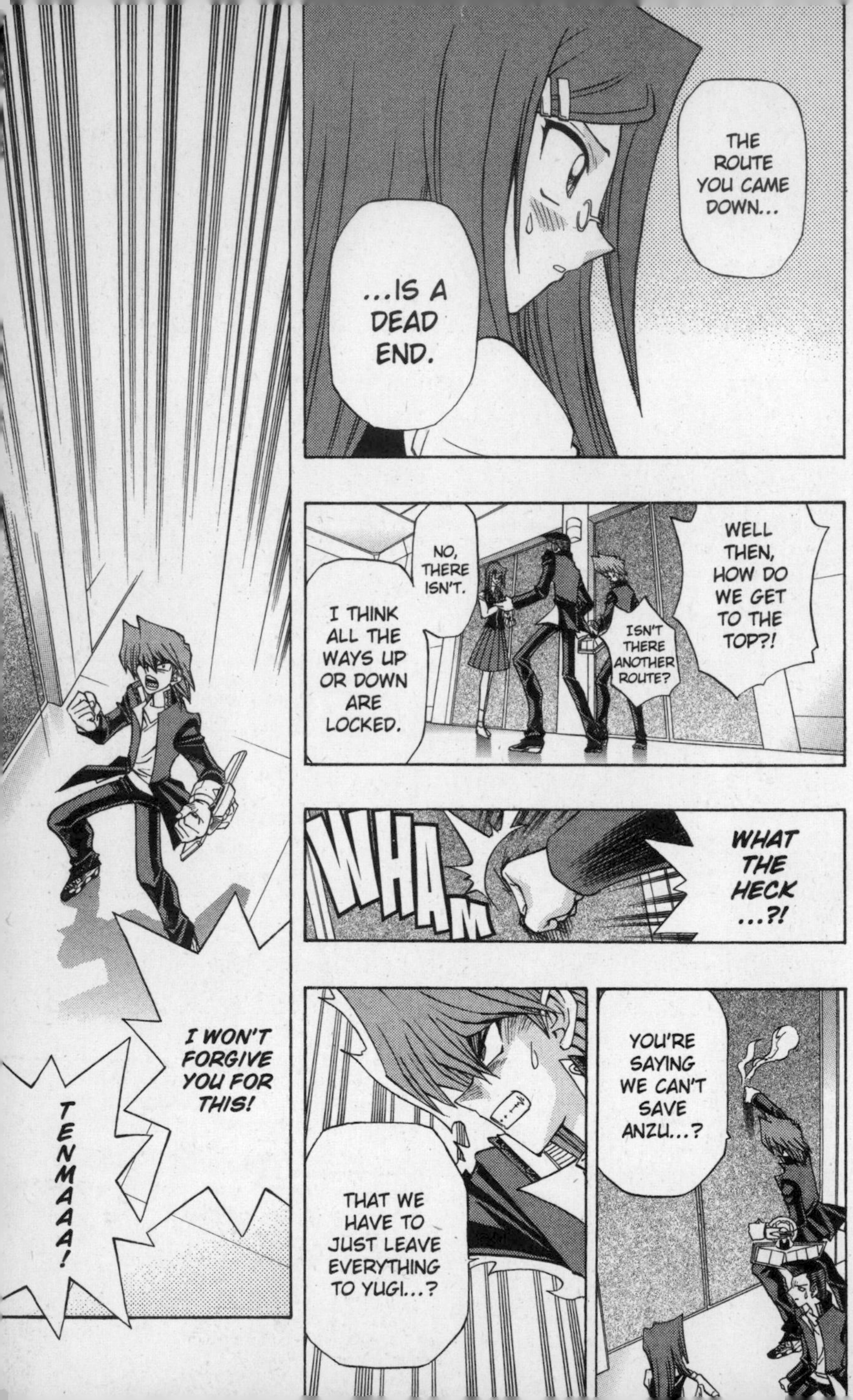
THE ROUTE YOU CAME DOWN...
...IS A DEAD END.
WELL THEN, HOW DO WE GET TO THE TOP?!
ISN'T THERE ANOTHER ROUTE?
NO, THERE ISN'T.
I THINK ALL THE WAYS UP OR DOWN ARE LOCKED.
WHAT THE HECK ...?!
WHAM
YOU'RE SAYING WE CAN'T SAVE ANZU...?
THAT WE HAVE TO JUST LEAVE EVERYTHING TO YUGI...?
I WON'T FORGIVE YOU FOR THIS!
TENMAAAA!

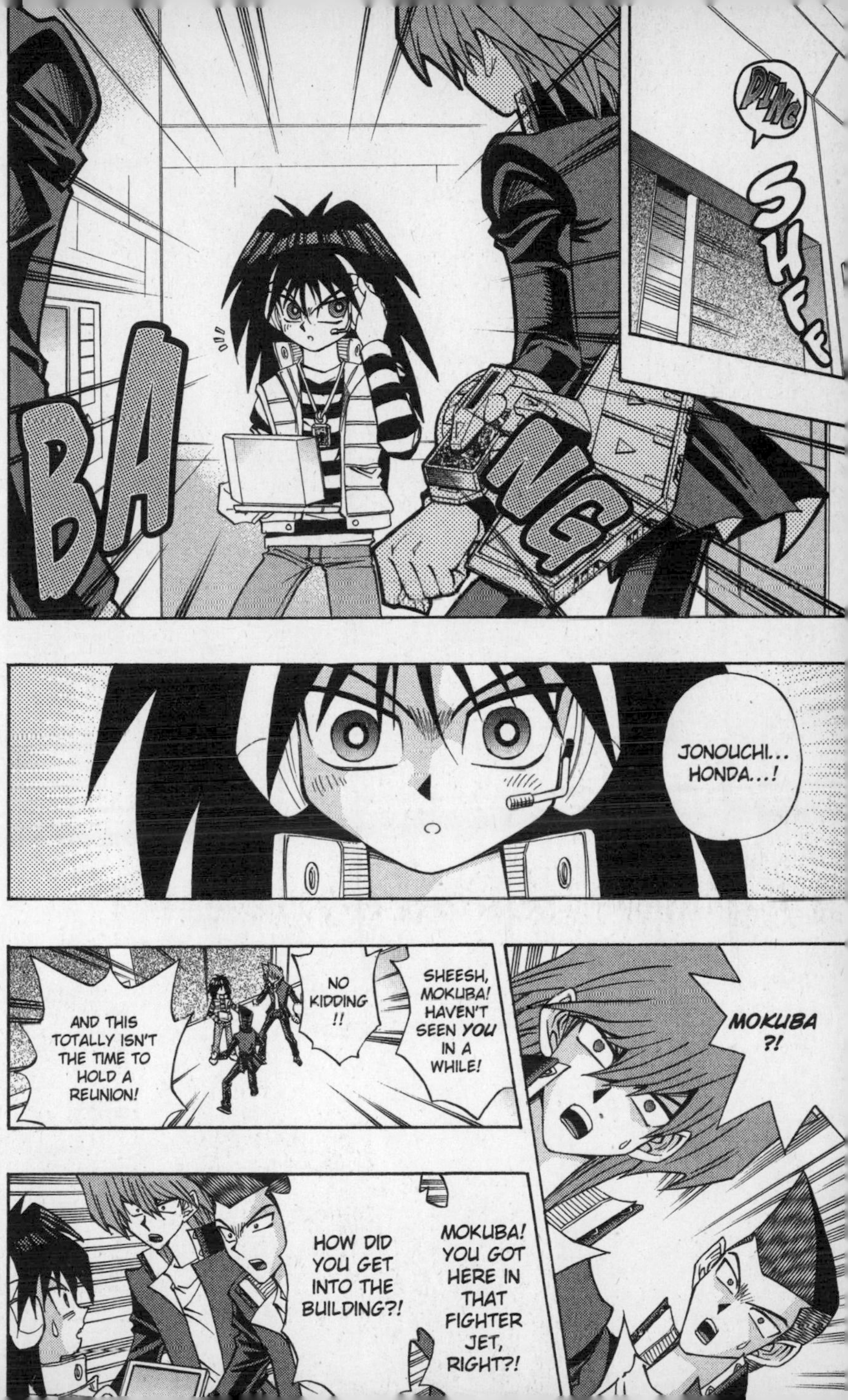
DING
SHFF
BA
NG
JONOUCHI... HONDA...!
MOKUBA ?!
MOKUBA! YOU GOT HERE IN THAT FIGHTER JET, RIGHT?!
SHEESH, MOKUBA! HAVEN'T SEEN *YOU* IN A WHILE!
NO KIDDING !!
AND THIS TOTALLY ISN'T THE TIME TO HOLD A REUNION!
HOW DID YOU GET INTO THE BUILDING?!

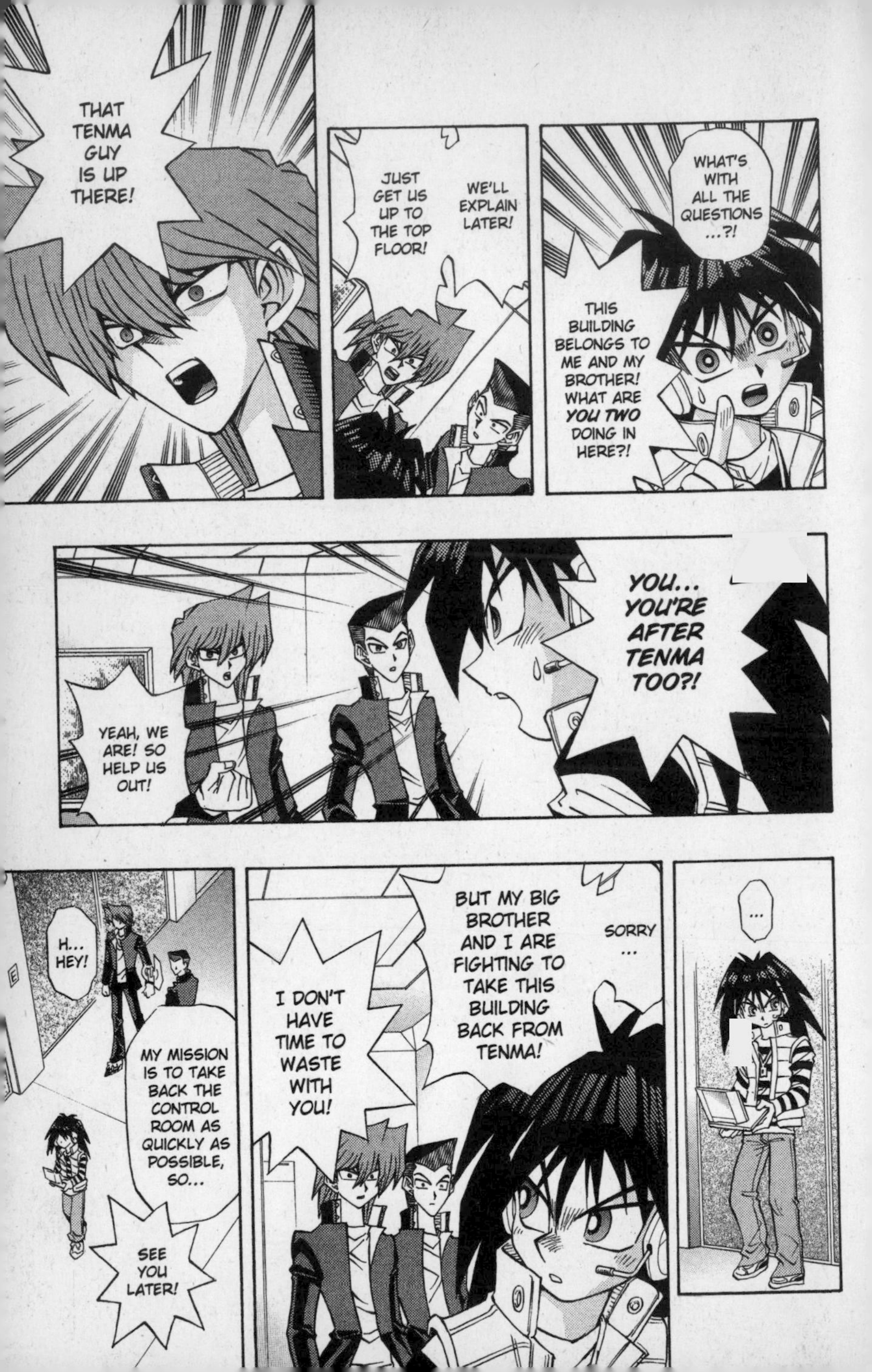
WHAT'S WITH ALL THE QUESTIONS ...?!
THIS BUILDING BELONGS TO ME AND MY BROTHER! WHAT ARE *YOU TWO* DOING IN HERE?!
WE'LL EXPLAIN LATER!
JUST GET US UP TO THE TOP FLOOR!
THAT TENMA GUY IS UP THERE!
YOU... YOU'RE AFTER TENMA TOO?!
YEAH, WE ARE! SO HELP US OUT!
...
SORRY ...
BUT MY BIG BROTHER AND I ARE FIGHTING TO TAKE THIS BUILDING BACK FROM TENMA!
I DON'T HAVE TIME TO WASTE WITH YOU!
H... HEY!
MY MISSION IS TO TAKE BACK THE CONTROL ROOM AS QUICKLY AS POSSIBLE, SO...
SEE YOU LATER!

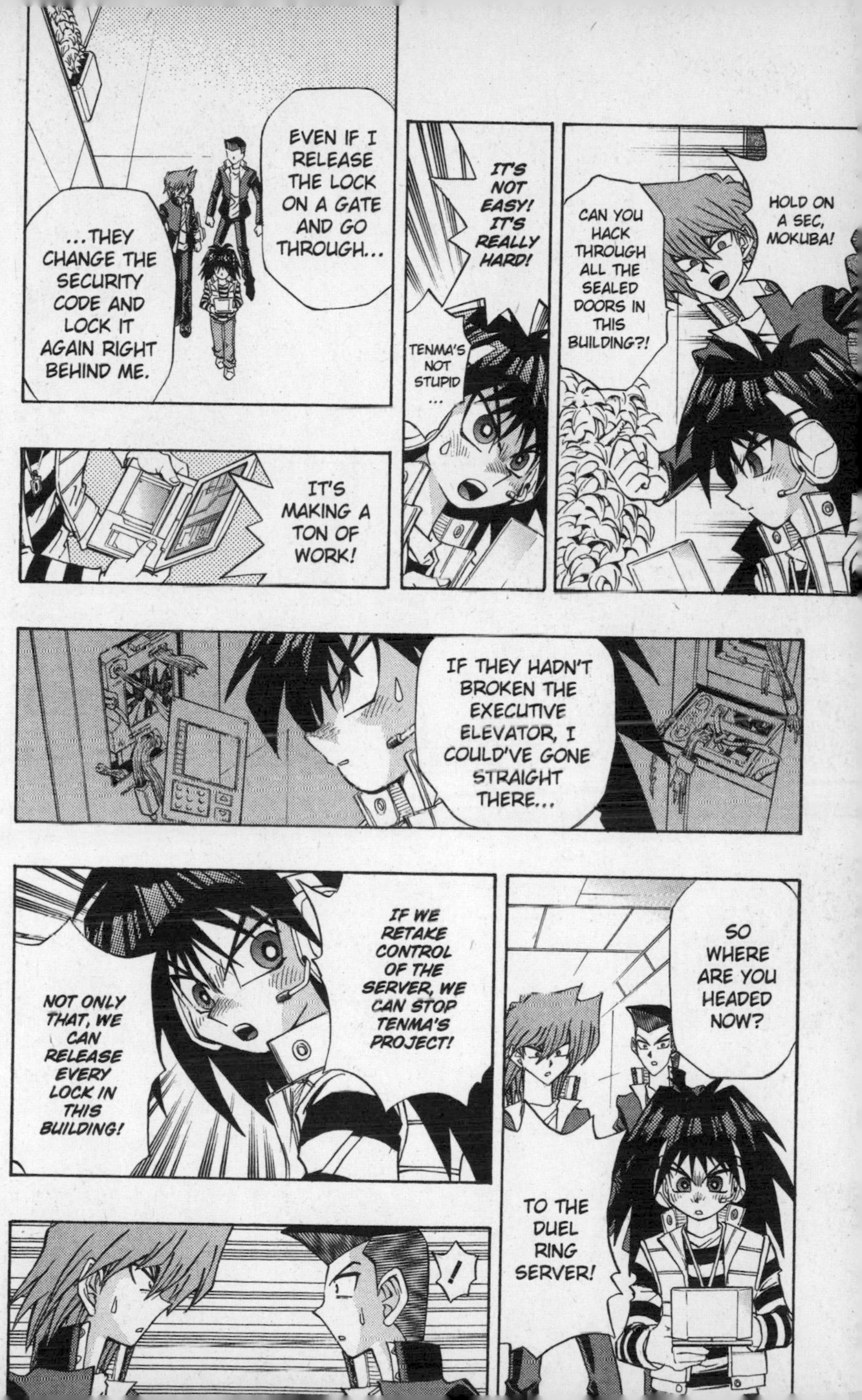
HOLD ON A SEC, MOKUBA!
CAN YOU HACK THROUGH ALL THE SEALED DOORS IN THIS BUILDING?!
IT'S NOT EASY! IT'S REALLY HARD!
TENMA'S NOT STUPID ...
EVEN IF I RELEASE THE LOCK ON A GATE AND GO THROUGH...
...THEY CHANGE THE SECURITY CODE AND LOCK IT AGAIN RIGHT BEHIND ME.
IT'S MAKING A TON OF WORK!
IF THEY HADN'T BROKEN THE EXECUTIVE ELEVATOR, I COULD'VE GONE STRAIGHT THERE...
SO WHERE ARE YOU HEADED NOW?
TO THE DUEL RING SERVER!
IF WE RETAKE CONTROL OF THE SERVER, WE CAN STOP TENMA'S PROJECT!
NOT ONLY THAT, WE CAN RELEASE EVERY LOCK IN THIS BUILDING!
!

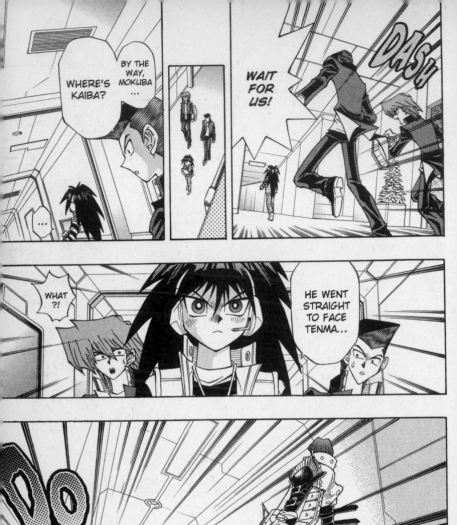

WHERE'S KAIBA?

BY THE WAY, MOKUBA...

...

WAIT FOR US!

DASH

WHAT ?!

HE WENT STRAIGHT TO FACE TENMA...

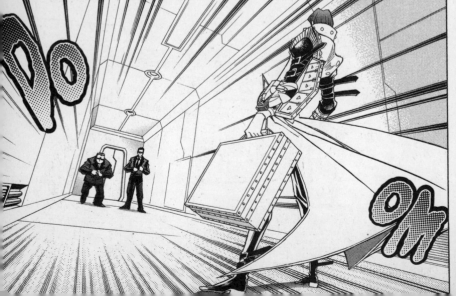

DO DO

VMM

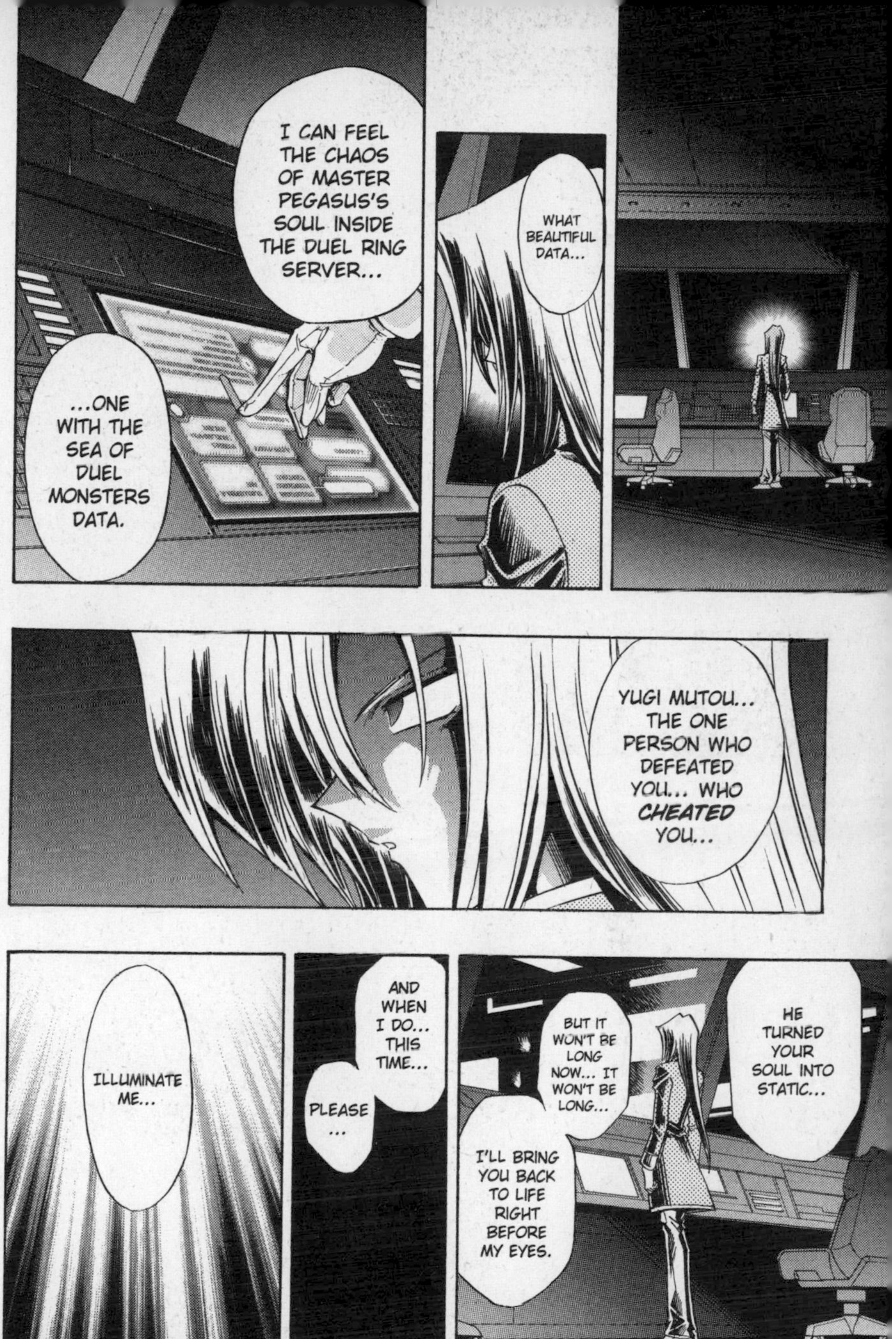
WHAT BEAUTIFUL DATA...
I CAN FEEL THE CHAOS OF MASTER PEGASUS'S SOUL INSIDE THE DUEL RING SERVER...
...ONE WITH THE SEA OF DUEL MONSTERS DATA.
YUGI MUTOU... THE ONE PERSON WHO DEFEATED YOU... WHO CHEATED YOU...
HE TURNED YOUR SOUL INTO STATIC...
BUT IT WON'T BE LONG NOW... IT WON'T BE LONG...
I'LL BRING YOU BACK TO LIFE RIGHT BEFORE MY EYES.
AND WHEN I DO... THIS TIME...
PLEASE...
ILLUMINATE ME...

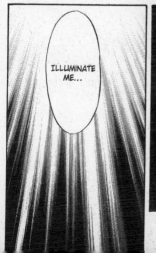

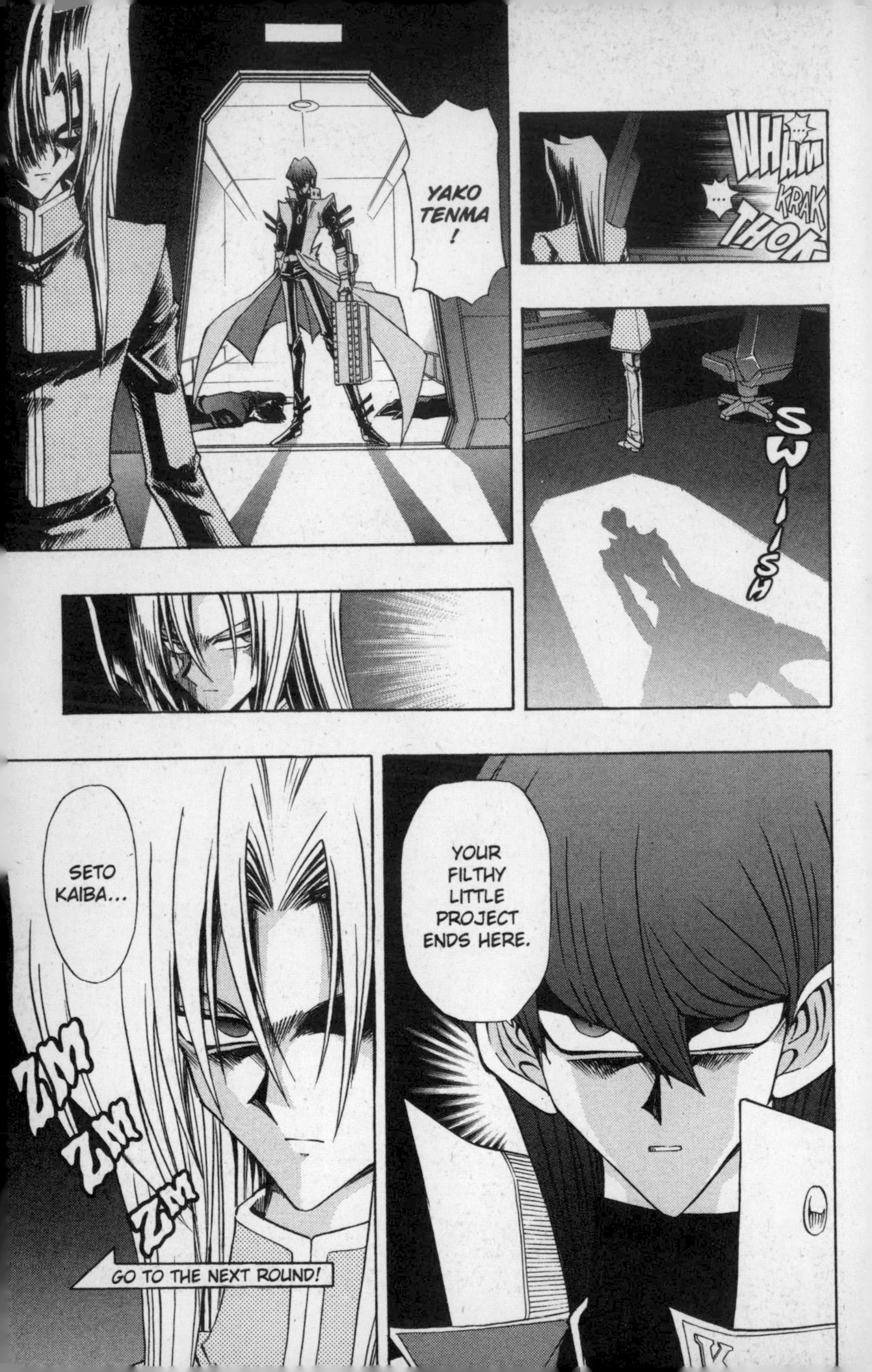

WHAM
...
...
KRAK
THOK
SWIIISH
YAKO TENMA!
YOUR FILTHY LITTLE PROJECT ENDS HERE.
SETO KAIBA...
ZM ZM ZM
GO TO THE NEXT ROUND!

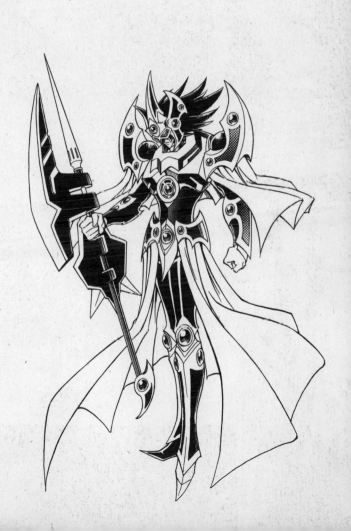

Duel Round 21: The Truth of the R.A. Project!!

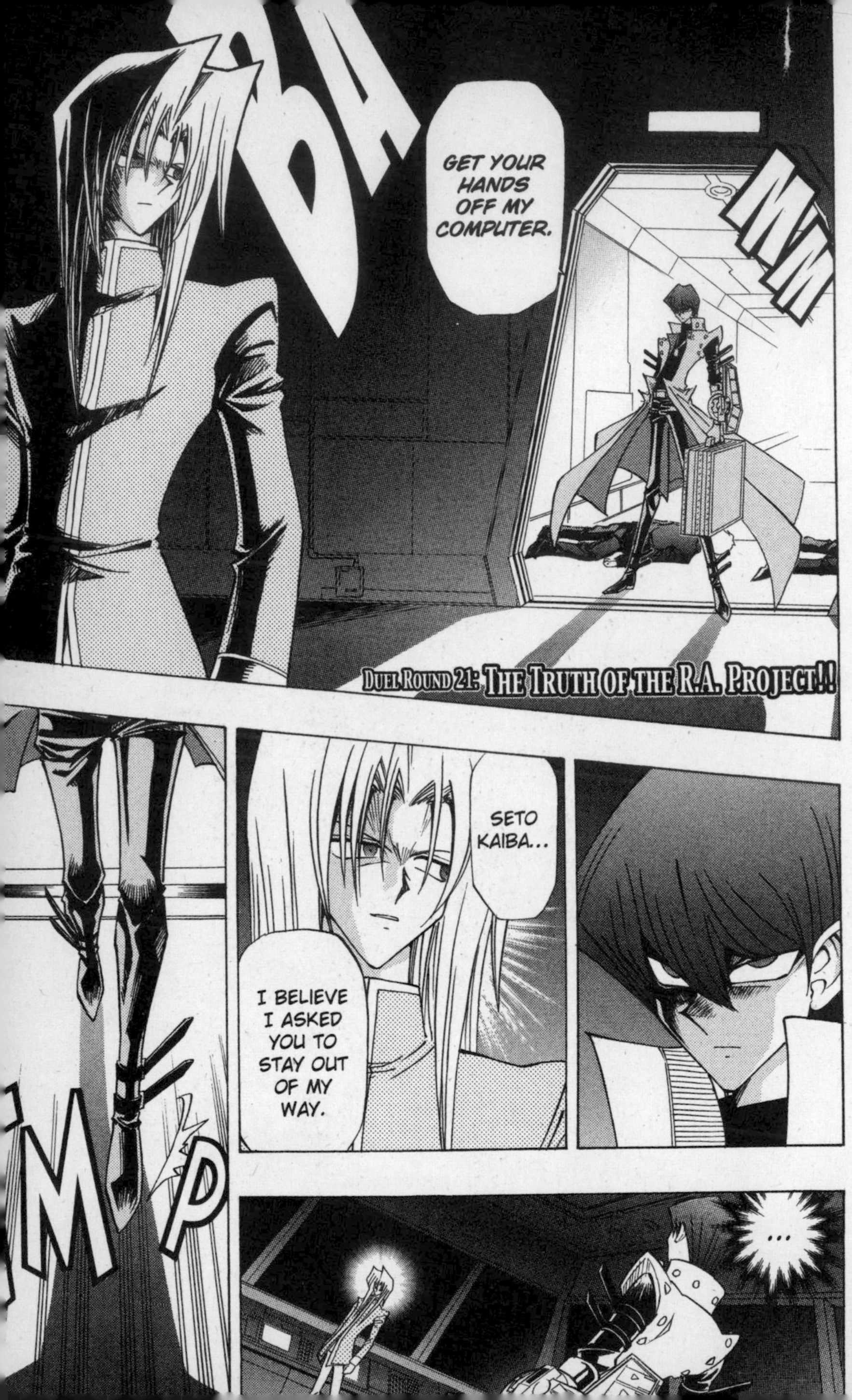
GET YOUR HANDS OFF MY COMPUTER.
SETO KAIBA...
I BELIEVE I ASKED YOU TO STAY OUT OF MY WAY.
...

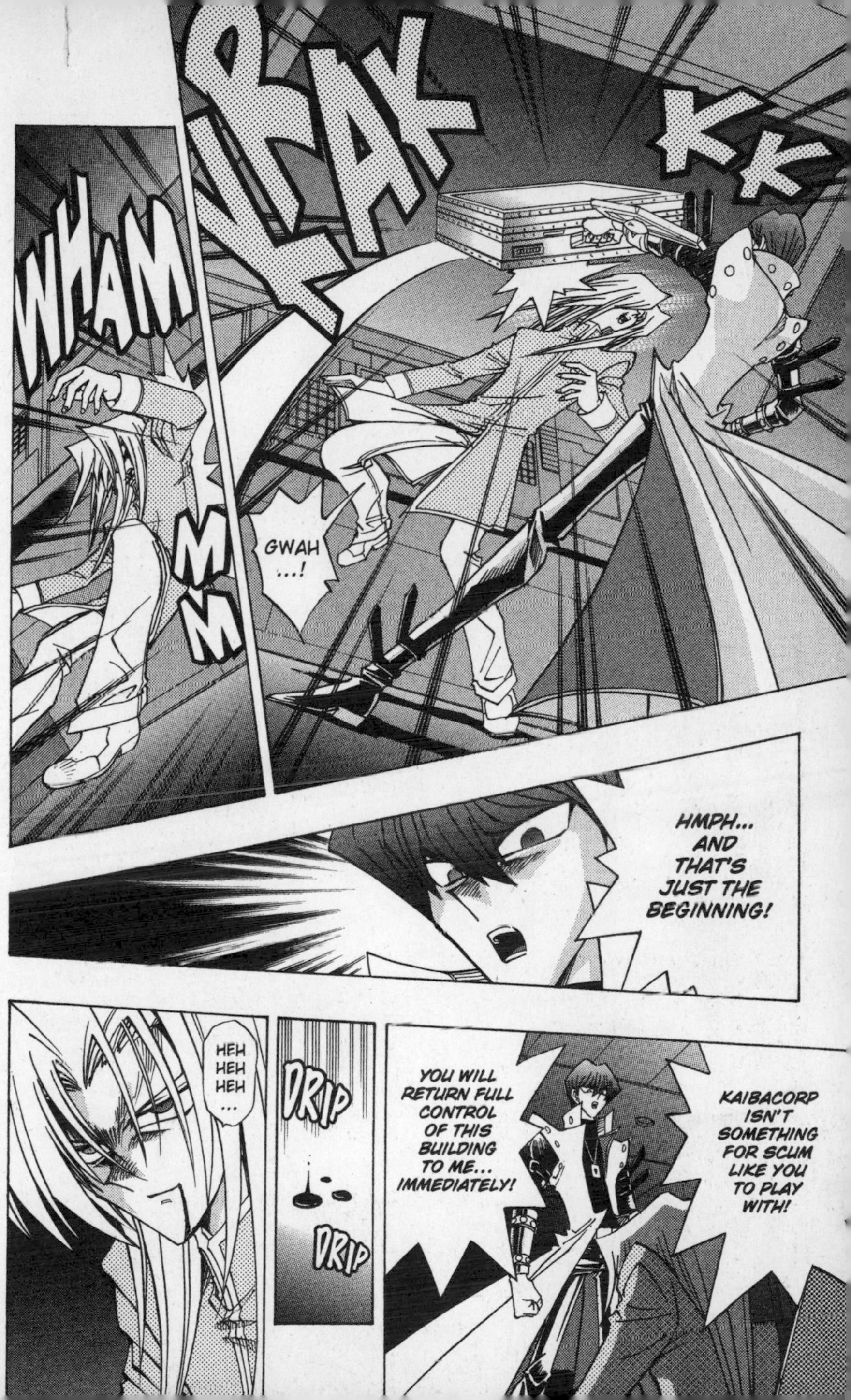
PAK
KK
GWAH ...!
WHAM
MMM
HMPH... AND THAT'S JUST THE BEGINNING!
KAIBACORP ISN'T SOMETHING FOR SCUM LIKE YOU TO PLAY WITH!
YOU WILL RETURN FULL CONTROL OF THIS BUILDING TO ME... IMMEDIATELY!
DRIP
DRIP
HEH HEH HEH ...

READ THIS WAY

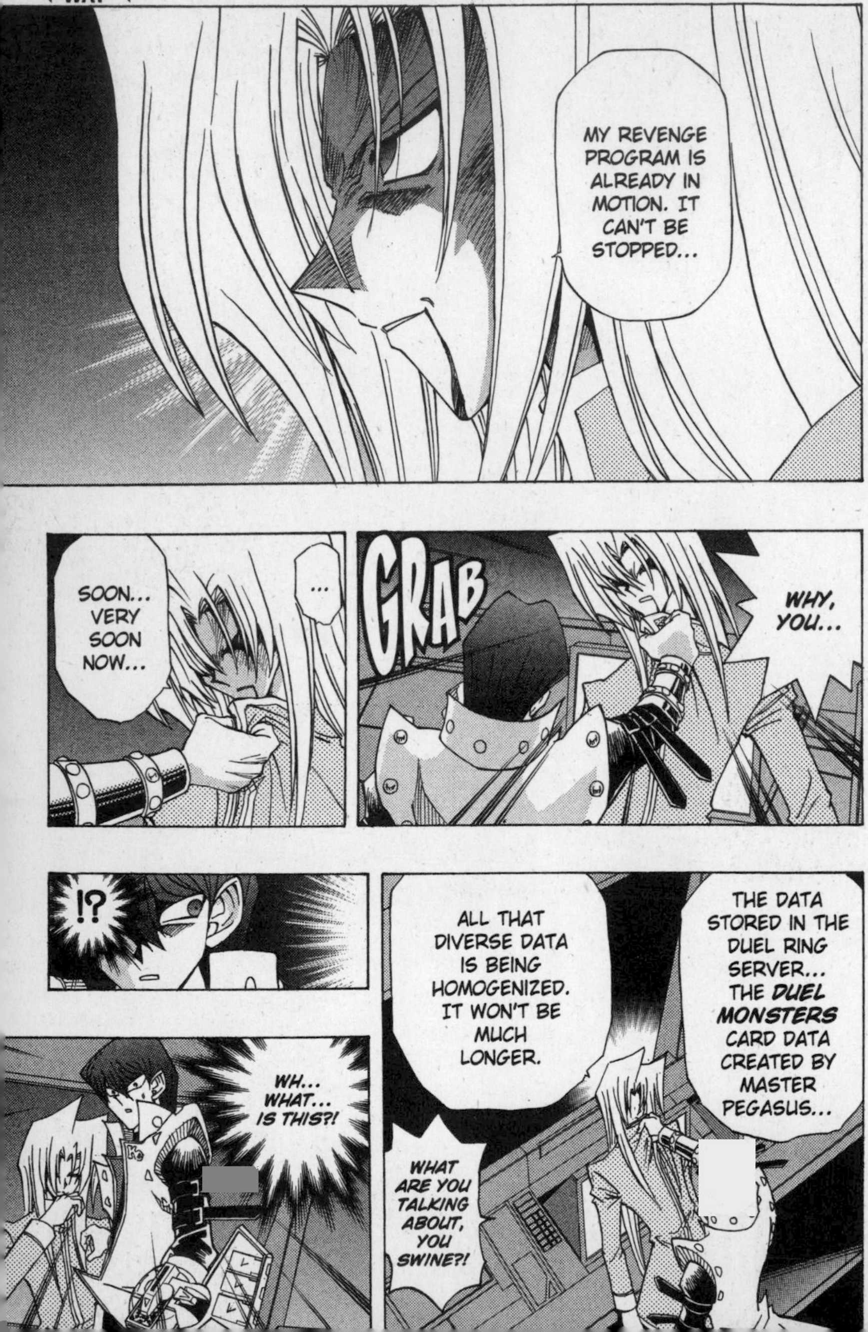

MY REVENGE PROGRAM IS ALREADY IN MOTION. IT CAN'T BE STOPPED...
GRAB
WHY, YOU...
...
SOON... VERY SOON NOW...
THE DATA STORED IN THE DUEL RING SERVER... THE ***DUEL MONSTERS*** CARD DATA CREATED BY MASTER PEGASUS...
ALL THAT DIVERSE DATA IS BEING HOMOGENIZED. IT WON'T BE MUCH LONGER.
WHAT ARE YOU TALKING ABOUT, YOU SWINE?!
!?
WH... WHAT... IS THIS?!

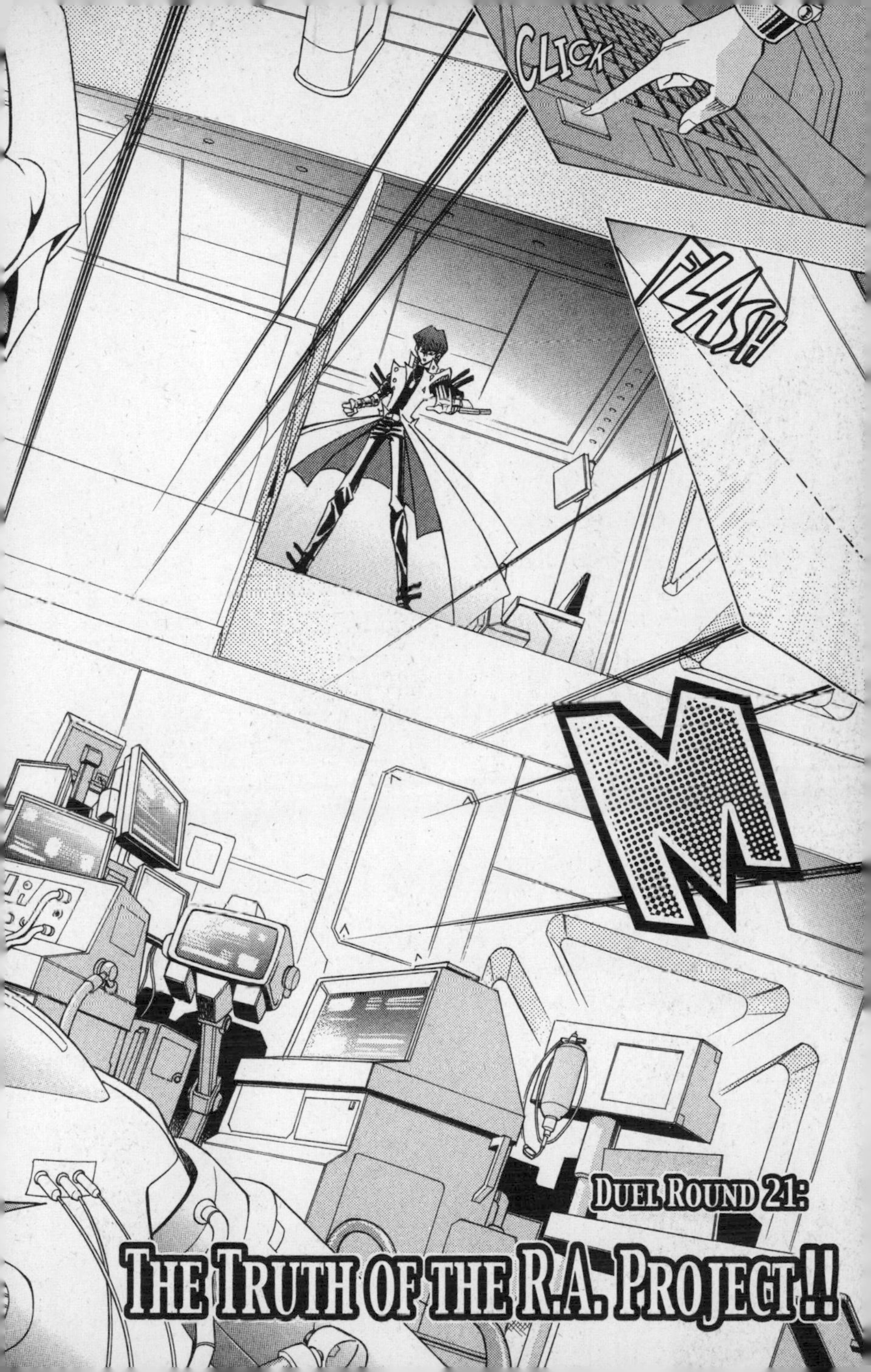
CLICK
FLASH
M
DUEL ROUND 21:
THE TRUTH OF THE R.A. PROJECT!!

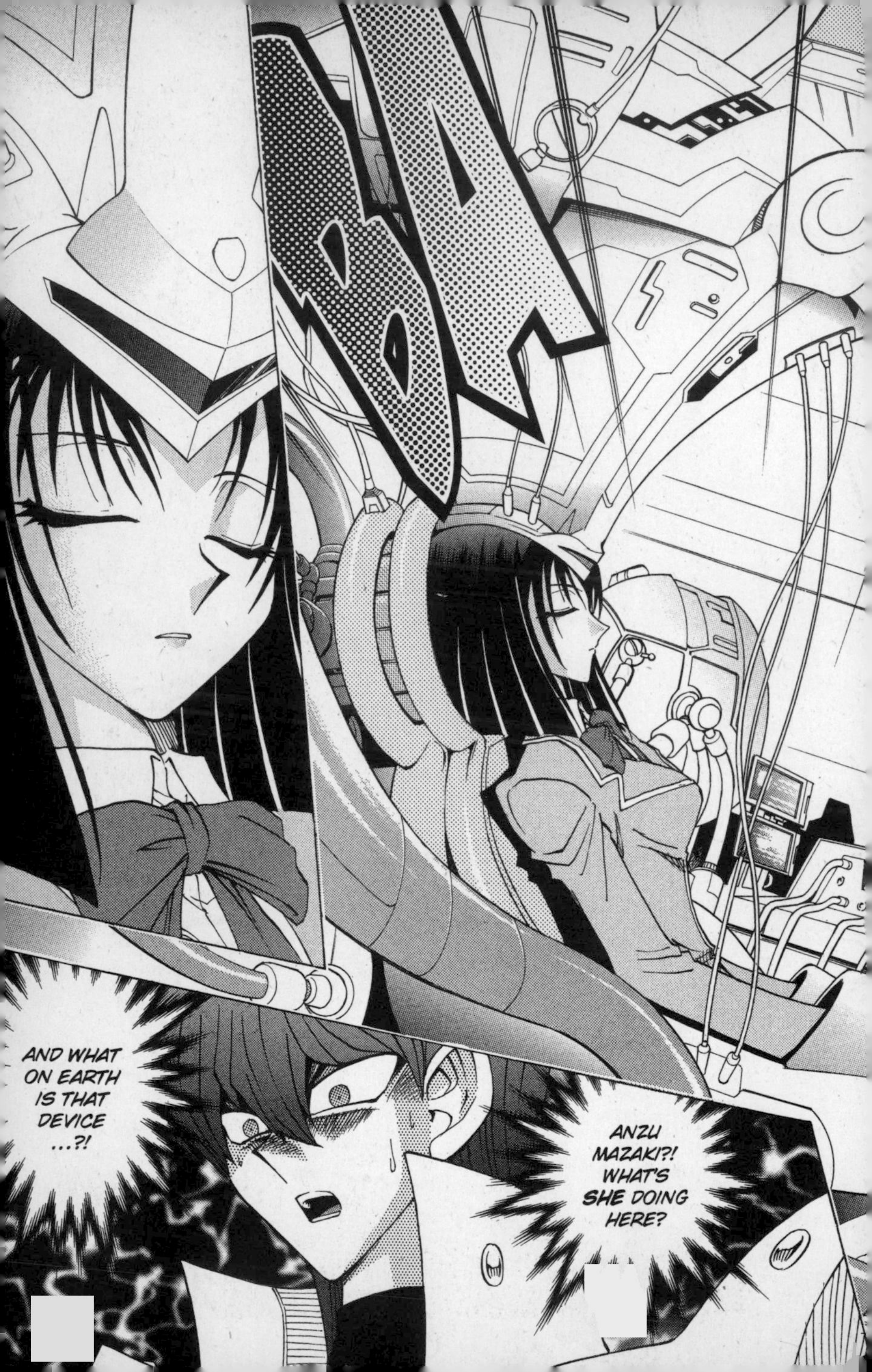
ANZU MAZAKI?! WHAT'S SHE DOING HERE?
AND WHAT ON EARTH IS THAT DEVICE ...?!

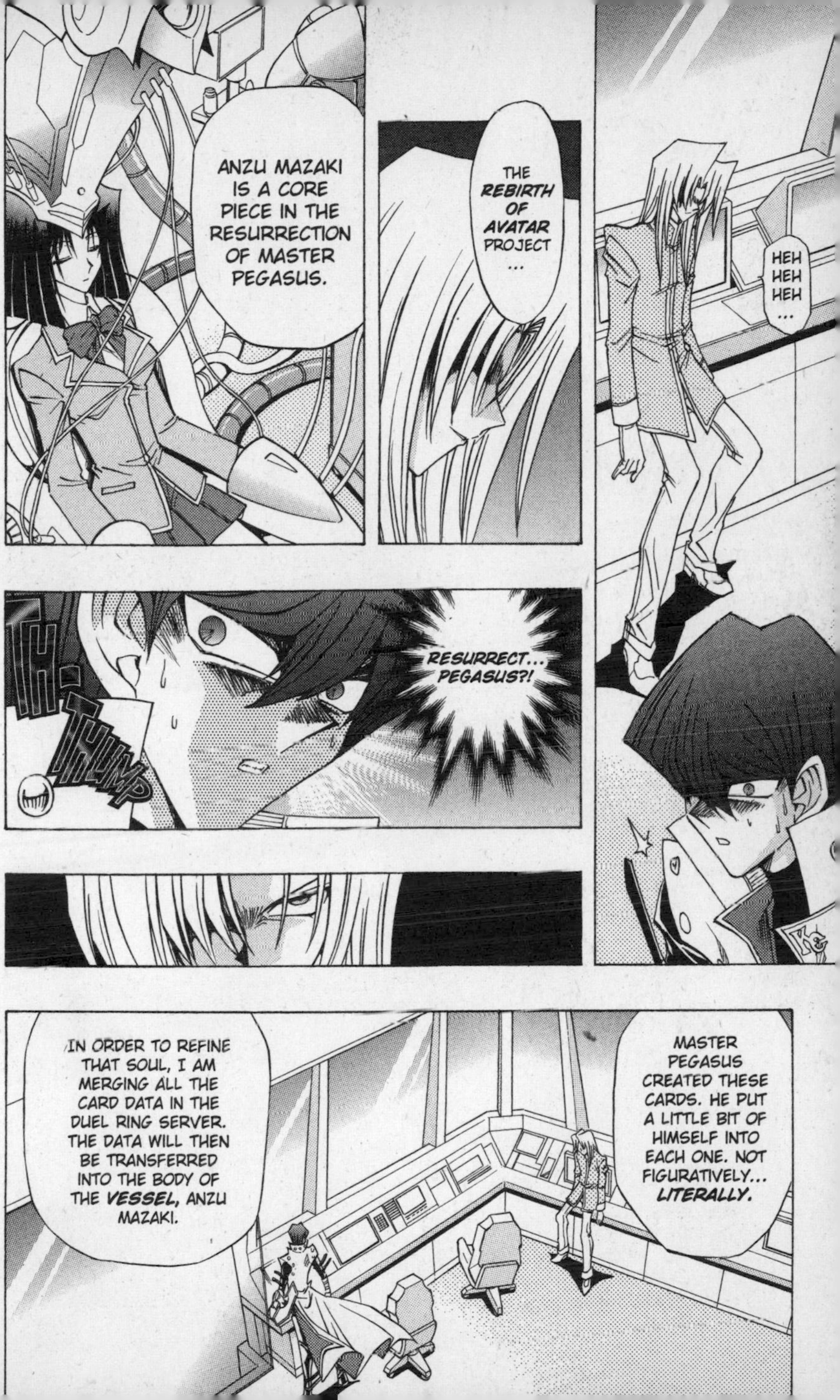
HEH HEH HEH ...
THE REBIRTH OF AVATAR PROJECT ...
ANZU MAZAKI IS A CORE PIECE IN THE RESURRECTION OF MASTER PEGASUS.
RESURRECT... PEGASUS?!
TH-THUMP
MASTER PEGASUS CREATED THESE CARDS. HE PUT A LITTLE BIT OF HIMSELF INTO EACH ONE. NOT FIGURATIVELY... LITERALLY.
IN ORDER TO REFINE THAT SOUL, I AM MERGING ALL THE CARD DATA IN THE DUEL RING SERVER. THE DATA WILL THEN BE TRANSFERRED INTO THE BODY OF THE VESSEL, ANZU MAZAKI.

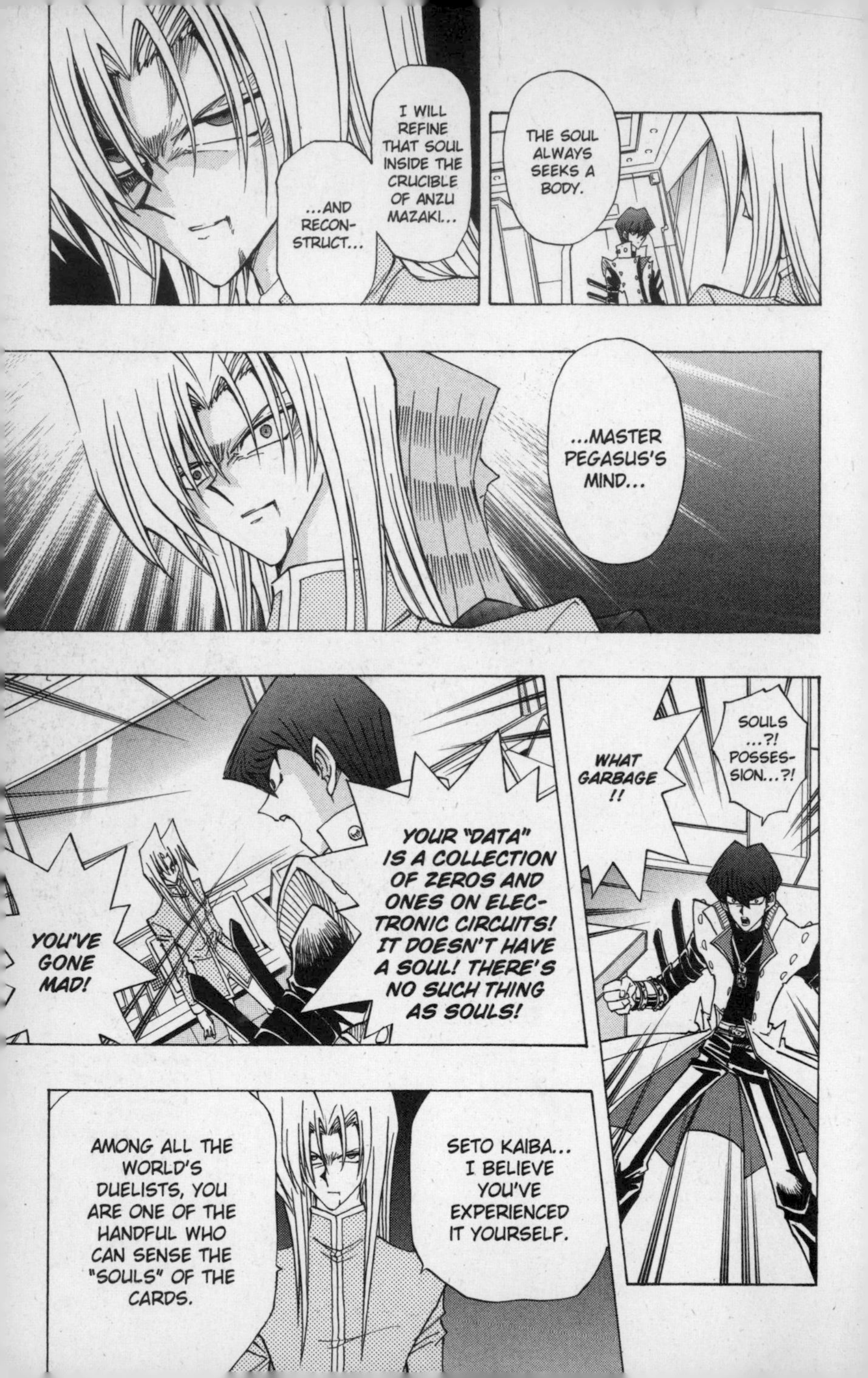
THE SOUL ALWAYS SEEKS A BODY.
I WILL REFINE THAT SOUL INSIDE THE CRUCIBLE OF ANZU MAZAKI...
...AND RECONSTRUCT...
...MASTER PEGASUS'S MIND...
SOULS...?! POSSESSION...?!
WHAT GARBAGE!!
YOUR "DATA" IS A COLLECTION OF ZEROS AND ONES ON ELECTRONIC CIRCUITS! IT DOESN'T HAVE A SOUL! THERE'S NO SUCH THING AS SOULS!
YOU'VE GONE MAD!
SETO KAIBA... I BELIEVE YOU'VE EXPERIENCED IT YOURSELF.
AMONG ALL THE WORLD'S DUELISTS, YOU ARE ONE OF THE HANDFUL WHO CAN SENSE THE "SOULS" OF THE CARDS.

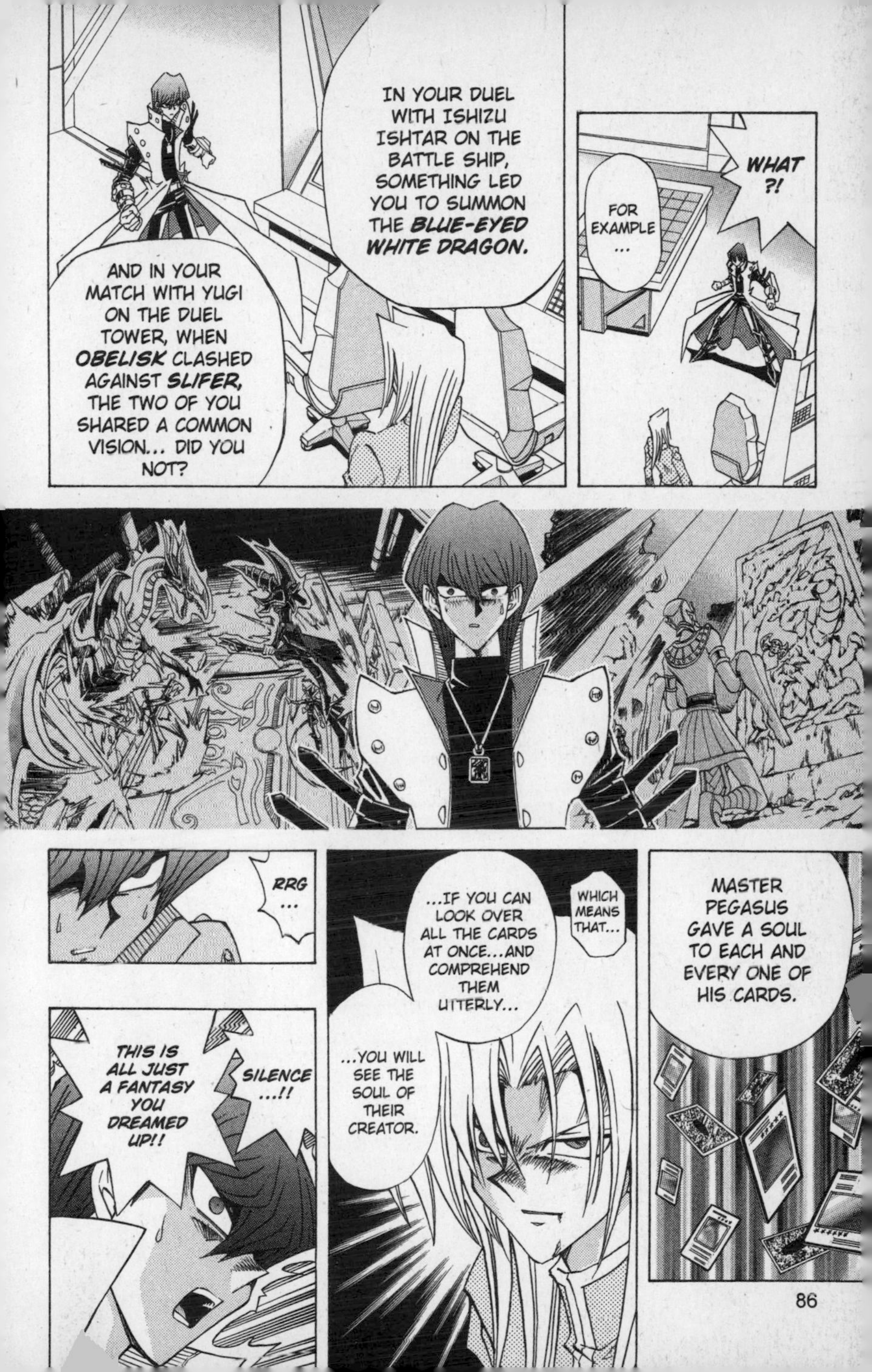
WHAT ?!
FOR EXAMPLE ...
IN YOUR DUEL WITH ISHIZU ISHTAR ON THE BATTLE SHIP, SOMETHING LED YOU TO SUMMON THE BLUE-EYED WHITE DRAGON.
AND IN YOUR MATCH WITH YUGI ON THE DUEL TOWER, WHEN OBELISK CLASHED AGAINST SLIFER, THE TWO OF YOU SHARED A COMMON VISION... DID YOU NOT?
MASTER PEGASUS GAVE A SOUL TO EACH AND EVERY ONE OF HIS CARDS.
WHICH MEANS THAT...
...IF YOU CAN LOOK OVER ALL THE CARDS AT ONCE...AND COMPREHEND THEM UTTERLY...
...YOU WILL SEE THE SOUL OF THEIR CREATOR.
RRG ...
SILENCE ...!!
THIS IS ALL JUST A FANTASY YOU DREAMED UP!!

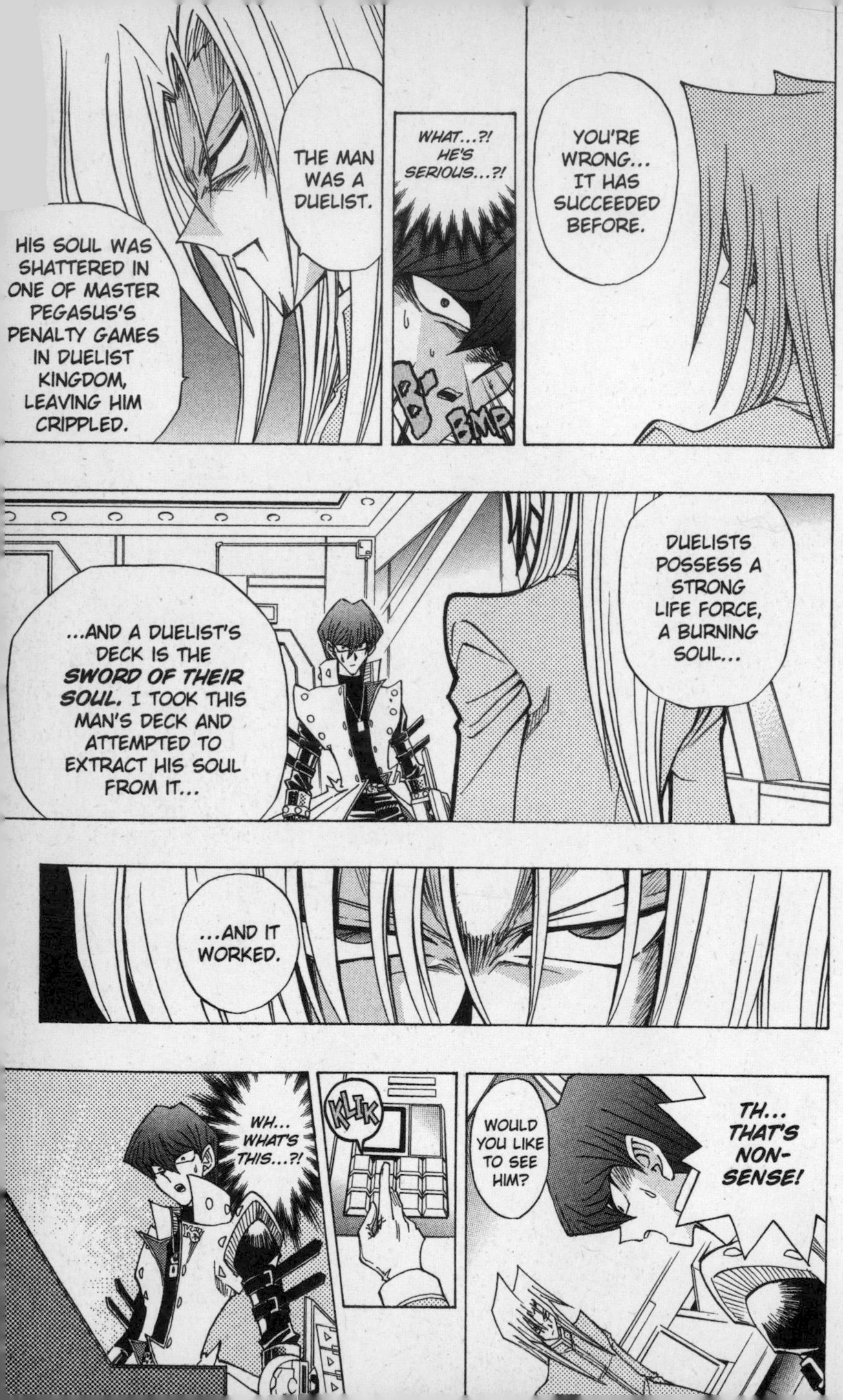
YOU'RE WRONG... IT HAS SUCCEEDED BEFORE.
WHAT...?! HE'S SERIOUS...?!
BMP
THE MAN WAS A DUELIST.
HIS SOUL WAS SHATTERED IN ONE OF MASTER PEGASUS'S PENALTY GAMES IN DUELIST KINGDOM, LEAVING HIM CRIPPLED.
DUELISTS POSSESS A STRONG LIFE FORCE, A BURNING SOUL...
...AND A DUELIST'S DECK IS THE ***SWORD OF THEIR SOUL.*** I TOOK THIS MAN'S DECK AND ATTEMPTED TO EXTRACT HIS SOUL FROM IT...
...AND IT WORKED.
TH... THAT'S NON-SENSE!
WOULD YOU LIKE TO SEE HIM?
KLIK
WH... WHAT'S THIS...?!

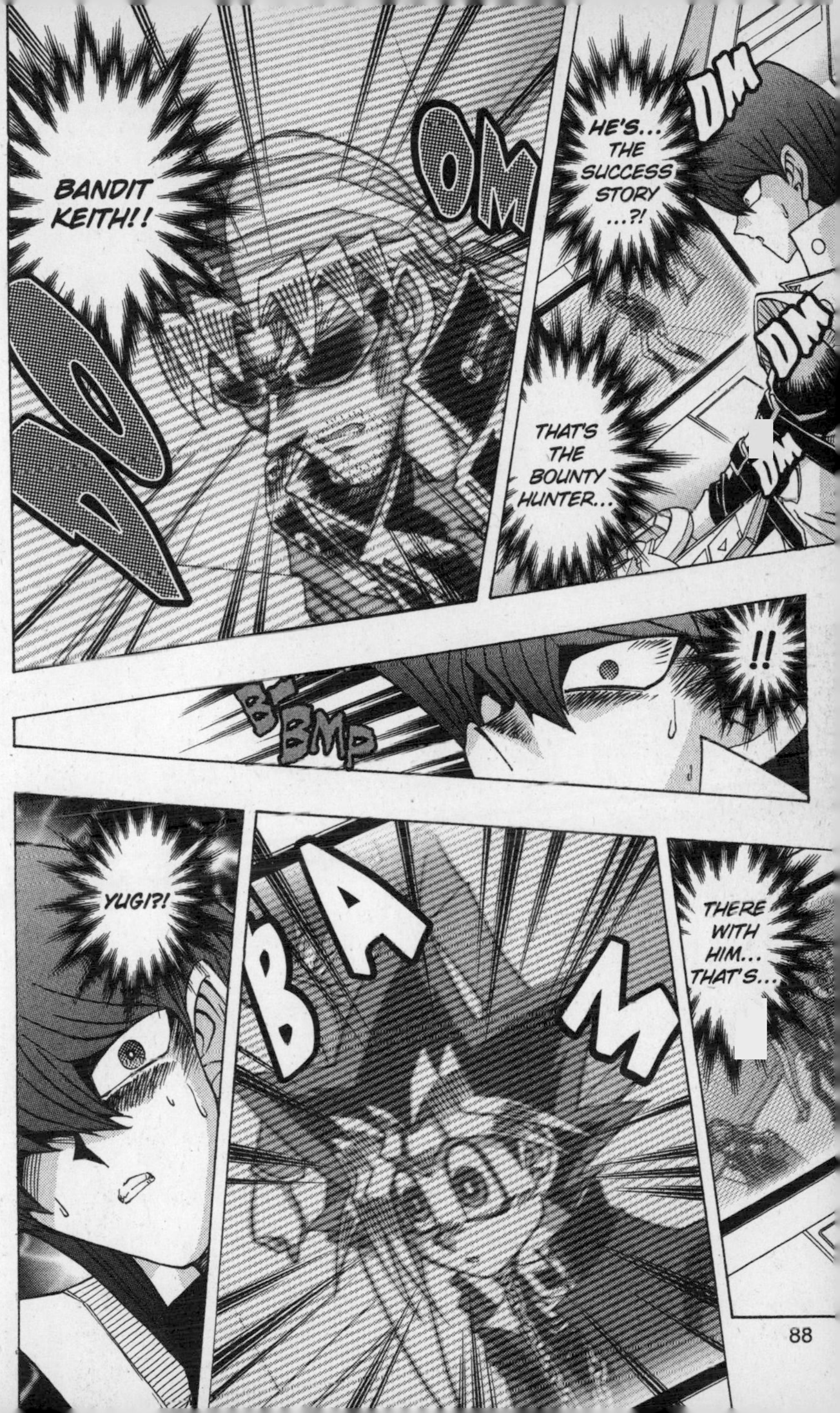
HE'S... THE SUCCESS STORY ...?!
DM
THAT'S THE BOUNTY HUNTER...
DM
DM
OM
BANDIT KEITH!!
!!
BBMP
THERE WITH HIM... THAT'S...
BAM
YUGI?!

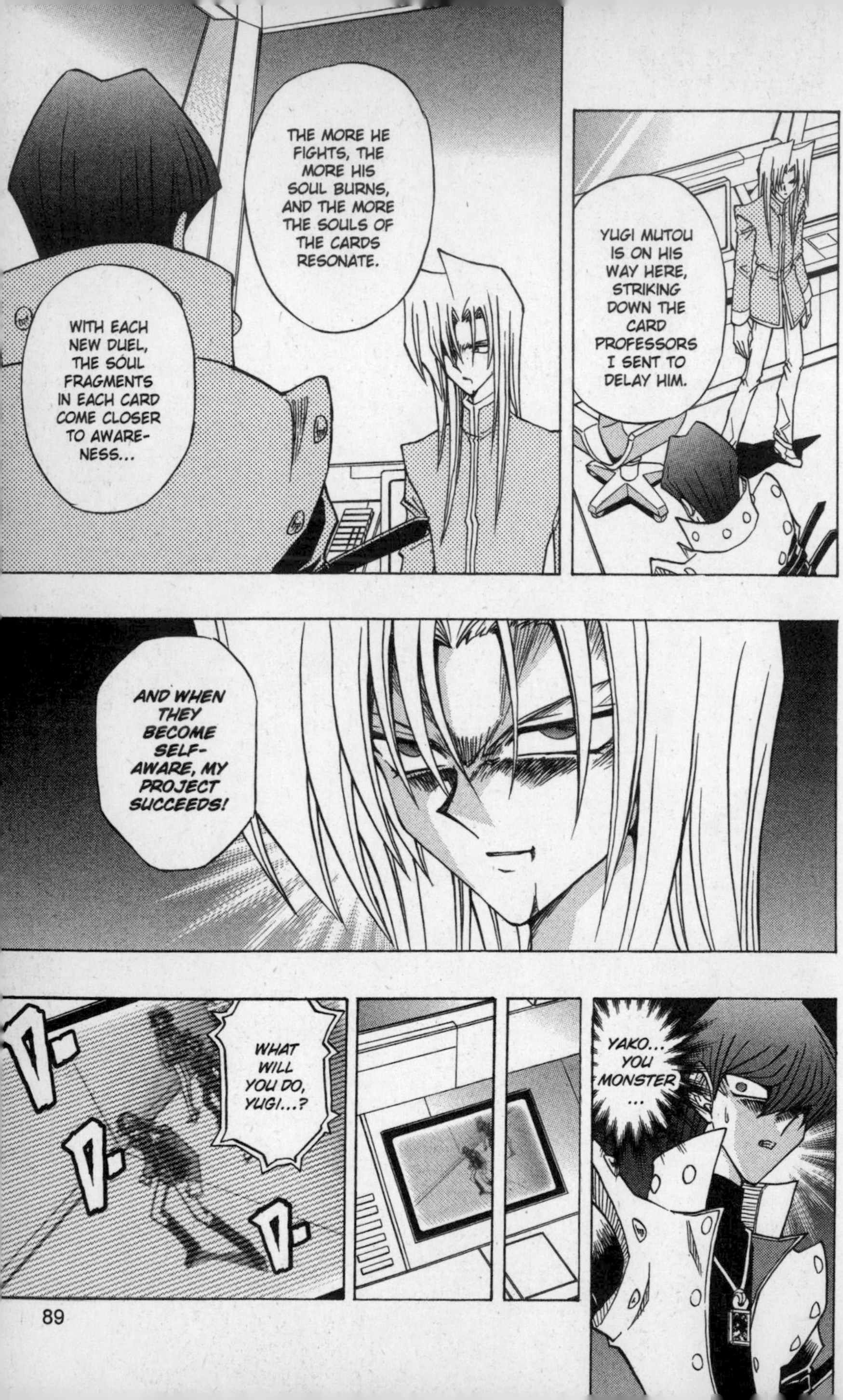
YUGI MUTOU IS ON HIS WAY HERE, STRIKING DOWN THE CARD PROFESSORS I SENT TO DELAY HIM.
THE MORE HE FIGHTS, THE MORE HIS SOUL BURNS, AND THE MORE THE SOULS OF THE CARDS RESONATE.
WITH EACH NEW DUEL, THE SOUL FRAGMENTS IN EACH CARD COME CLOSER TO AWARENESS...
AND WHEN THEY BECOME SELF-AWARE, MY PROJECT SUCCEEDS!
YAKO... YOU MONSTER...
WHAT WILL YOU DO, YUGI...?

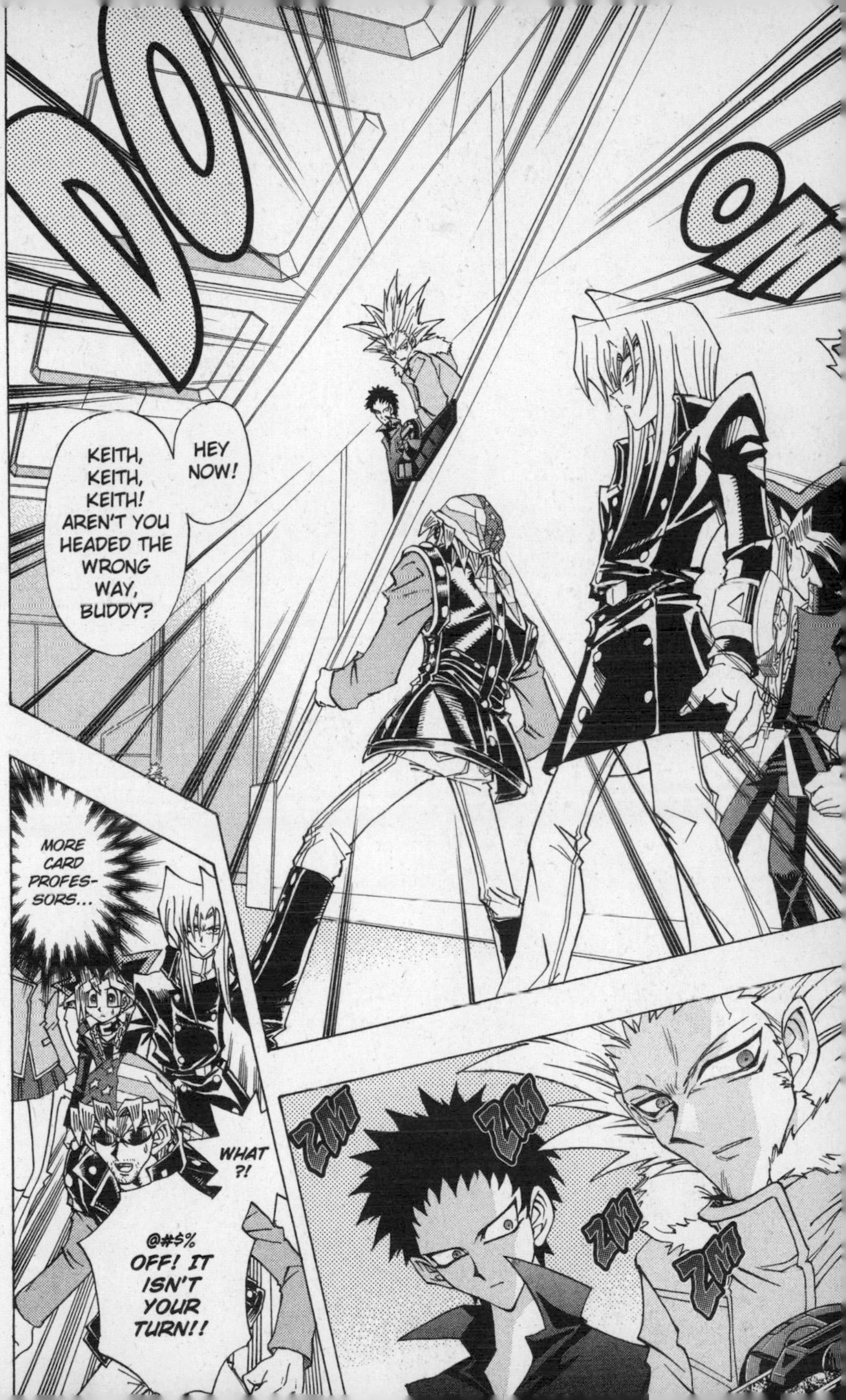

DO
OM
HEY NOW!
KEITH, KEITH, KEITH! AREN'T YOU HEADED THE WRONG WAY, BUDDY?
ZM
ZM
ZM
ZM
MORE CARD PROFES-SORS...
WHAT?!
@#$% OFF! IT ISN'T YOUR TURN!!

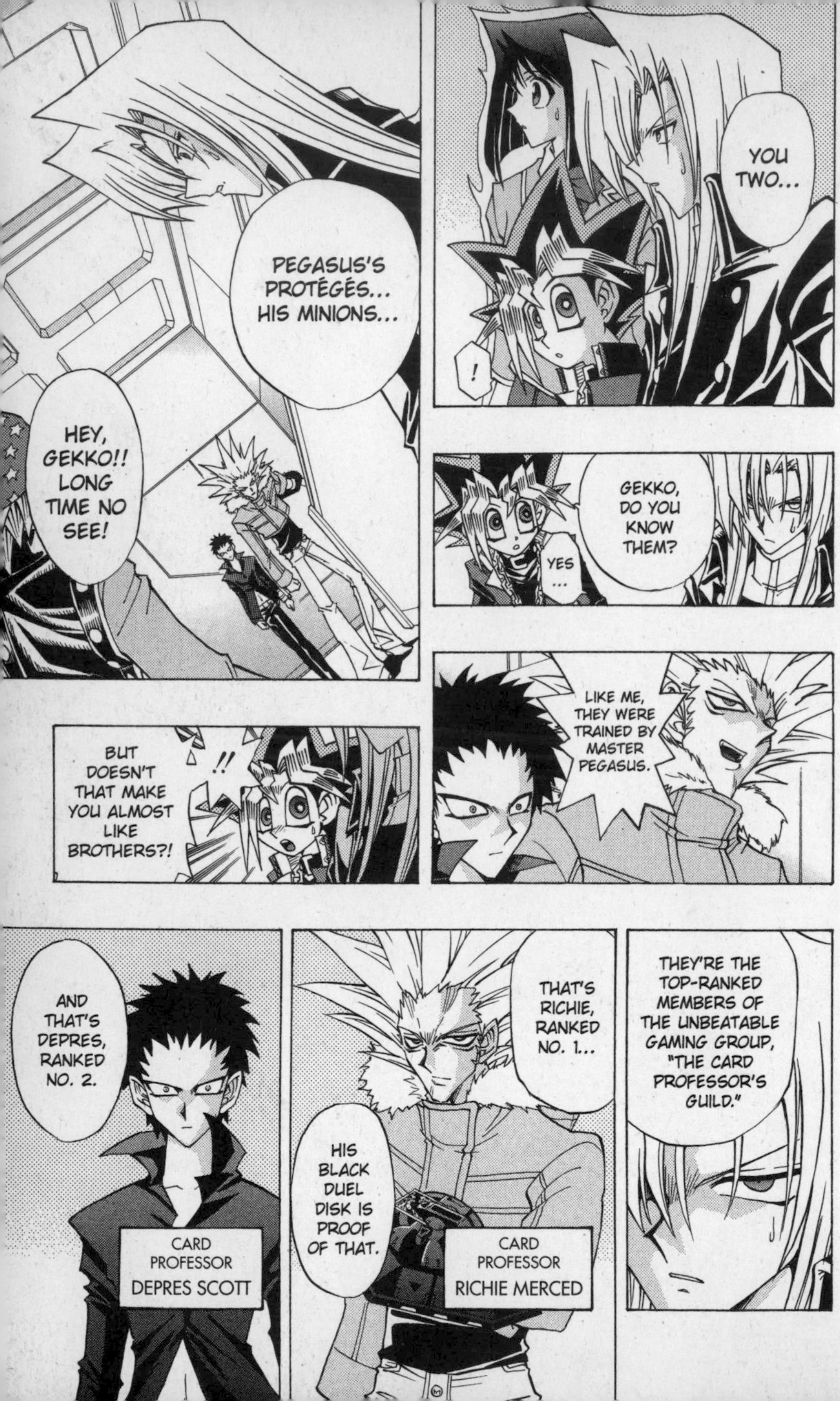

YOU TWO...
!
GEKKO, DO YOU KNOW THEM?
YES...
PEGASUS'S PROTÉGÉS... HIS MINIONS...
HEY, GEKKO!! LONG TIME NO SEE!
LIKE ME, THEY WERE TRAINED BY MASTER PEGASUS.
!!
BUT DOESN'T THAT MAKE YOU ALMOST LIKE BROTHERS?!
THEY'RE THE TOP-RANKED MEMBERS OF THE UNBEATABLE GAMING GROUP, "THE CARD PROFESSOR'S GUILD."
THAT'S RICHIE, RANKED NO. 1...
HIS BLACK DUEL DISK IS PROOF OF THAT.
CARD PROFESSOR RICHIE MERCED
AND THAT'S DEPRES, RANKED NO. 2.
CARD PROFESSOR DEPRES SCOTT

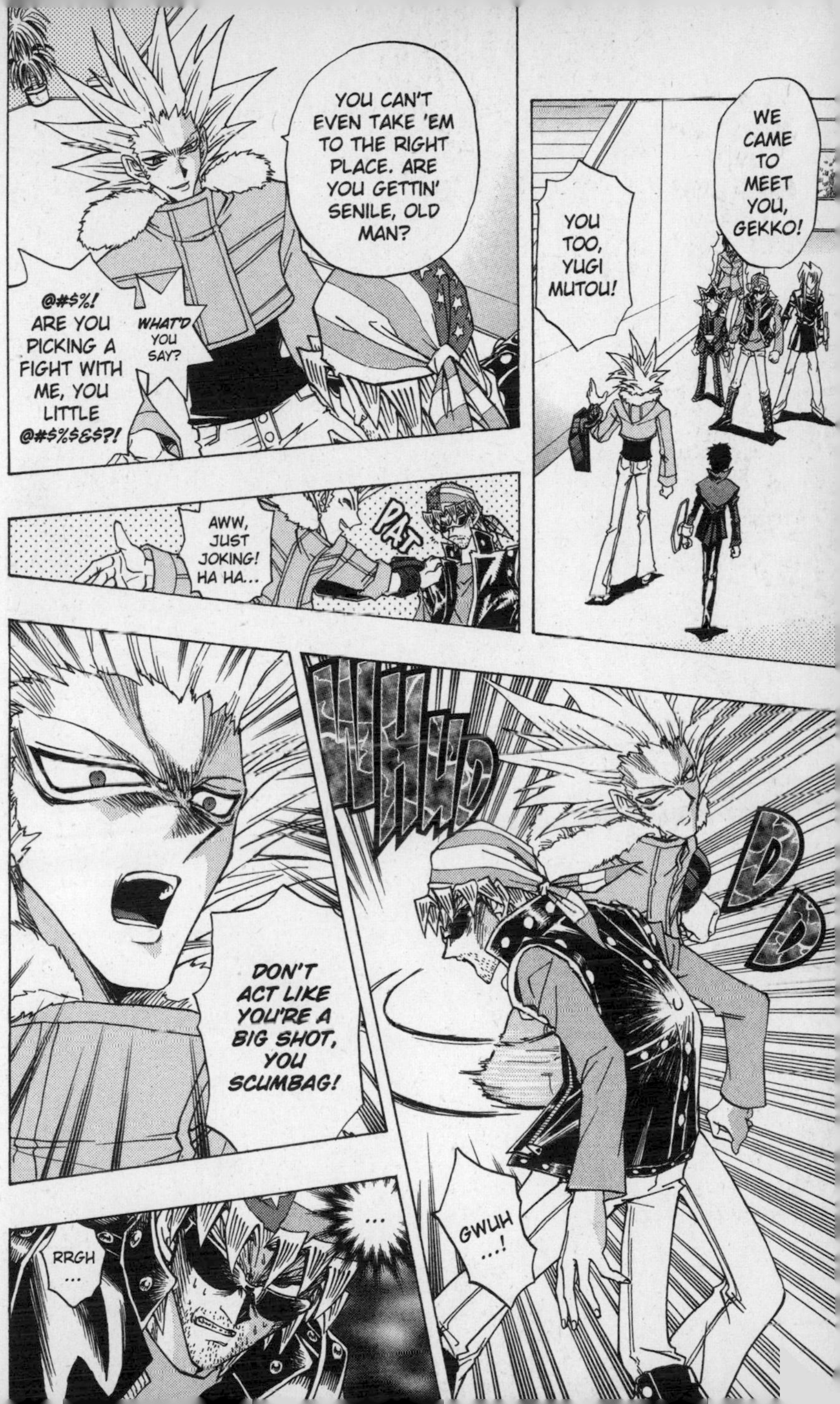
WE CAME TO MEET YOU, GEKKO!
YOU TOO, YUGI MUTOU!
YOU CAN'T EVEN TAKE 'EM TO THE RIGHT PLACE. ARE YOU GETTIN' SENILE, OLD MAN?
WHAT'D YOU SAY?
@#$%! ARE YOU PICKING A FIGHT WITH ME, YOU LITTLE @#$%$&$?!
AWW, JUST JOKING! HA HA...
PAT
WHUD
DD
GWUH ...!
DON'T ACT LIKE YOU'RE A BIG SHOT, YOU SCUMBAG!
...
RRGH ...

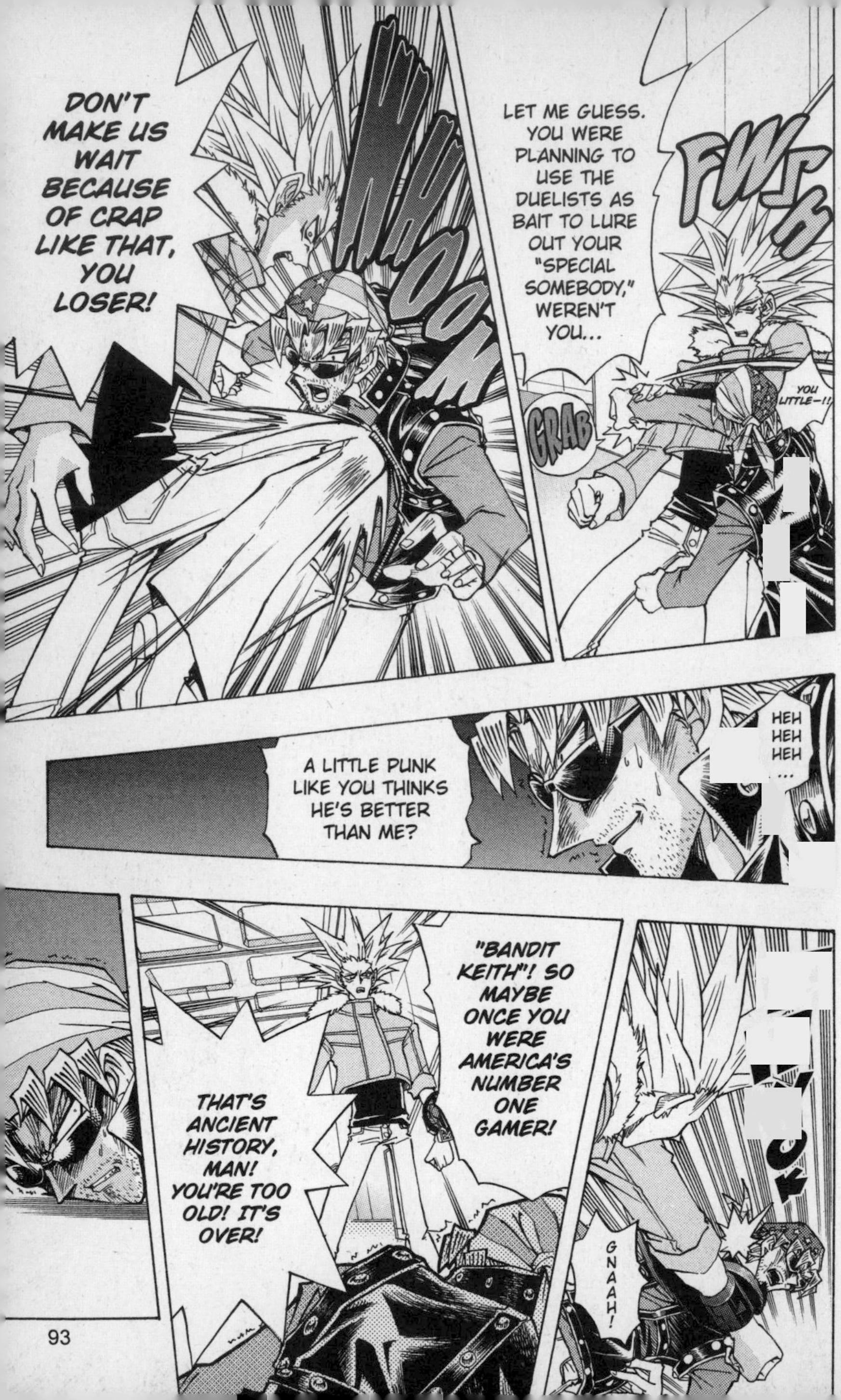
LET ME GUESS. YOU WERE PLANNING TO USE THE DUELISTS AS BAIT TO LURE OUT YOUR "SPECIAL SOMEBODY," WEREN'T YOU...
FWSH
YOU LITTLE—!!
GRAB
DON'T MAKE US WAIT BECAUSE OF CRAP LIKE THAT, YOU LOSER!
HEH HEH HEH...
A LITTLE PUNK LIKE YOU THINKS HE'S BETTER THAN ME?
GNAAH!
"BANDIT KEITH"! SO MAYBE ONCE YOU WERE AMERICA'S NUMBER ONE GAMER!
THAT'S ANCIENT HISTORY, MAN! YOU'RE TOO OLD! IT'S OVER!

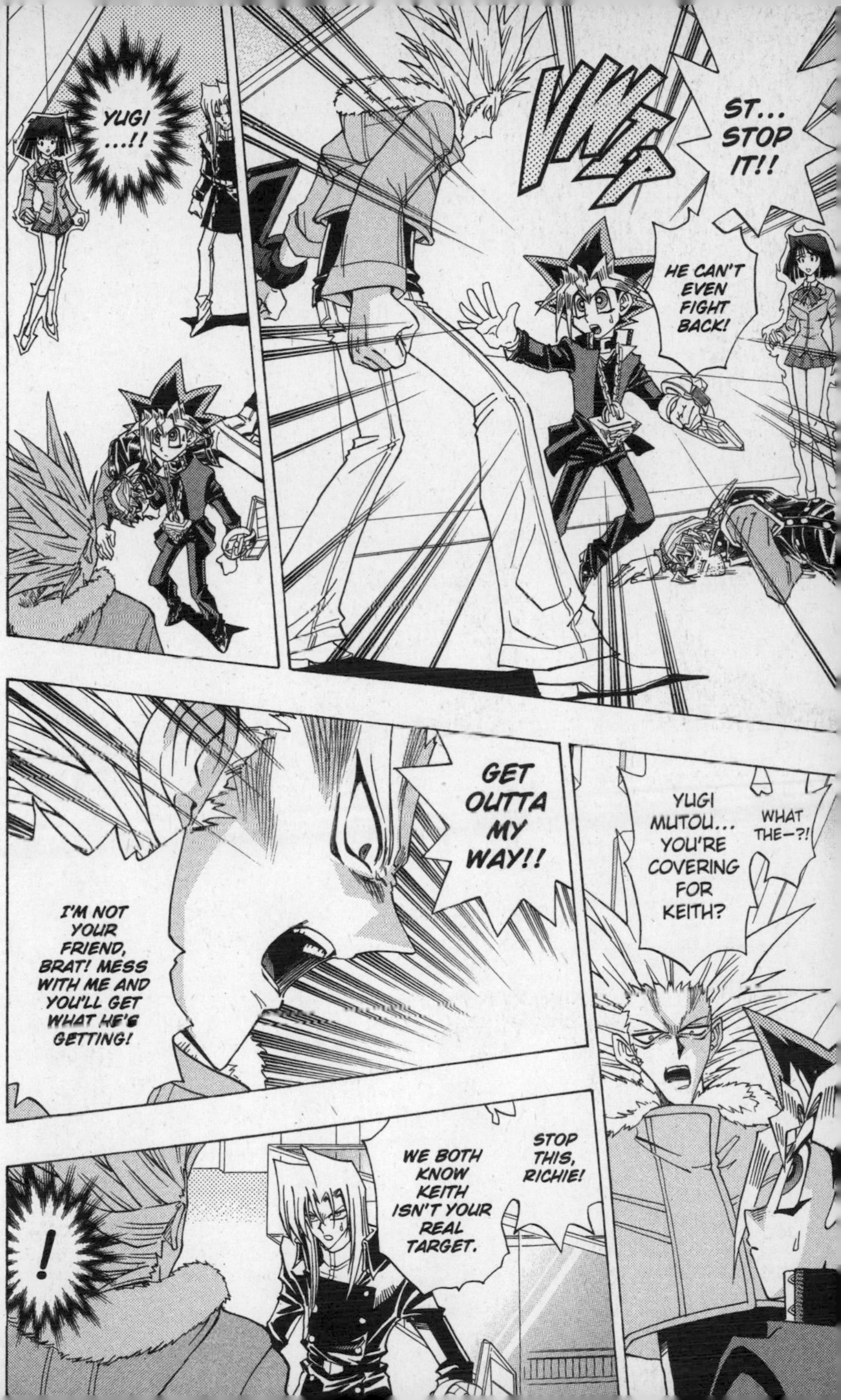
VWIP
ST... STOP IT!!
HE CAN'T EVEN FIGHT BACK!
YUGI ...!!
WHAT THE—?!
YUGI MUTOU... YOU'RE COVERING FOR KEITH?
GET OUTTA MY WAY!!
I'M NOT YOUR FRIEND, BRAT! MESS WITH ME AND YOU'LL GET WHAT HE'S GETTING!
STOP THIS, RICHIE!
WE BOTH KNOW KEITH ISN'T YOUR REAL TARGET.
!

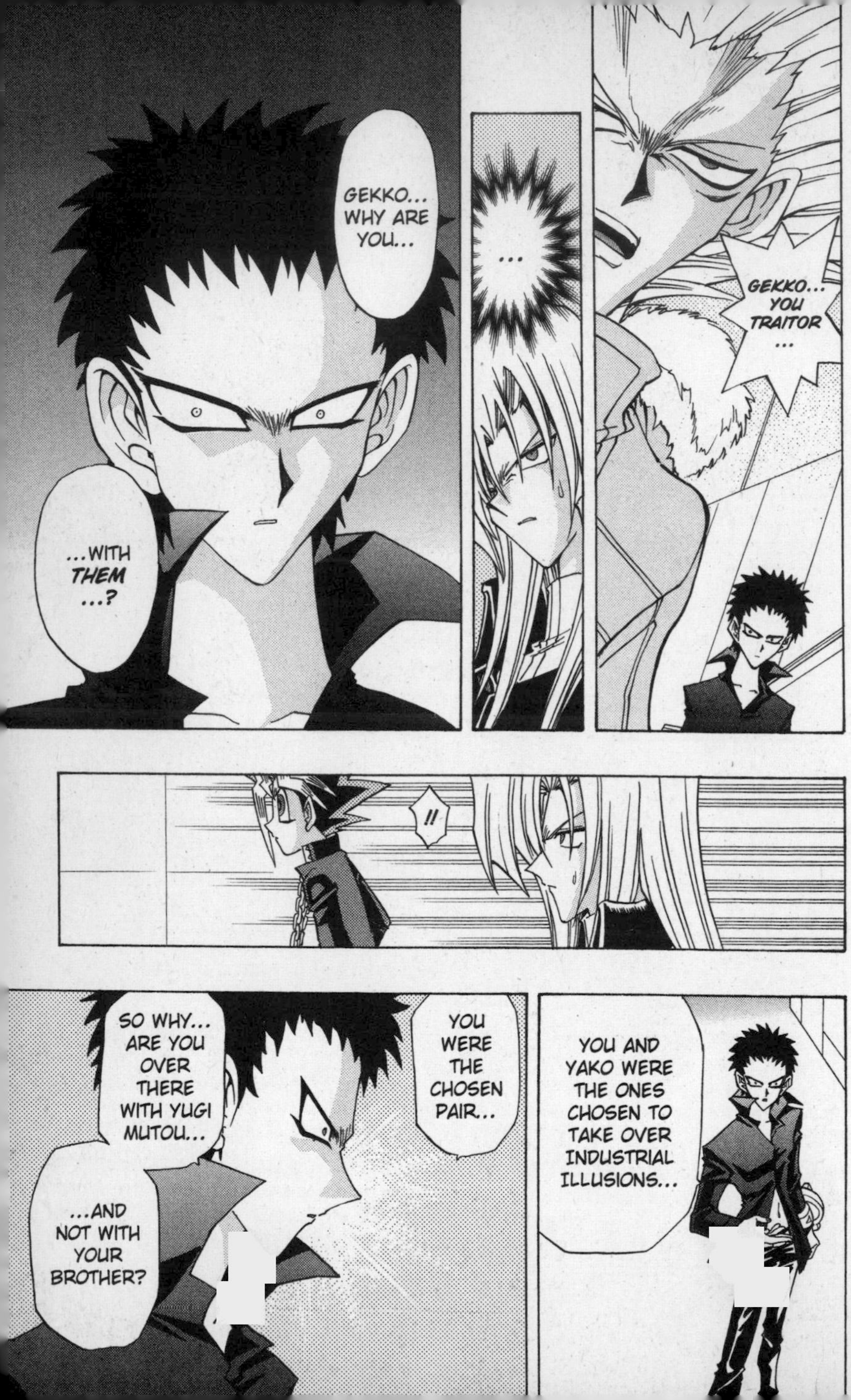
GEKKO... YOU TRAITOR ...
...
GEKKO... WHY ARE YOU...
...WITH *THEM* ...?
!!
YOU AND YAKO WERE THE ONES CHOSEN TO TAKE OVER INDUSTRIAL ILLUSIONS...
YOU WERE THE CHOSEN PAIR...
SO WHY... ARE YOU OVER THERE WITH YUGI MUTOU...
...AND NOT WITH YOUR BROTHER?

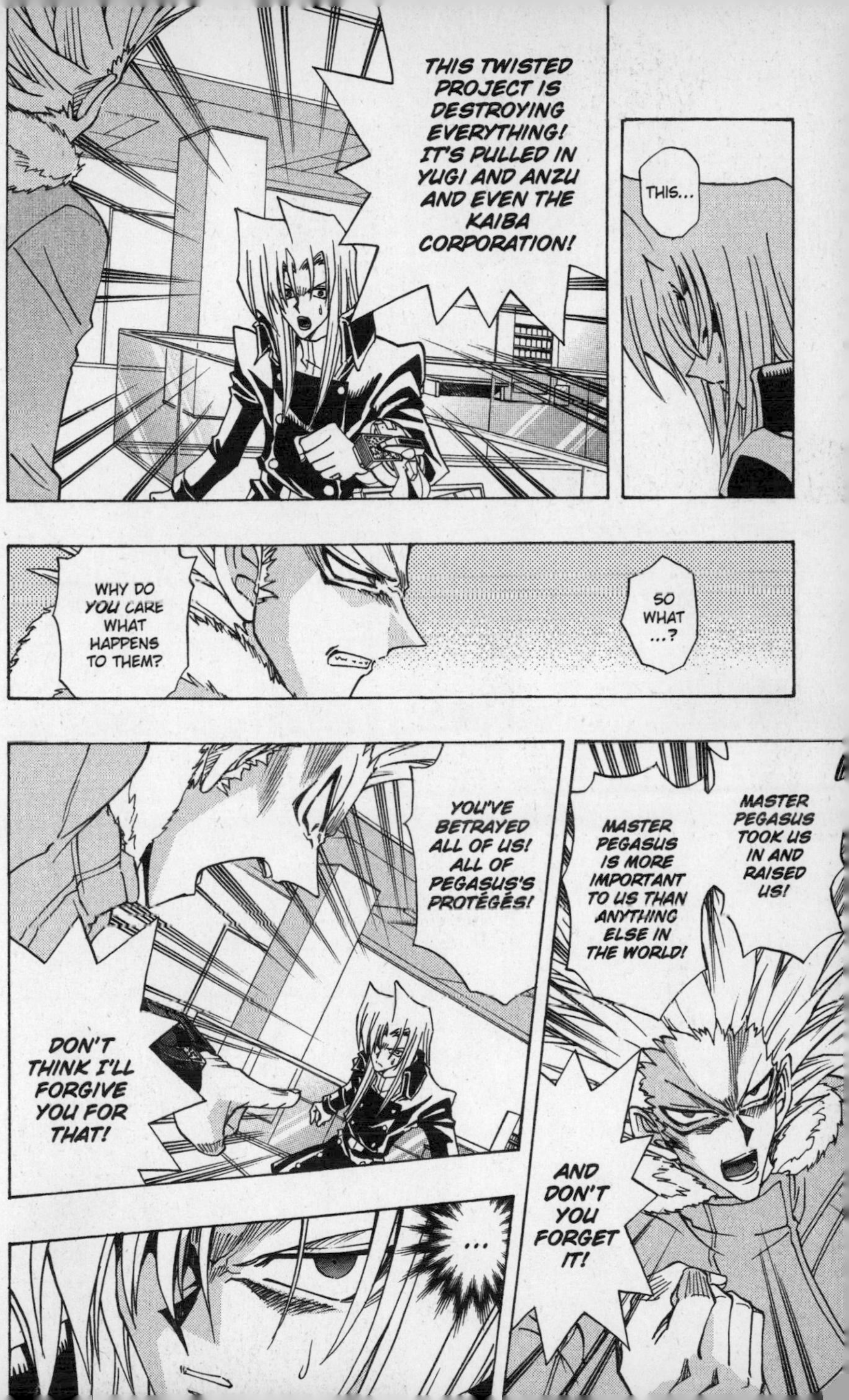
THIS...
THIS TWISTED PROJECT IS DESTROYING EVERYTHING! IT'S PULLED IN YUGI AND ANZU AND EVEN THE KAIBA CORPORATION!
SO WHAT ...?
WHY DO YOU CARE WHAT HAPPENS TO THEM?
MASTER PEGASUS TOOK US IN AND RAISED US!
MASTER PEGASUS IS MORE IMPORTANT TO US THAN ANYTHING ELSE IN THE WORLD!
AND DON'T YOU FORGET IT!
YOU'VE BETRAYED ALL OF US! ALL OF PEGASUS'S PROTÉGÉS!
DON'T THINK I'LL FORGIVE YOU FOR THAT!
...

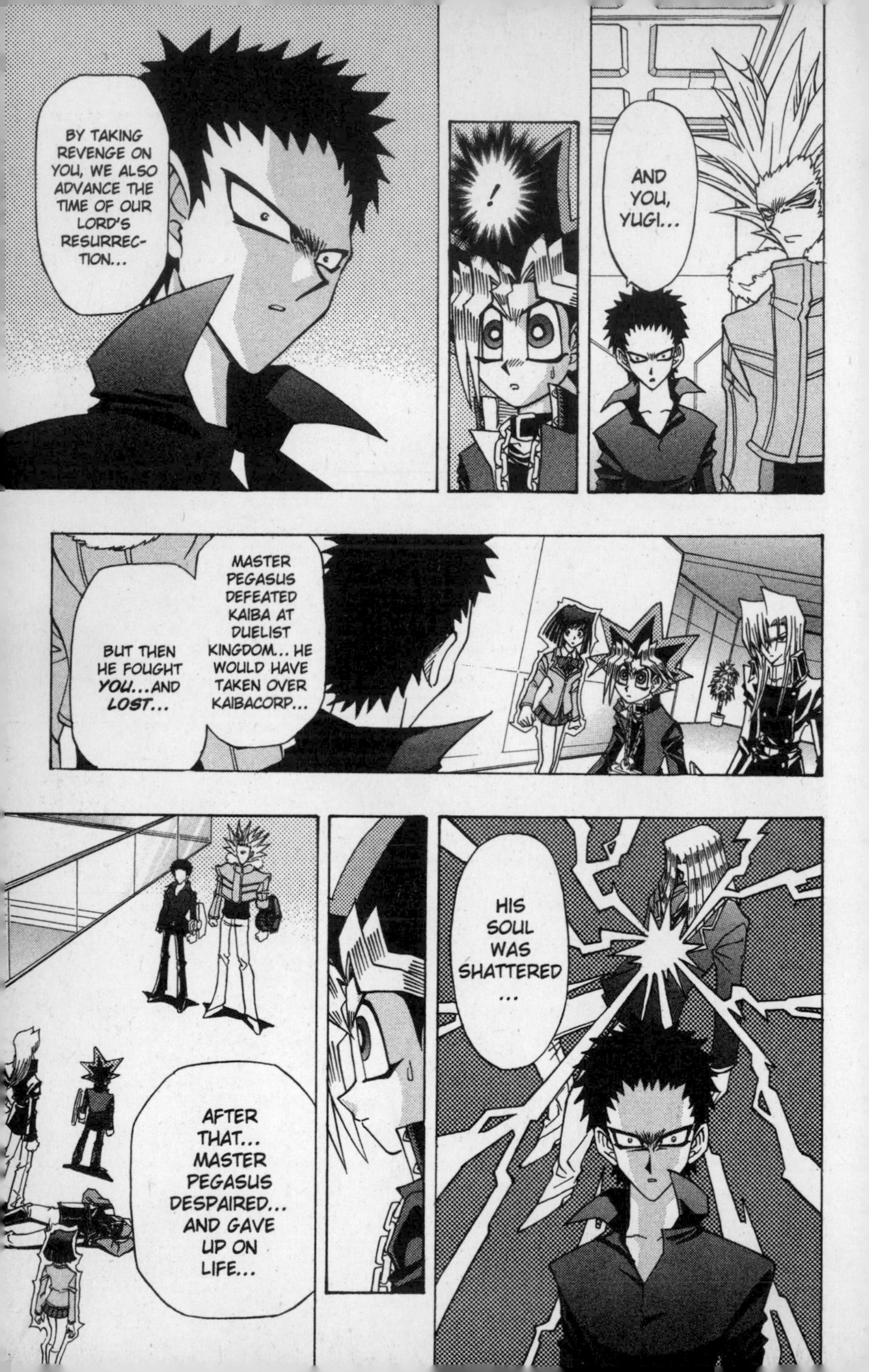
AND YOU, YUGI...
!
BY TAKING REVENGE ON YOU, WE ALSO ADVANCE THE TIME OF OUR LORD'S RESURRECTION...
MASTER PEGASUS DEFEATED KAIBA AT DUELIST KINGDOM... HE WOULD HAVE TAKEN OVER KAIBACORP...
BUT THEN HE FOUGHT *YOU*...AND *LOST*...
HIS SOUL WAS SHATTERED...
AFTER THAT... MASTER PEGASUS DESPAIRED... AND GAVE UP ON LIFE...

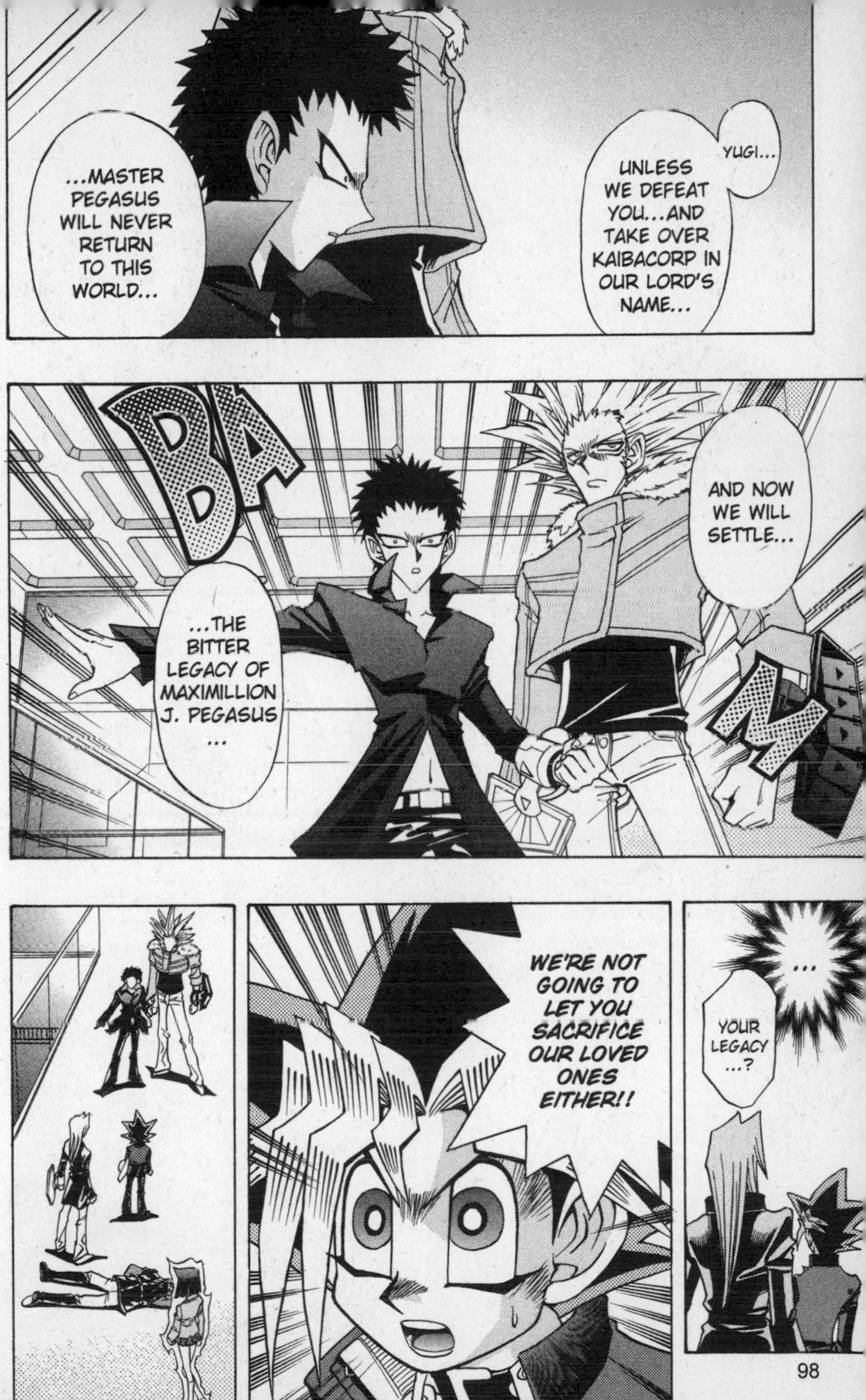
YUGI...
UNLESS WE DEFEAT YOU...AND TAKE OVER KAIBACORP IN OUR LORD'S NAME...
...MASTER PEGASUS WILL NEVER RETURN TO THIS WORLD...
AND NOW WE WILL SETTLE...
...THE BITTER LEGACY OF MAXIMILLION J. PEGASUS ...
BAM
...
YOUR LEGACY ...?
WE'RE NOT GOING TO LET YOU SACRIFICE OUR LOVED ONES EITHER!!

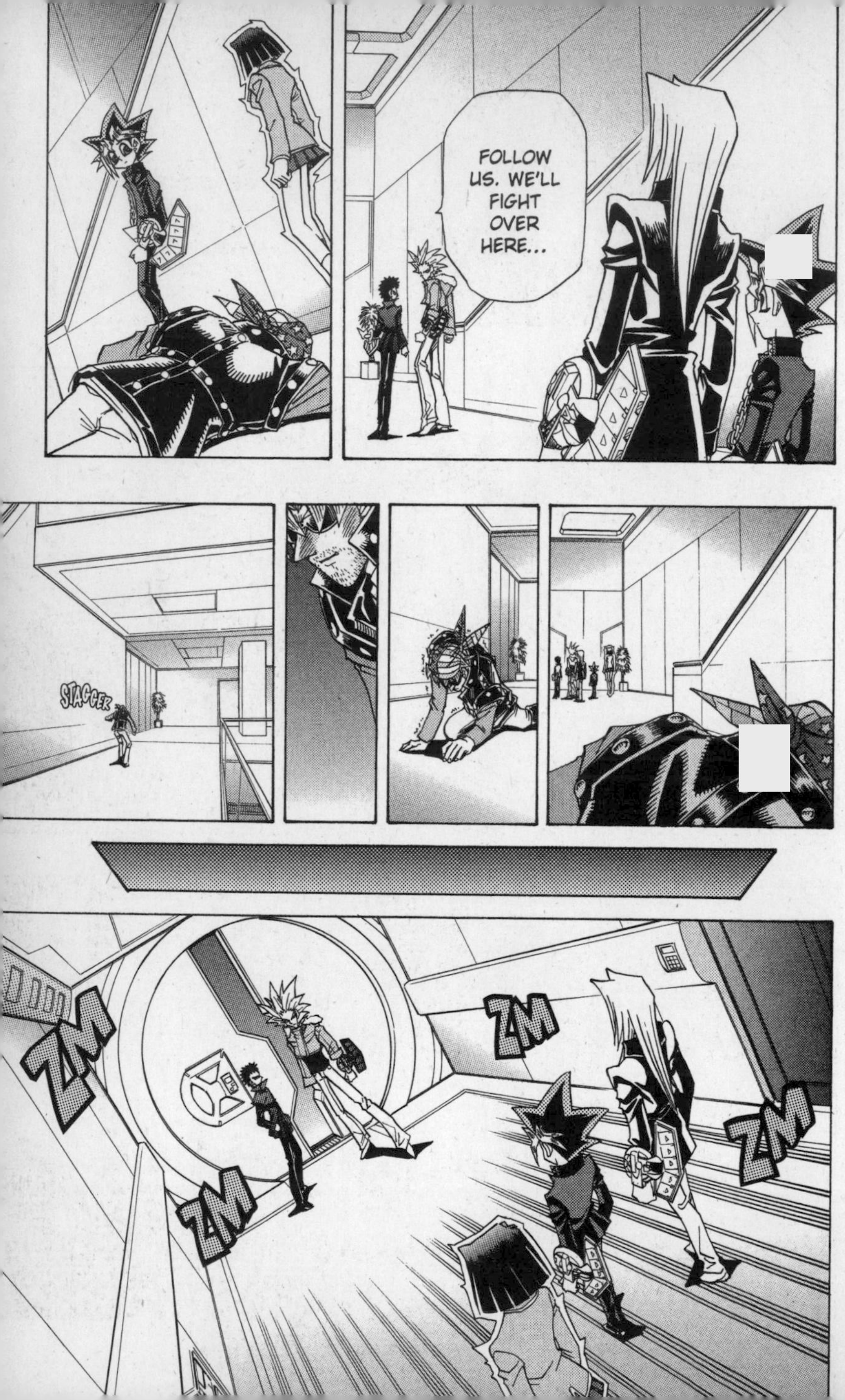
FOLLOW US. WE'LL FIGHT OVER HERE...
STAGGER
ZM
ZM
ZM
ZM

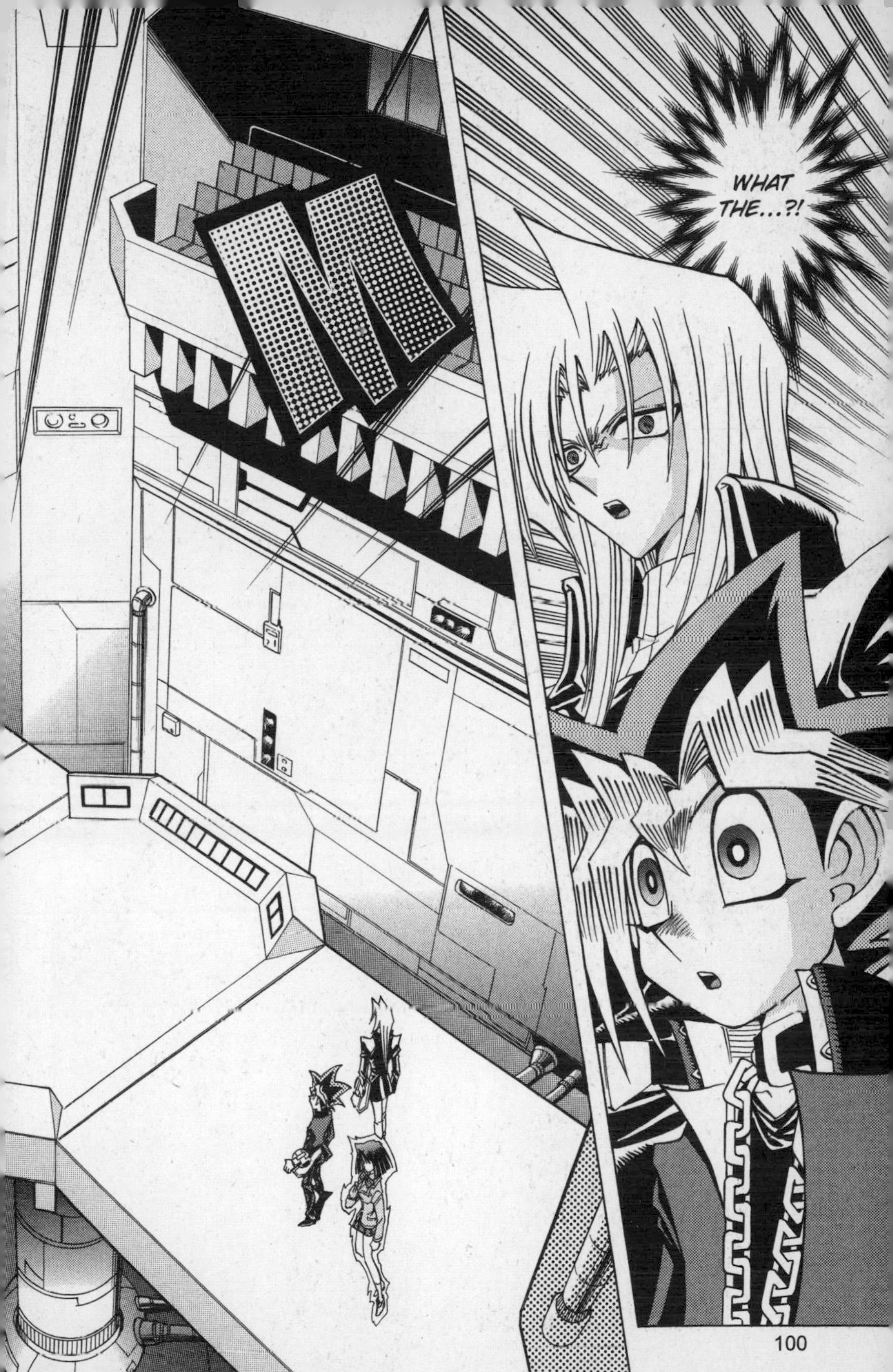
WHAT THE...?!

READ THIS WAY

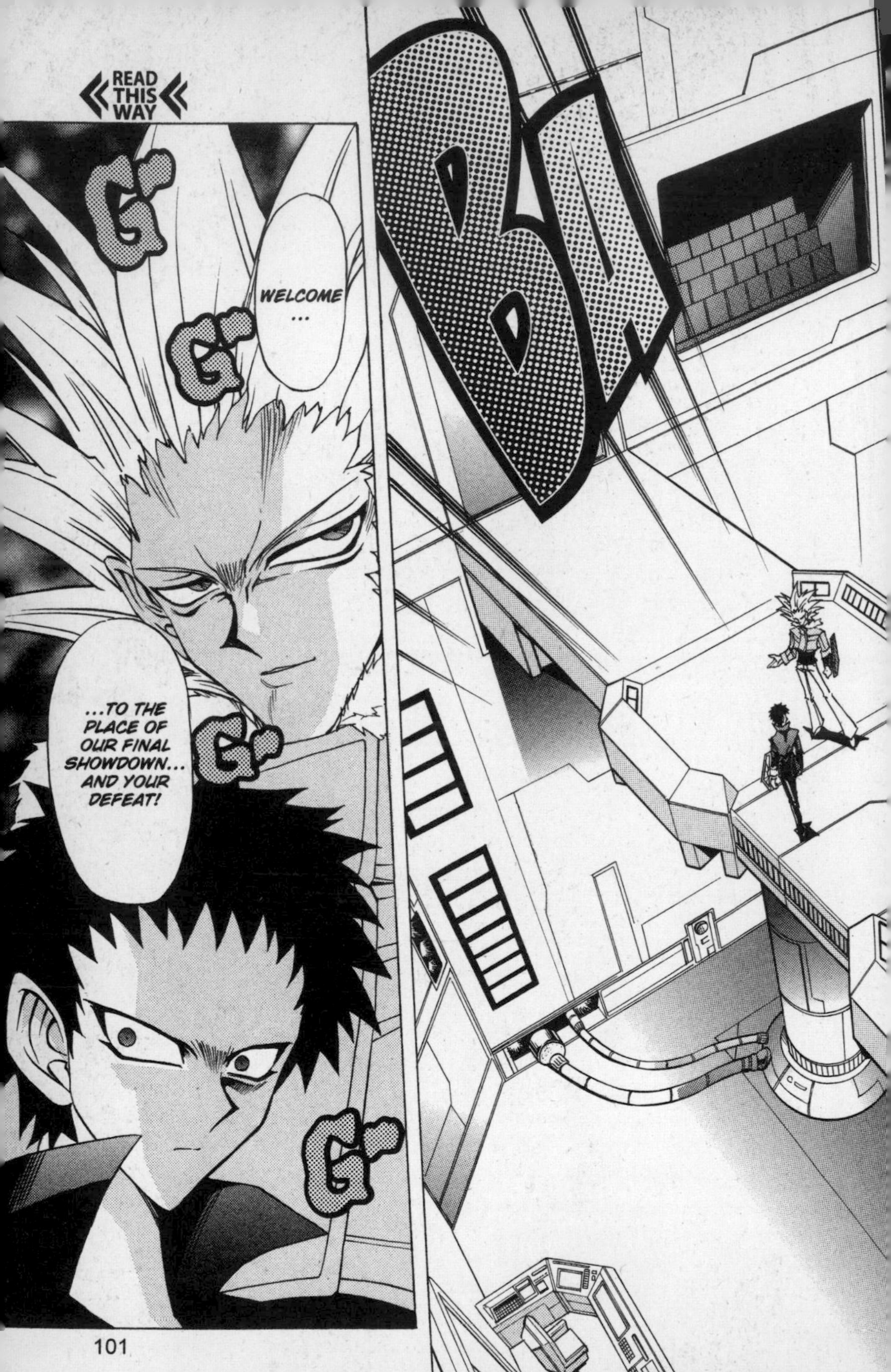
BA!
G
G
WELCOME ...
...TO THE PLACE OF OUR FINAL SHOWDOWN... AND YOUR DEFEAT!
G
G

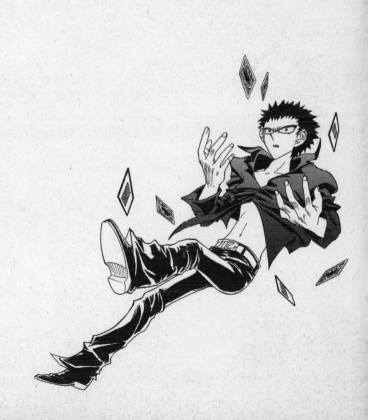

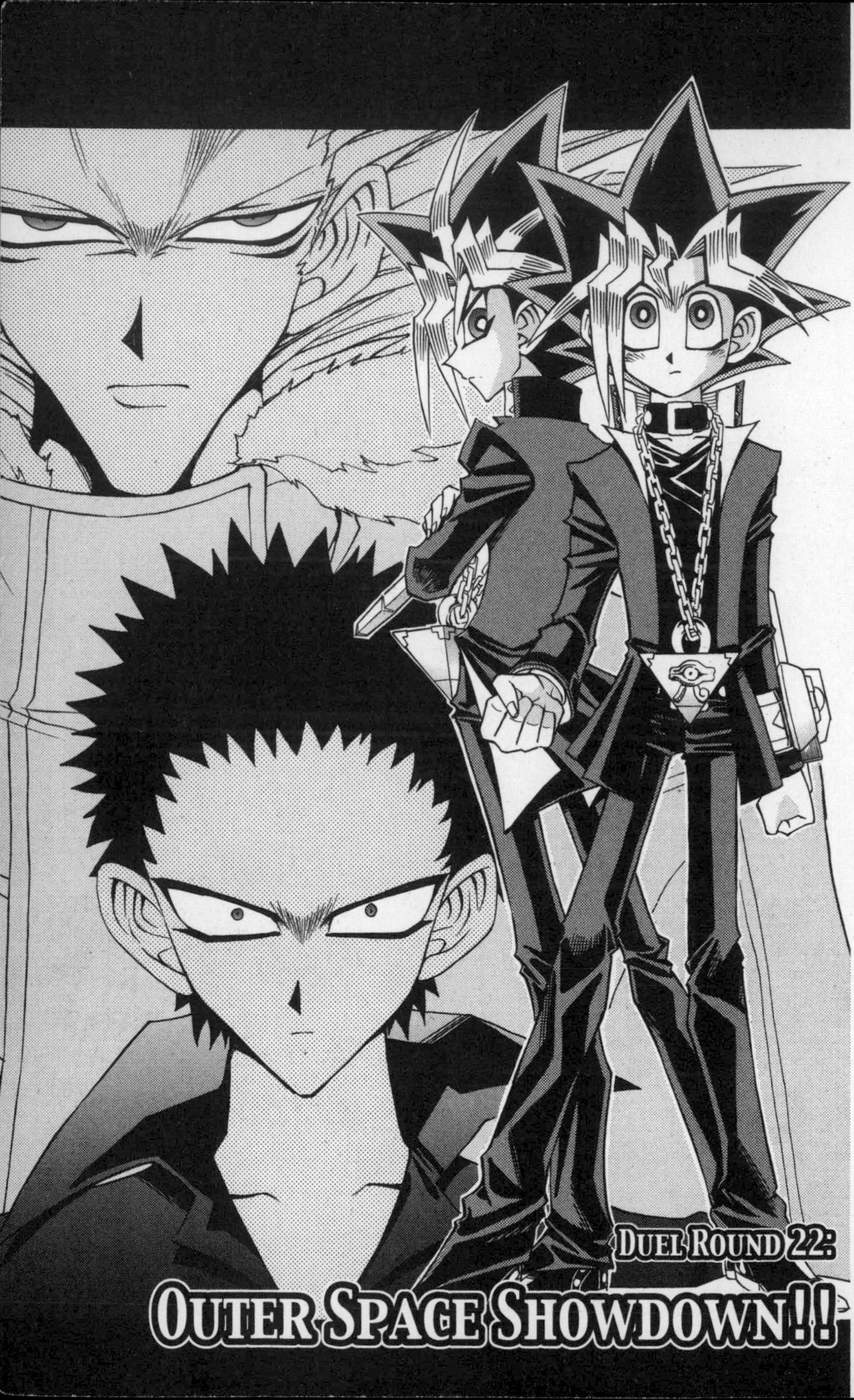
DUEL ROUND 22:
OUTER SPACE SHOWDOWN!!

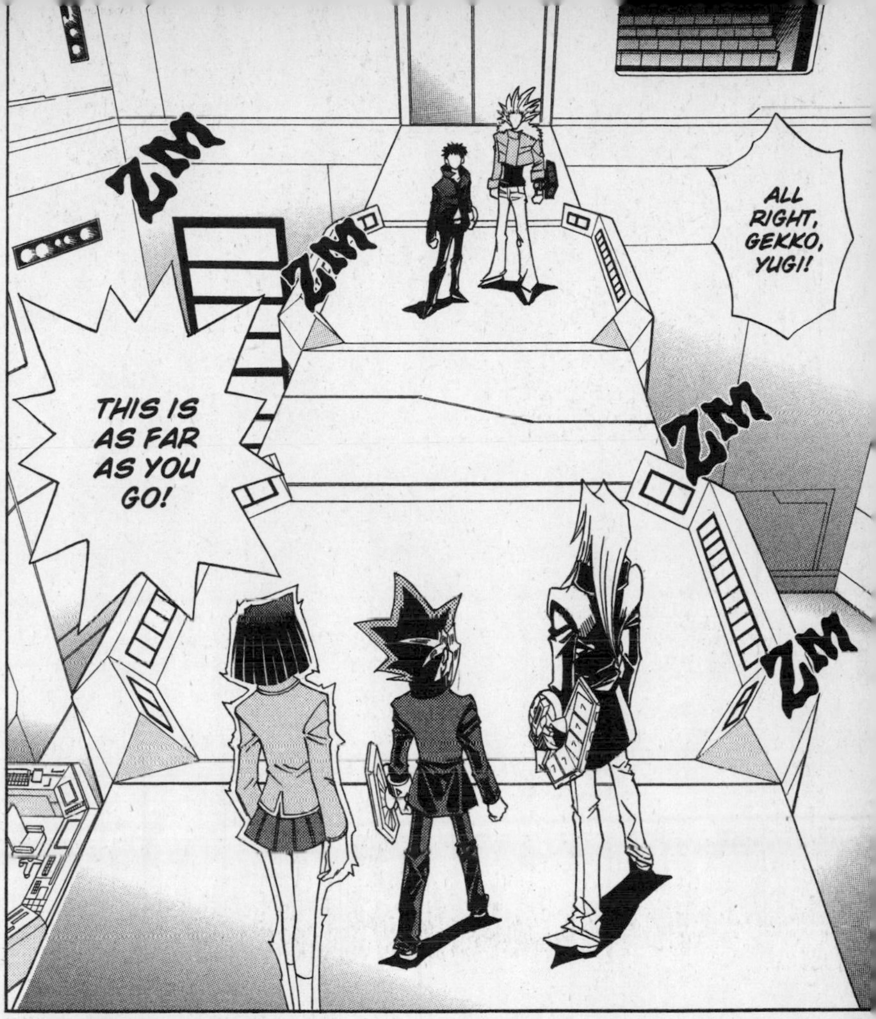
ALL RIGHT, GEKKO, YUGI!
ZM
ZM
THIS IS AS FAR AS YOU GO!
ZM
ZM

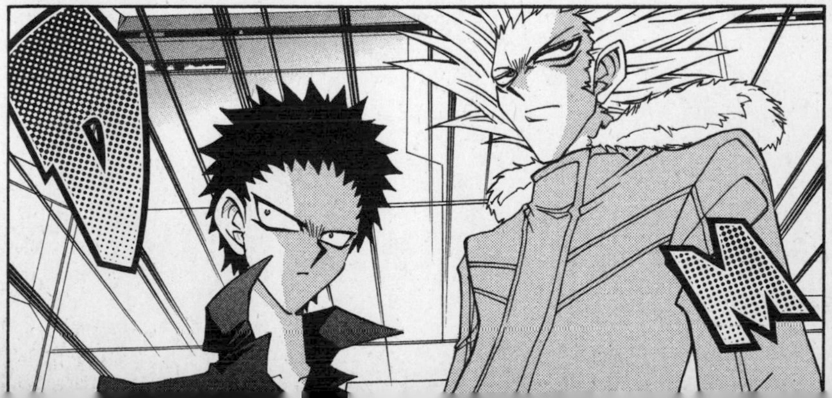
D
M

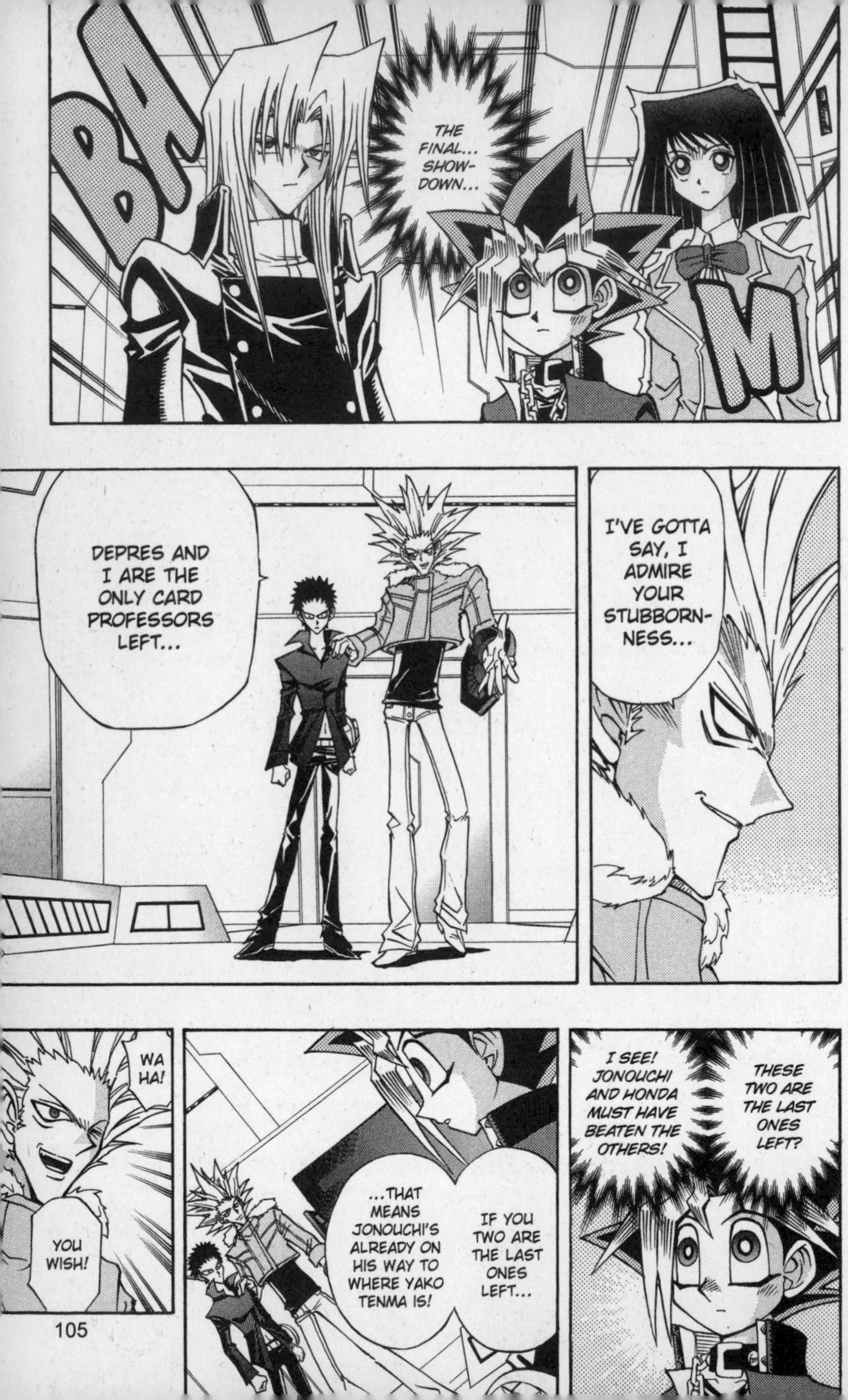
THE FINAL... SHOW-DOWN...
BAM
I'VE GOTTA SAY, I ADMIRE YOUR STUBBORN-NESS...
DEPRES AND I ARE THE ONLY CARD PROFESSORS LEFT...
THESE TWO ARE THE LAST ONES LEFT?
I SEE! JONOUCHI AND HONDA MUST HAVE BEATEN THE OTHERS!
IF YOU TWO ARE THE LAST ONES LEFT...
...THAT MEANS JONOUCHI'S ALREADY ON HIS WAY TO WHERE YAKO TENMA IS!
WA HA!
YOU WISH!

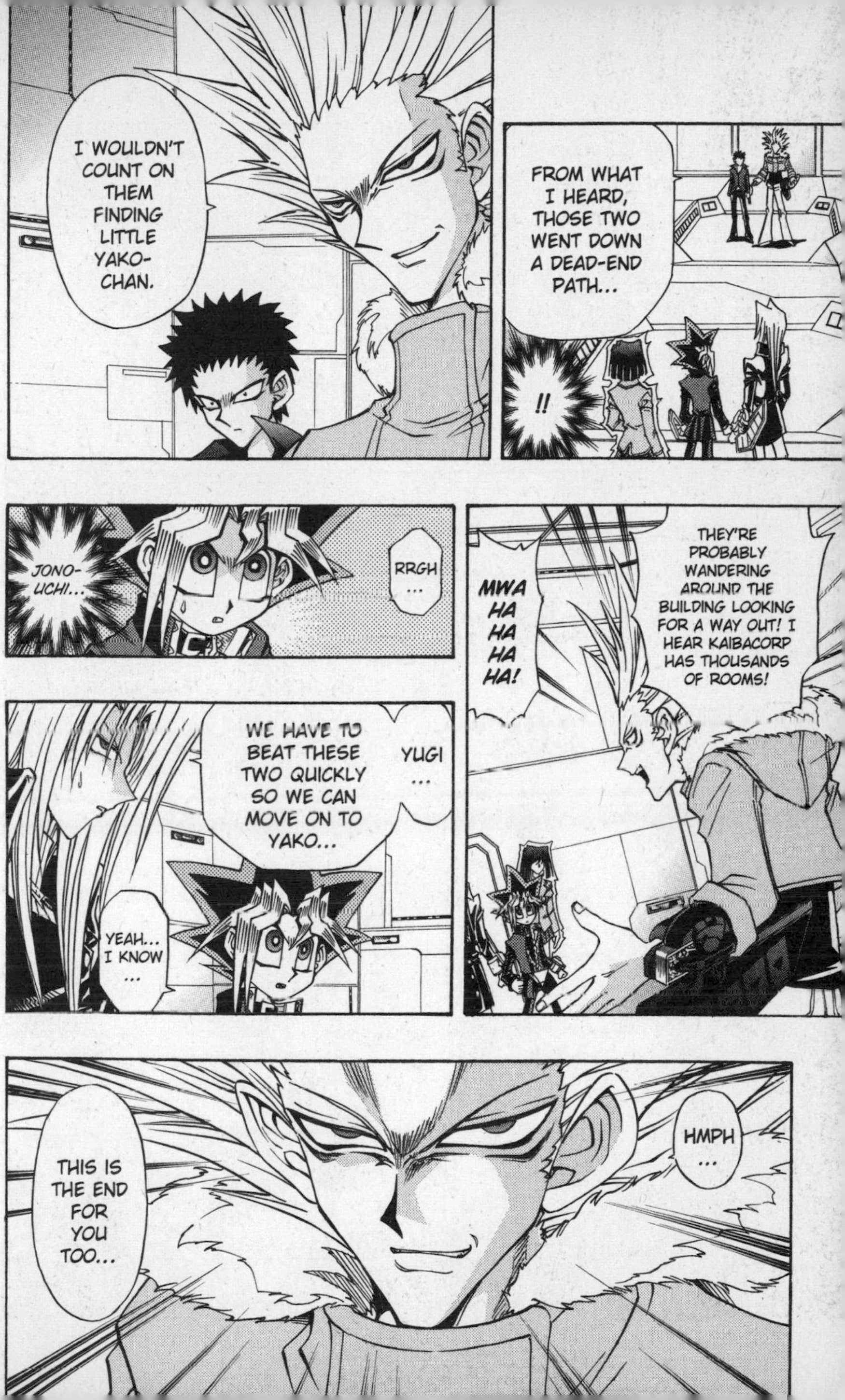
FROM WHAT I HEARD, THOSE TWO WENT DOWN A DEAD-END PATH...
!!
I WOULDN'T COUNT ON THEM FINDING LITTLE YAKO-CHAN.
THEY'RE PROBABLY WANDERING AROUND THE BUILDING LOOKING FOR A WAY OUT! I HEAR KAIBACORP HAS THOUSANDS OF ROOMS!
MWA HA HA HA HA!
RRGH...
JONO-UCHI...
YUGI...
WE HAVE TO BEAT THESE TWO QUICKLY SO WE CAN MOVE ON TO YAKO...
YEAH... I KNOW...
HMPH...
THIS IS THE END FOR YOU TOO...

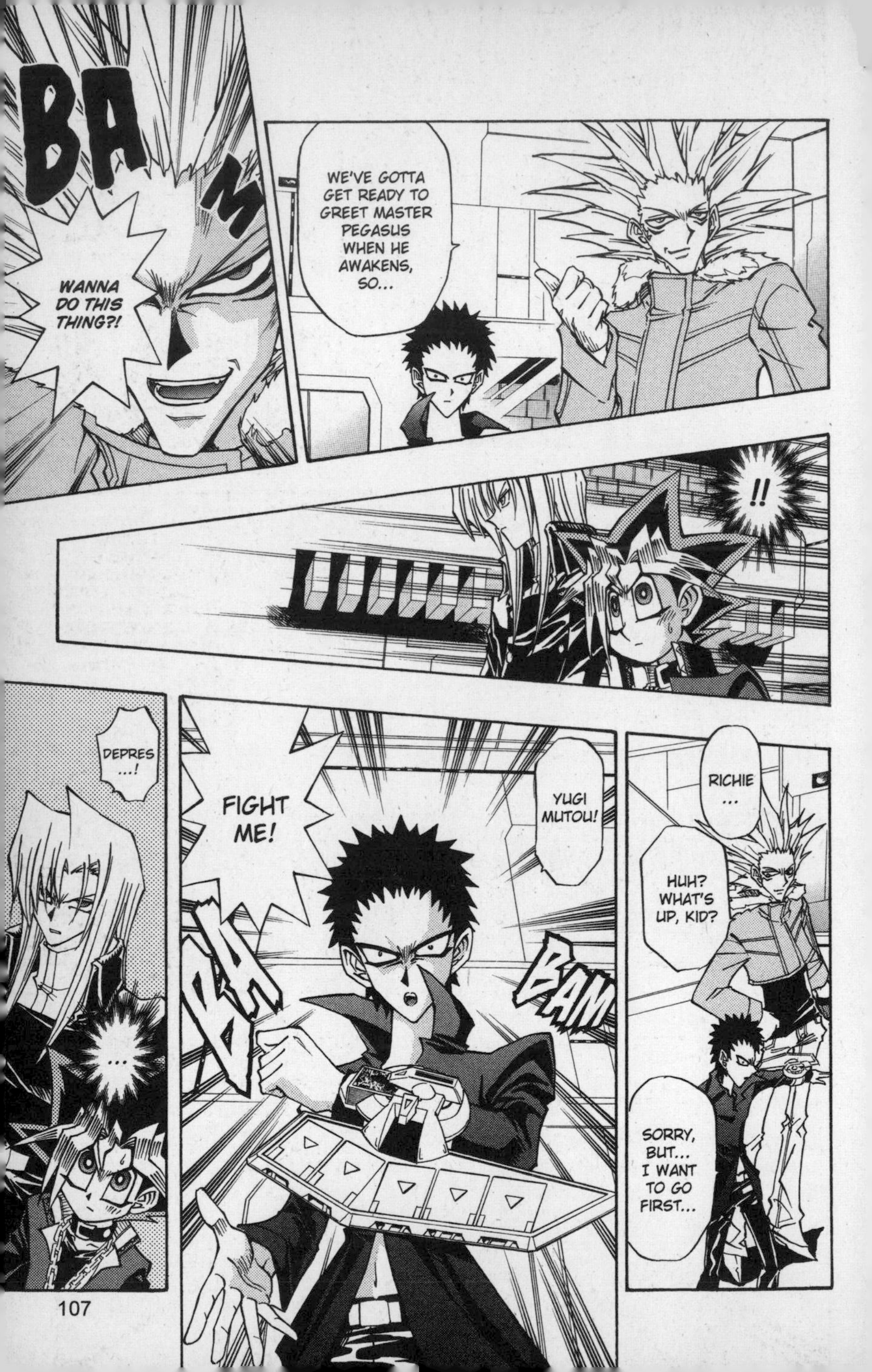
WE'VE GOTTA GET READY TO GREET MASTER PEGASUS WHEN HE AWAKENS, SO...
BAM
WANNA DO THIS THING?!
!!
RICHIE...
HUH? WHAT'S UP, KID?
SORRY, BUT... I WANT TO GO FIRST...
YUGI MUTOU!
FIGHT ME!
BAM
BAM
DEPRES...!
...

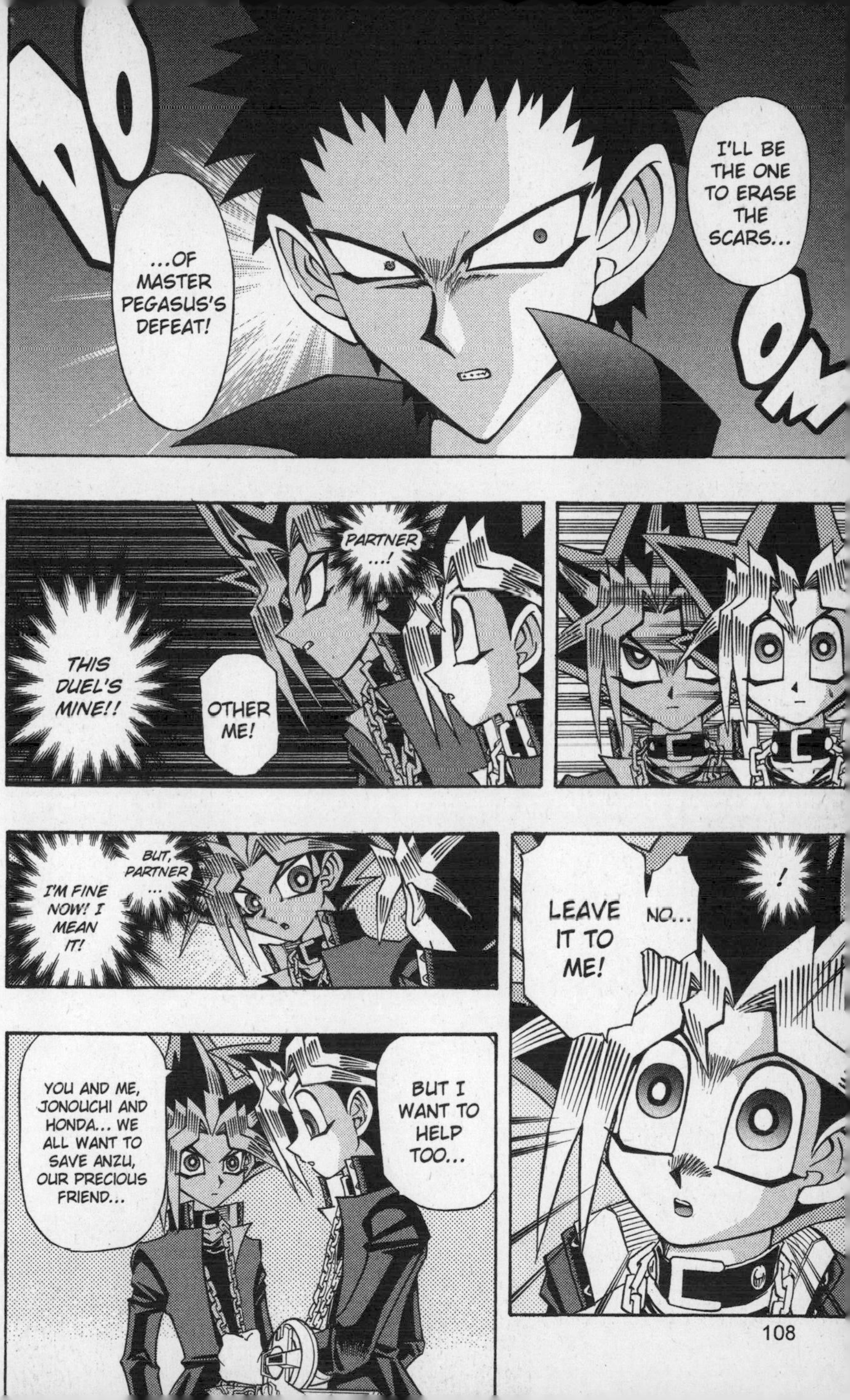

I'LL BE THE ONE TO ERASE THE SCARS...
...OF MASTER PEGASUS'S DEFEAT!
DO
OM
PARTNER ...!
OTHER ME!
THIS DUEL'S MINE!!
!
NO...
LEAVE IT TO ME!
BUT, PARTNER ...
I'M FINE NOW! I MEAN IT!
BUT I WANT TO HELP TOO...
YOU AND ME, JONOUCHI AND HONDA... WE ALL WANT TO SAVE ANZU, OUR PRECIOUS FRIEND...

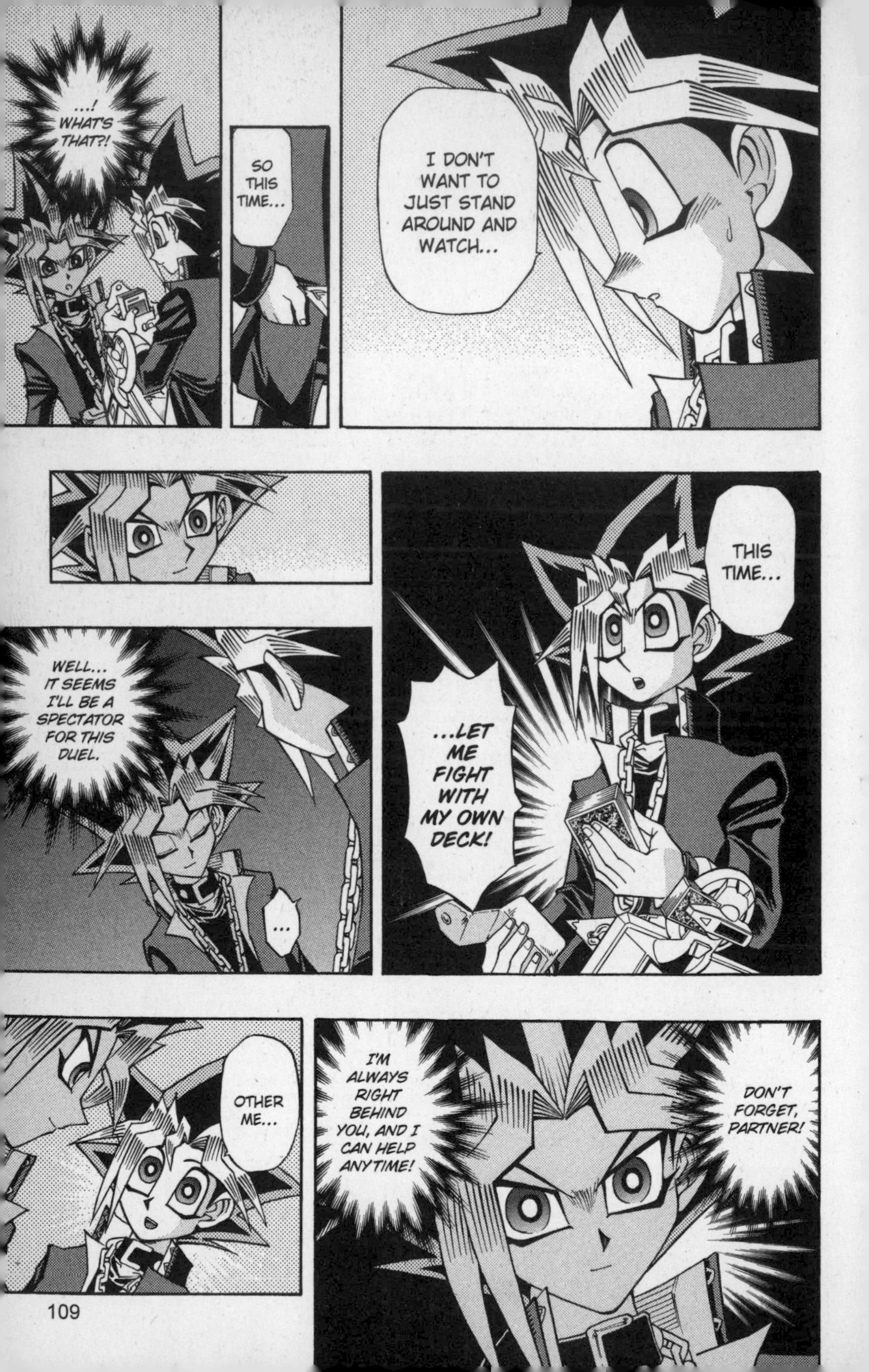
I DON'T WANT TO JUST STAND AROUND AND WATCH...
SO THIS TIME...
...! WHAT'S THAT?!
THIS TIME...
...LET ME FIGHT WITH MY OWN DECK!
WELL... IT SEEMS I'LL BE A SPECTATOR FOR THIS DUEL.
...
DON'T FORGET, PARTNER!
I'M ALWAYS RIGHT BEHIND YOU, AND I CAN HELP ANYTIME!
OTHER ME...

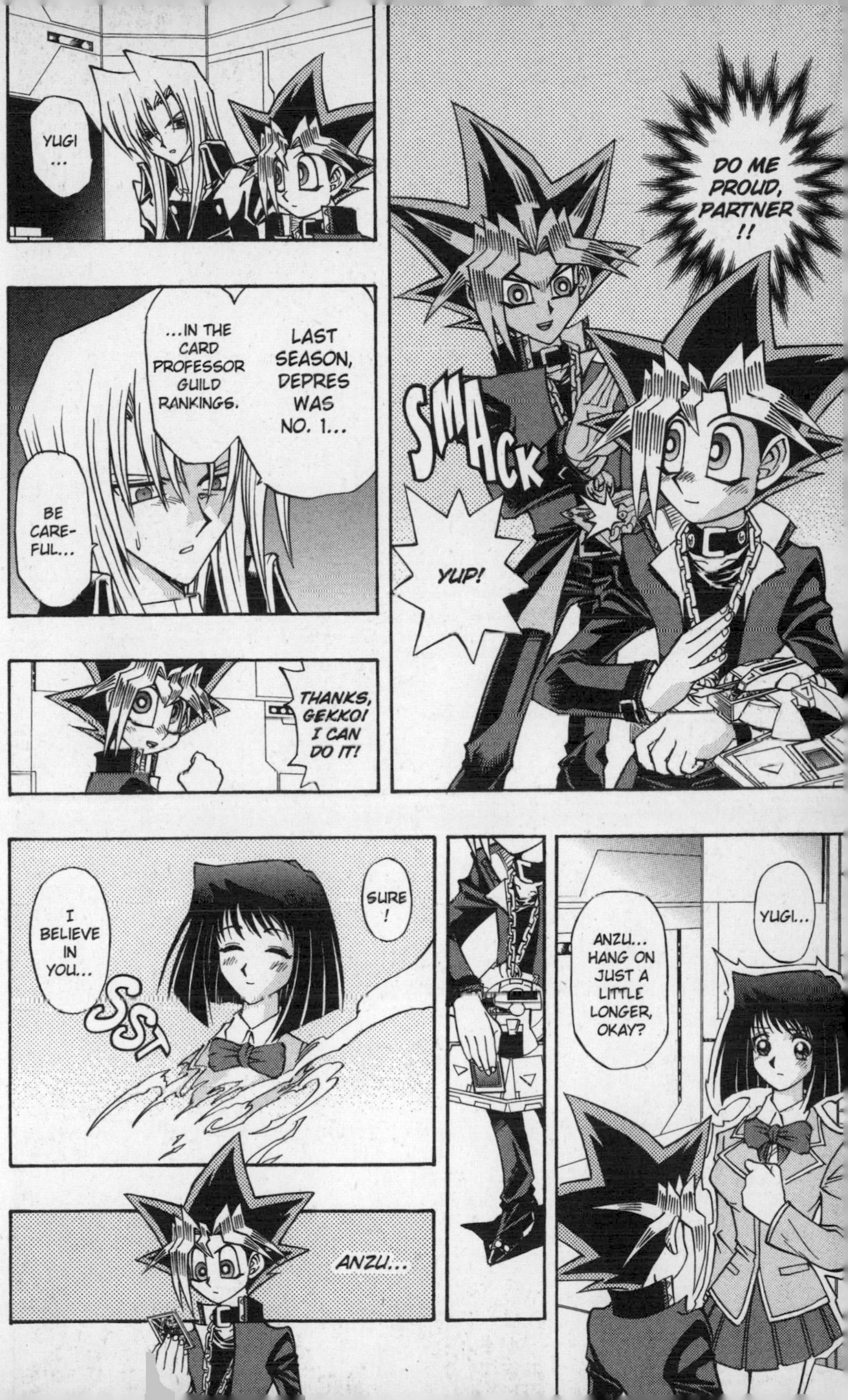
DO ME PROUD, PARTNER !!
SMACK
YUP!
YUGI ...
LAST SEASON, DEPRES WAS NO. 1...
...IN THE CARD PROFESSOR GUILD RANKINGS.
BE CARE-FUL...
THANKS, GEKKO! I CAN DO IT!
YUGI...
ANZU... HANG ON JUST A LITTLE LONGER, OKAY?
SURE !
I BELIEVE IN YOU...
SST
ANZU...

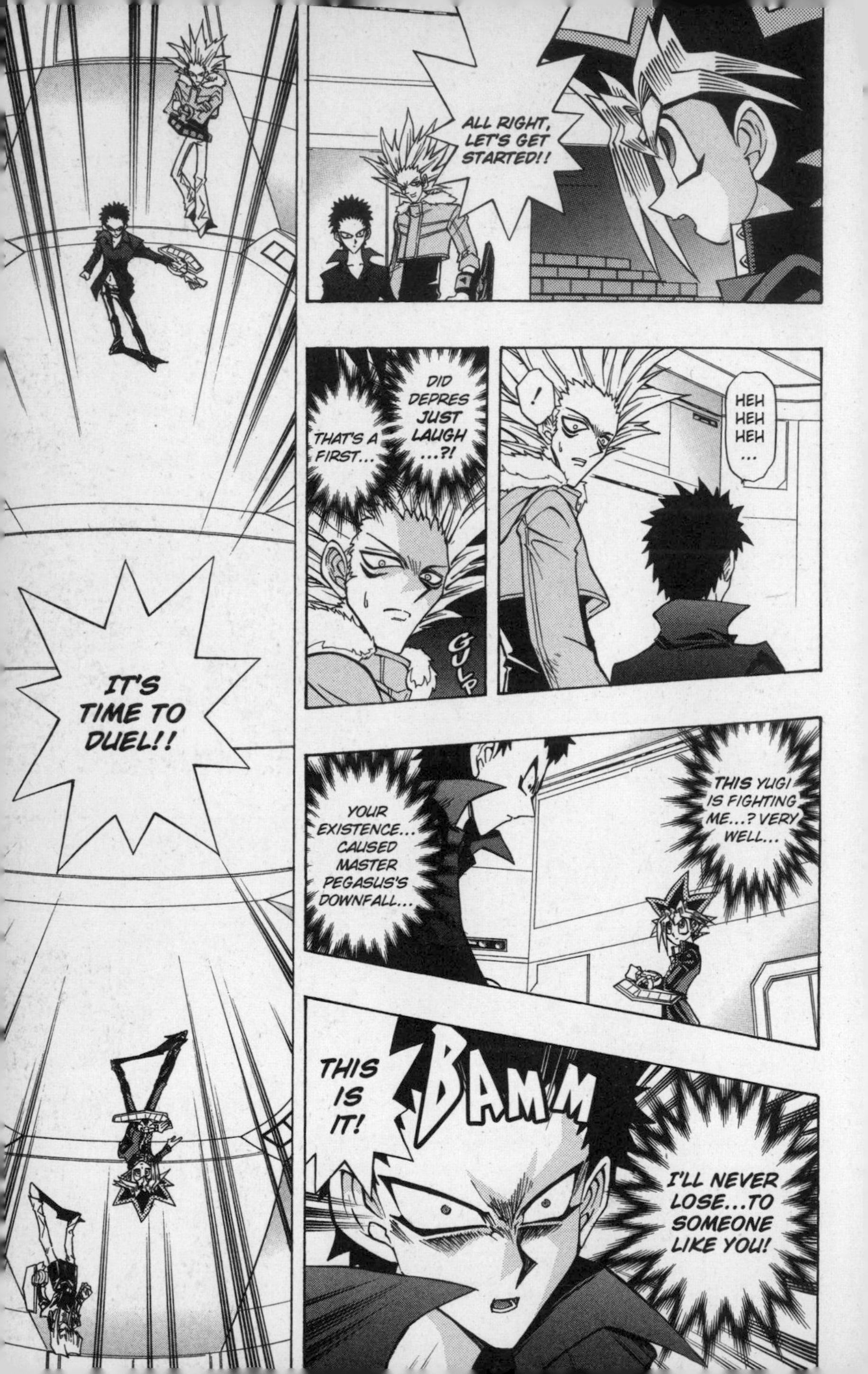
ALL RIGHT, LET'S GET STARTED!!
!
HEH HEH HEH ...
DID DEPRES JUST LAUGH ...?!
THAT'S A FIRST...
GULP
THIS YUGI IS FIGHTING ME...? VERY WELL...
YOUR EXISTENCE... CAUSED MASTER PEGASUS'S DOWNFALL...
BAMM
THIS IS IT!
I'LL NEVER LOSE...TO SOMEONE LIKE YOU!
IT'S TIME TO DUEL!!

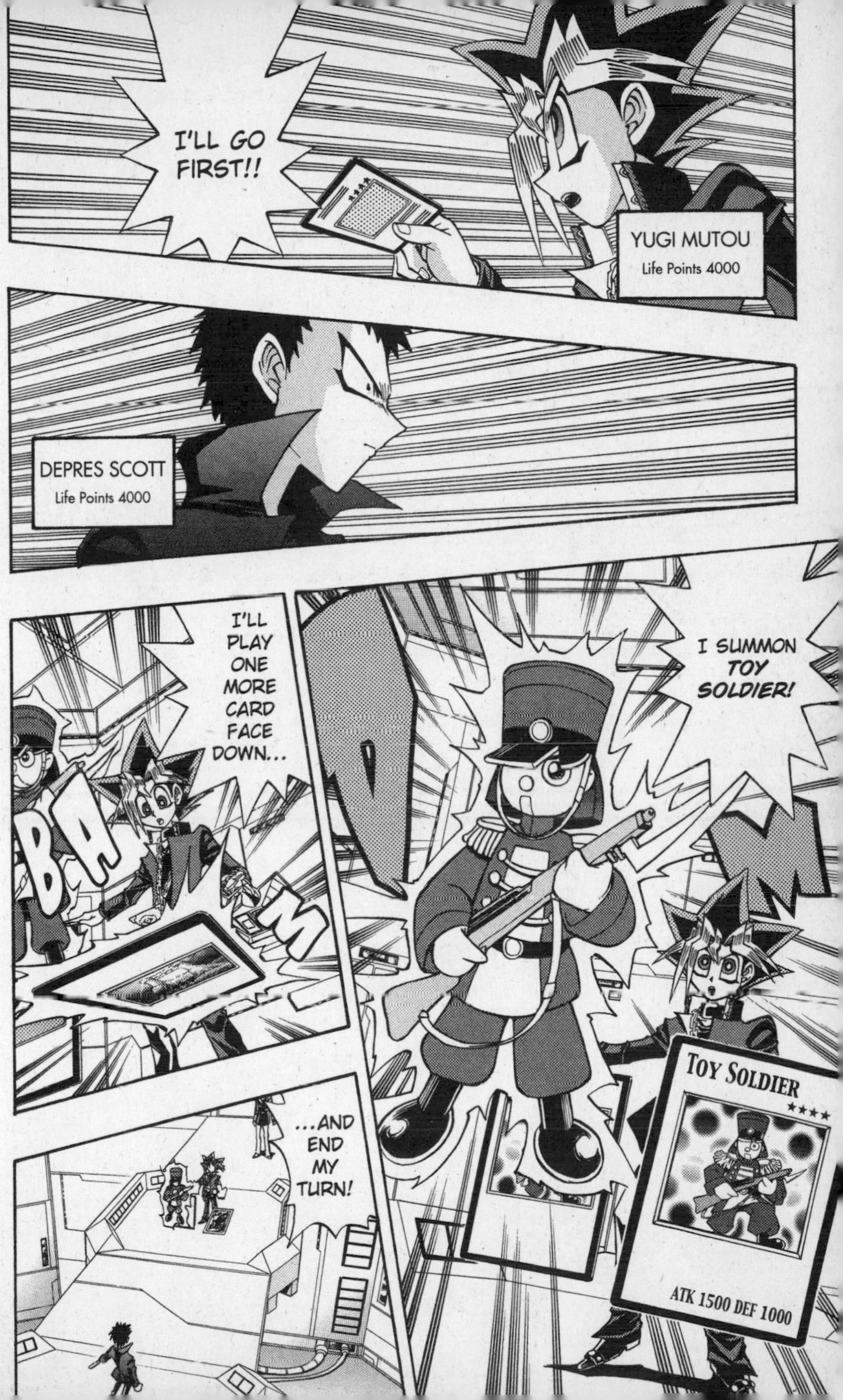
I'LL GO FIRST!!
YUGI MUTOU
Life Points 4000
DEPRES SCOTT
Life Points 4000
I SUMMON TOY SOLDIER!
TOY SOLDIER
ATK 1500 DEF 1000
I'LL PLAY ONE MORE CARD FACE DOWN...
BAM
...AND END MY TURN!

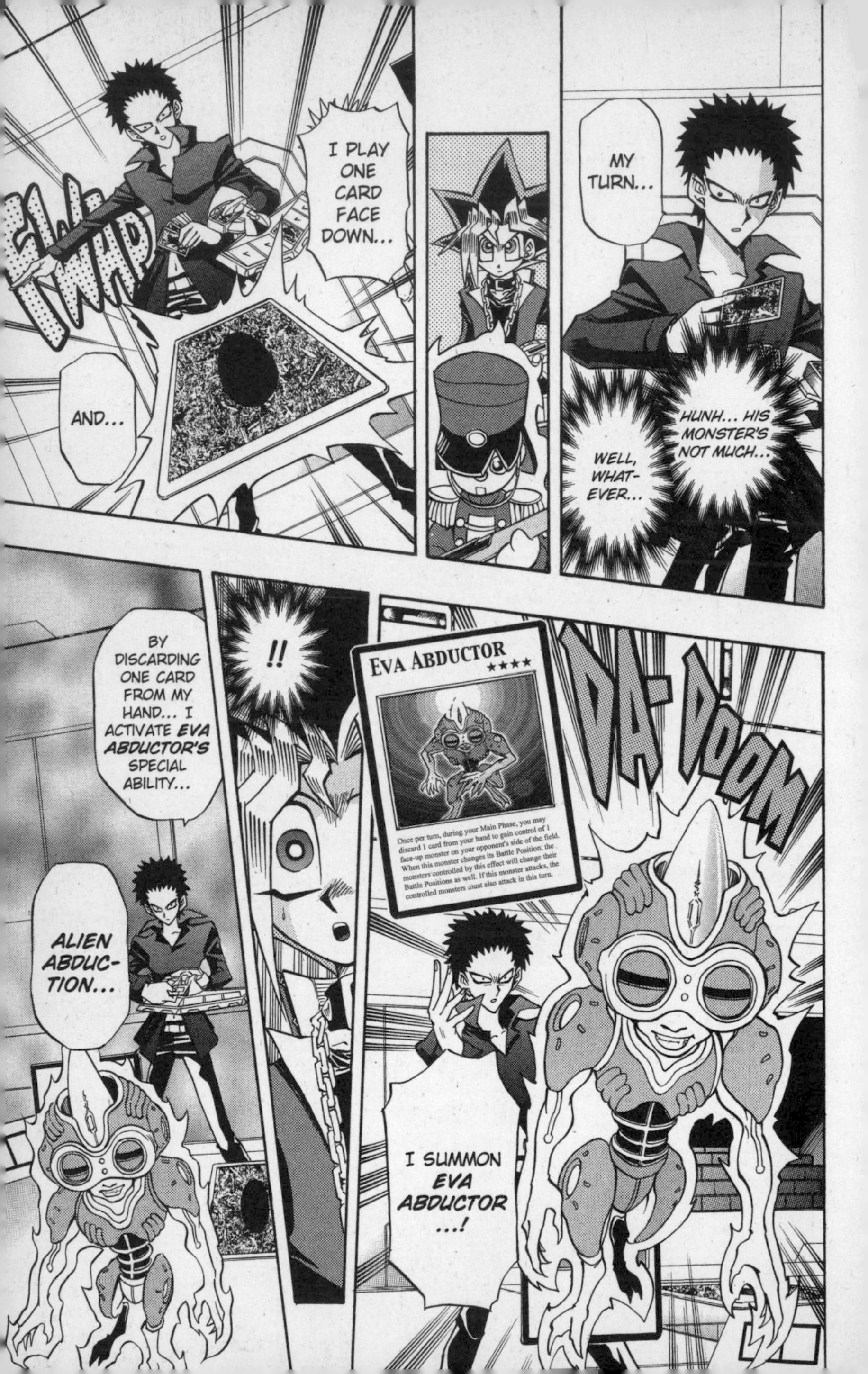
MY TURN...
HUNH... HIS MONSTER'S NOT MUCH...
WELL, WHAT-EVER...
I PLAY ONE CARD FACE DOWN...
AND...
DA-DOOM
EVA ABDUCTOR
Once per turn, during your Main Phase, you may discard 1 card from your hand to gain control of 1 face-up monster on your opponent's side of the field. When this monster changes its Battle Position, the monsters controlled by this effect will change their Battle Positions as well. If this monster attacks, the controlled monsters must also attack in this turn.
I SUMMON EVA ABDUCTOR ...!
!!
BY DISCARDING ONE CARD FROM MY HAND... I ACTIVATE EVA ABDUCTOR'S SPECIAL ABILITY...
ALIEN ABDUC-TION...

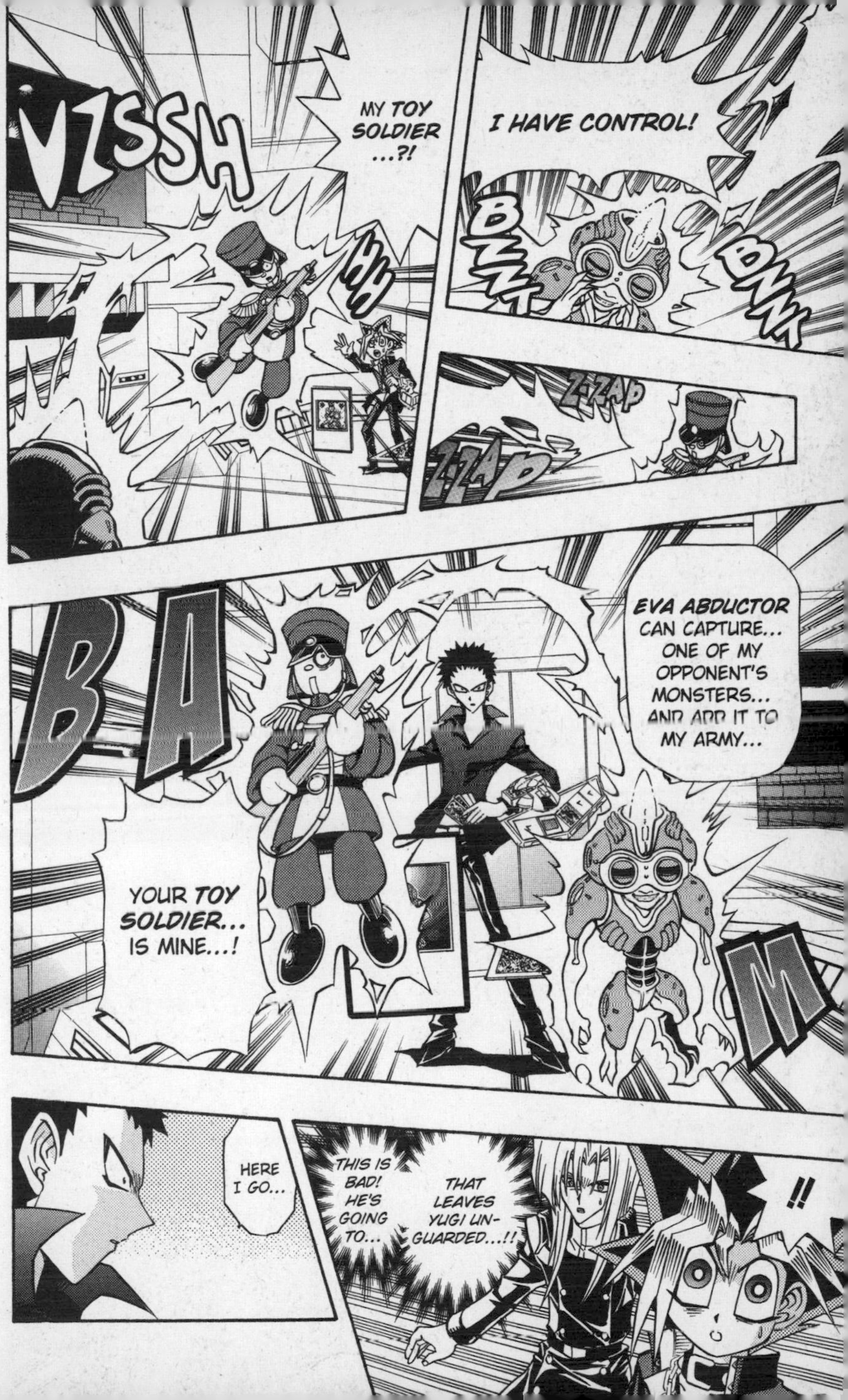
I HAVE CONTROL!
BZZZT
BONK
Z-ZAP
Z-ZAP
VISSH
MY TOY SOLDIER ...?!
EVA ABDUCTOR CAN CAPTURE... ONE OF MY OPPONENT'S MONSTERS... AND ADD IT TO MY ARMY...
YOUR TOY SOLDIER... IS MINE...!
BA
M
!!
THAT LEAVES YUGI UN-GUARDED...!!
THIS IS BAD! HE'S GOING TO...
HERE I GO...

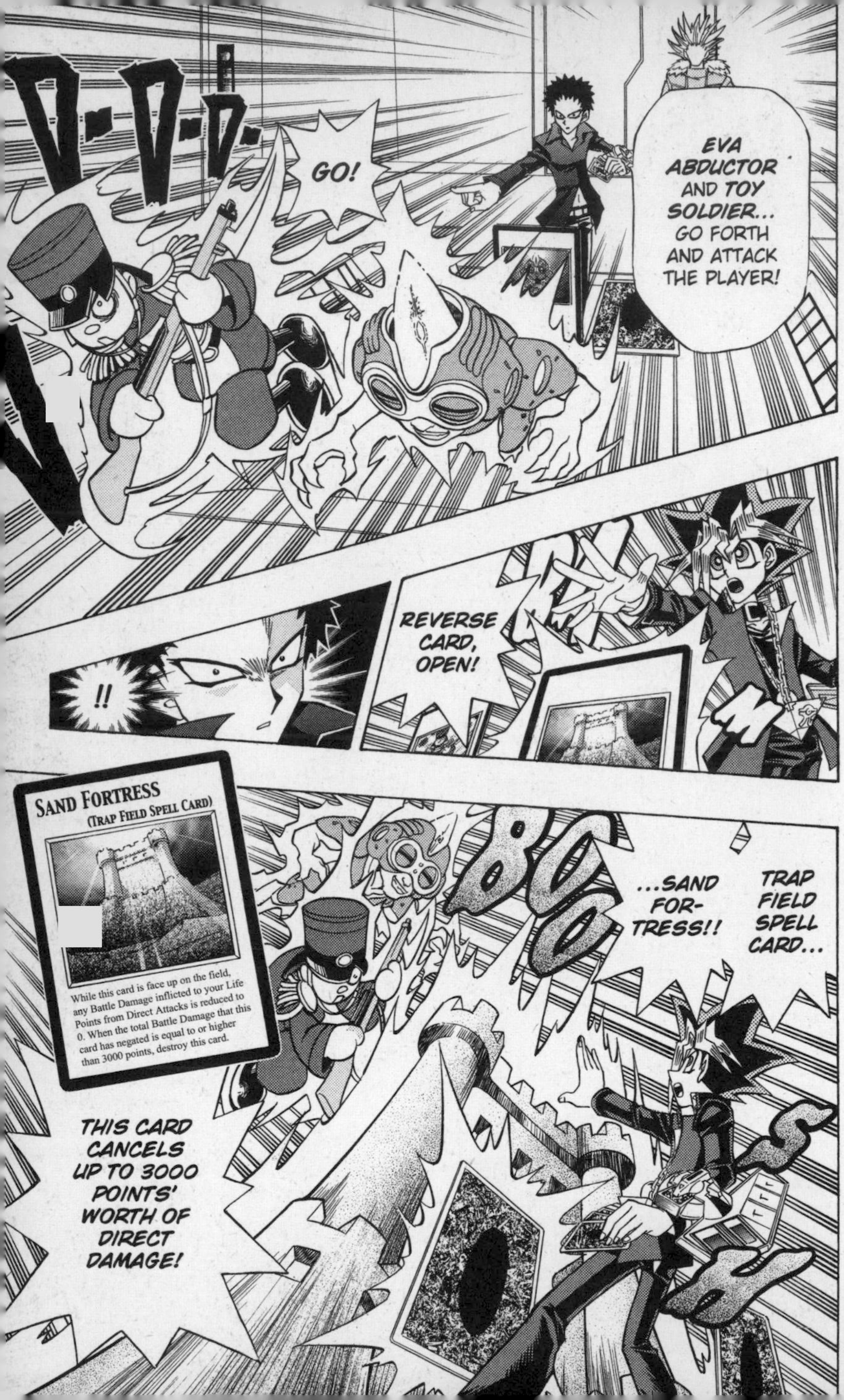
EVA ABDUCTOR AND TOY SOLDIER... GO FORTH AND ATTACK THE PLAYER!
GO!
D-D-D
REVERSE CARD, OPEN!
!!
TRAP FIELD SPELL CARD...
...SAND FOR-TRESS!!
BOO
SAND FORTRESS
(TRAP FIELD SPELL CARD)
While this card is face up on the field, any Battle Damage inflicted to your Life Points from Direct Attacks is reduced to 0. When the total Battle Damage that this card has negated is equal to or higher than 3000 points, destroy this card.
THIS CARD CANCELS UP TO 3000 POINTS' WORTH OF DIRECT DAMAGE!

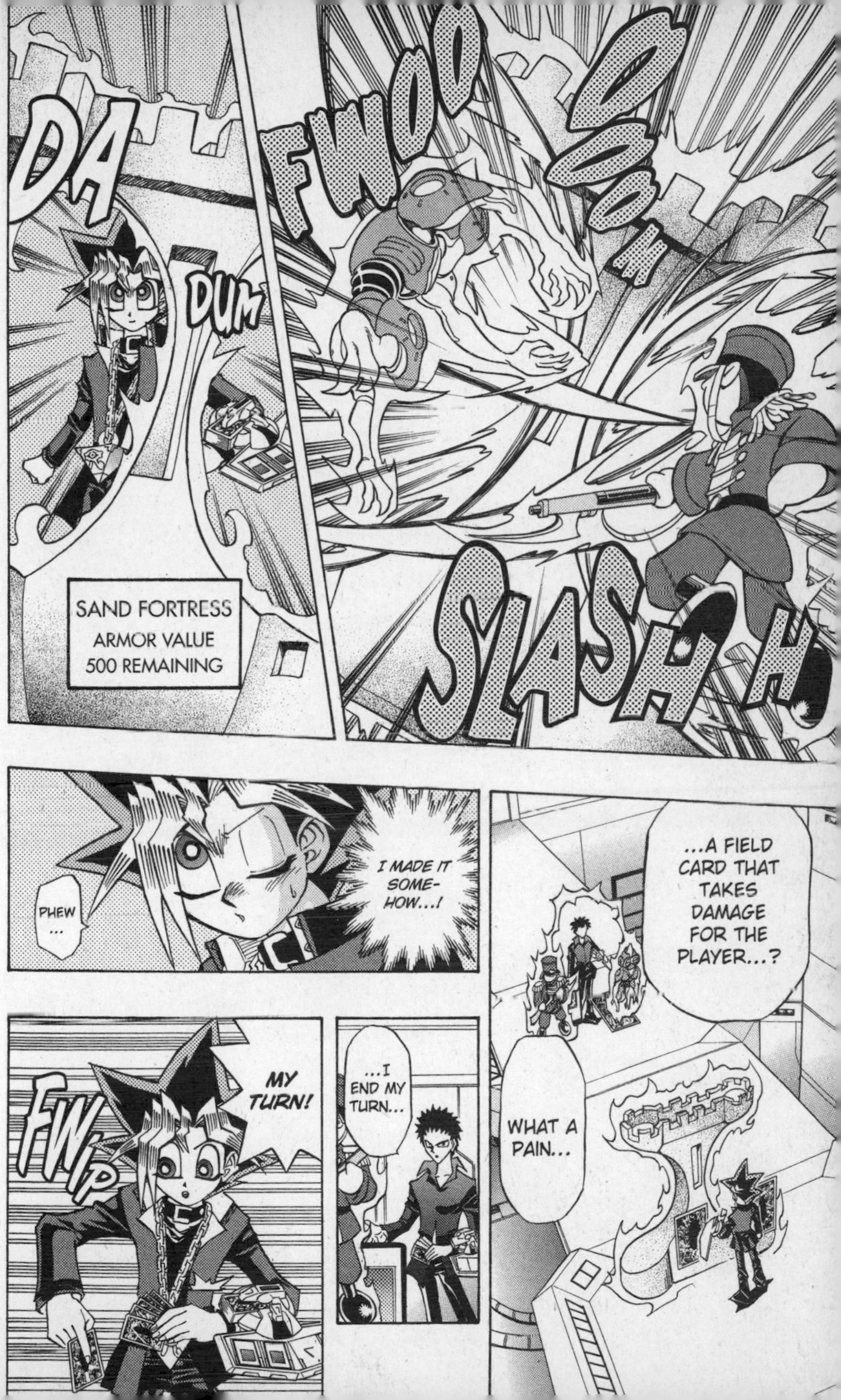
FWOOOOOOM
SLASHH
DA
DUM
SAND FORTRESS
ARMOR VALUE
500 REMAINING
...A FIELD CARD THAT TAKES DAMAGE FOR THE PLAYER...?
WHAT A PAIN...
I MADE IT SOME-HOW...!
PHEW...
...I END MY TURN...
MY TURN!
FWIP

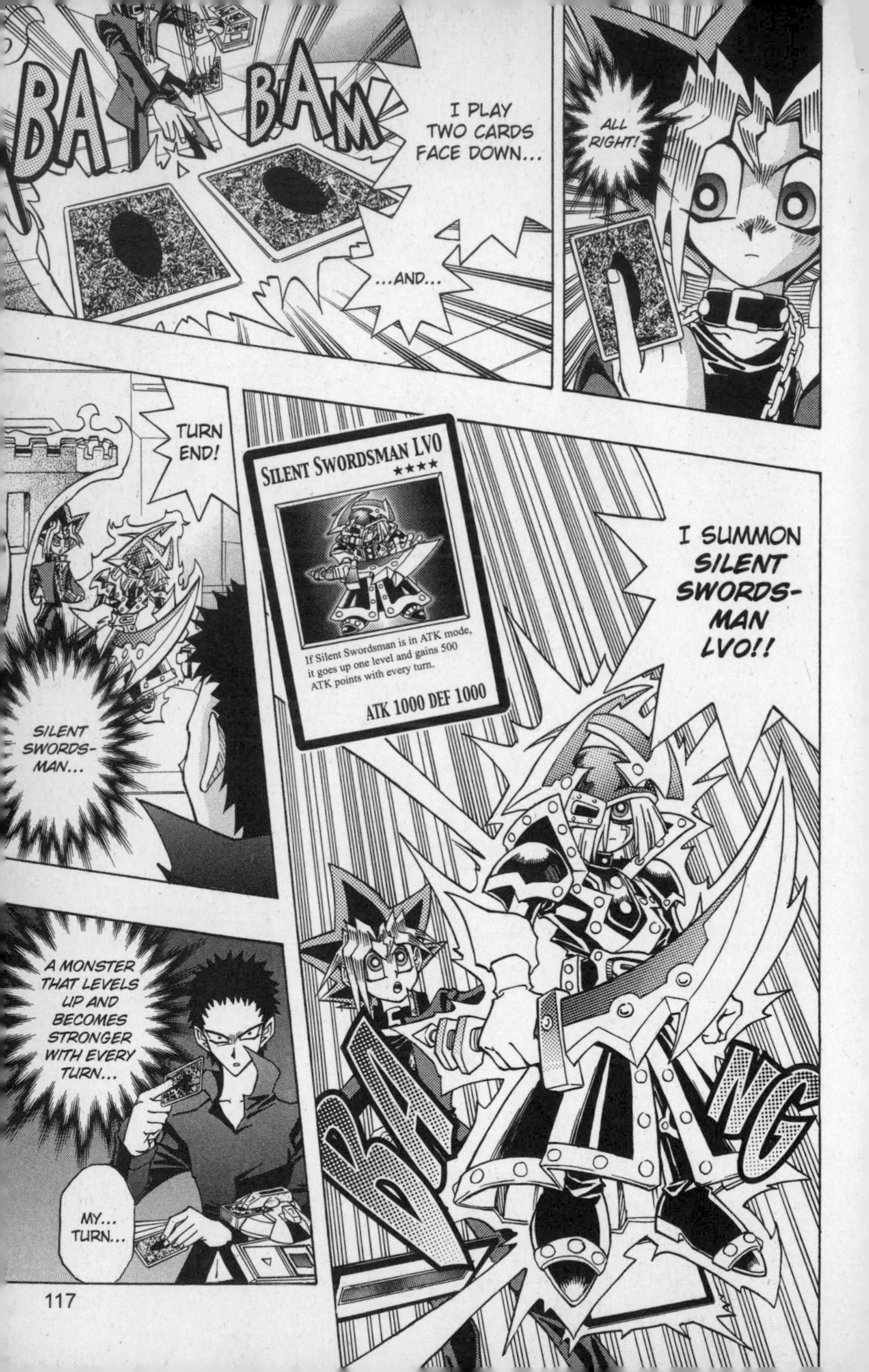
ALL RIGHT!
BA BAM
I PLAY TWO CARDS FACE DOWN...
...AND...
I SUMMON SILENT SWORDSMAN LVO!!
SILENT SWORDSMAN LVO
★★★★
If Silent Swordsman is in ATK mode, it goes up one level and gains 500 ATK points with every turn.
ATK 1000 DEF 1000
TURN END!
SILENT SWORDSMAN...
A MONSTER THAT LEVELS UP AND BECOMES STRONGER WITH EVERY TURN...
MY... TURN...

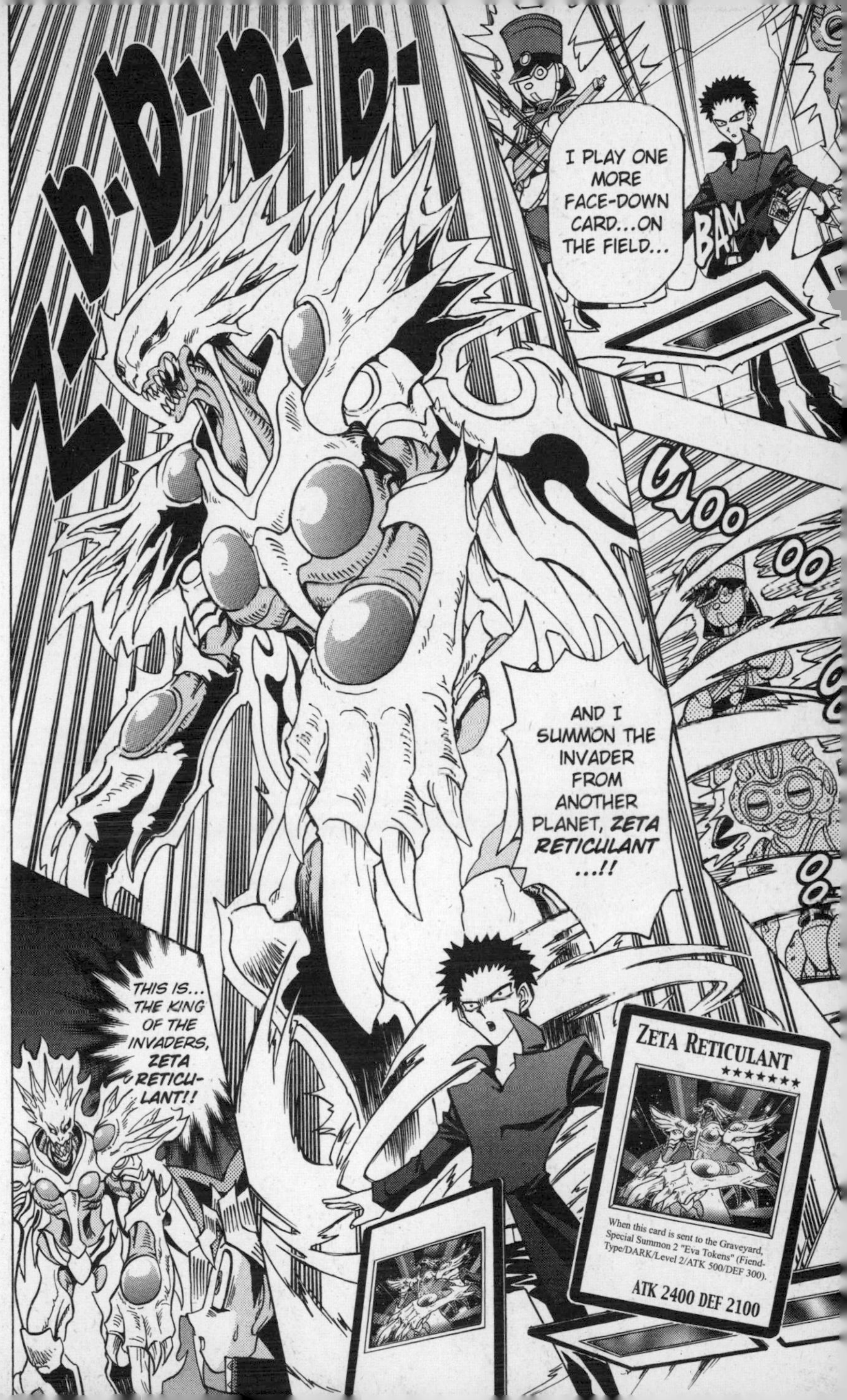
I PLAY ONE MORE FACE-DOWN CARD...ON THE FIELD...
BAM
WOOOOOOOOO
Z-D-D-D-D-
AND I SUMMON THE INVADER FROM ANOTHER PLANET, ZETA RETICULANT ...!!
THIS IS... THE KING OF THE INVADERS, ZETA RETICULANT!!
ZETA RETICULANT
When this card is sent to the Graveyard, Special Summon 2 "Eva Tokens" (Fiend-Type/DARK/Level 2/ATK 500/DEF 300).
ATK 2400 DEF 2100

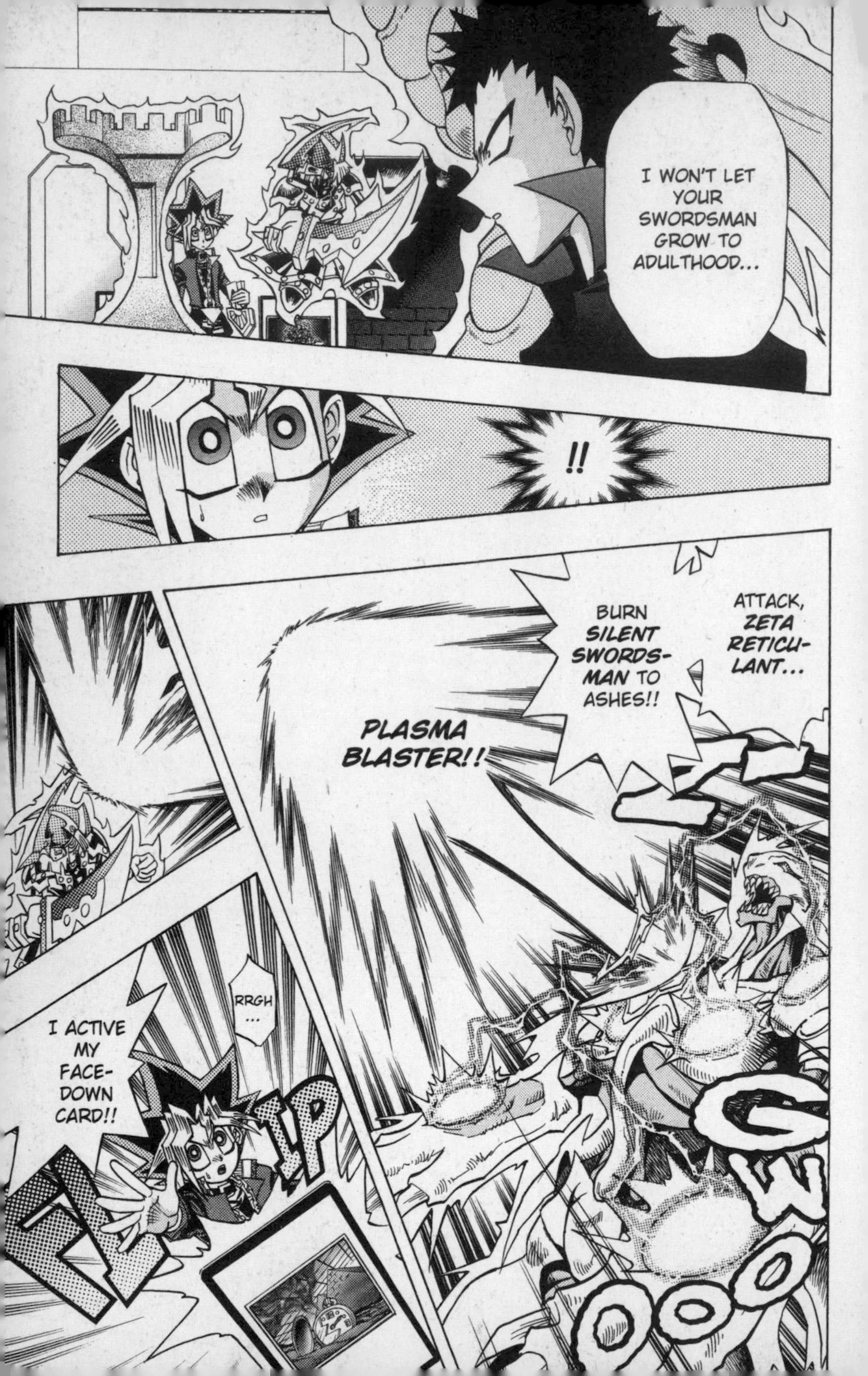
I WON'T LET YOUR SWORDSMAN GROW TO ADULTHOOD...
!!
ATTACK, ZETA RETICULANT...
BURN SILENT SWORDSMAN TO ASHES!!
PLASMA BLASTER!!
RRGH...
I ACTIVE MY FACE-DOWN CARD!!

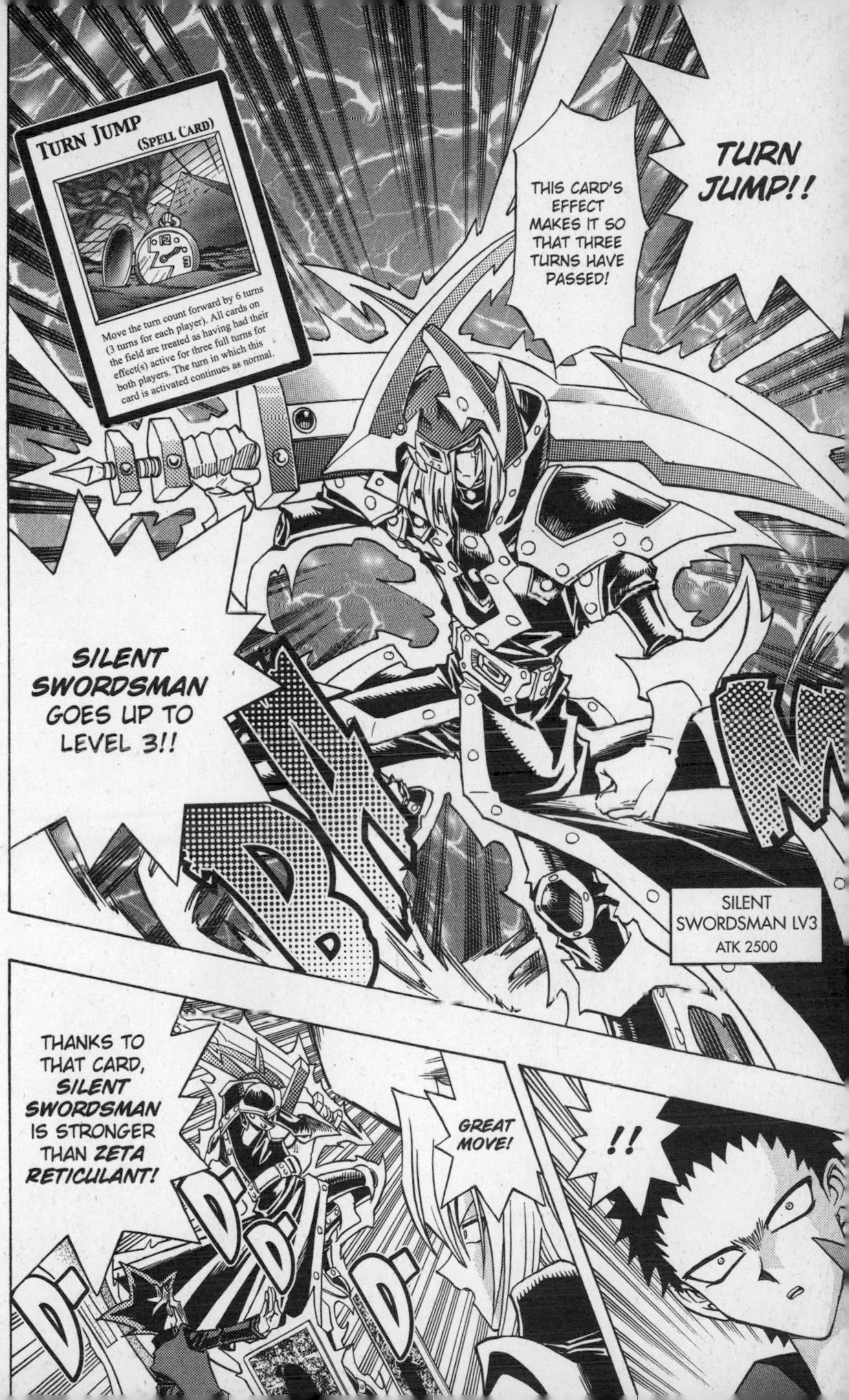
TURN JUMP!!
THIS CARD'S EFFECT MAKES IT SO THAT THREE TURNS HAVE PASSED!
TURN JUMP (SPELL CARD)
Move the turn count forward by 6 turns (3 turns for each player). All cards on the field are treated as having had their effect(s) active for three full turns for both players. The turn in which this card is activated continues as normal.
SILENT SWORDSMAN GOES UP TO LEVEL 3!!
SILENT SWORDSMAN LV3
ATK 2500
!!
GREAT MOVE!
THANKS TO THAT CARD, SILENT SWORDSMAN IS STRONGER THAN ZETA RETICULANT!

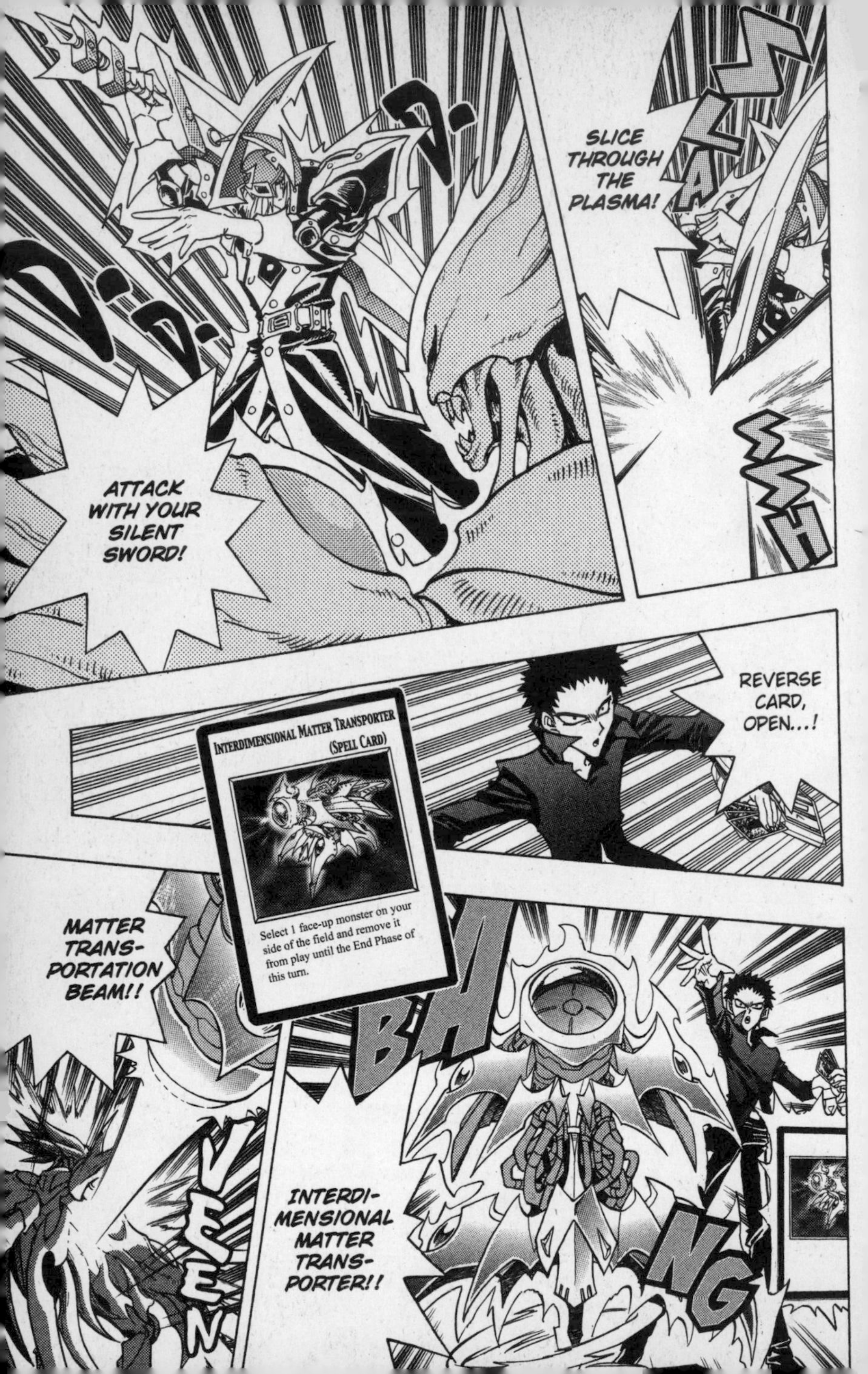
SLICE THROUGH THE PLASMA!
ATTACK WITH YOUR SILENT SWORD!
REVERSE CARD, OPEN...!
INTERDIMENSIONAL MATTER TRANSPORTER
(SPELL CARD)
Select 1 face-up monster on your side of the field and remove it from play until the End Phase of this turn.
INTERDI-MENSIONAL MATTER TRANS-PORTER!!
MATTER TRANS-PORTATION BEAM!!

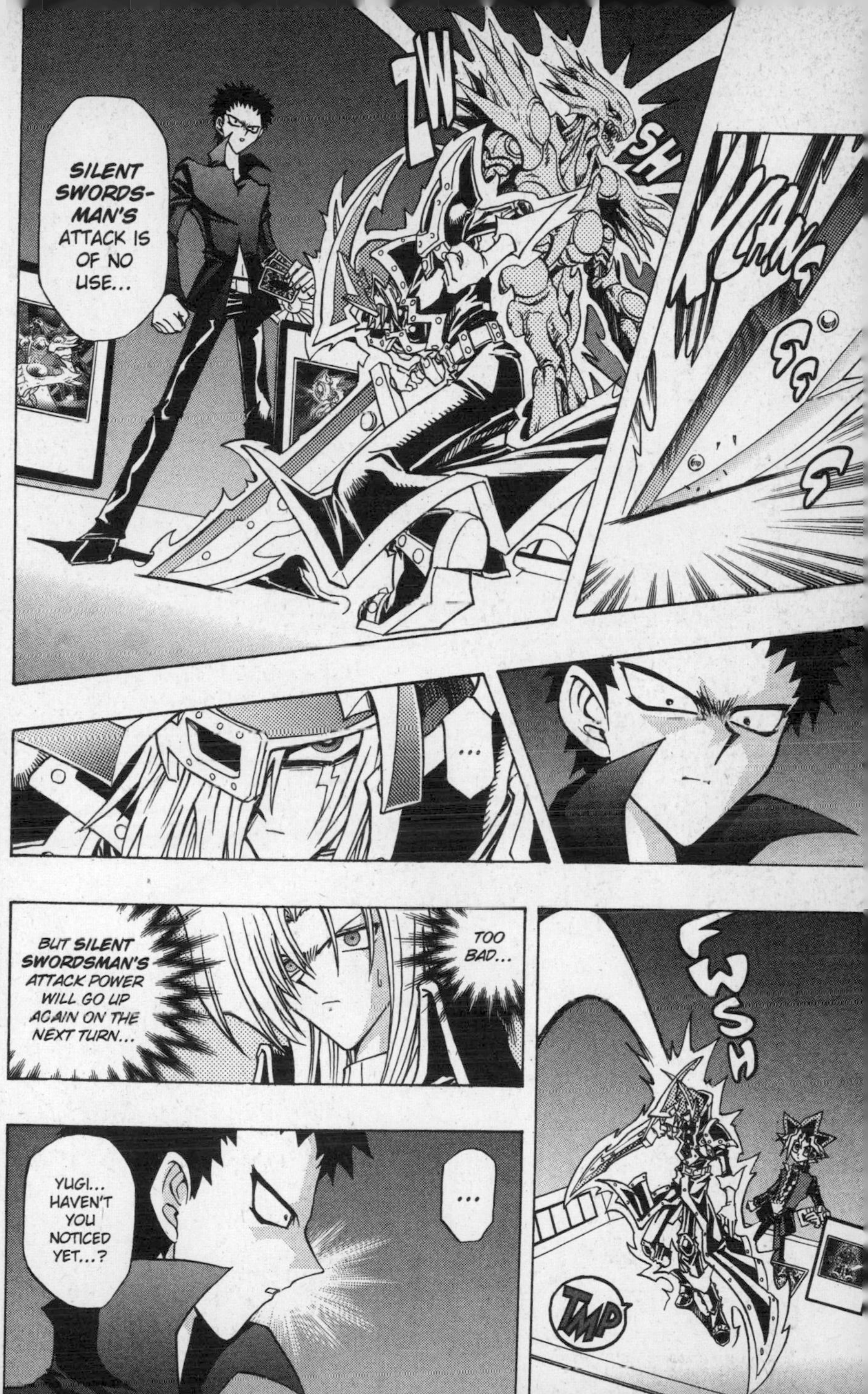
KLANG
GG
G
ZW
SH
SILENT SWORDSMAN'S ATTACK IS OF NO USE...
...
FWSH
TMP
TOO BAD...
BUT SILENT SWORDSMAN'S ATTACK POWER WILL GO UP AGAIN ON THE NEXT TURN...
...
YUGI... HAVEN'T YOU NOTICED YET...?

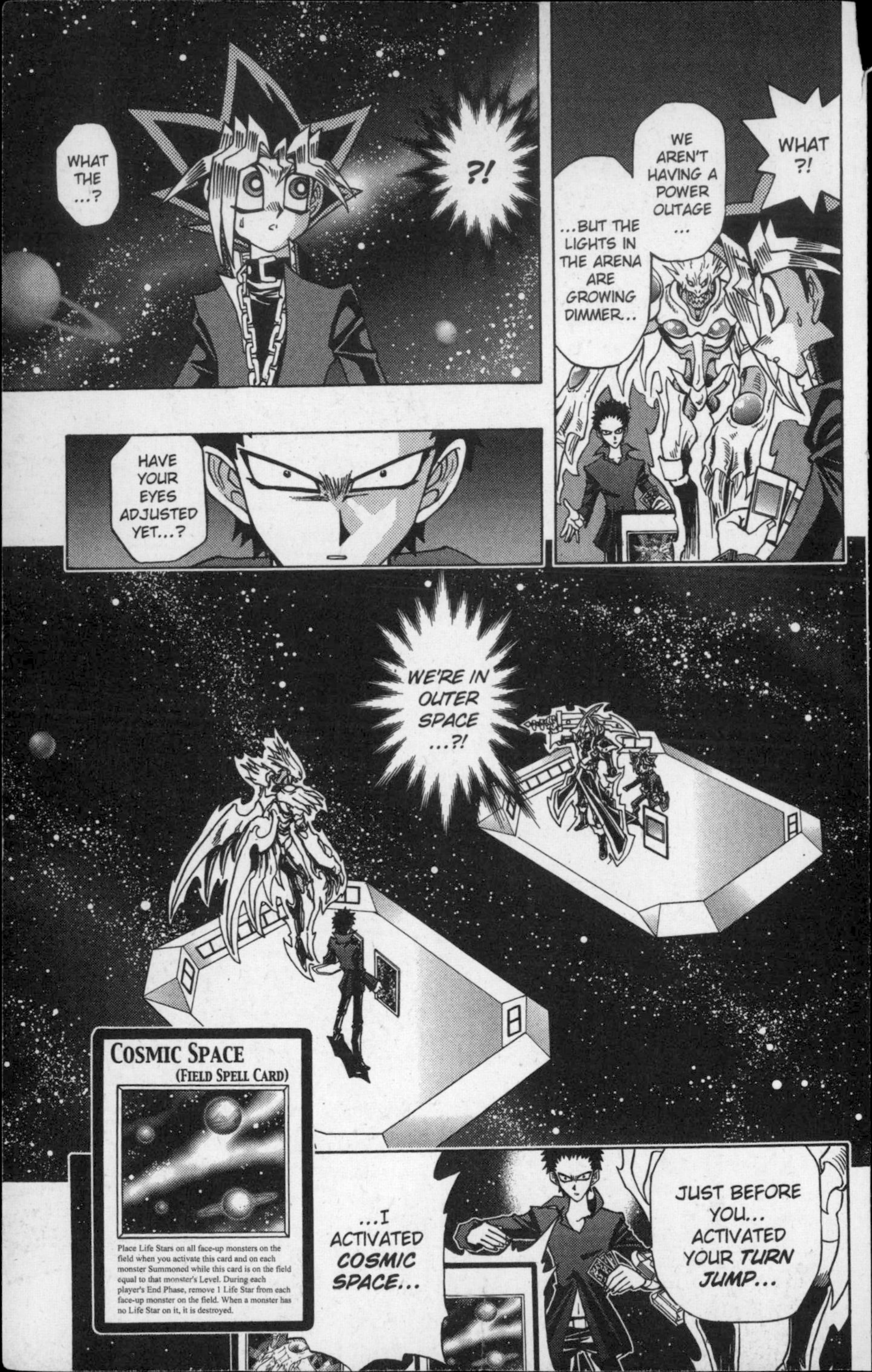
WHAT ?!
WE AREN'T HAVING A POWER OUTAGE ...
...BUT THE LIGHTS IN THE ARENA ARE GROWING DIMMER...
?!
WHAT THE ...?
HAVE YOUR EYES ADJUSTED YET...?
WE'RE IN OUTER SPACE ...?!
JUST BEFORE YOU... ACTIVATED YOUR TURN JUMP...
...I ACTIVATED COSMIC SPACE...
COSMIC SPACE
(FIELD SPELL CARD)
Place Life Stars on all face-up monsters on the field when you activate this card and on each monster Summoned while this card is on the field equal to that monster's Level. During each player's End Phase, remove 1 Life Star from each face-up monster on the field. When a monster has no Life Star on it, it is destroyed.

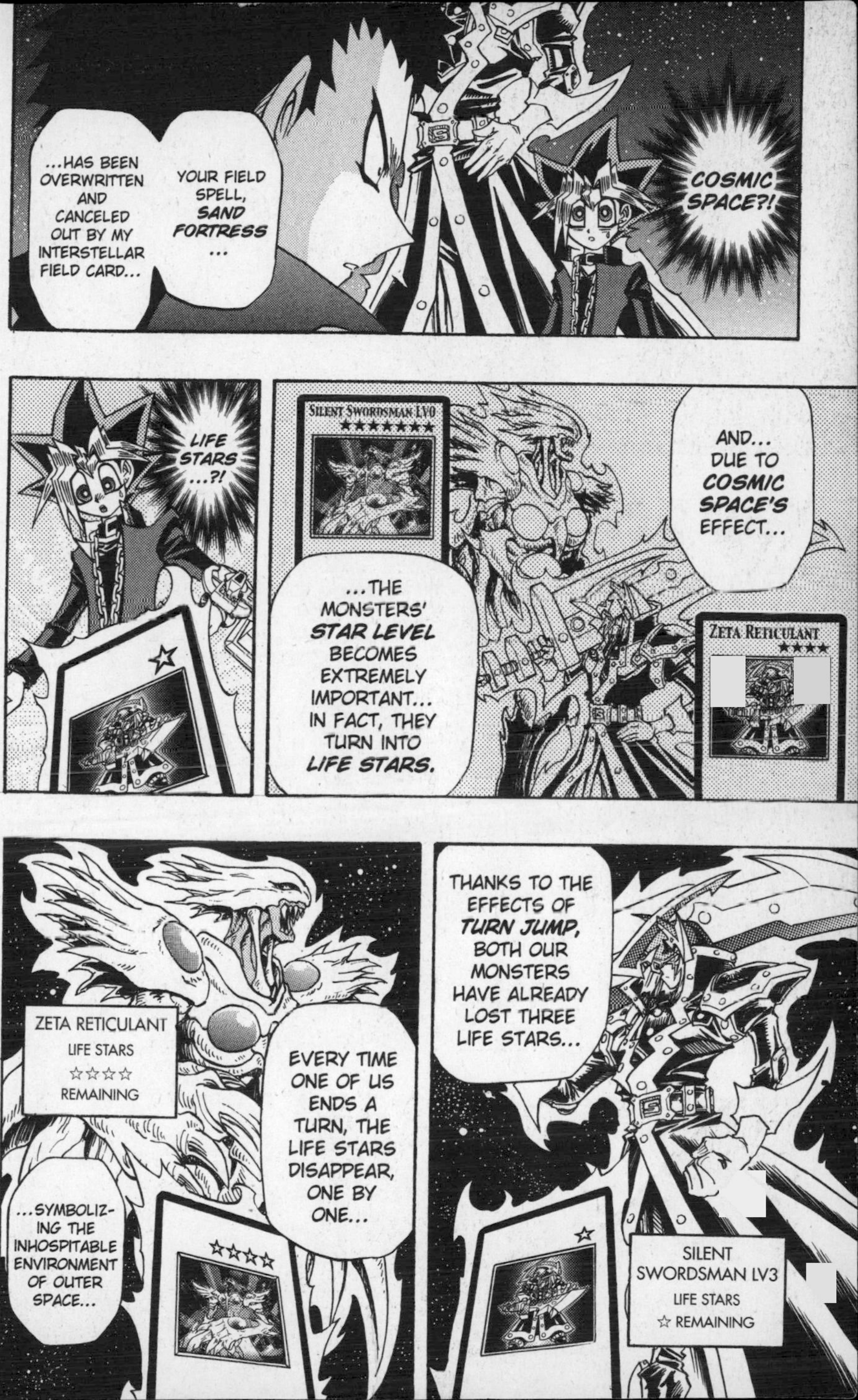
COSMIC SPACE?!
YOUR FIELD SPELL, SAND FORTRESS...
...HAS BEEN OVERWRITTEN AND CANCELED OUT BY MY INTERSTELLAR FIELD CARD...
AND... DUE TO COSMIC SPACE'S EFFECT...
SILENT SWORDSMAN LV0
...THE MONSTERS' STAR LEVEL BECOMES EXTREMELY IMPORTANT... IN FACT, THEY TURN INTO LIFE STARS.
ZETA RETICULANT
LIFE STARS...?!
THANKS TO THE EFFECTS OF TURN JUMP, BOTH OUR MONSTERS HAVE ALREADY LOST THREE LIFE STARS...
SILENT SWORDSMAN LV3 LIFE STARS ☆ REMAINING
EVERY TIME ONE OF US ENDS A TURN, THE LIFE STARS DISAPPEAR, ONE BY ONE...
ZETA RETICULANT LIFE STARS ☆☆☆☆ REMAINING
...SYMBOLIZING THE INHOSPITABLE ENVIRONMENT OF OUTER SPACE...

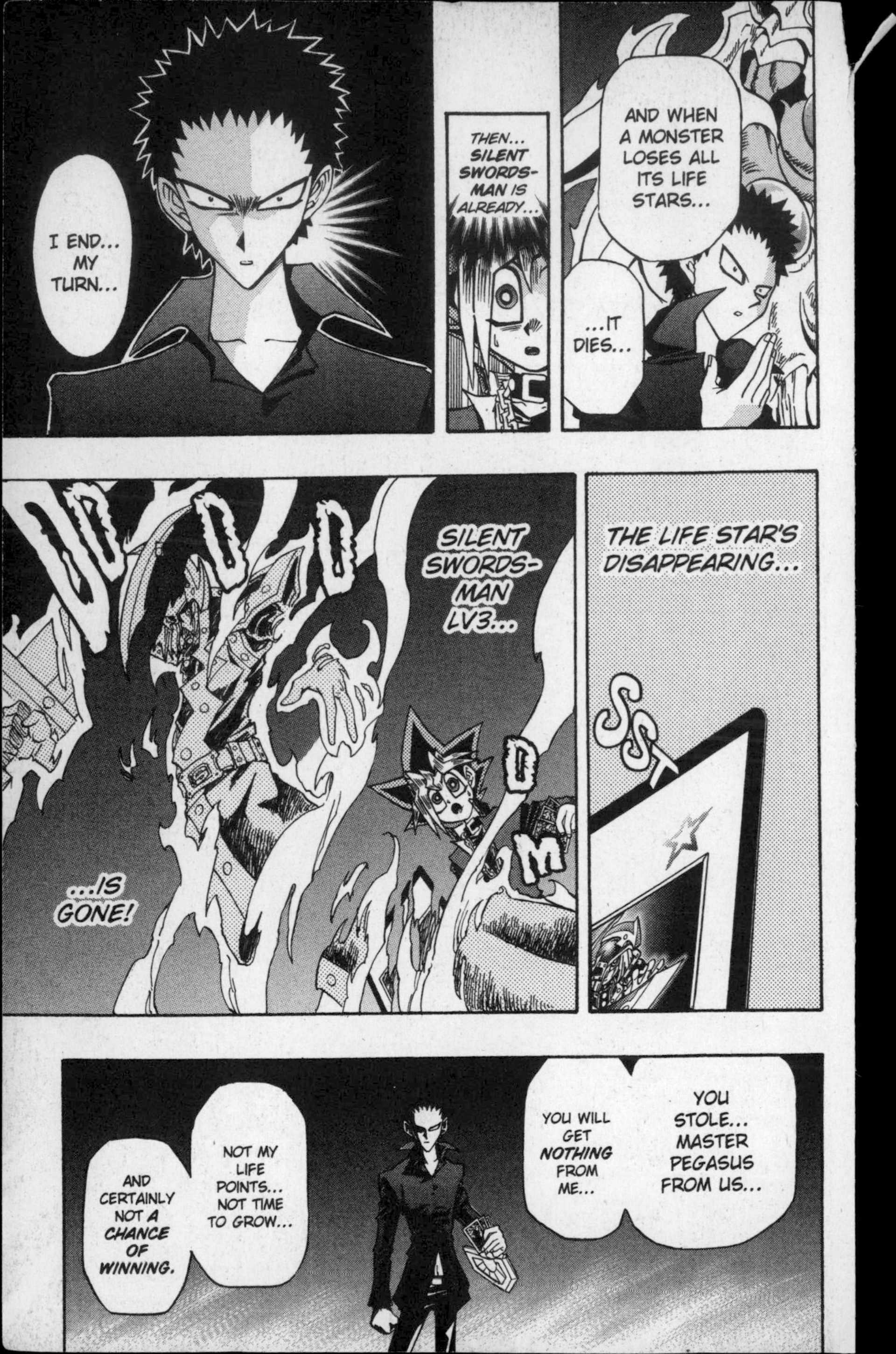
AND WHEN A MONSTER LOSES ALL ITS LIFE STARS...
...IT DIES...
THEN... SILENT SWORDSMAN IS ALREADY...
I END... MY TURN...
THE LIFE STAR'S DISAPPEARING...
SST
SILENT SWORDSMAN LV3...
...IS GONE!
YOU STOLE... MASTER PEGASUS FROM US...
YOU WILL GET NOTHING FROM ME...
NOT MY LIFE POINTS... NOT TIME TO GROW...
AND CERTAINLY NOT A CHANCE OF WINNING.

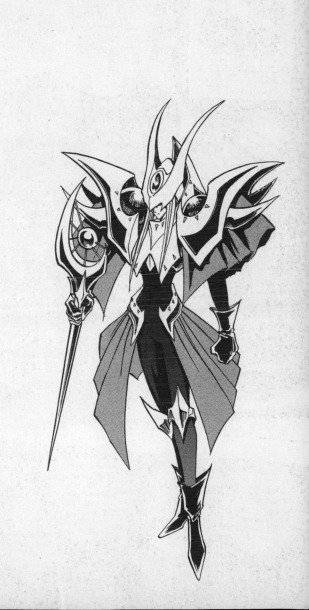

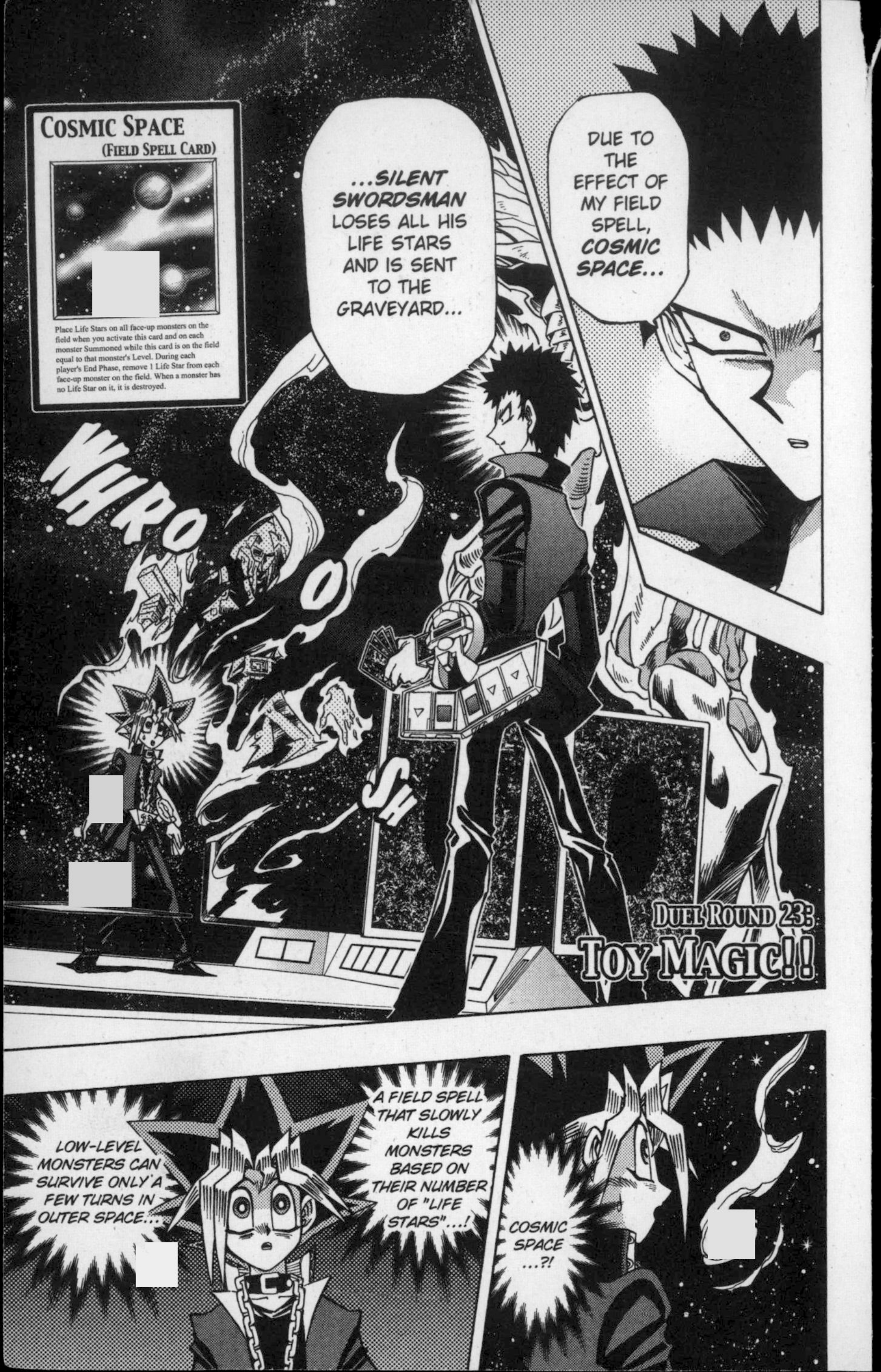
DUE TO THE EFFECT OF MY FIELD SPELL, COSMIC SPACE...
...SILENT SWORDSMAN LOSES ALL HIS LIFE STARS AND IS SENT TO THE GRAVEYARD...
COSMIC SPACE
(FIELD SPELL CARD)
Place Life Stars on all face-up monsters on the field when you activate this card and on each monster Summoned while this card is on the field equal to that monster's Level. During each player's End Phase, remove 1 Life Star from each face-up monster on the field. When a monster has no Life Star on it, it is destroyed.
WHROOOSH
DUEL ROUND 23:
TOY MAGIC!!
COSMIC SPACE ...?!
A FIELD SPELL THAT SLOWLY KILLS MONSTERS BASED ON THEIR NUMBER OF "LIFE STARS"...!
LOW-LEVEL MONSTERS CAN SURVIVE ONLY A FEW TURNS IN OUTER SPACE...

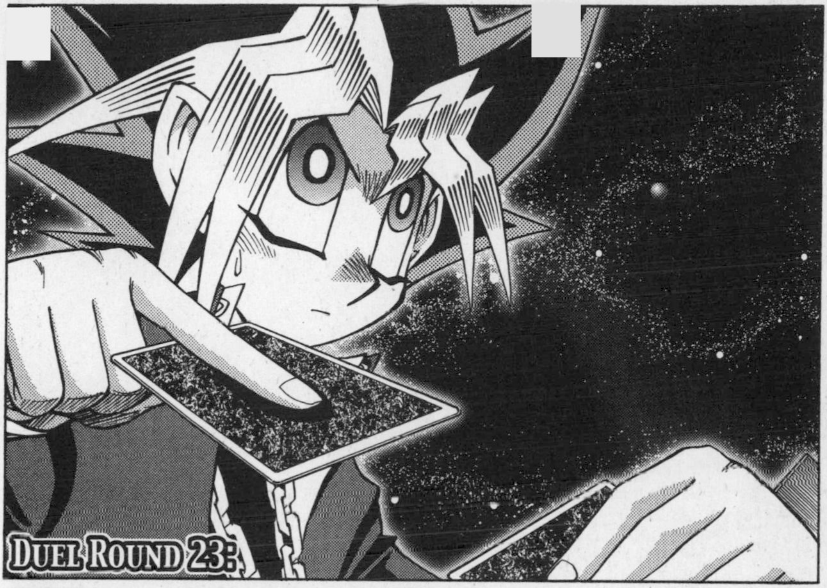

Duel Round 23: Toy Magic!!

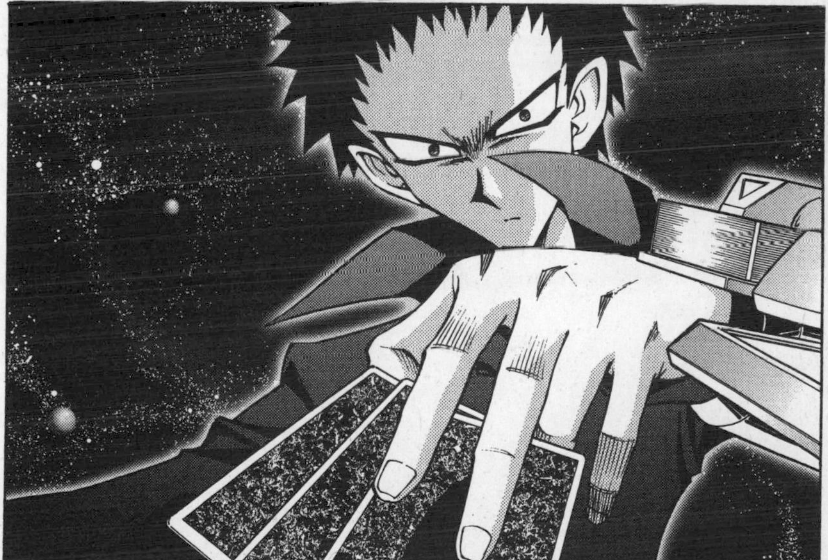

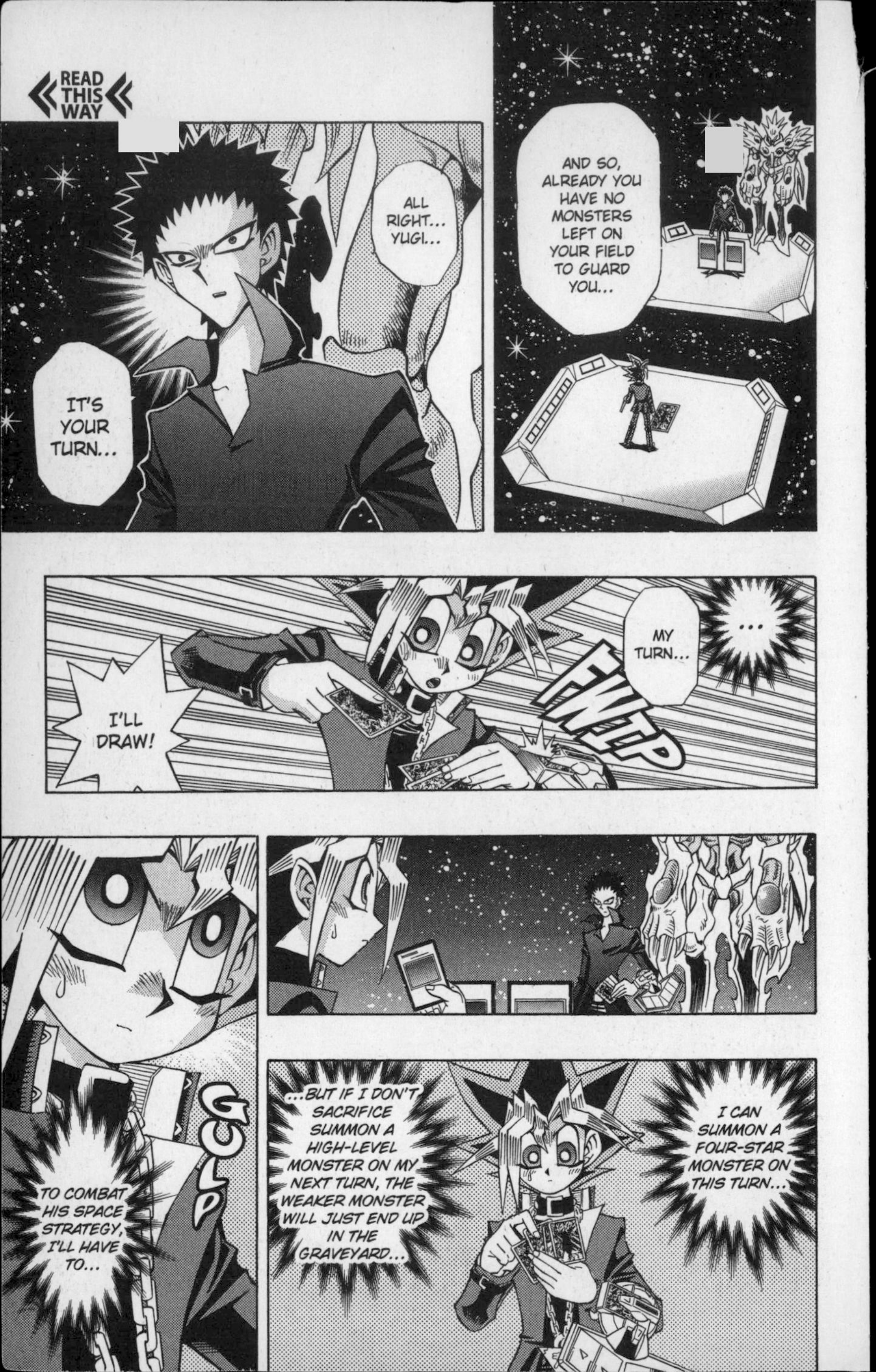
READ THIS WAY
AND SO, ALREADY YOU HAVE NO MONSTERS LEFT ON YOUR FIELD TO GUARD YOU...
ALL RIGHT... YUGI...
IT'S YOUR TURN...
...
MY TURN...
FWIP
I'LL DRAW!
I CAN SUMMON A FOUR-STAR MONSTER ON THIS TURN...
...BUT IF I DON'T SACRIFICE SUMMON A HIGH-LEVEL MONSTER ON MY NEXT TURN, THE WEAKER MONSTER WILL JUST END UP IN THE GRAVEYARD...
GULP
TO COMBAT HIS SPACE STRATEGY, I'LL HAVE TO...

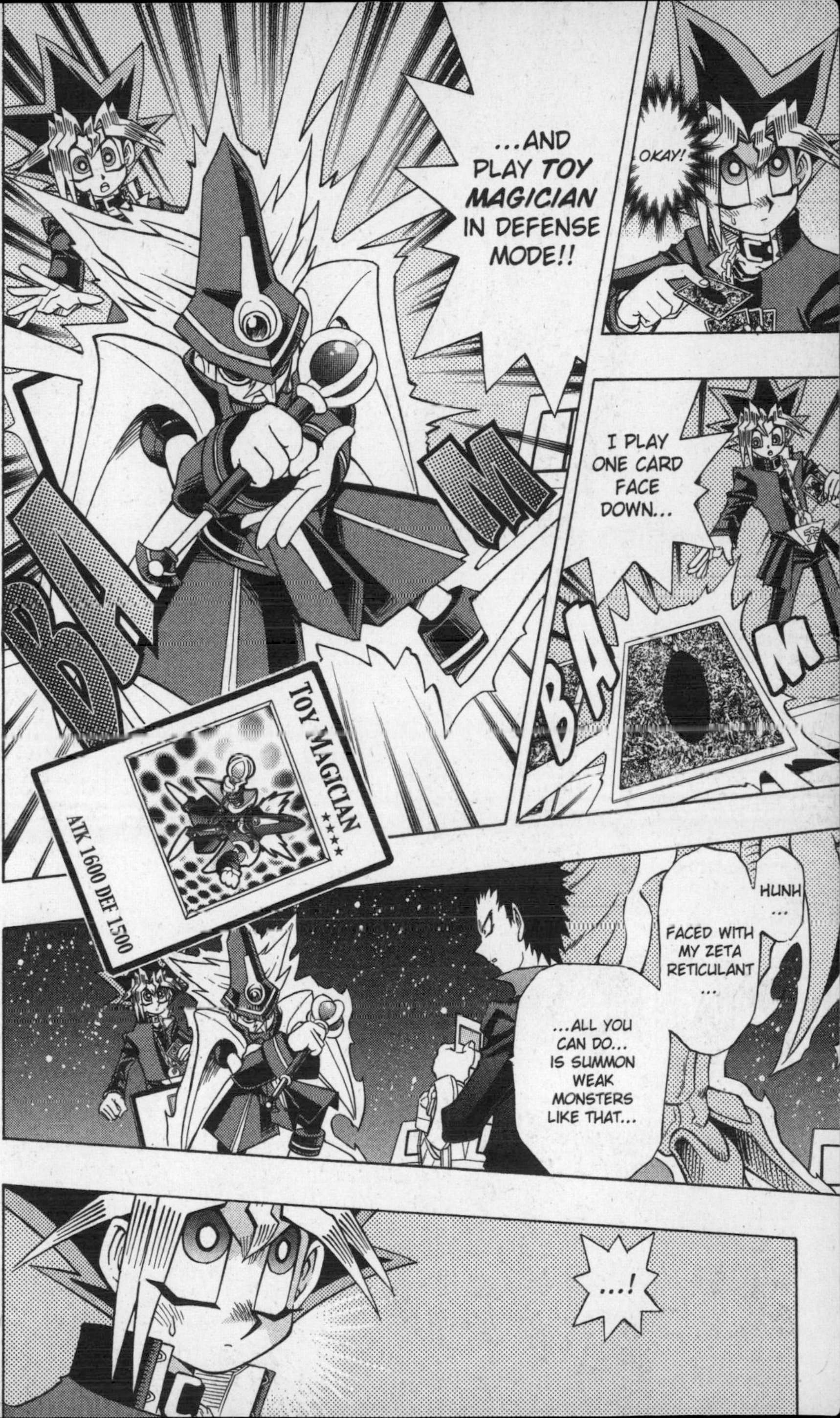
OKAY!
I PLAY ONE CARD FACE DOWN...
BAM
...AND PLAY TOY MAGICIAN IN DEFENSE MODE!!
TOY MAGICIAN
ATK 1600 DEF 1500
HUNH...
FACED WITH MY ZETA RETICULANT...
...ALL YOU CAN DO... IS SUMMON WEAK MONSTERS LIKE THAT...
...!

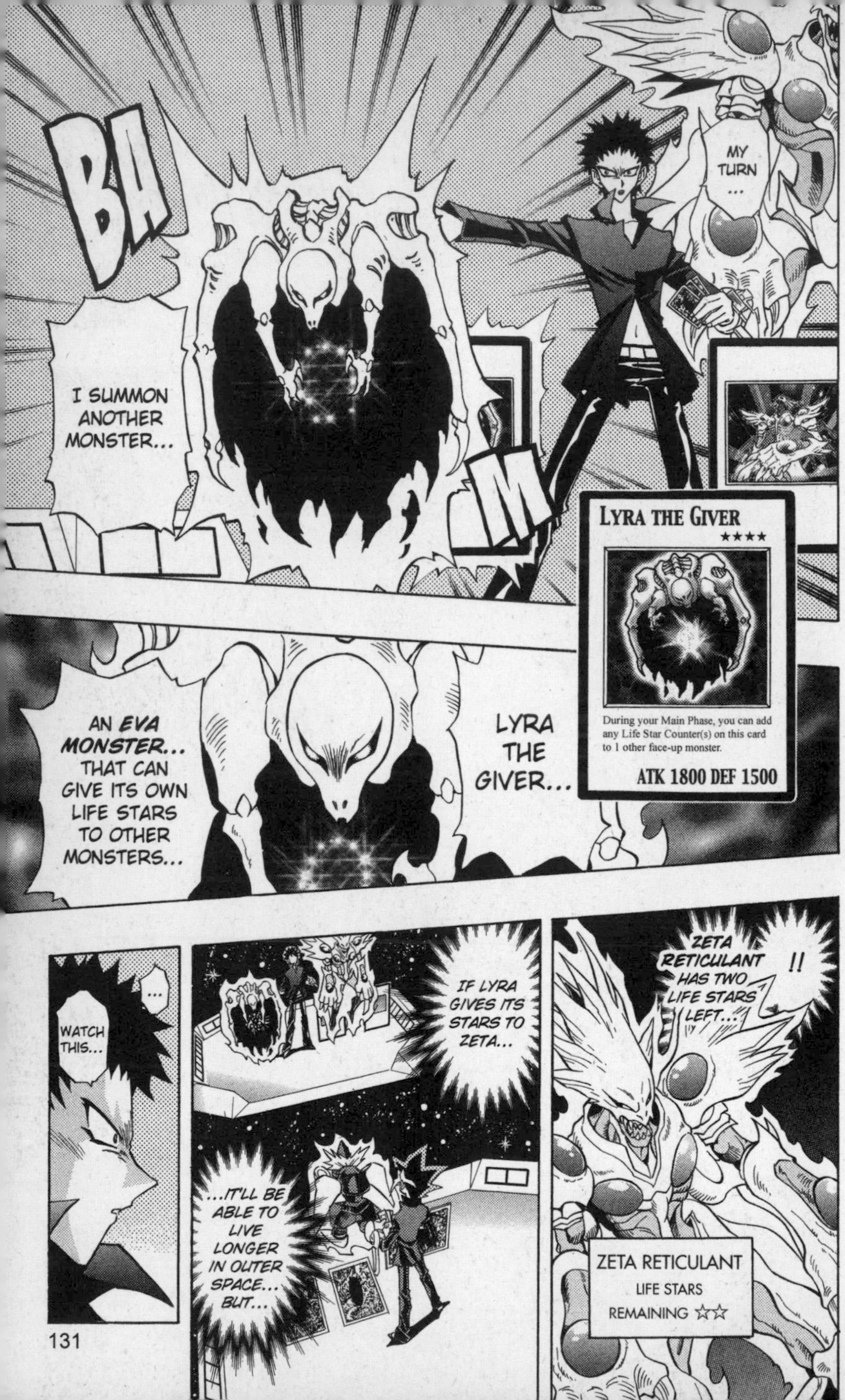
MY TURN...
BA
M
I SUMMON ANOTHER MONSTER...
LYRA THE GIVER
★★★★
During your Main Phase, you can add any Life Star Counter(s) on this card to 1 other face-up monster.
ATK 1800 DEF 1500
LYRA THE GIVER...
AN EVA MONSTER... THAT CAN GIVE ITS OWN LIFE STARS TO OTHER MONSTERS...
ZETA RETICULANT HAS TWO LIFE STARS LEFT...
!!
ZETA RETICULANT
LIFE STARS
REMAINING ☆☆
IF LYRA GIVES ITS STARS TO ZETA...
...IT'LL BE ABLE TO LIVE LONGER IN OUTER SPACE... BUT...
...
WATCH THIS...

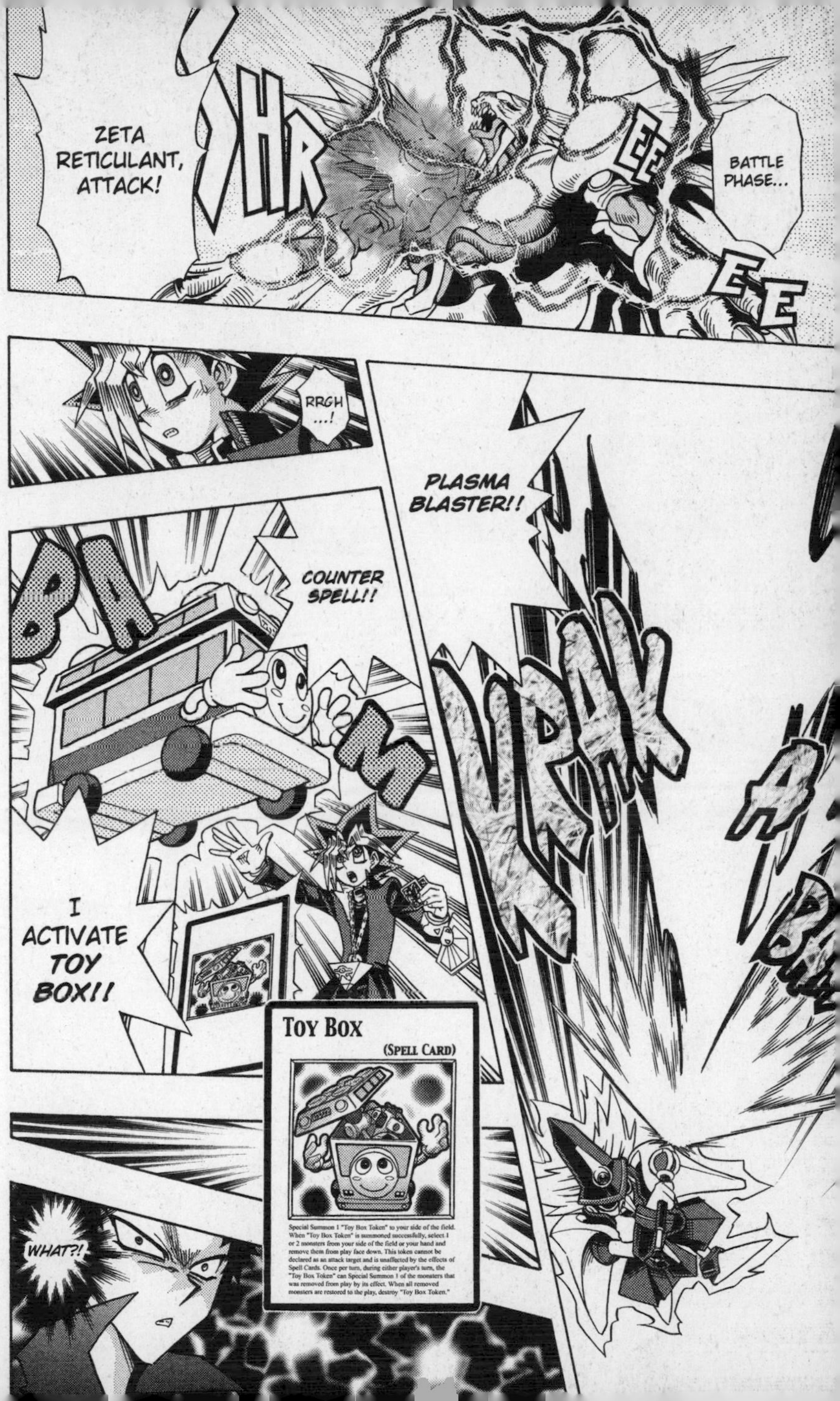
BATTLE PHASE...
ZETA RETICULANT, ATTACK!
PLASMA BLASTER!!
RRGH ...!
COUNTER SPELL!!
I ACTIVATE TOY BOX!!
TOY BOX
(SPELL CARD)
Special Summon 1 "Toy Box Token" to your side of the field. When "Toy Box Token" is summoned successfully, select 1 or 2 monsters from your side of the field or your hand and remove them from play face down. This token cannot be declared as an attack target and is unaffected by the effects of Spell Cards. Once per turn, during either player's turn, the "Toy Box Token" can Special Summon 1 of the monsters that was removed from play by its effect. When all removed monsters are restored to the play, destroy "Toy Box Token."
WHAT?!

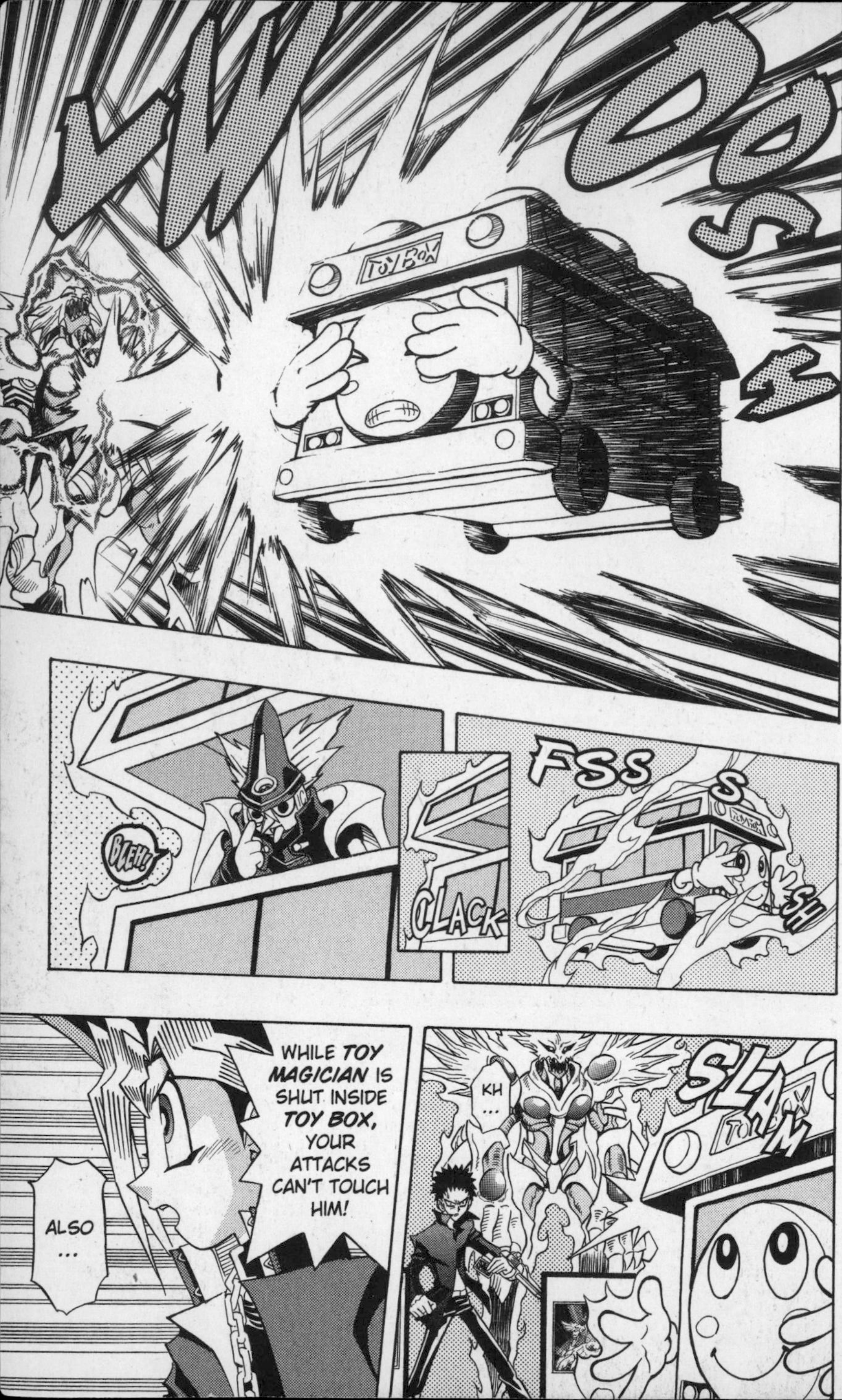
WHOOSH
TOY BOX
FSS S
SH
CLACK
BLEH!
SLAM
KH ...
WHILE TOY MAGICIAN IS SHUT INSIDE TOY BOX, YOUR ATTACKS CAN'T TOUCH HIM!
ALSO ...

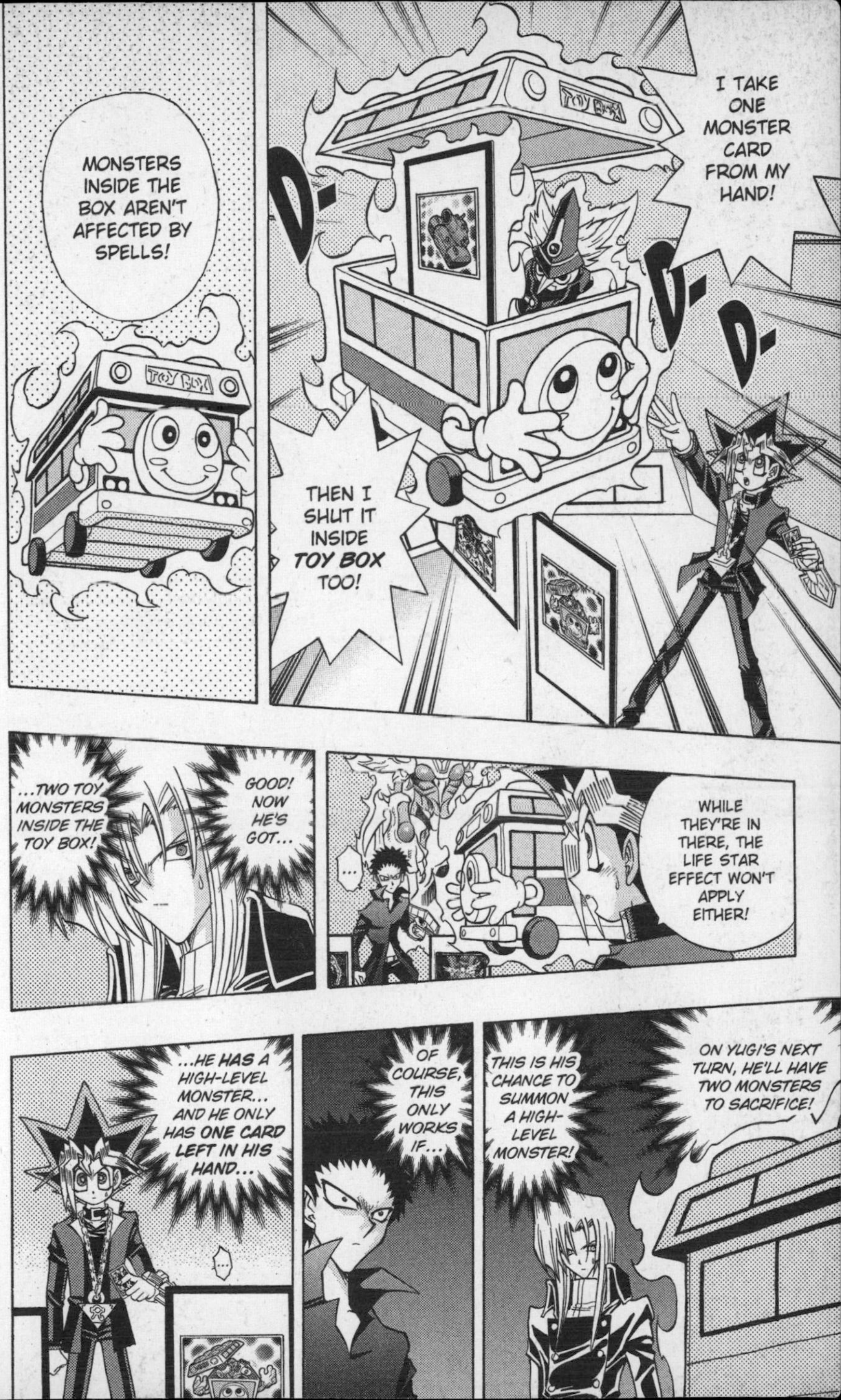
I TAKE ONE MONSTER CARD FROM MY HAND!
TOY BOX
D- D- D-
THEN I SHUT IT INSIDE *TOY BOX* TOO!
MONSTERS INSIDE THE BOX AREN'T AFFECTED BY SPELLS!
TOY BOX
WHILE THEY'RE IN THERE, THE LIFE STAR EFFECT WON'T APPLY EITHER!
...
GOOD! NOW HE'S GOT...
...TWO TOY MONSTERS INSIDE THE TOY BOX!
ON YUGI'S NEXT TURN, HE'LL HAVE TWO MONSTERS TO SACRIFICE!
THIS IS HIS CHANCE TO SUMMON A HIGH-LEVEL MONSTER!
OF COURSE, THIS ONLY WORKS IF...
...HE HAS A HIGH-LEVEL MONSTER... AND HE ONLY HAS ONE CARD LEFT IN HIS HAND...
...

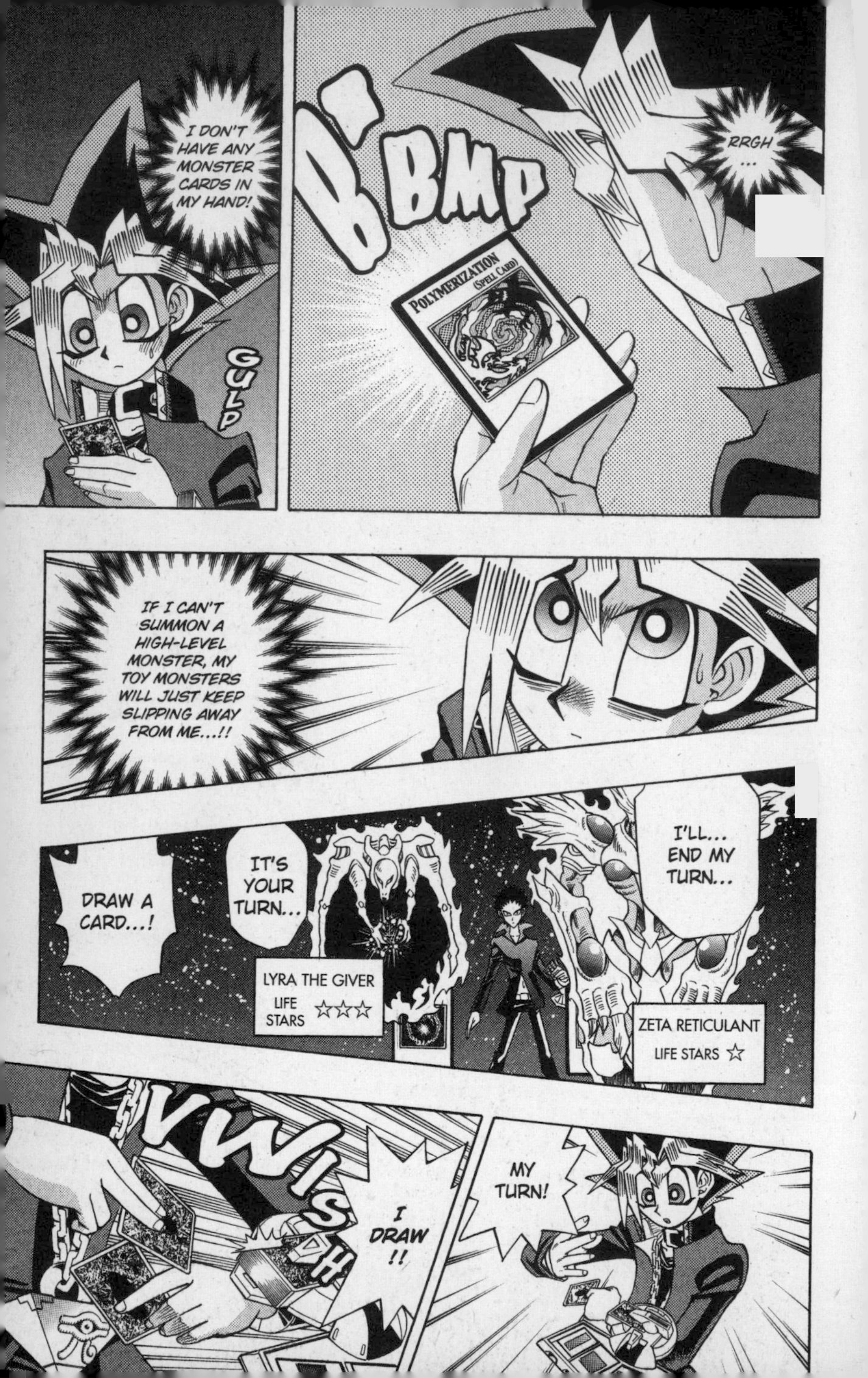
RRGH...
BMP
POLYMERIZATION
(SPELL CARD)
I DON'T HAVE ANY MONSTER CARDS IN MY HAND!
GULP
IF I CAN'T SUMMON A HIGH-LEVEL MONSTER, MY TOY MONSTERS WILL JUST KEEP SLIPPING AWAY FROM ME...!!
I'LL... END MY TURN...
ZETA RETICULANT
LIFE STARS ☆
IT'S YOUR TURN...
LYRA THE GIVER
LIFE STARS ☆☆☆
DRAW A CARD...!
MY TURN!
I DRAW!!
VWISH

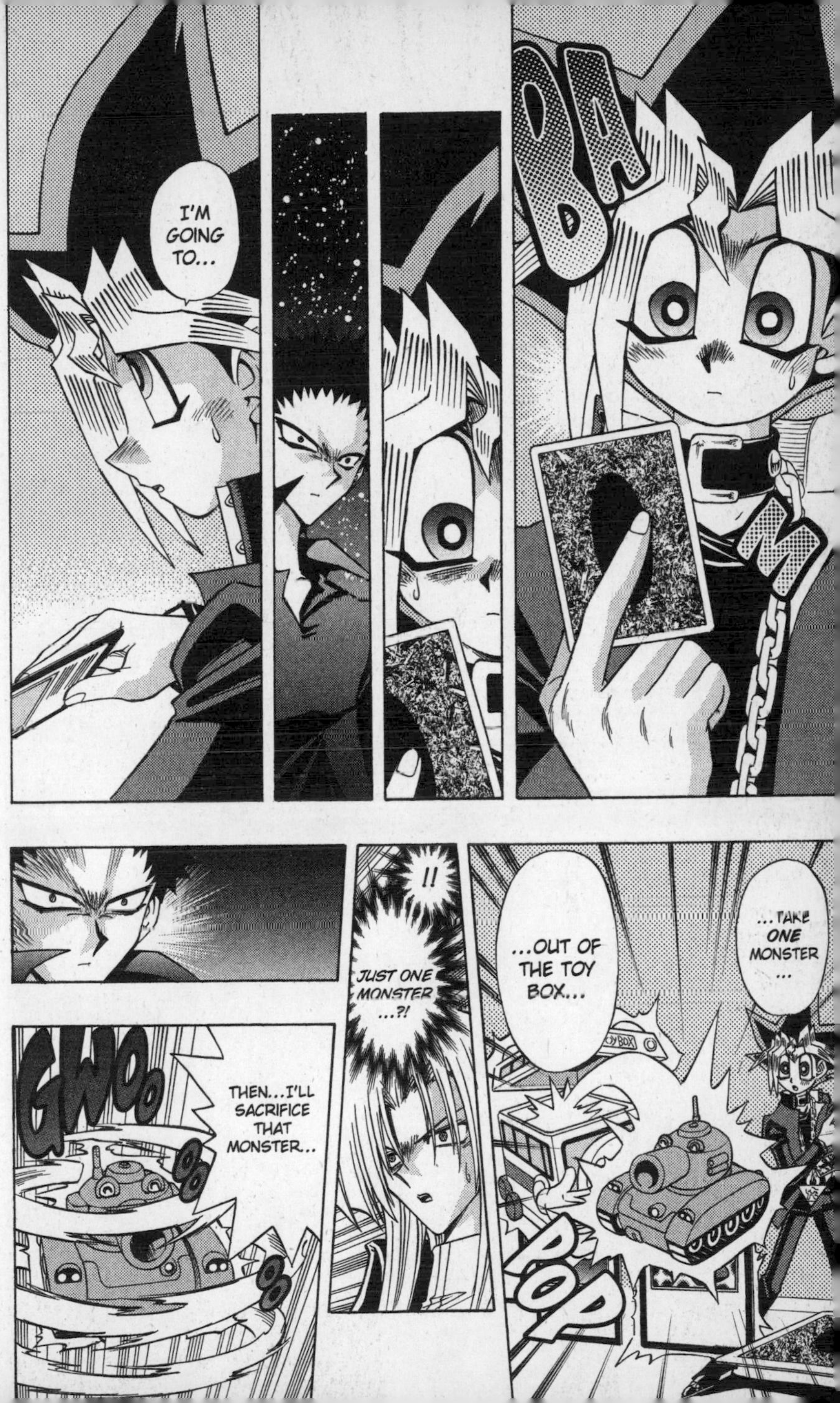
BAM
I'M GOING TO...
...TAKE ONE MONSTER...
...OUT OF THE TOY BOX...
POP
!!
JUST ONE MONSTER...?!
GWOOO
THEN...I'LL SACRIFICE THAT MONSTER...

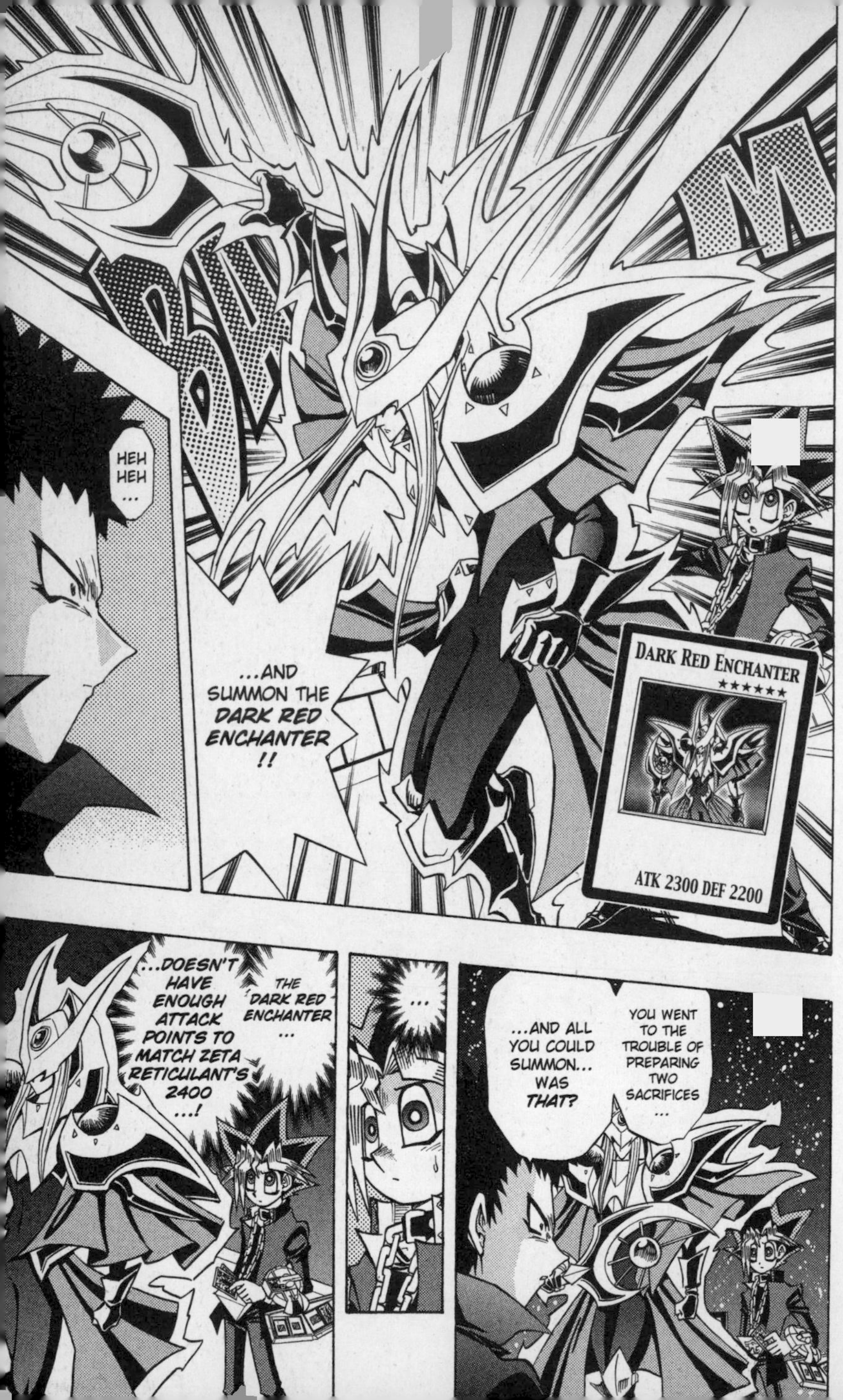
...AND SUMMON THE DARK RED ENCHANTER !!
DARK RED ENCHANTER
ATK 2300 DEF 2200
HEH HEH ...
YOU WENT TO THE TROUBLE OF PREPARING TWO SACRIFICES ...
...AND ALL YOU COULD SUMMON... WAS THAT?
...
THE DARK RED ENCHANTER ...
...DOESN'T HAVE ENOUGH ATTACK POINTS TO MATCH ZETA RETICULANT'S 2400 ...!

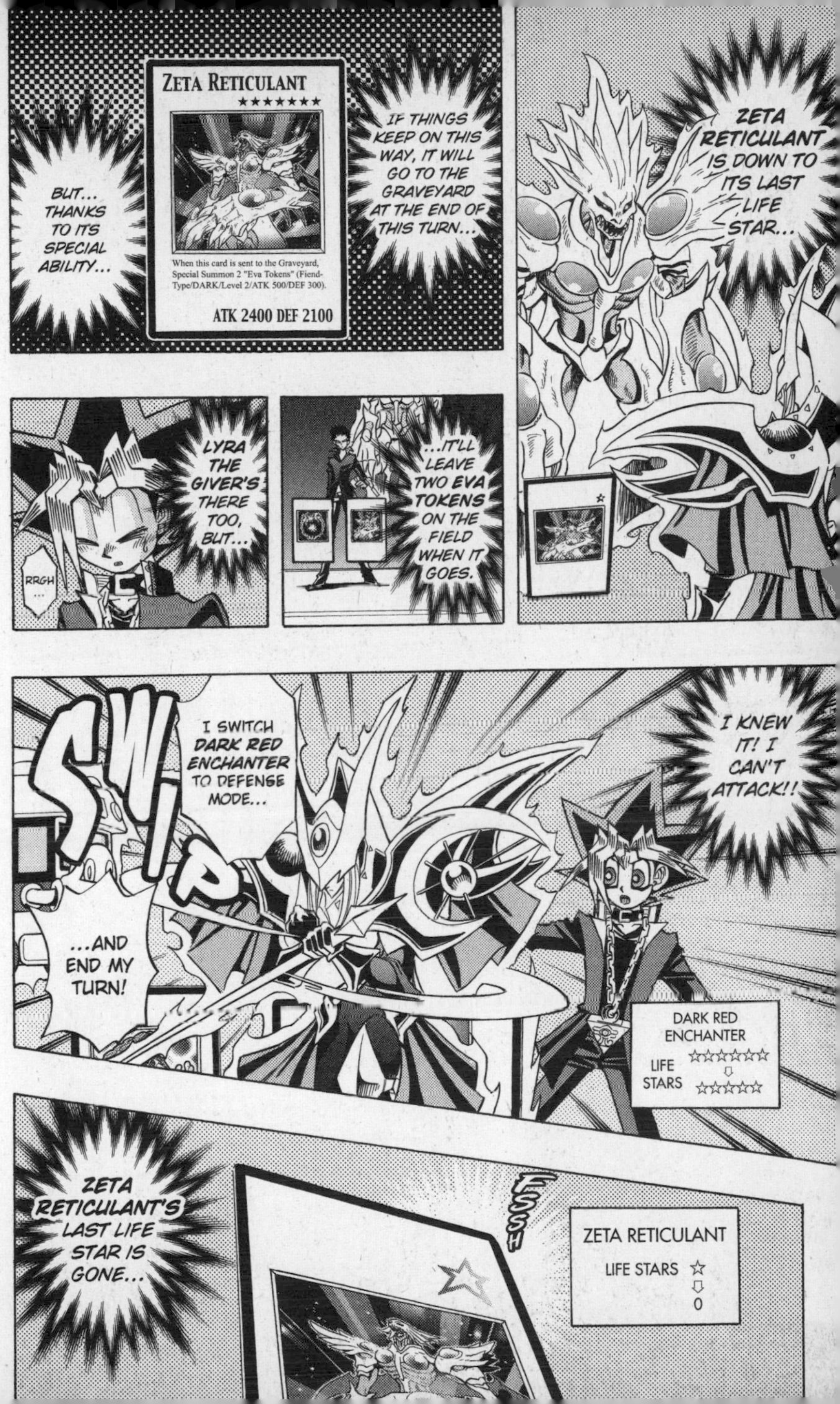
ZETA RETICULANT IS DOWN TO ITS LAST LIFE STAR...
IF THINGS KEEP ON THIS WAY, IT WILL GO TO THE GRAVEYARD AT THE END OF THIS TURN...
ZETA RETICULANT
★★★★★★★
When this card is sent to the Graveyard, Special Summon 2 "Eva Tokens" (Fiend-Type/DARK/Level 2/ATK 500/DEF 300).
ATK 2400 DEF 2100
BUT... THANKS TO ITS SPECIAL ABILITY...
...IT'LL LEAVE TWO EVA TOKENS ON THE FIELD WHEN IT GOES.
LYRA THE GIVER'S THERE TOO, BUT...
RRGH...
I KNEW IT! I CAN'T ATTACK!!
SWIP
I SWITCH DARK RED ENCHANTER TO DEFENSE MODE...
...AND END MY TURN!
DARK RED ENCHANTER
LIFE STARS ☆☆☆☆☆☆ ⇩ ☆☆☆☆☆
ZETA RETICULANT
LIFE STARS ☆ ⇩ 0
FSSH
ZETA RETICULANT'S LAST LIFE STAR IS GONE...

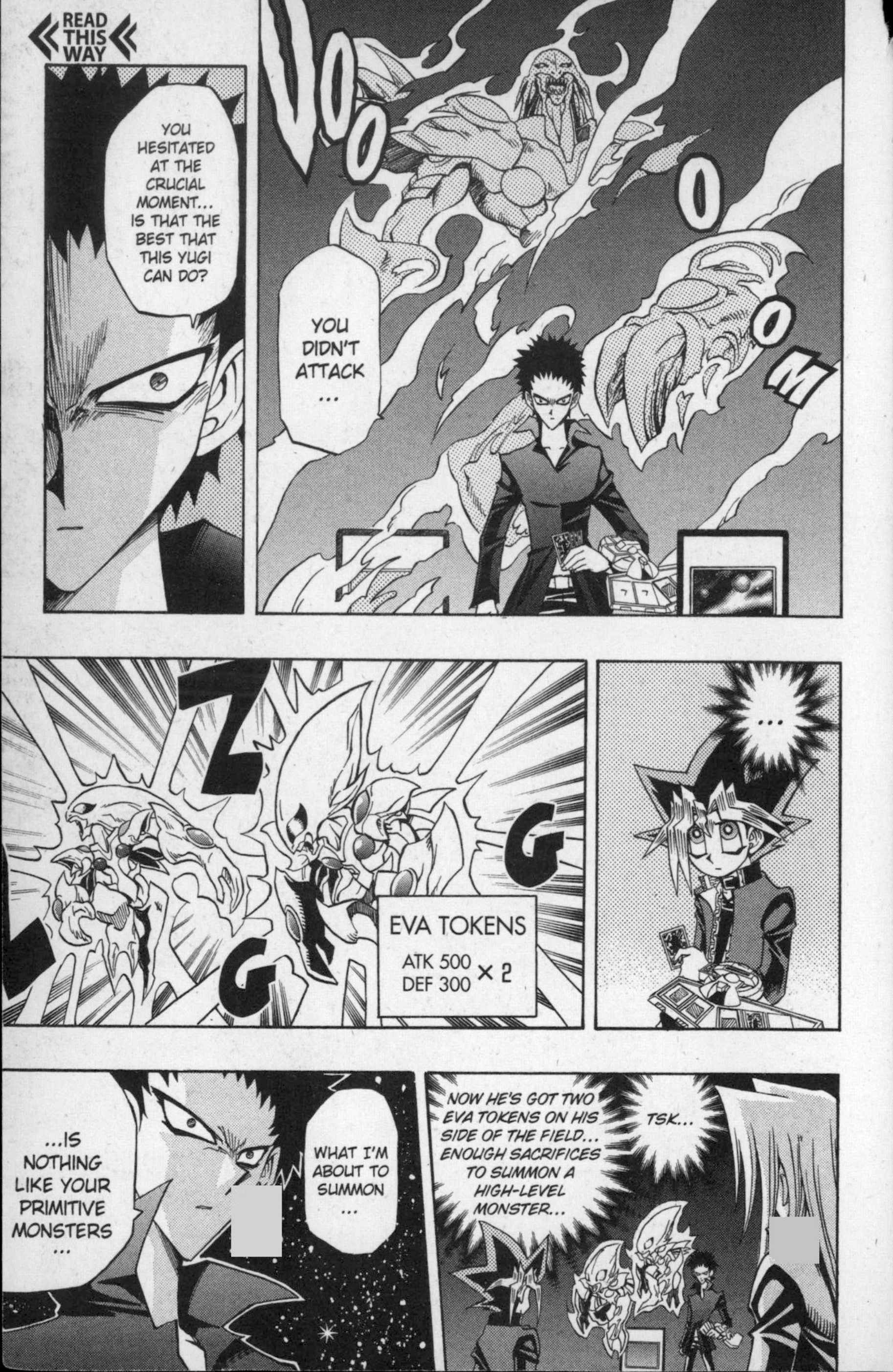
READ THIS WAY
DOOOOOOM
YOU DIDN'T ATTACK ...
YOU HESITATED AT THE CRUCIAL MOMENT... IS THAT THE BEST THAT THIS YUGI CAN DO?
...
Z
G
G
EVA TOKENS
ATK 500 DEF 300 × 2
TSK...
NOW HE'S GOT TWO EVA TOKENS ON HIS SIDE OF THE FIELD... ENOUGH SACRIFICES TO SUMMON A HIGH-LEVEL MONSTER...
WHAT I'M ABOUT TO SUMMON ...
...IS NOTHING LIKE YOUR PRIMITIVE MONSTERS ...

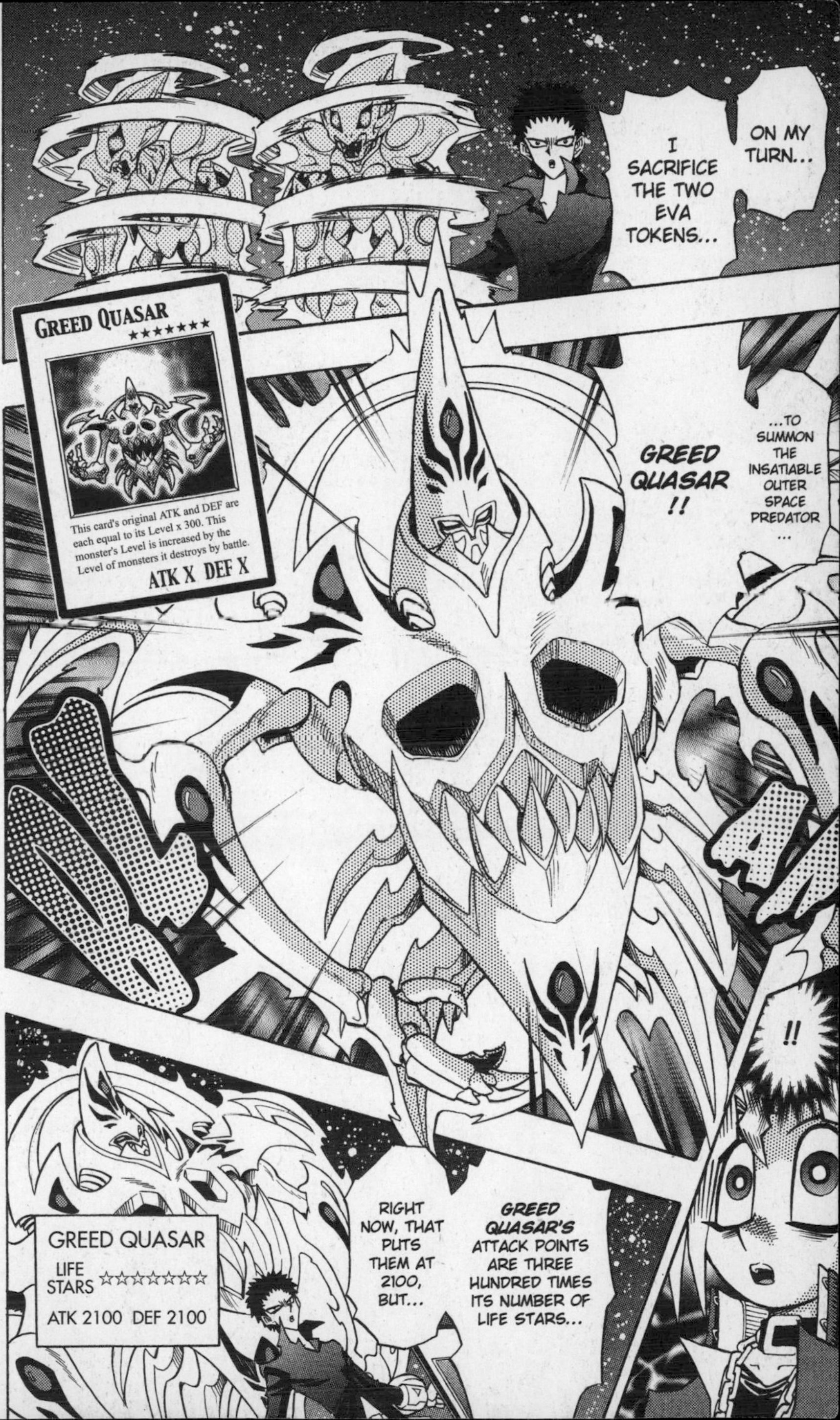
ON MY TURN...
I SACRIFICE THE TWO EVA TOKENS...
...TO SUMMON THE INSATIABLE OUTER SPACE PREDATOR...
GREED QUASAR !!
GREED QUASAR
★★★★★★★
This card's original ATK and DEF are each equal to its Level x 300. This monster's Level is increased by the Level of monsters it destroys by battle.
ATK X DEF X
!!
GREED QUASAR'S ATTACK POINTS ARE THREE HUNDRED TIMES ITS NUMBER OF LIFE STARS...
RIGHT NOW, THAT PUTS THEM AT 2100, BUT...
GREED QUASAR
LIFE STARS ☆☆☆☆☆☆☆
ATK 2100 DEF 2100

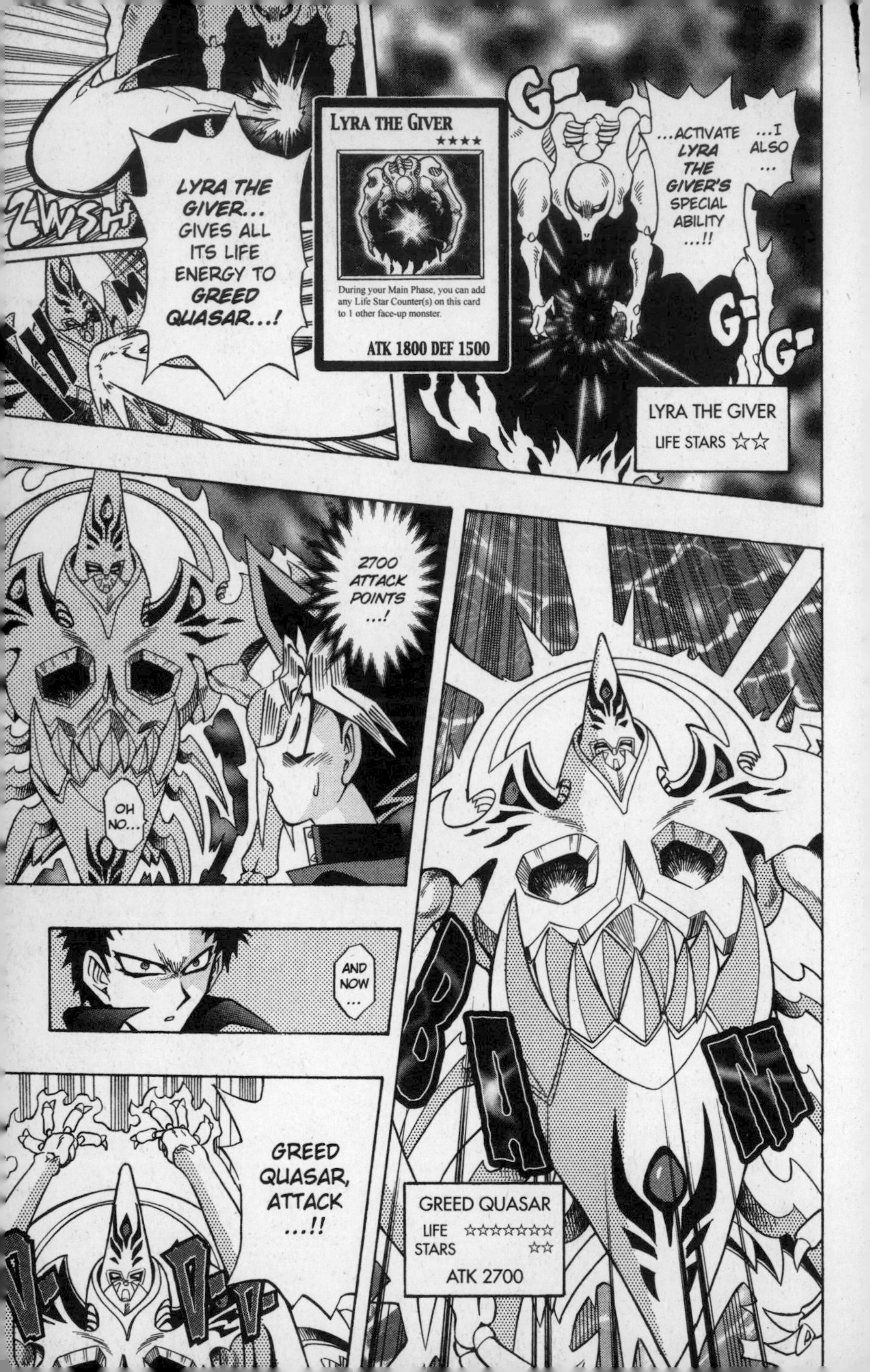
...I ALSO ...
...ACTIVATE LYRA THE GIVER'S SPECIAL ABILITY ...!!
G- G- G-
LYRA THE GIVER LIFE STARS ☆☆
LYRA THE GIVER ★★★★
During your Main Phase, you can add any Life Star Counter(s) on this card to 1 other face-up monster.
ATK 1800 DEF 1500
LYRA THE GIVER... GIVES ALL ITS LIFE ENERGY TO GREED QUASAR...!
ZWSH
BAM
GREED QUASAR LIFE STARS ☆☆☆☆☆☆☆ ☆☆ ATK 2700
2700 ATTACK POINTS ...!
OH NO...
AND NOW ...
GREED QUASAR, ATTACK ...!!

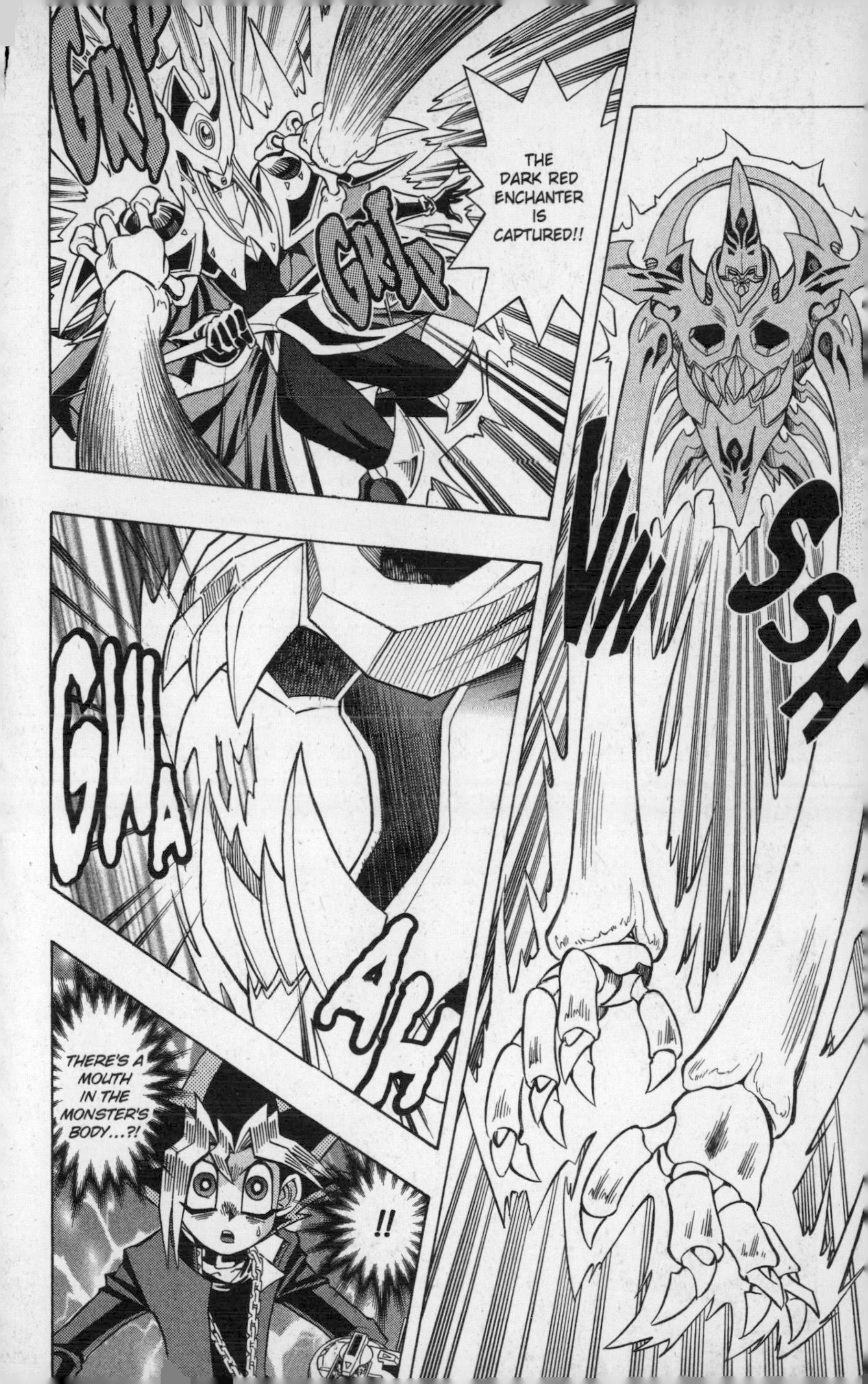
THE DARK RED ENCHANTER IS CAPTURED!!
WHSSH
GRIP
GRIP
GWAA
AAH
THERE'S A MOUTH IN THE MONSTER'S BODY...?!
!!

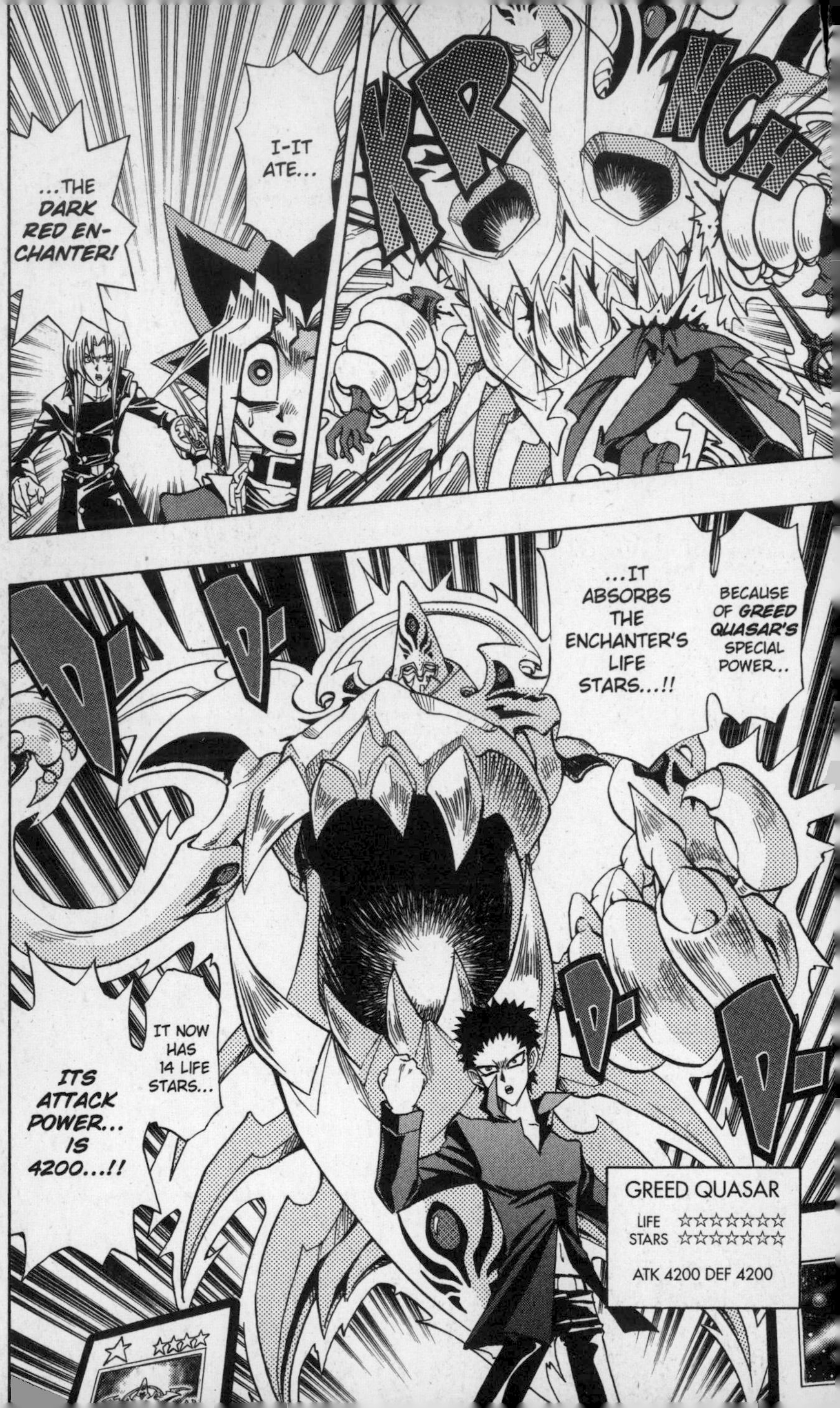

I-IT ATE...
...THE DARK RED EN-CHANTER!
BECAUSE OF GREED QUASAR'S SPECIAL POWER...
...IT ABSORBS THE ENCHANTER'S LIFE STARS...!!
IT NOW HAS 14 LIFE STARS...
ITS ATTACK POWER... IS 4200...!!
GREED QUASAR
LIFE STARS ☆☆☆☆☆☆☆☆☆☆☆☆☆☆
ATK 4200 DEF 4200

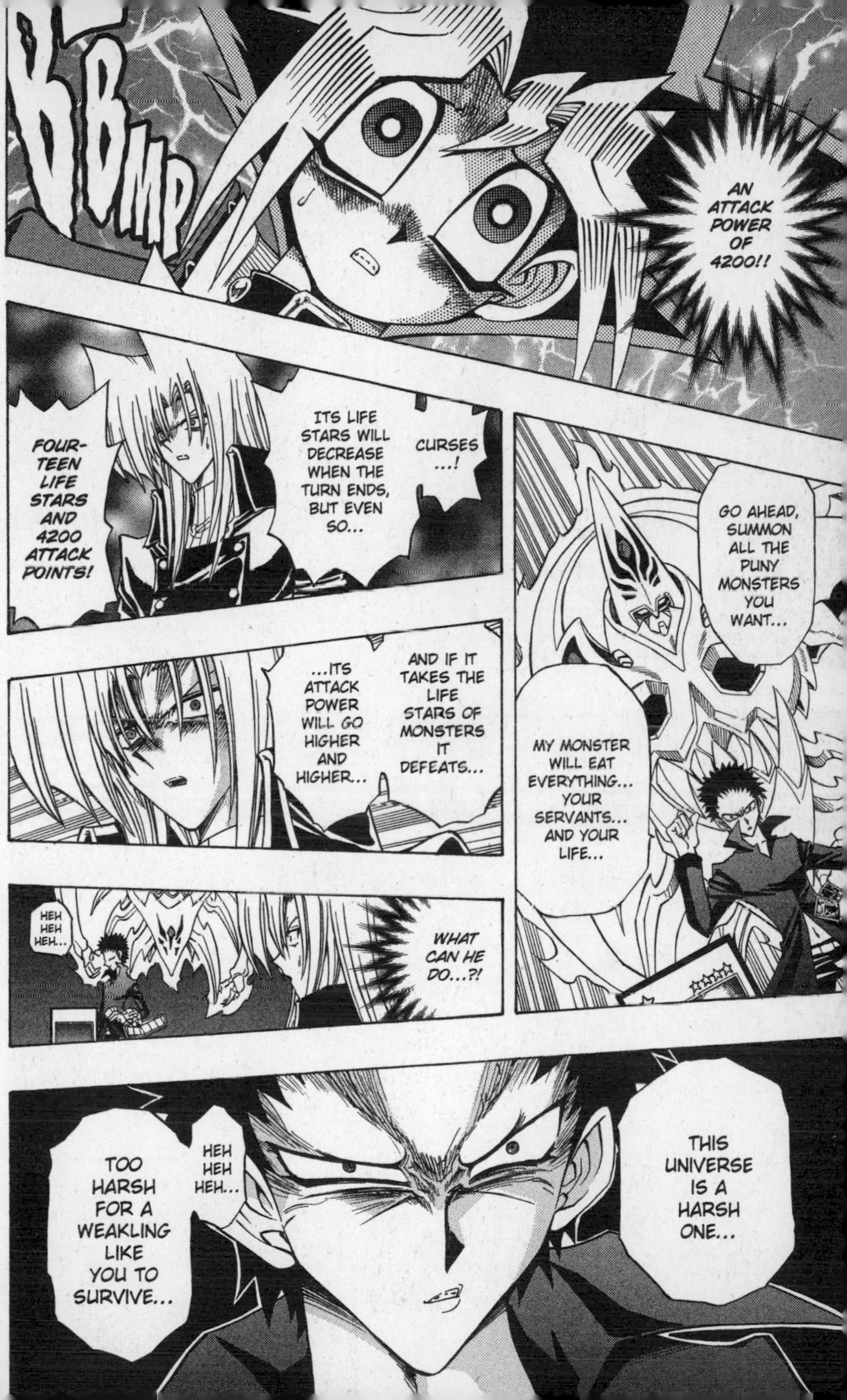
AN ATTACK POWER OF 4200!!
BBUMP
GO AHEAD, SUMMON ALL THE PUNY MONSTERS YOU WANT...
MY MONSTER WILL EAT EVERYTHING... YOUR SERVANTS... AND YOUR LIFE...
CURSES ...!
ITS LIFE STARS WILL DECREASE WHEN THE TURN ENDS, BUT EVEN SO...
FOURTEEN LIFE STARS AND 4200 ATTACK POINTS!
AND IF IT TAKES THE LIFE STARS OF MONSTERS IT DEFEATS...
...ITS ATTACK POWER WILL GO HIGHER AND HIGHER...
WHAT CAN HE DO...?!
HEH HEH HEH...
THIS UNIVERSE IS A HARSH ONE...
HEH HEH HEH...
TOO HARSH FOR A WEAKLING LIKE YOU TO SURVIVE...

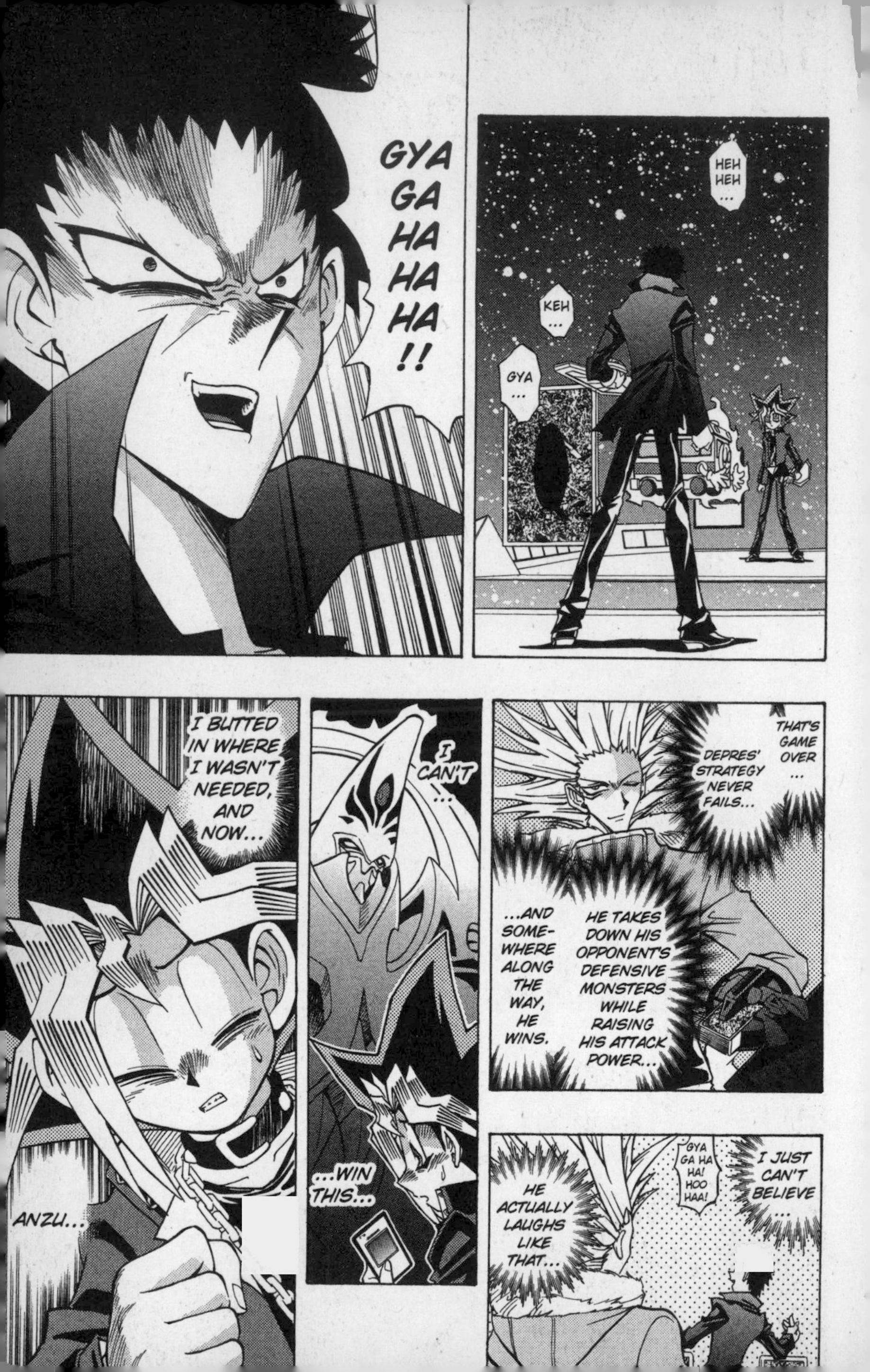
HEH HEH ...
KEH ...
GYA ...
GYA GA HA HA HA!!
THAT'S GAME OVER ...
DEPRES' STRATEGY NEVER FAILS...
HE TAKES DOWN HIS OPPONENT'S DEFENSIVE MONSTERS WHILE RAISING HIS ATTACK POWER...
...AND SOMEWHERE ALONG THE WAY, HE WINS.
I JUST CAN'T BELIEVE ...
GYA GA HA HA! HOO HAA!
HE ACTUALLY LAUGHS LIKE THAT...
I CAN'T ...
...WIN THIS...
I BUTTED IN WHERE I WASN'T NEEDED, AND NOW...
ANZU...

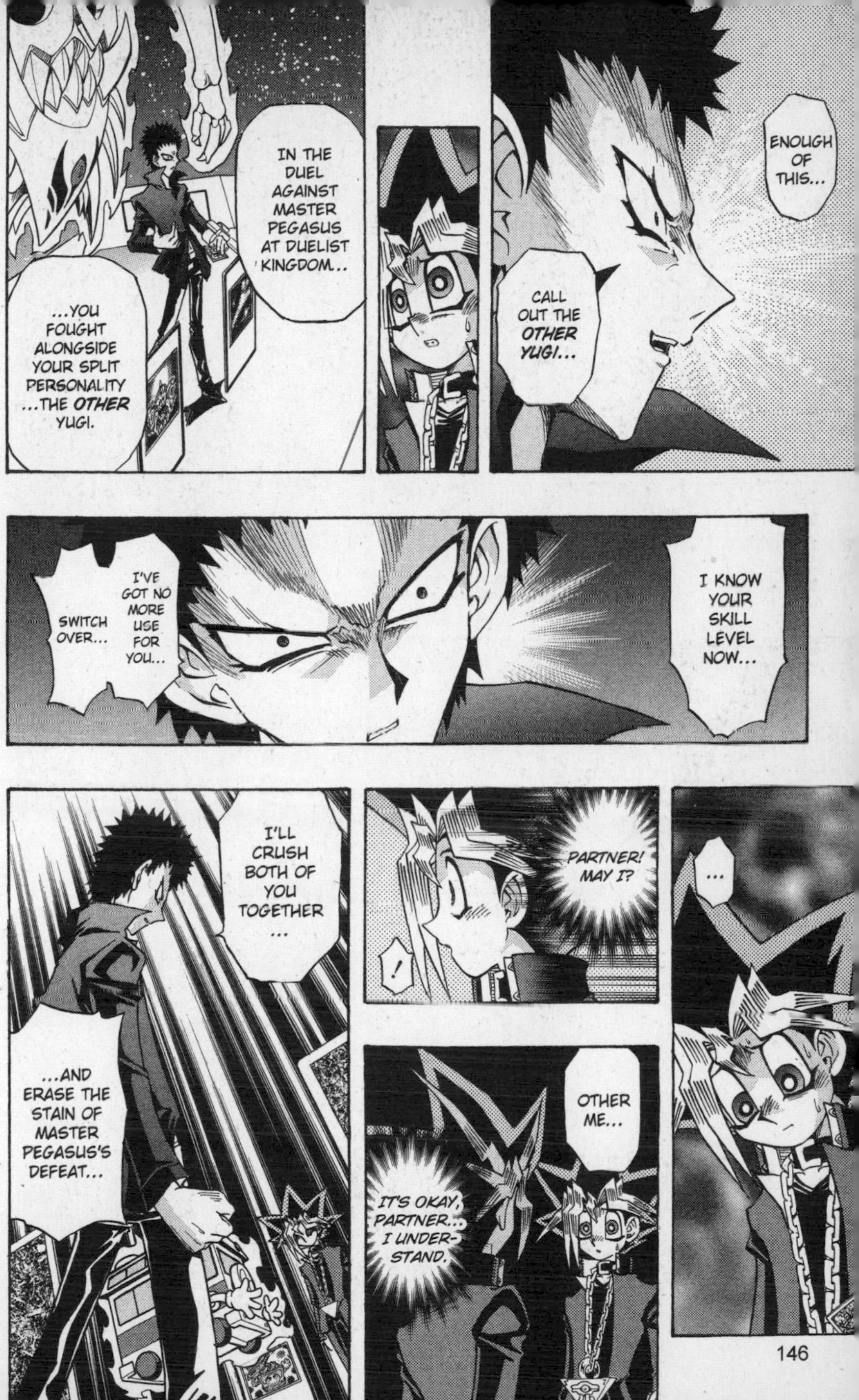
ENOUGH OF THIS...
CALL OUT THE *OTHER YUGI*...
IN THE DUEL AGAINST MASTER PEGASUS AT DUELIST KINGDOM...
...YOU FOUGHT ALONGSIDE YOUR SPLIT PERSONALITY ...THE *OTHER* YUGI.
I KNOW YOUR SKILL LEVEL NOW...
I'VE GOT NO MORE USE FOR YOU...
SWITCH OVER...
...
PARTNER! MAY I?
!
OTHER ME...
IT'S OKAY, PARTNER... I UNDERSTAND.
I'LL CRUSH BOTH OF YOU TOGETHER...
...AND ERASE THE STAIN OF MASTER PEGASUS'S DEFEAT...

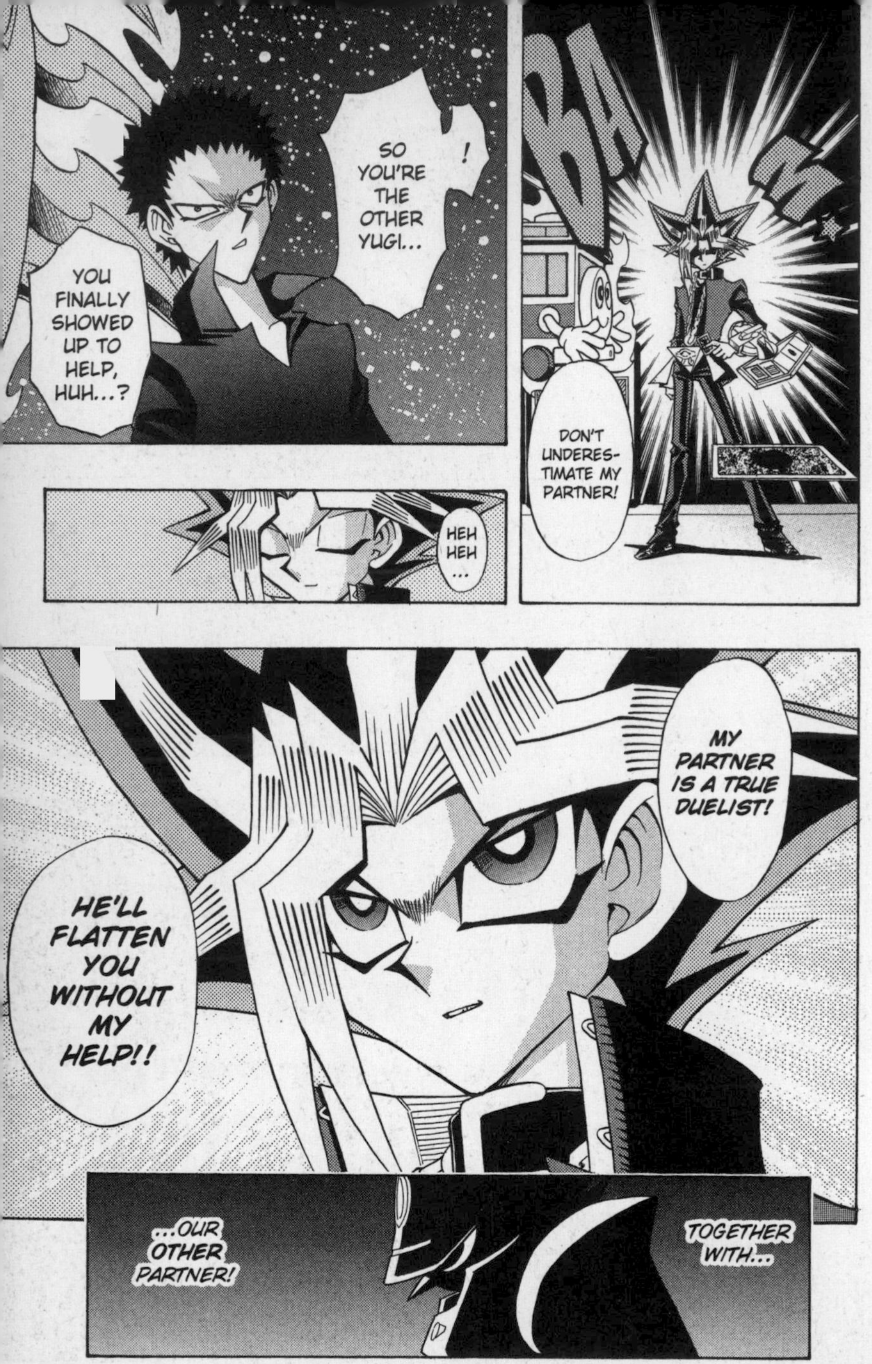
BAM
DON'T UNDERES-TIMATE MY PARTNER!
SO YOU'RE THE OTHER YUGI...!
YOU FINALLY SHOWED UP TO HELP, HUH...?
HEH HEH ...
MY PARTNER IS A TRUE DUELIST!
HE'LL FLATTEN YOU WITHOUT MY HELP!!
TOGETHER WITH...
...OUR OTHER PARTNER!

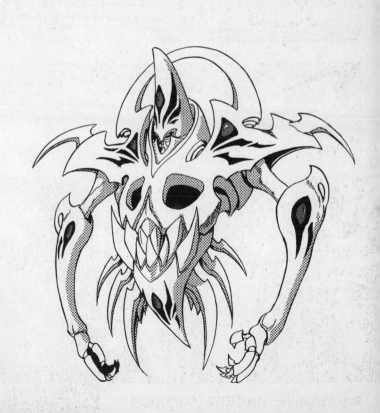

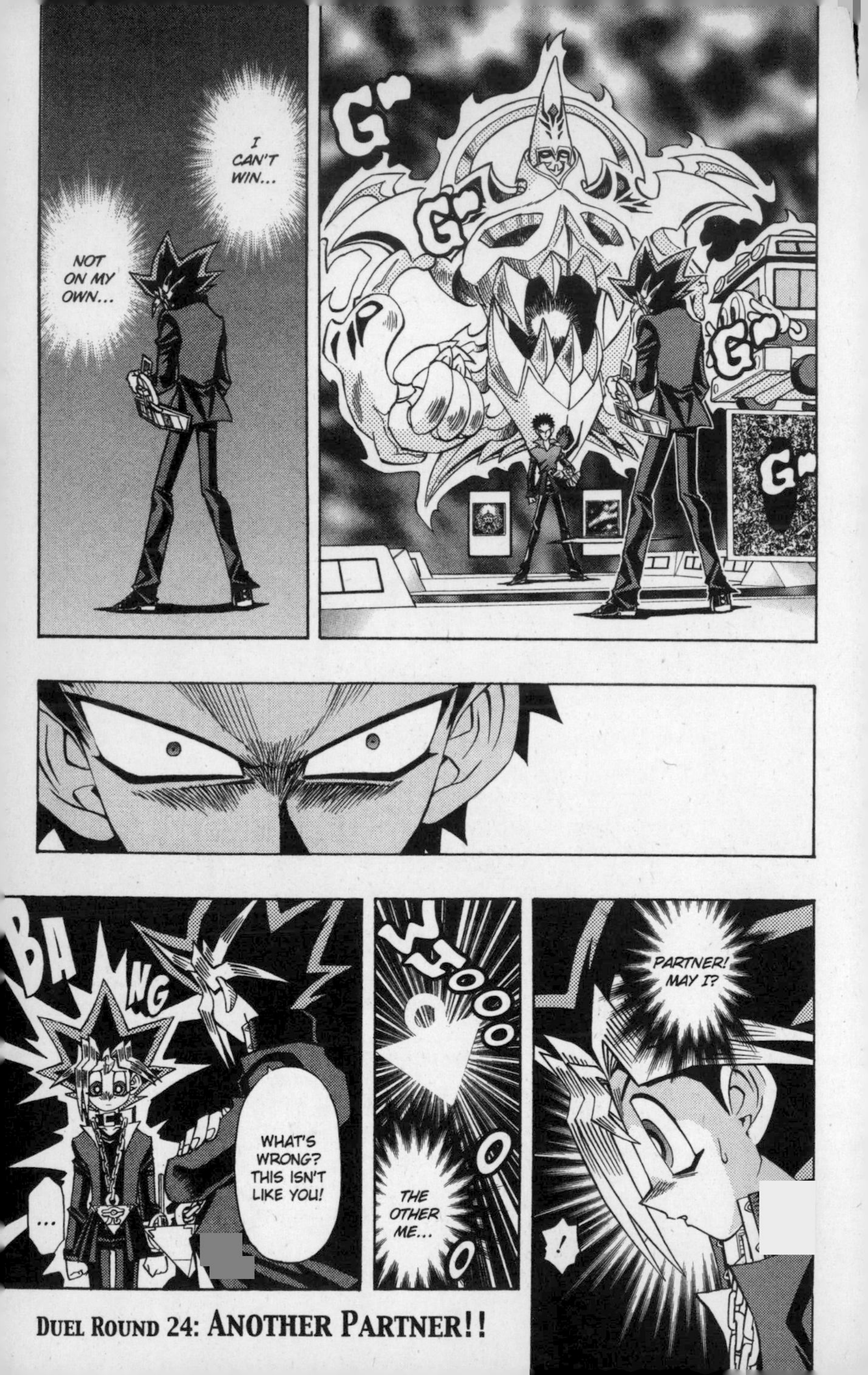
G
G
G
G
I CAN'T WIN...
NOT ON MY OWN...
PARTNER! MAY I?
!
WHOOOOO
THE OTHER ME...
BA NG
WHAT'S WRONG? THIS ISN'T LIKE YOU!
...

DUEL ROUND 24: ANOTHER PARTNER!!

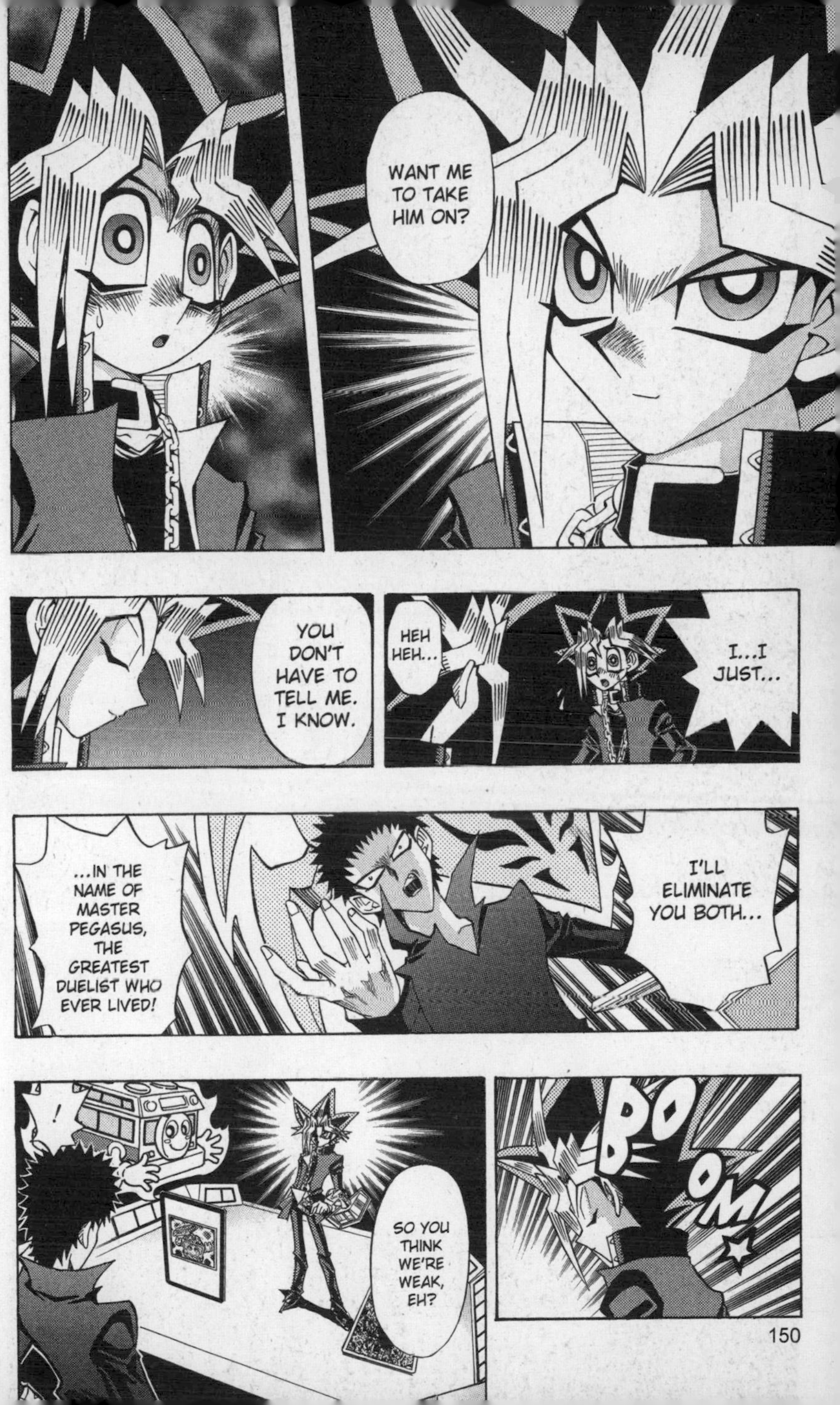
WANT ME TO TAKE HIM ON?
I...I JUST...
HEH HEH...
YOU DON'T HAVE TO TELL ME. I KNOW.
I'LL ELIMINATE YOU BOTH...
...IN THE NAME OF MASTER PEGASUS, THE GREATEST DUELIST WHO EVER LIVED!
BOOM
!
SO YOU THINK WE'RE WEAK, EH?

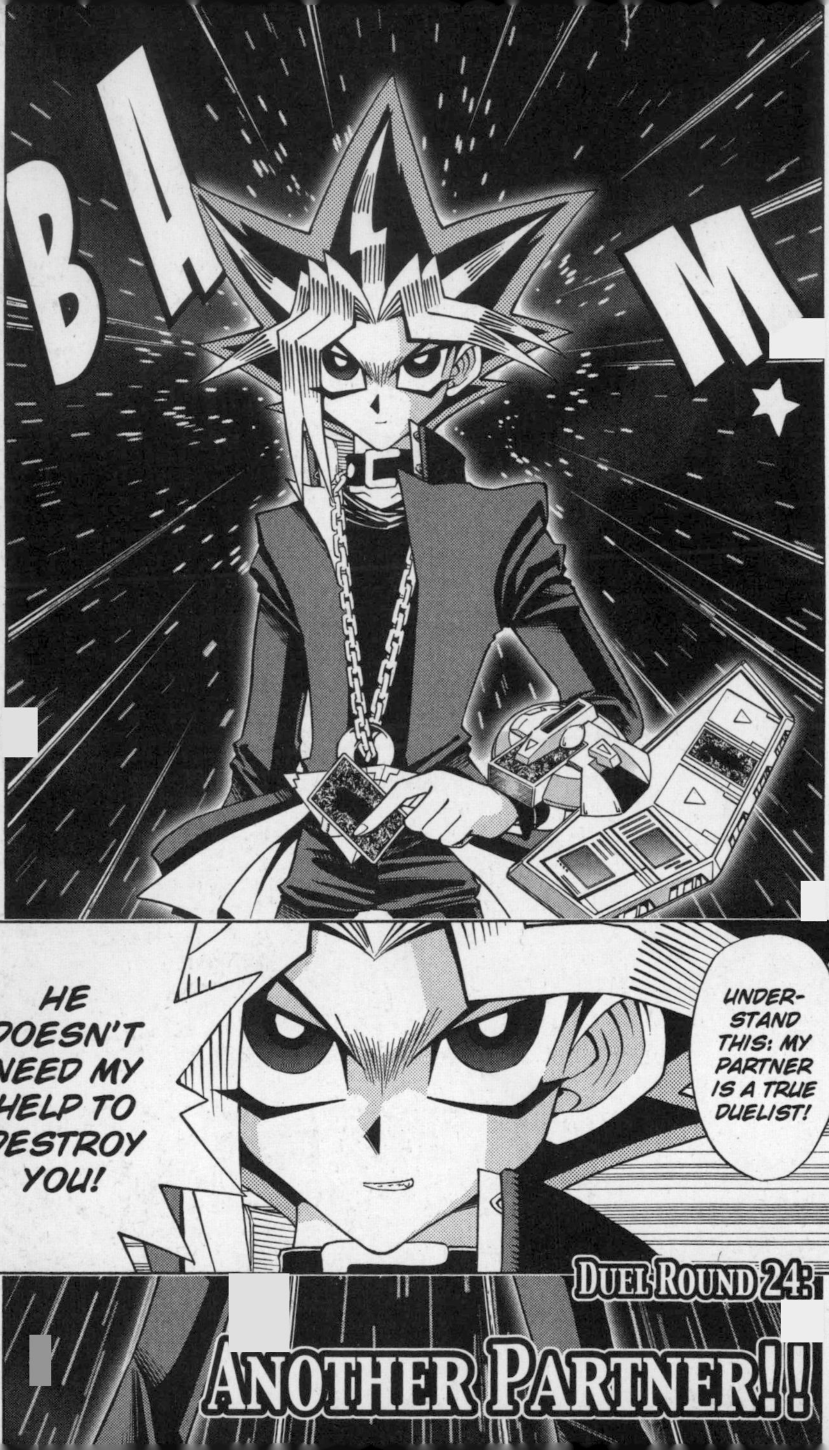
BAM
UNDER-STAND THIS: MY PARTNER IS A TRUE DUELIST!
HE DOESN'T NEED MY HELP TO DESTROY YOU!
DUEL ROUND 24:
ANOTHER PARTNER!!

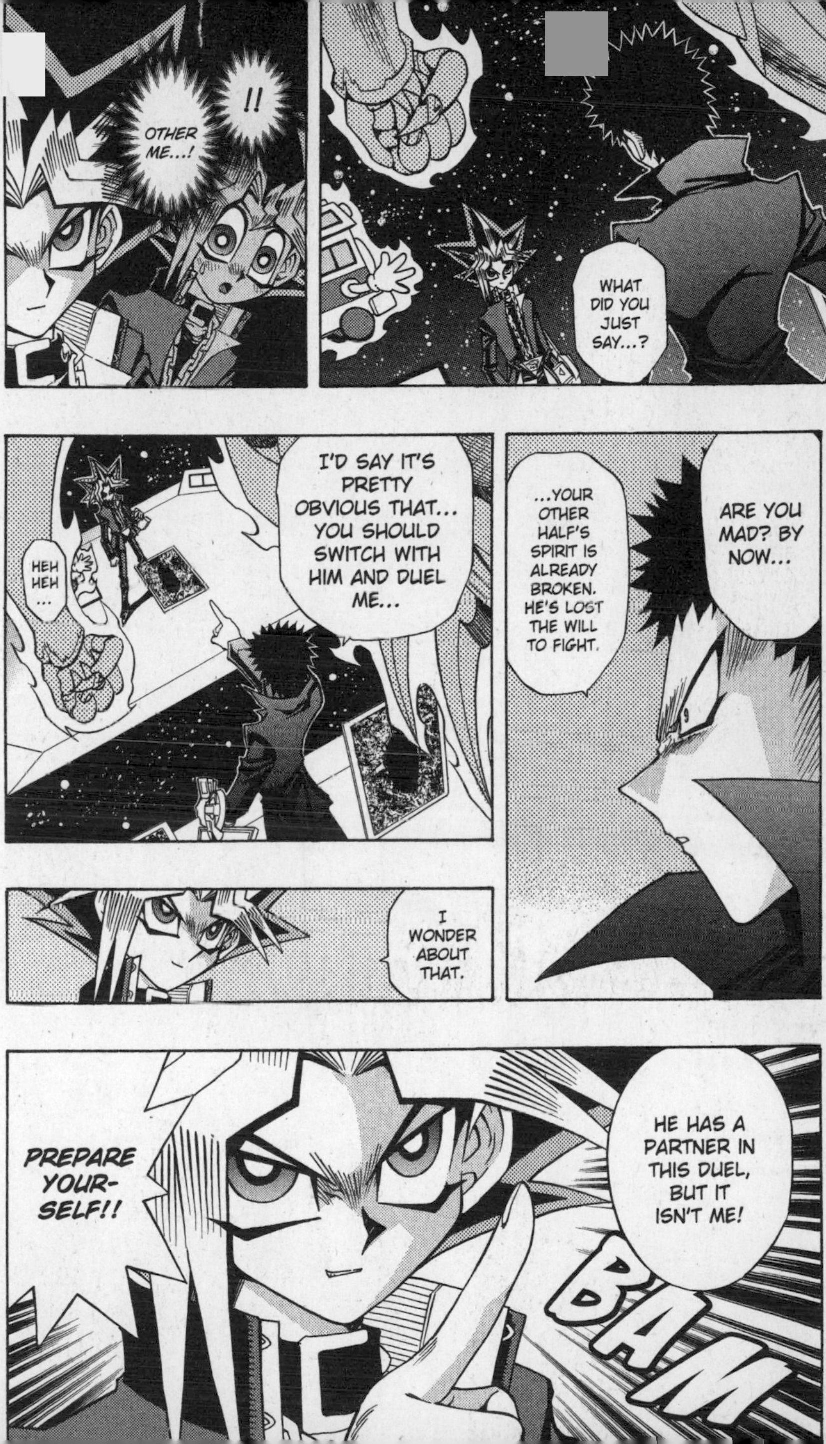
WHAT DID YOU JUST SAY...?
!!
OTHER ME...!
ARE YOU MAD? BY NOW...
...YOUR OTHER HALF'S SPIRIT IS ALREADY BROKEN. HE'S LOST THE WILL TO FIGHT.
I'D SAY IT'S PRETTY OBVIOUS THAT... YOU SHOULD SWITCH WITH HIM AND DUEL ME...
HEH HEH ...
I WONDER ABOUT THAT.
HE HAS A PARTNER IN THIS DUEL, BUT IT ISN'T ME!
BAM
PREPARE YOUR-SELF!!

READ THIS WAY

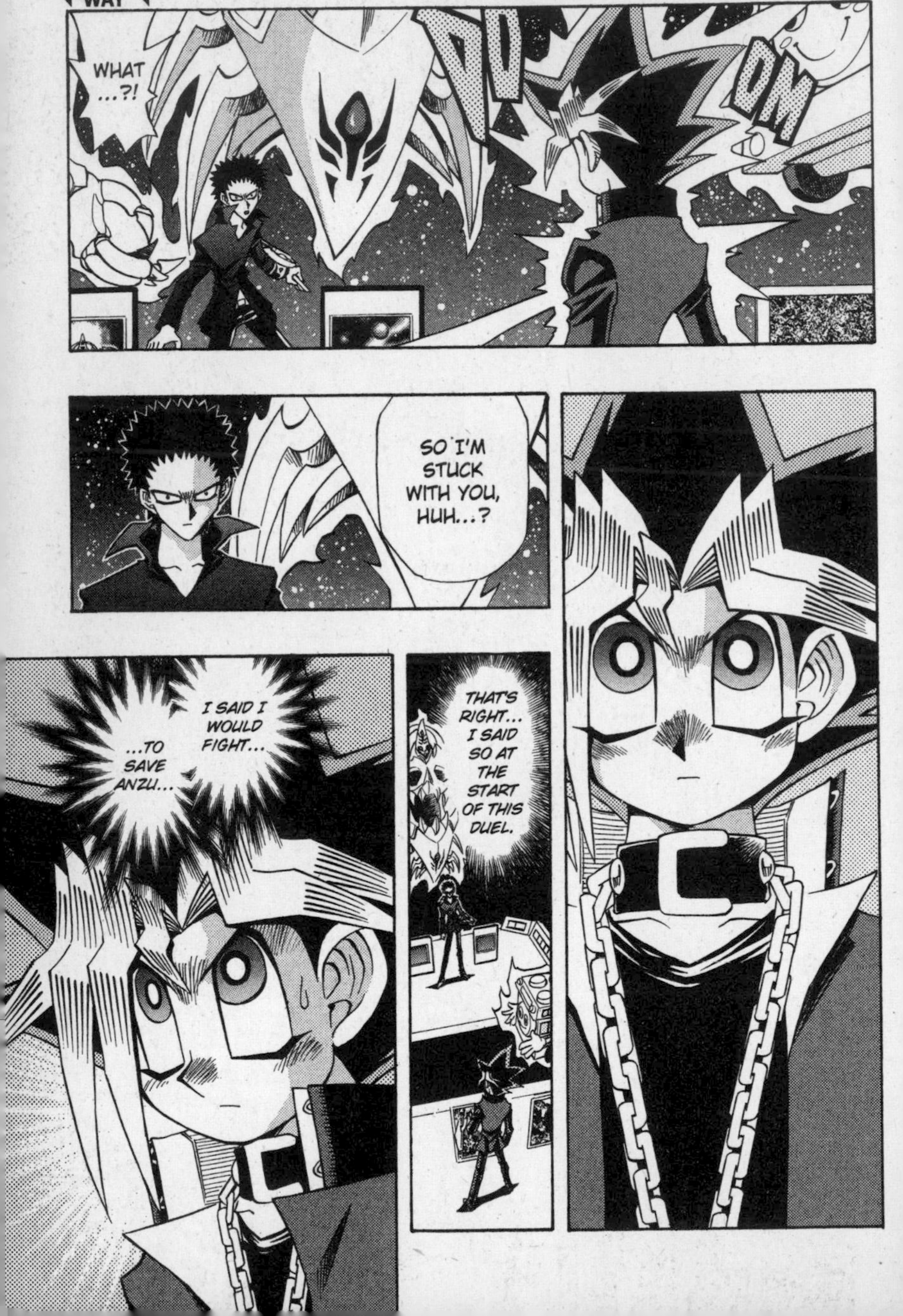
DOOM
WHAT ...?!
SO I'M STUCK WITH YOU, HUH...?
THAT'S RIGHT... I SAID SO AT THE START OF THIS DUEL.
I SAID I WOULD FIGHT...
...TO SAVE ANZU...

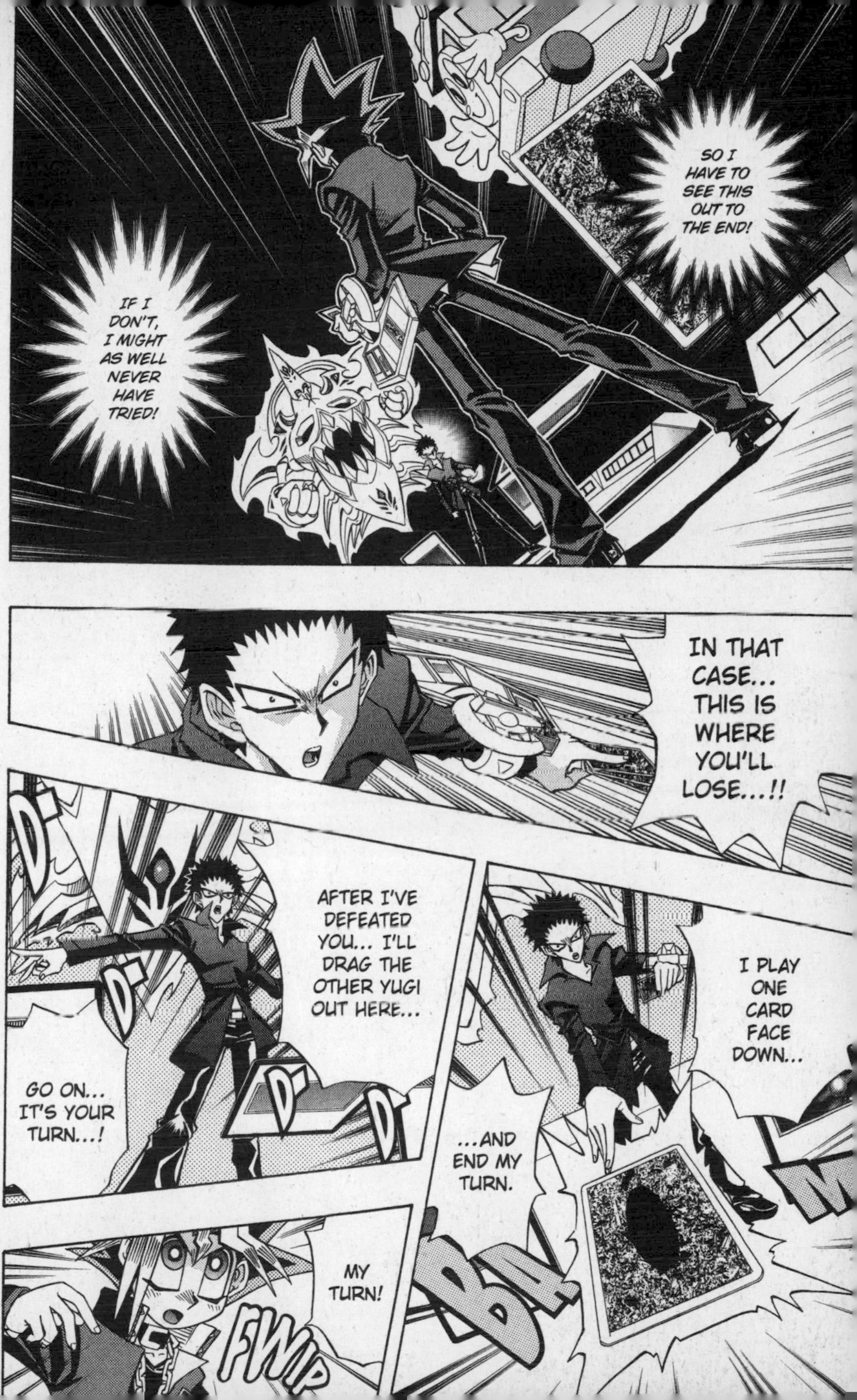
SO I HAVE TO SEE THIS OUT TO THE END!
IF I DON'T, I MIGHT AS WELL NEVER HAVE TRIED!
IN THAT CASE... THIS IS WHERE YOU'LL LOSE...!!
I PLAY ONE CARD FACE DOWN...
...AND END MY TURN.
AFTER I'VE DEFEATED YOU... I'LL DRAG THE OTHER YUGI OUT HERE...
GO ON... IT'S YOUR TURN...!
MY TURN!
FWIP

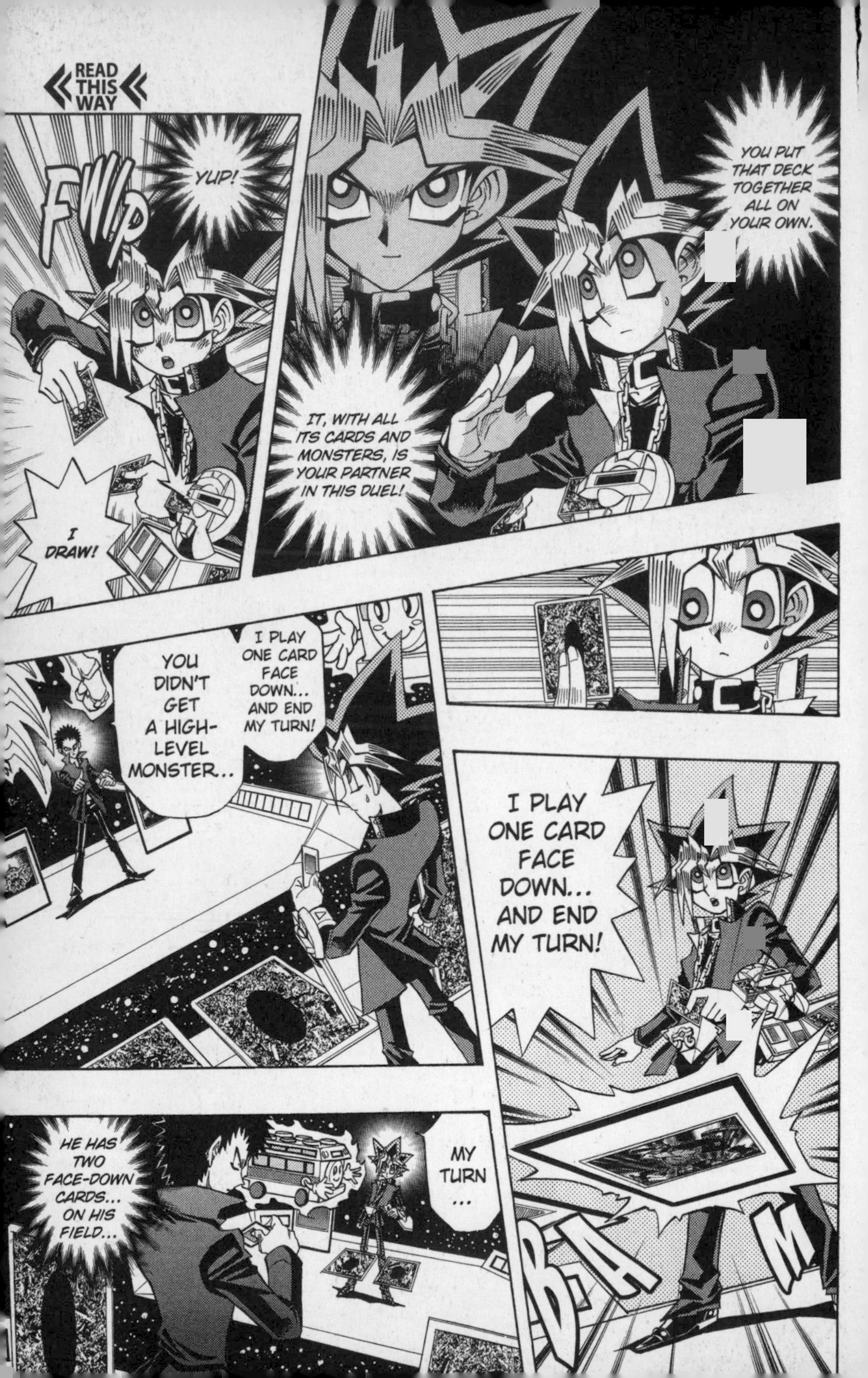

READ THIS WAY
YOU PUT THAT DECK TOGETHER ALL ON YOUR OWN.
IT, WITH ALL ITS CARDS AND MONSTERS, IS YOUR PARTNER IN THIS DUEL!
YUP!
FWIP
I DRAW!
I PLAY ONE CARD FACE DOWN... AND END MY TURN!
YOU DIDN'T GET A HIGH-LEVEL MONSTER...
I PLAY ONE CARD FACE DOWN... AND END MY TURN!
BAM
MY TURN...
HE HAS TWO FACE-DOWN CARDS... ON HIS FIELD...

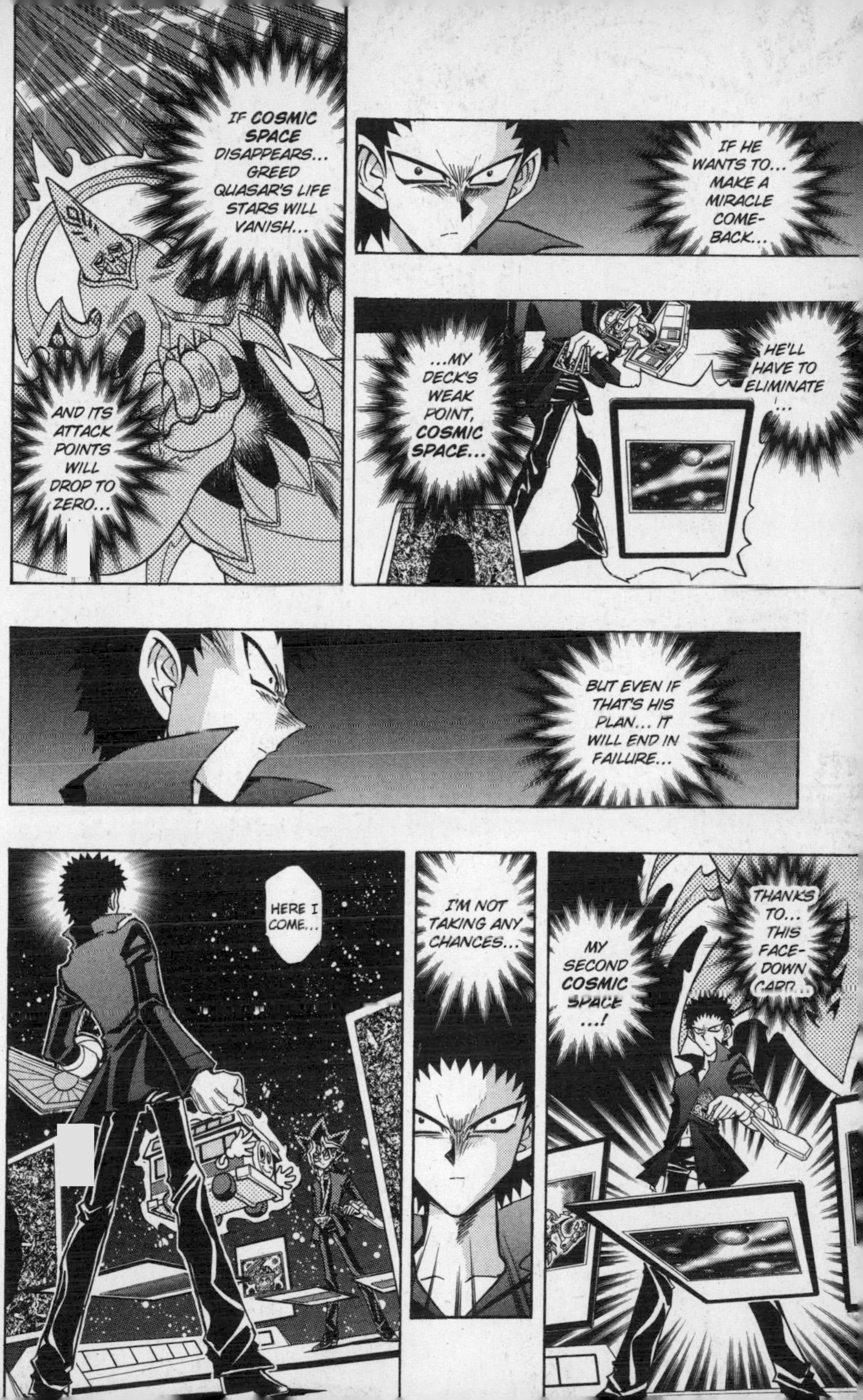
IF HE WANTS TO... MAKE A MIRACLE COME-BACK...
HE'LL HAVE TO ELIMINATE ...
...MY DECK'S WEAK POINT, COSMIC SPACE...
IF COSMIC SPACE DISAPPEARS... GREED QUASAR'S LIFE STARS WILL VANISH...
AND ITS ATTACK POINTS WILL DROP TO ZERO...
BUT EVEN IF THAT'S HIS PLAN... IT WILL END IN FAILURE...
THANKS TO... THIS FACE-DOWN CARD...
MY SECOND COSMIC SPACE ...!
I'M NOT TAKING ANY CHANCES...
HERE I COME...

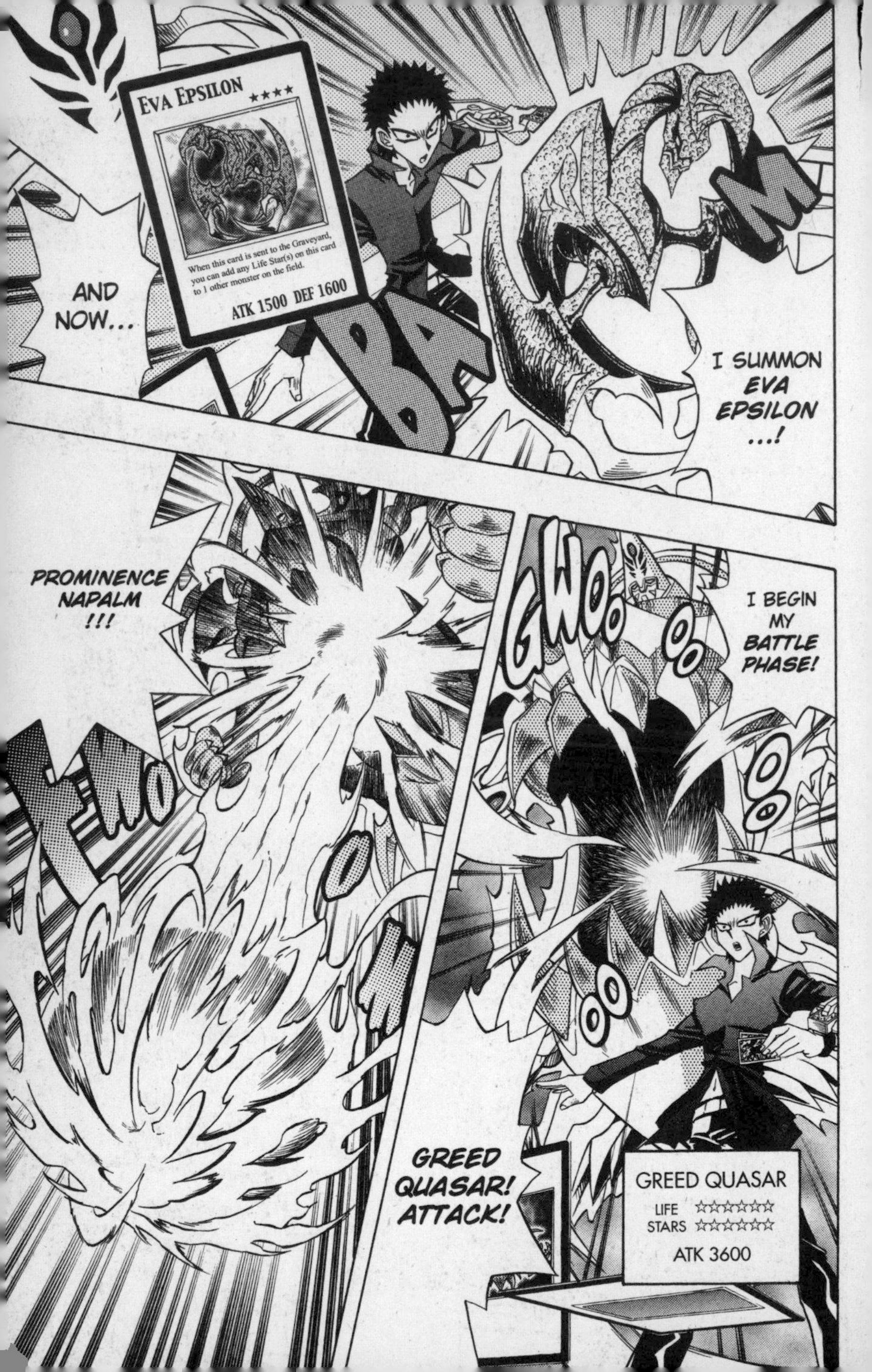
EVA EPSILON ★★★★
When this card is sent to the Graveyard, you can add any Life Star(s) on this card to 1 other monster on the field.
ATK 1500 DEF 1600
AND NOW...
I SUMMON EVA EPSILON ...!
I BEGIN MY BATTLE PHASE!
GREED QUASAR! ATTACK!
GREED QUASAR
LIFE ☆☆☆☆☆☆☆
STARS ☆☆☆☆☆☆☆
ATK 3600
PROMINENCE NAPALM !!!

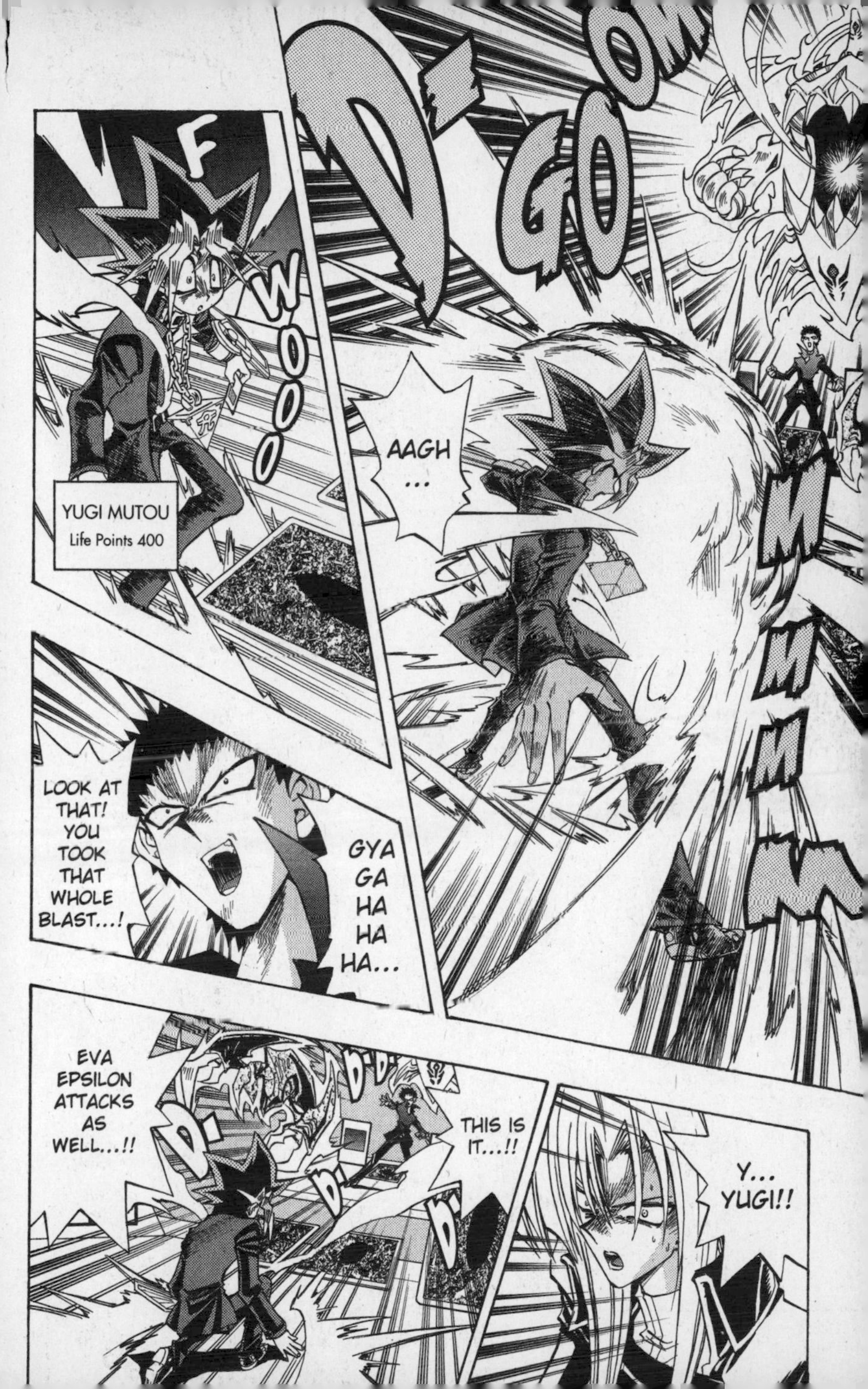
DGOOOM
AAGH...
MMMMM
FWOOOO
YUGI MUTOU
Life Points 400
GYA GA HA HA HA...
LOOK AT THAT! YOU TOOK THAT WHOLE BLAST...!
Y... YUGI!!
THIS IS IT...!!
EVA EPSILON ATTACKS AS WELL...!!

READ THIS WAY

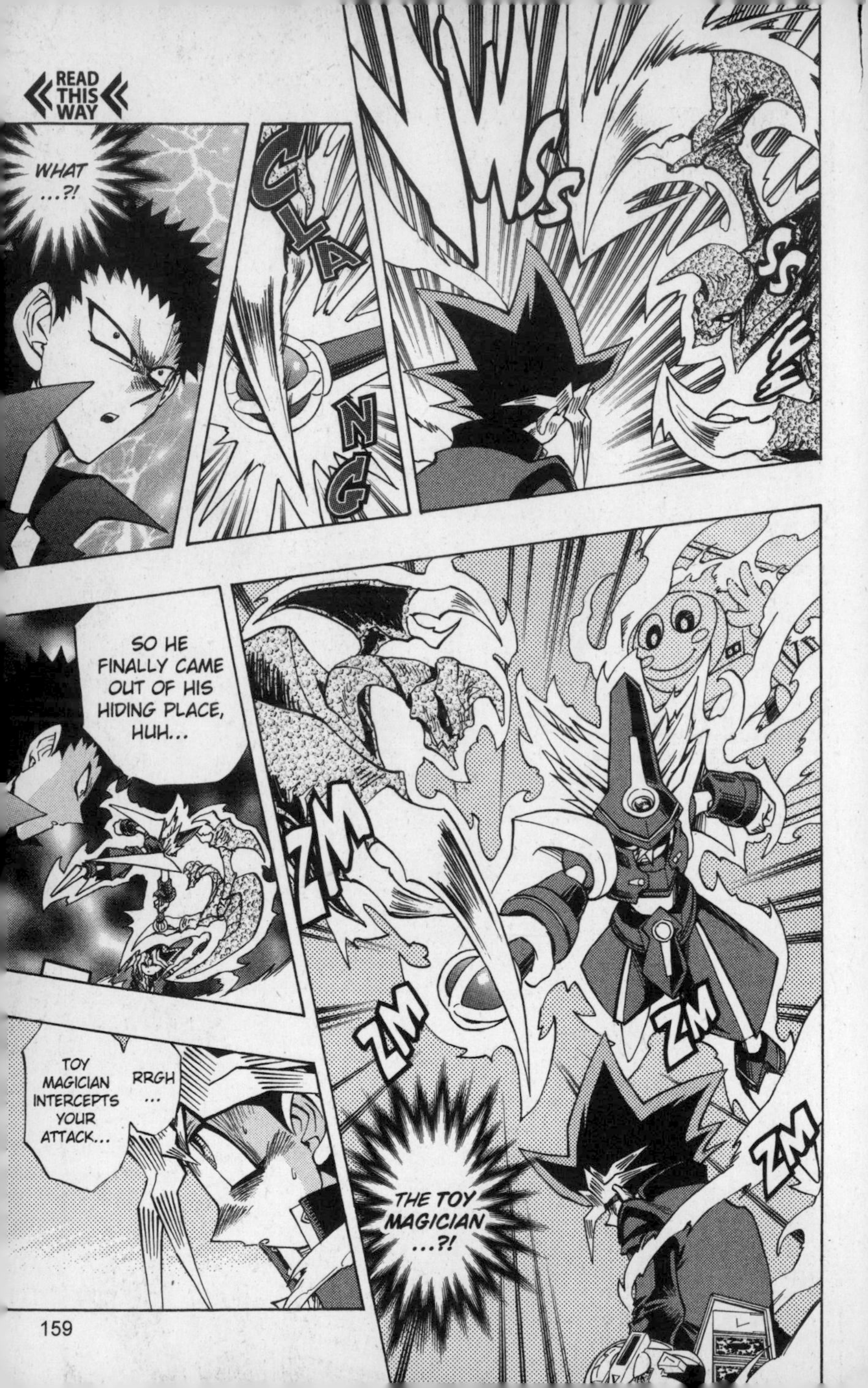

CLANG
WHAT ...?!
ZM
ZM
ZM
ZM
ZM
THE TOY MAGICIAN ...?!
SO HE FINALLY CAME OUT OF HIS HIDING PLACE, HUH...
TOY MAGICIAN INTERCEPTS YOUR ATTACK...
RRGH ...

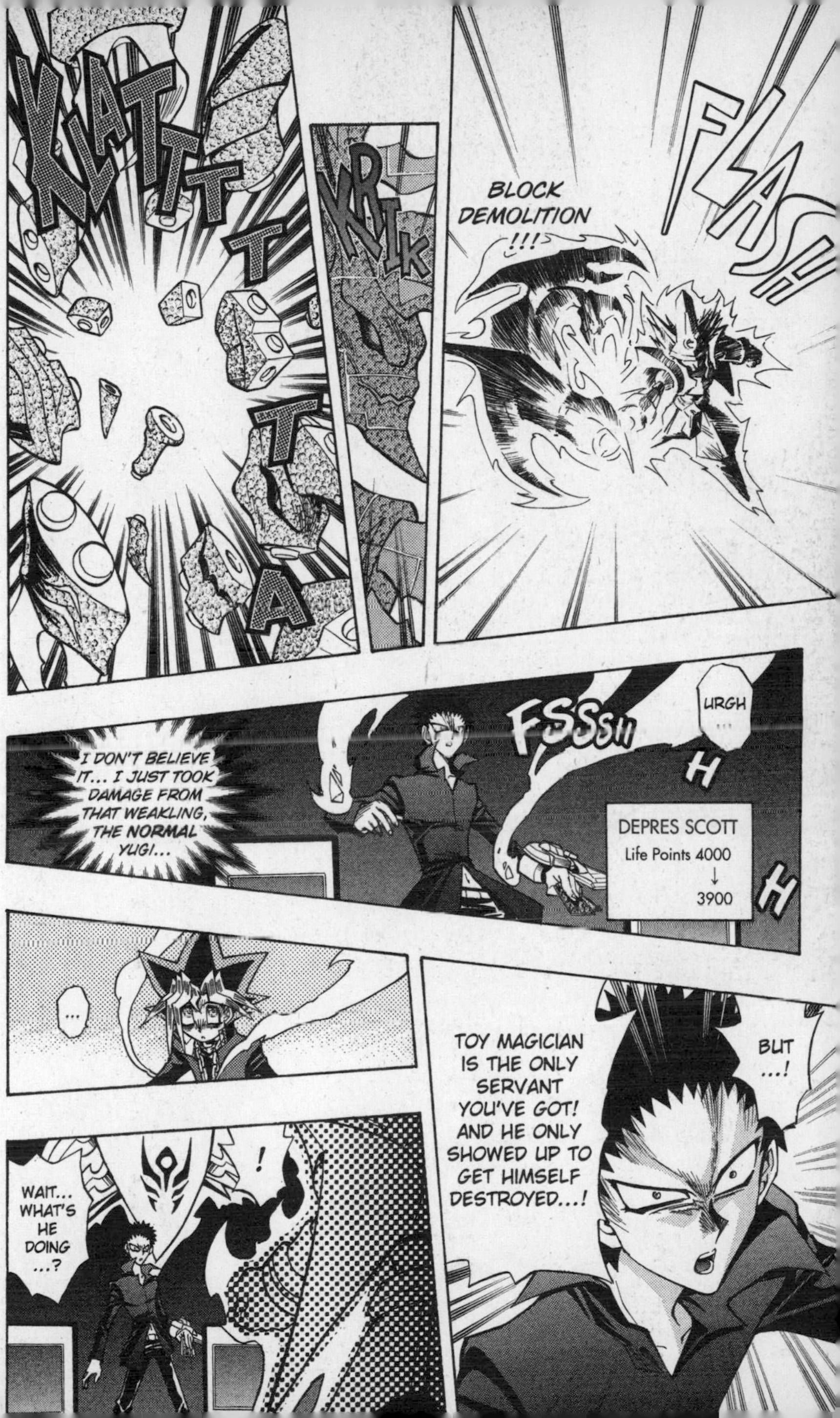
FLASH
BLOCK DEMOLITION !!!
KRIK
KLATTTTTA
URGH...
FSSSHHH
I DON'T BELIEVE IT... I JUST TOOK DAMAGE FROM THAT WEAKLING, THE NORMAL YUGI...
DEPRES SCOTT
Life Points 4000
↓
3900
BUT...!
TOY MAGICIAN IS THE ONLY SERVANT YOU'VE GOT! AND HE ONLY SHOWED UP TO GET HIMSELF DESTROYED...!
...
!
WAIT... WHAT'S HE DOING...?

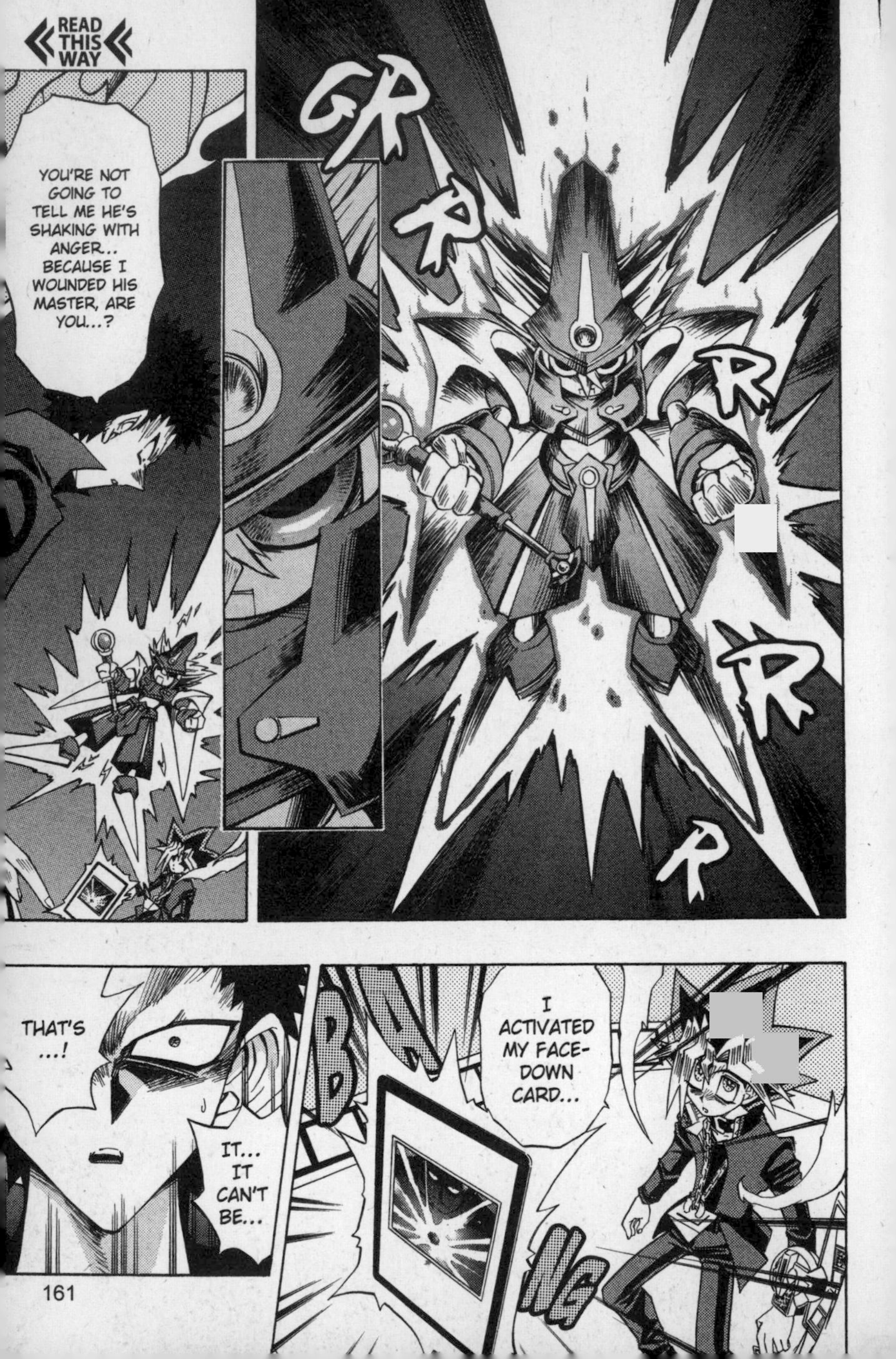
READ THIS WAY
GR
R
R
R
R
YOU'RE NOT GOING TO TELL ME HE'S SHAKING WITH ANGER... BECAUSE I WOUNDED HIS MASTER, ARE YOU...?
I ACTIVATED MY FACE-DOWN CARD...
BA
NG
THAT'S ...!
IT... IT CAN'T BE...

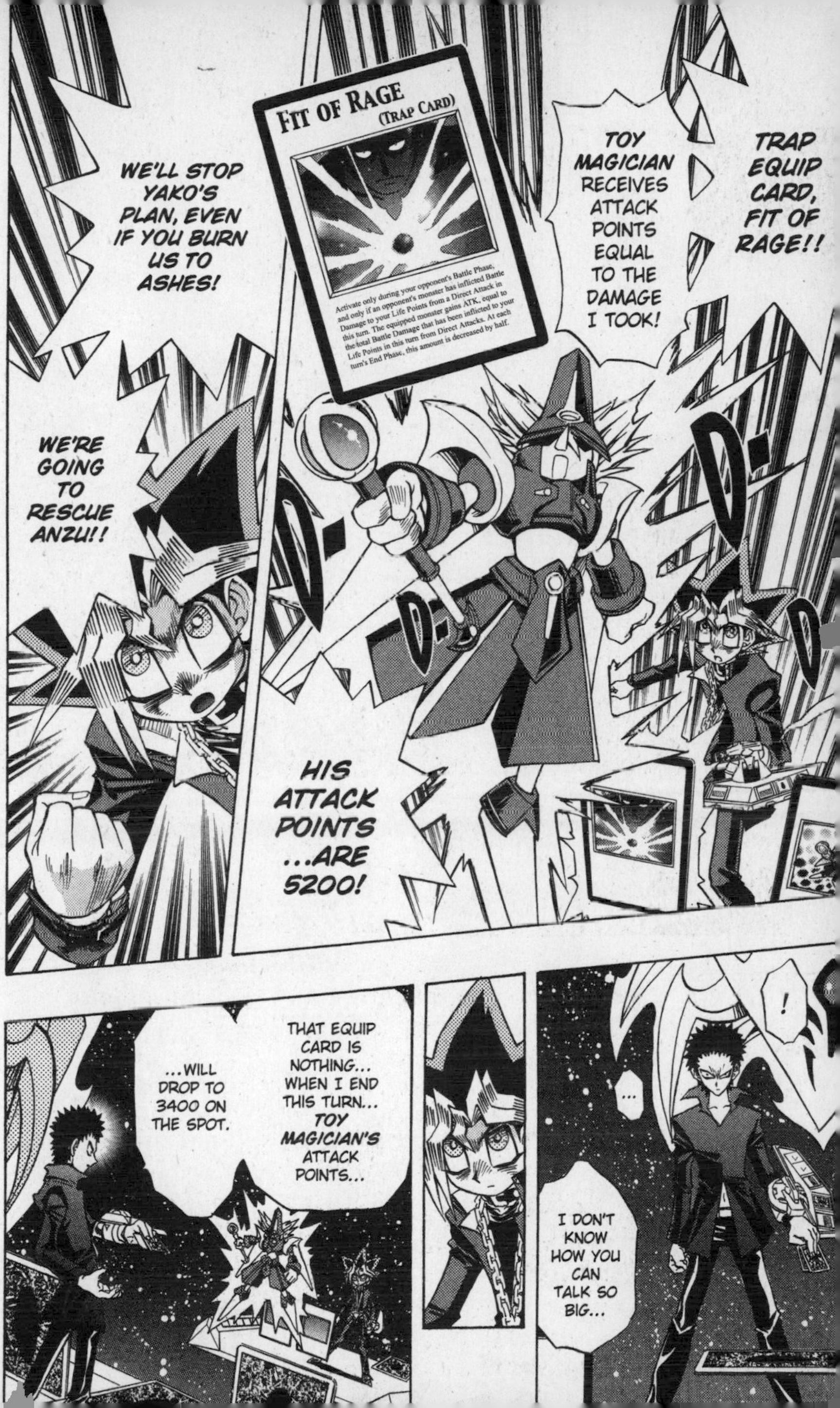
TRAP EQUIP CARD, FIT OF RAGE!!
TOY MAGICIAN RECEIVES ATTACK POINTS EQUAL TO THE DAMAGE I TOOK!
FIT OF RAGE (TRAP CARD)
Activate only during your opponent's Battle Phase, and only if an opponent's monster has inflicted Battle Damage to your Life Points from a Direct Attack in this turn. The equipped monster gains ATK, equal to the total Battle Damage that has been inflicted to your Life Points in this turn from Direct Attacks. At each turn's End Phase, this amount is decreased by half.
HIS ATTACK POINTS ...ARE 5200!
WE'LL STOP YAKO'S PLAN, EVEN IF YOU BURN US TO ASHES!
WE'RE GOING TO RESCUE ANZU!!
!
...
I DON'T KNOW HOW YOU CAN TALK SO BIG...
THAT EQUIP CARD IS NOTHING... WHEN I END THIS TURN... TOY MAGICIAN'S ATTACK POINTS...
...WILL DROP TO 3400 ON THE SPOT.

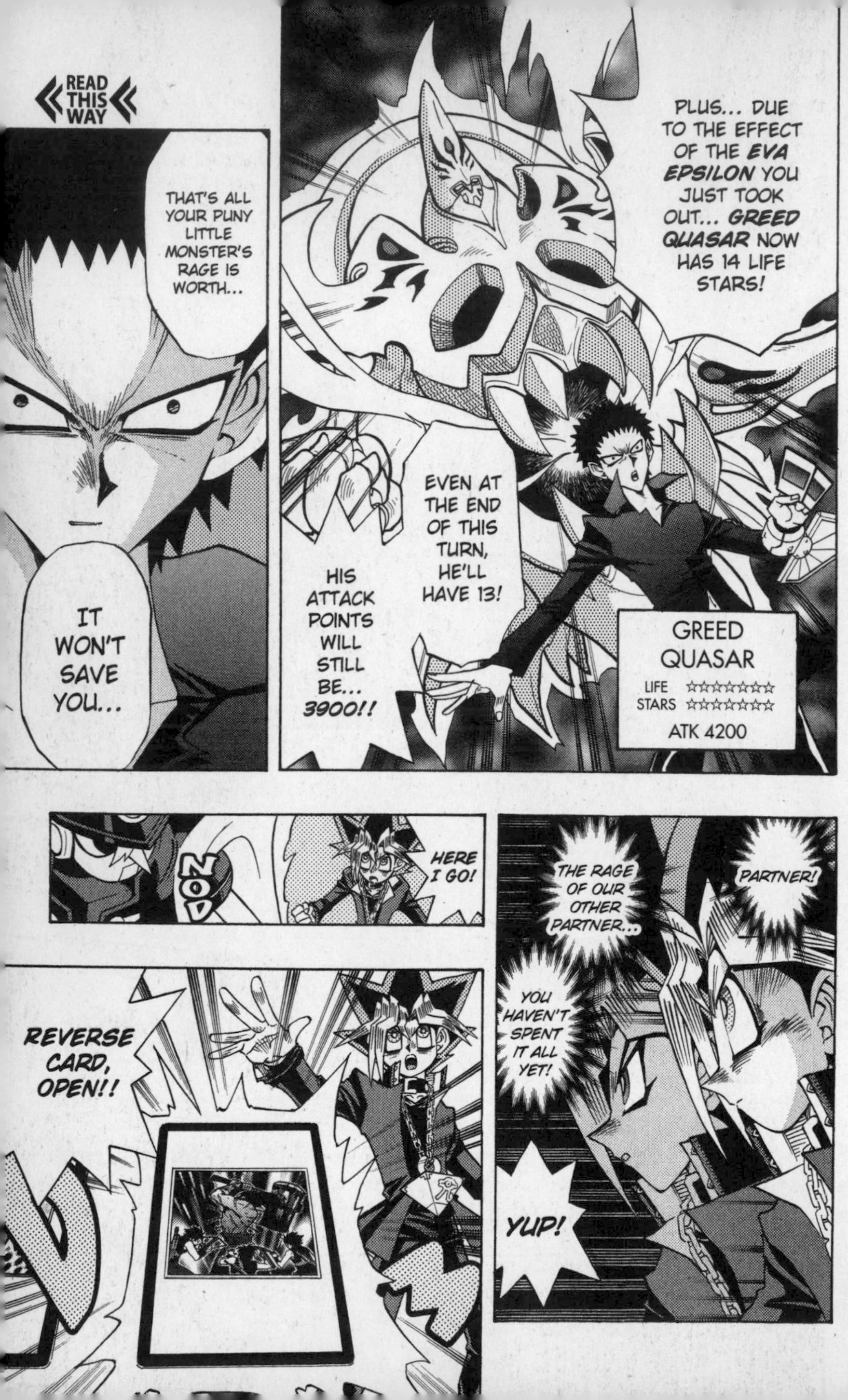
READ THIS WAY
PLUS... DUE TO THE EFFECT OF THE EVA EPSILON YOU JUST TOOK OUT... GREED QUASAR NOW HAS 14 LIFE STARS!
EVEN AT THE END OF THIS TURN, HE'LL HAVE 13!
HIS ATTACK POINTS WILL STILL BE... 3900!!
GREED QUASAR
LIFE STARS ☆☆☆☆☆☆☆☆☆☆☆☆☆☆
ATK 4200
THAT'S ALL YOUR PUNY LITTLE MONSTER'S RAGE IS WORTH...
IT WON'T SAVE YOU...
PARTNER!
THE RAGE OF OUR OTHER PARTNER...
YOU HAVEN'T SPENT IT ALL YET!
YUP!
HERE I GO!
NOD
REVERSE CARD, OPEN!!

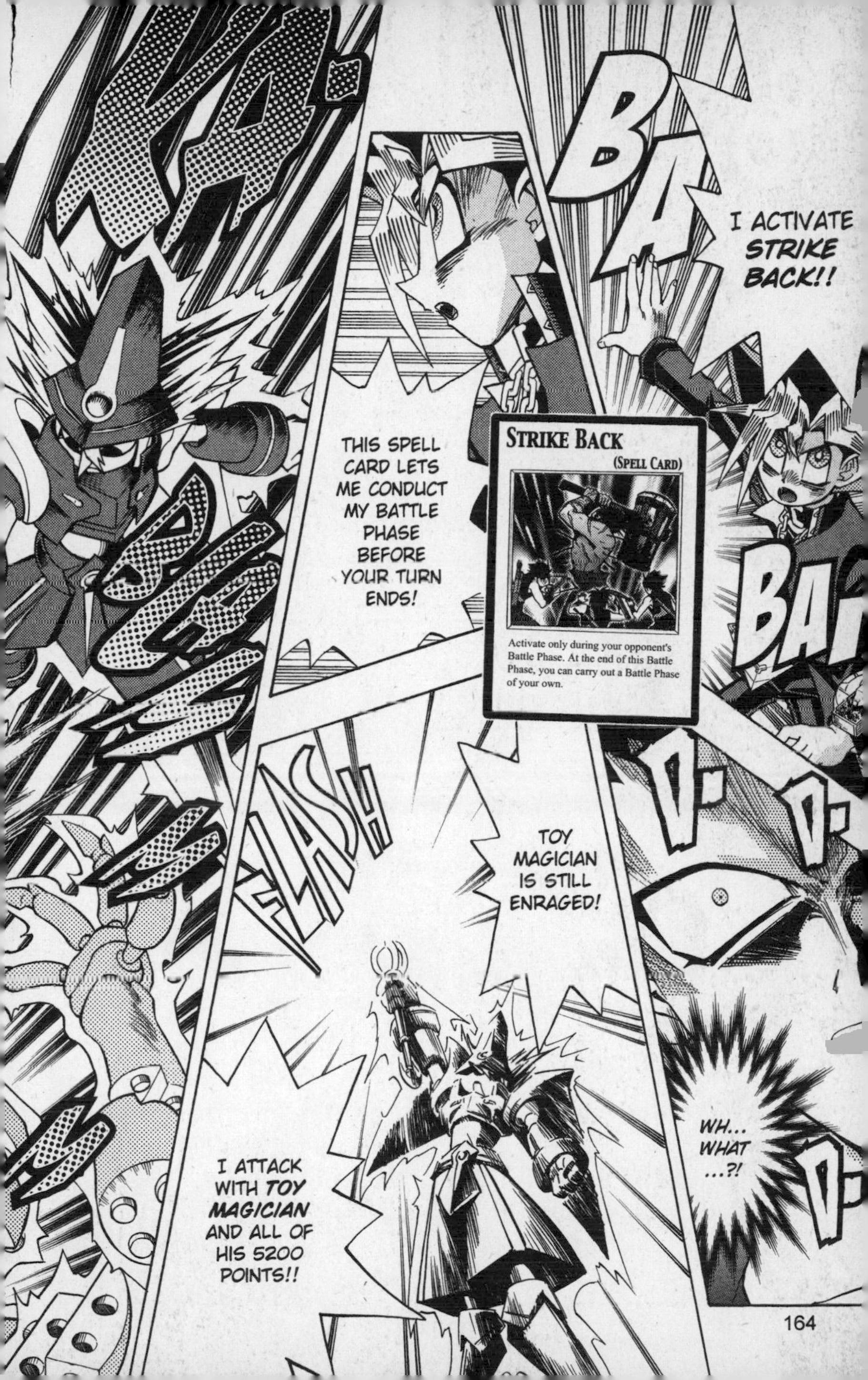
BA
I ACTIVATE STRIKE BACK!!
BA
STRIKE BACK
(SPELL CARD)
Activate only during your opponent's Battle Phase. At the end of this Battle Phase, you can carry out a Battle Phase of your own.
THIS SPELL CARD LETS ME CONDUCT MY BATTLE PHASE BEFORE YOUR TURN ENDS!
WH... WHAT ...?!
TOY MAGICIAN IS STILL ENRAGED!
I ATTACK WITH TOY MAGICIAN AND ALL OF HIS 5200 POINTS!!

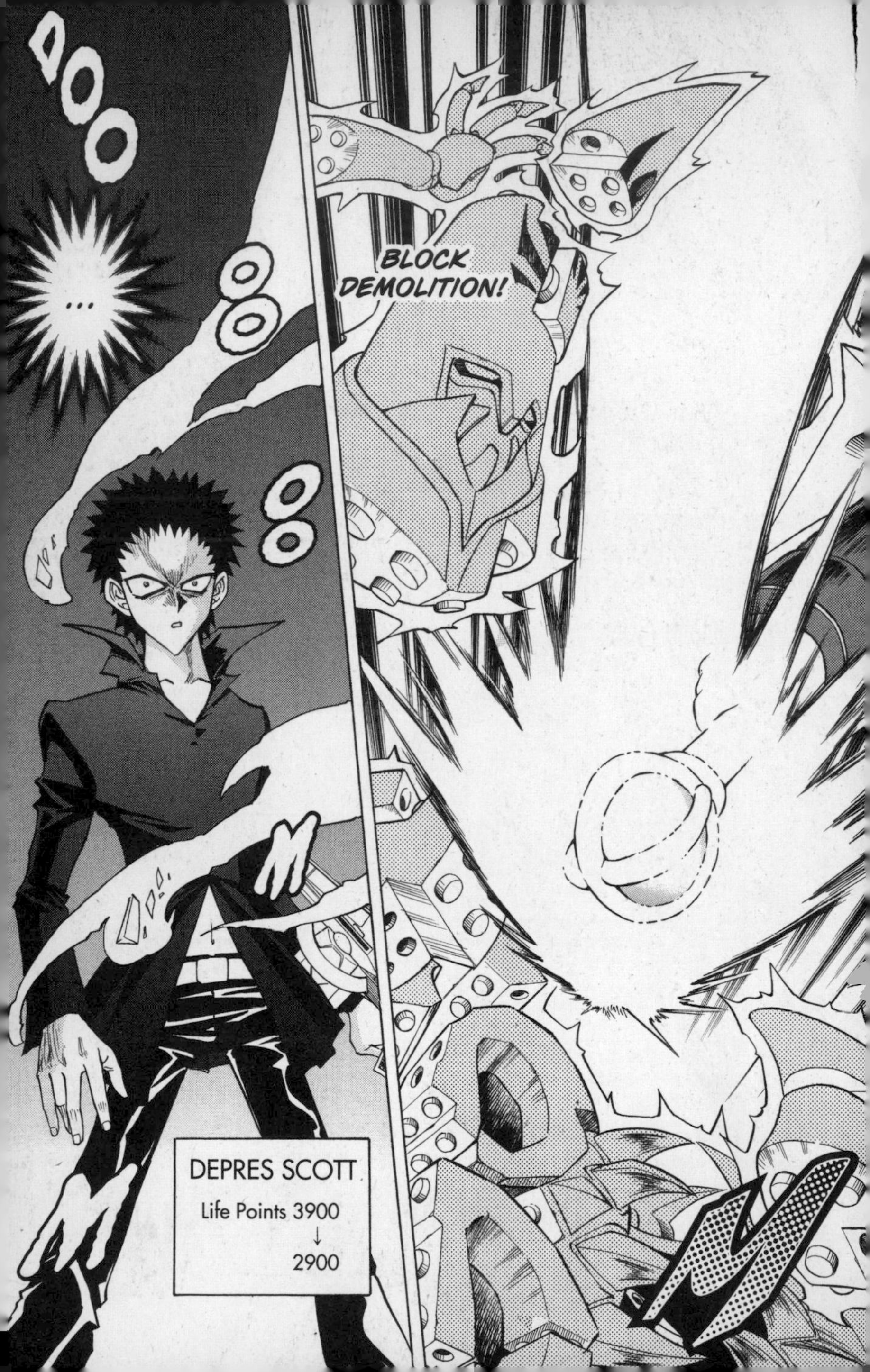
BLOCK DEMOLITION!
...
DEPRES SCOTT
Life Points 3900
↓
2900

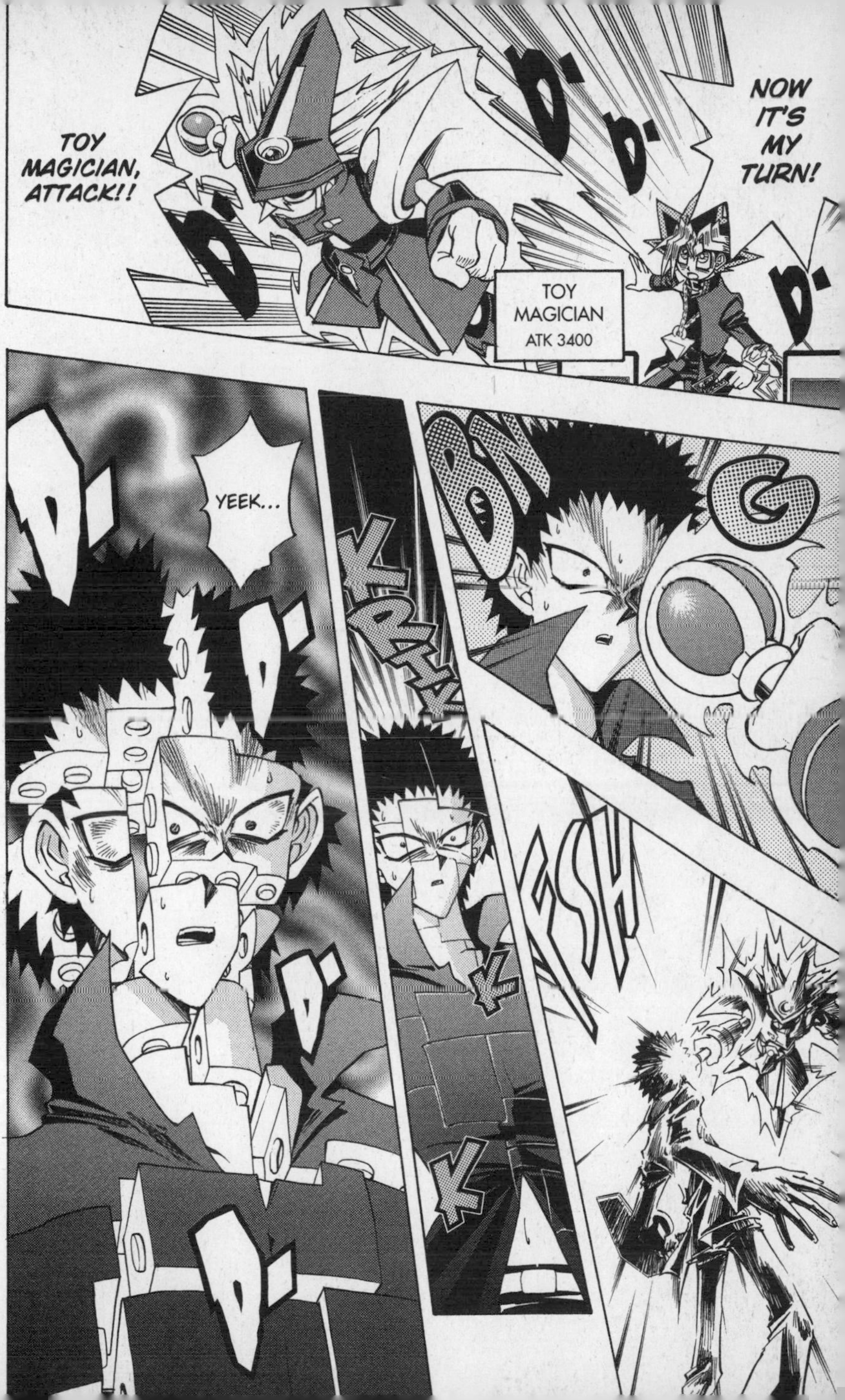
NOW IT'S MY TURN!
TOY MAGICIAN, ATTACK!!
TOY MAGICIAN
ATK 3400
YEEK...

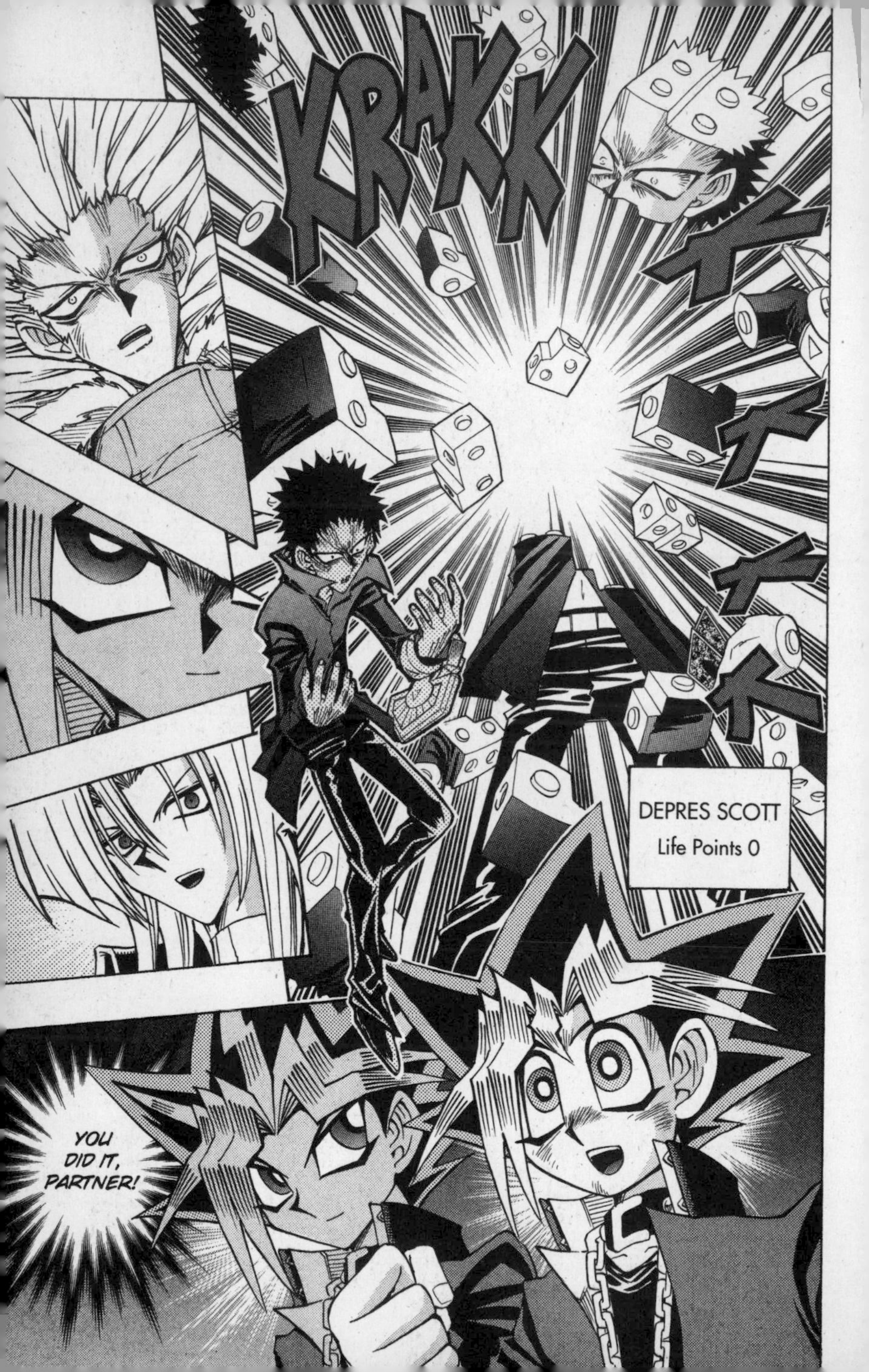
KRAKK
DEPRES SCOTT
Life Points 0
YOU DID IT, PARTNER!

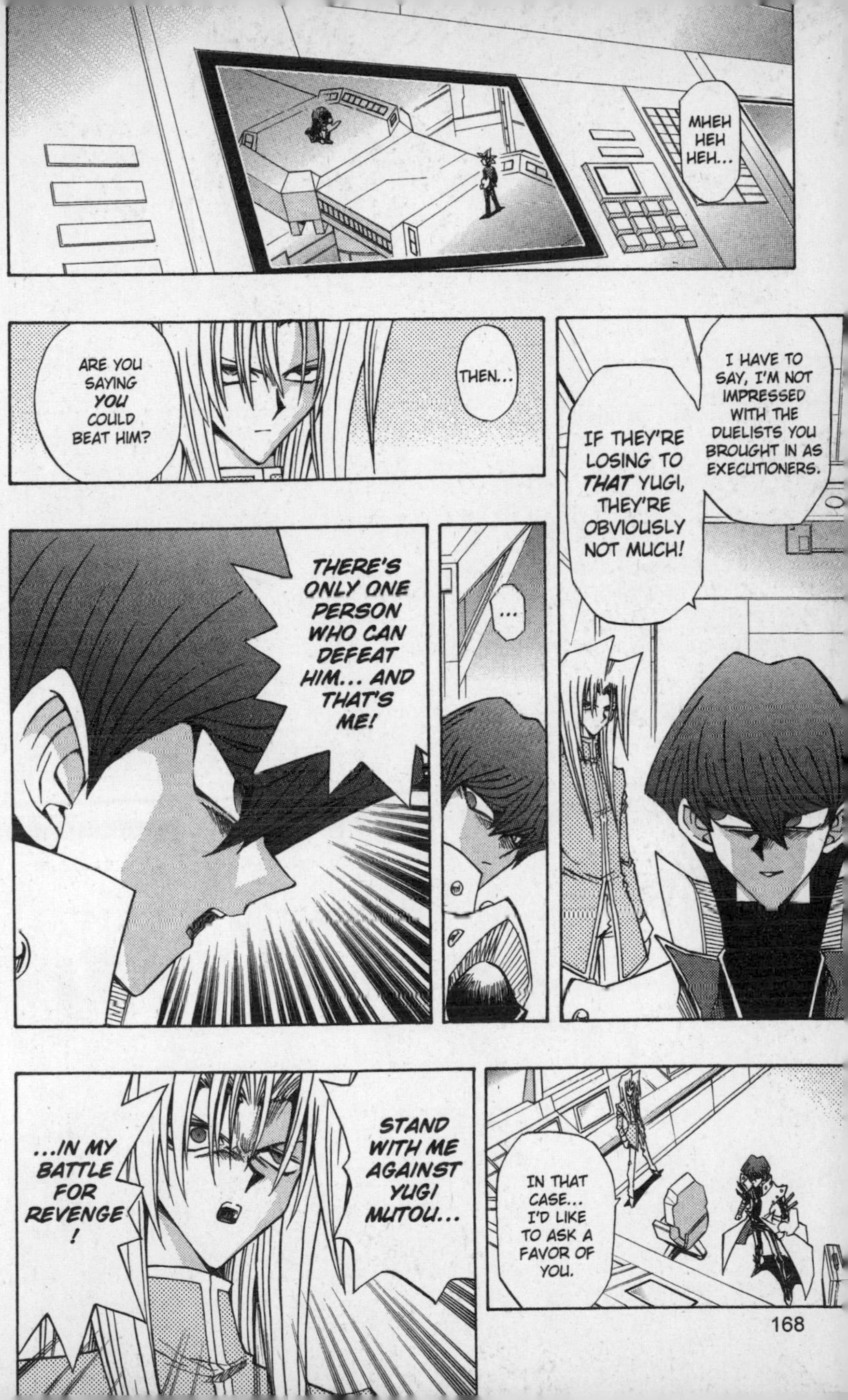
MHEH HEH HEH...
I HAVE TO SAY, I'M NOT IMPRESSED WITH THE DUELISTS YOU BROUGHT IN AS EXECUTIONERS.
IF THEY'RE LOSING TO THAT YUGI, THEY'RE OBVIOUSLY NOT MUCH!
THEN...
ARE YOU SAYING YOU COULD BEAT HIM?
...
THERE'S ONLY ONE PERSON WHO CAN DEFEAT HIM... AND THAT'S ME!
IN THAT CASE... I'D LIKE TO ASK A FAVOR OF YOU.
STAND WITH ME AGAINST YUGI MUTOU...
...IN MY BATTLE FOR REVENGE!

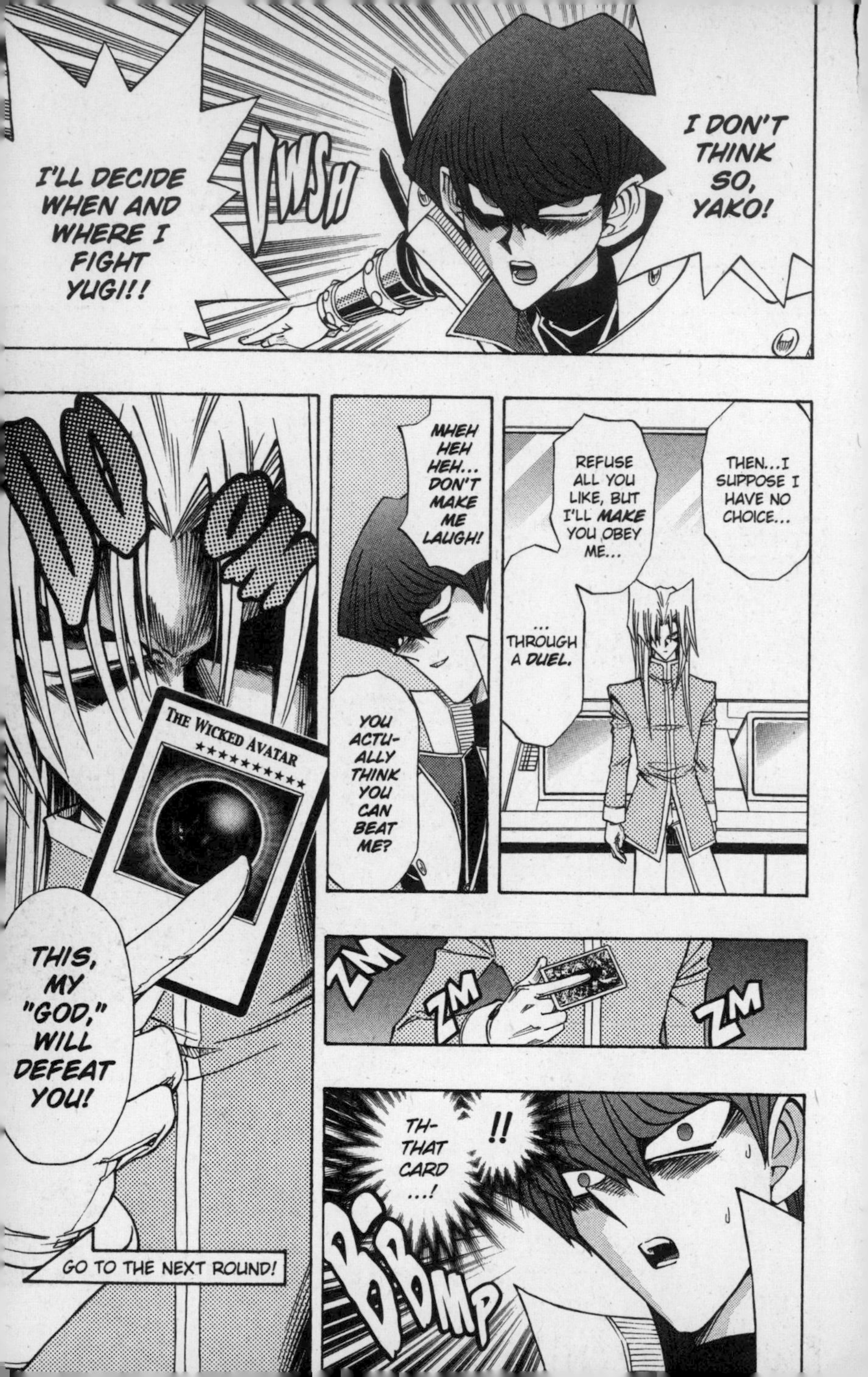
I DON'T THINK SO, YAKO!
VWSH
I'LL DECIDE WHEN AND WHERE I FIGHT YUGI!!
THEN...I SUPPOSE I HAVE NO CHOICE...
REFUSE ALL YOU LIKE, BUT I'LL MAKE YOU OBEY ME...
...THROUGH A DUEL.
MHEH HEH HEH... DON'T MAKE ME LAUGH!
YOU ACTU-ALLY THINK YOU CAN BEAT ME?
ZM
ZM
ZM
!!
TH-THAT CARD ...!
BBOMP
DOOM
THE WICKED AVATAR
THIS, MY "GOD," WILL DEFEAT YOU!
GO TO THE NEXT ROUND!

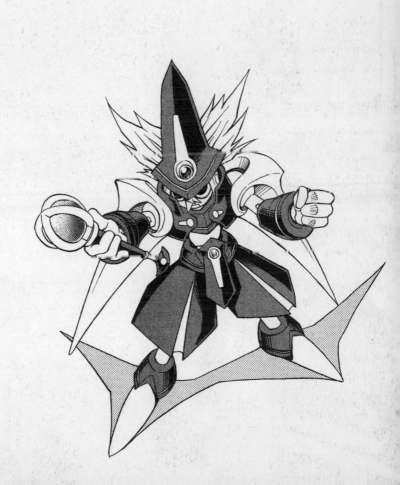

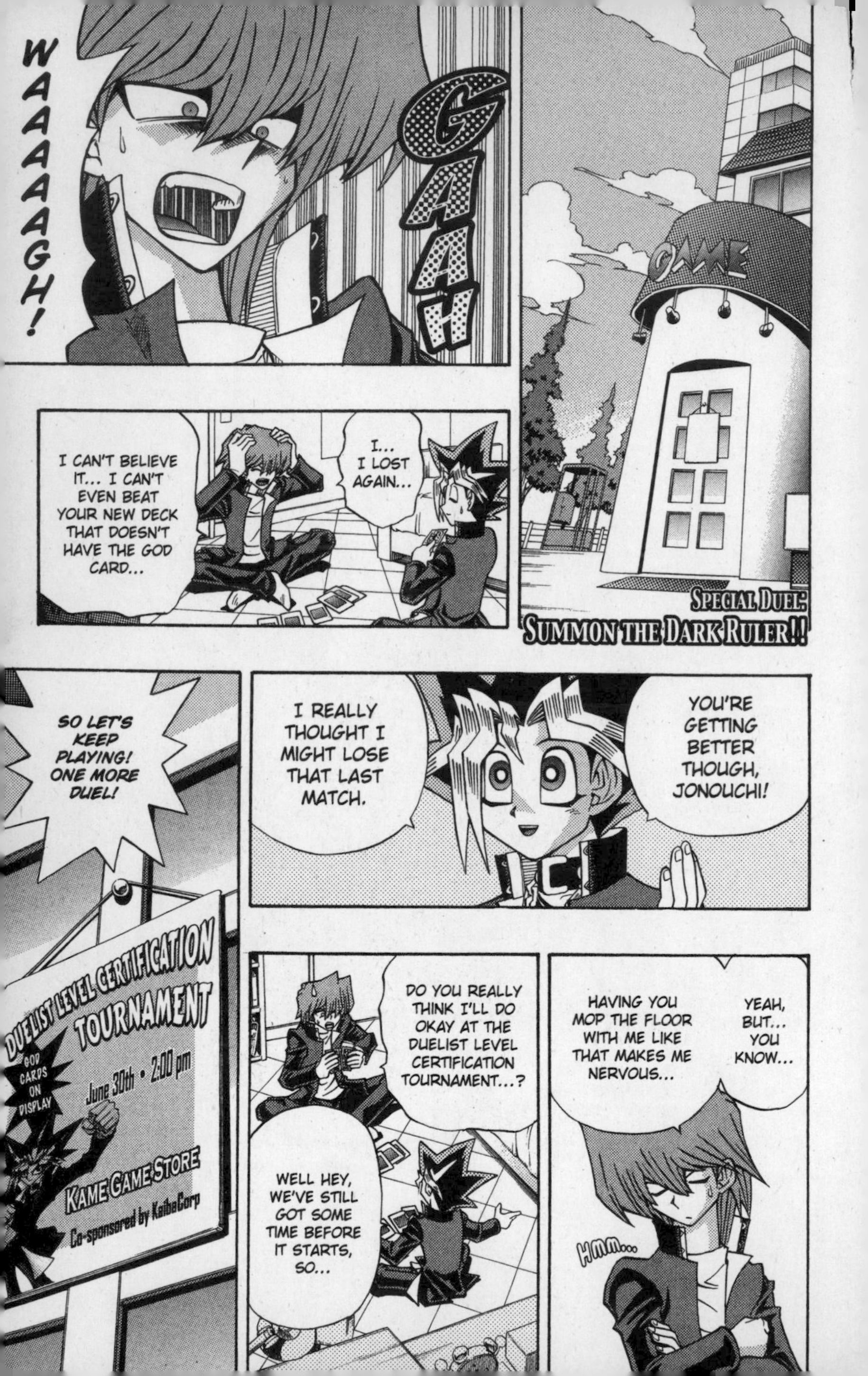
GAME
SPECIAL DUEL: SUMMON THE DARK RULER!!
WAAAAAAGH!
GAAH
I... I LOST AGAIN...
I CAN'T BELIEVE IT... I CAN'T EVEN BEAT YOUR NEW DECK THAT DOESN'T HAVE THE GOD CARD...
YOU'RE GETTING BETTER THOUGH, JONOUCHI!
I REALLY THOUGHT I MIGHT LOSE THAT LAST MATCH.
YEAH, BUT... YOU KNOW...
HAVING YOU MOP THE FLOOR WITH ME LIKE THAT MAKES ME NERVOUS...
HMM...
DO YOU REALLY THINK I'LL DO OKAY AT THE DUELIST LEVEL CERTIFICATION TOURNAMENT...?
WELL HEY, WE'VE STILL GOT SOME TIME BEFORE IT STARTS, SO...
SO LET'S KEEP PLAYING! ONE MORE DUEL!
DUELIST LEVEL CERTIFICATION TOURNAMENT
GOD CARDS ON DISPLAY
June 30th • 2:00 pm
KAME GAME STORE
Co-sponsored by KaibaCorp

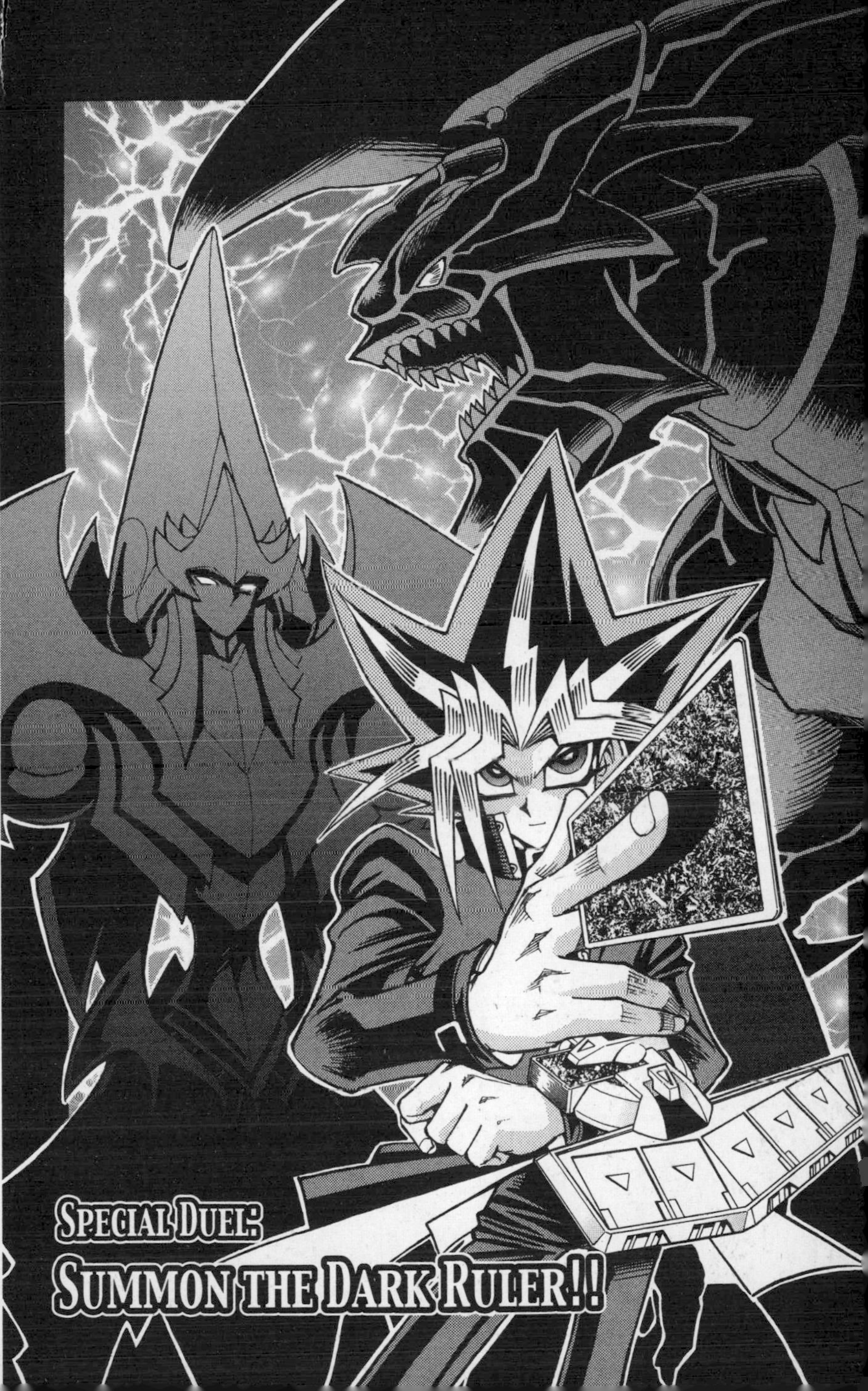
SPECIAL DUEL:
SUMMON THE DARK RULER!!

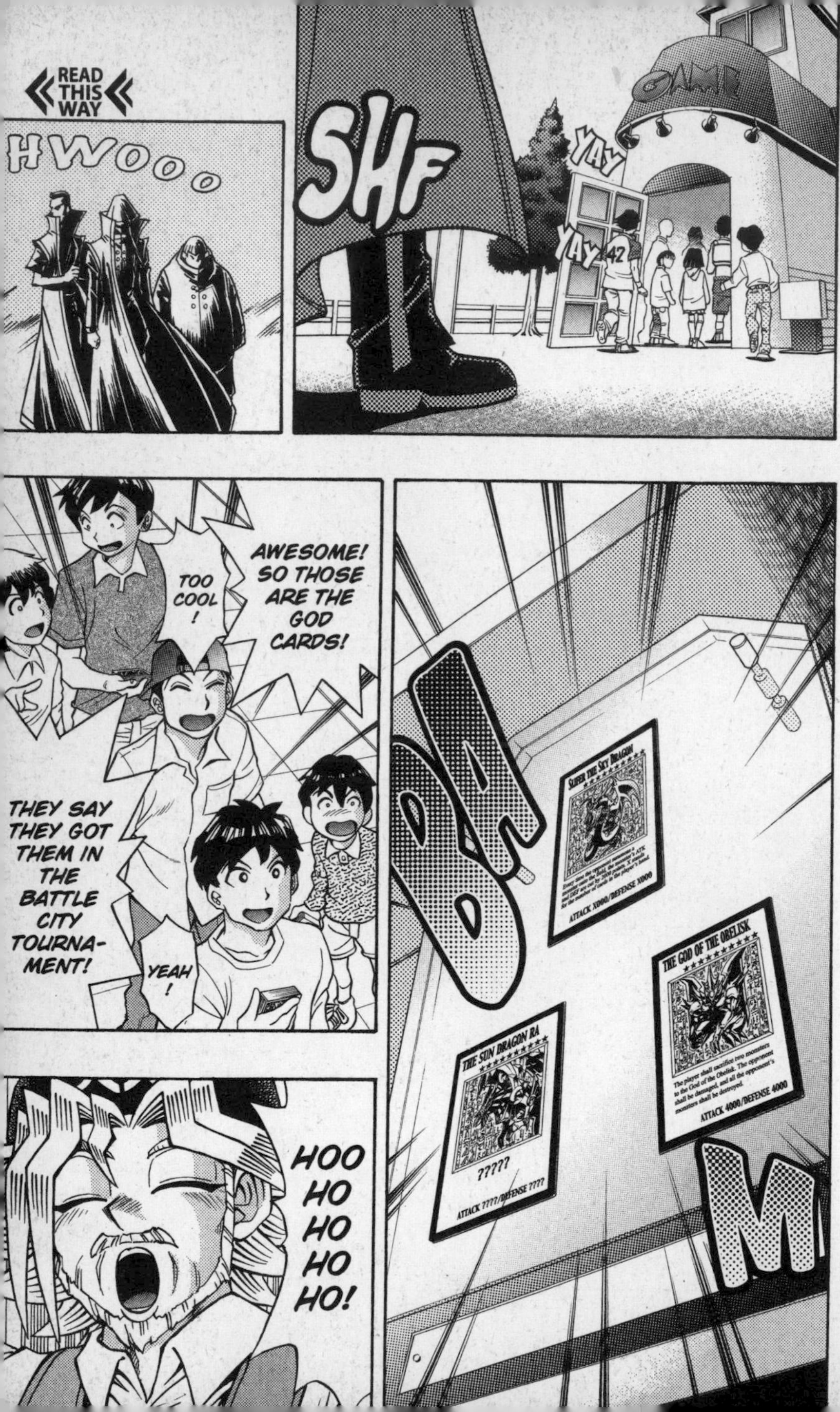
READ THIS WAY
GAME
SHF
YAY
YAY
HWOOO
SLIFER THE SKY DRAGON
ATTACK X000/DEFENSE X000
THE GOD OF THE OBELISK
The player shall sacrifice two monsters to the God of the Obelisk. The opponent shall be damaged, and all the opponent's monsters shall be destroyed.
ATTACK 4000/DEFENSE 4000
THE SUN DRAGON RA
?????
ATTACK ????/DEFENSE ????
AWESOME! SO THOSE ARE THE GOD CARDS!
TOO COOL!
THEY SAY THEY GOT THEM IN THE BATTLE CITY TOURNAMENT!
YEAH!
HOO HO HO HO HO!

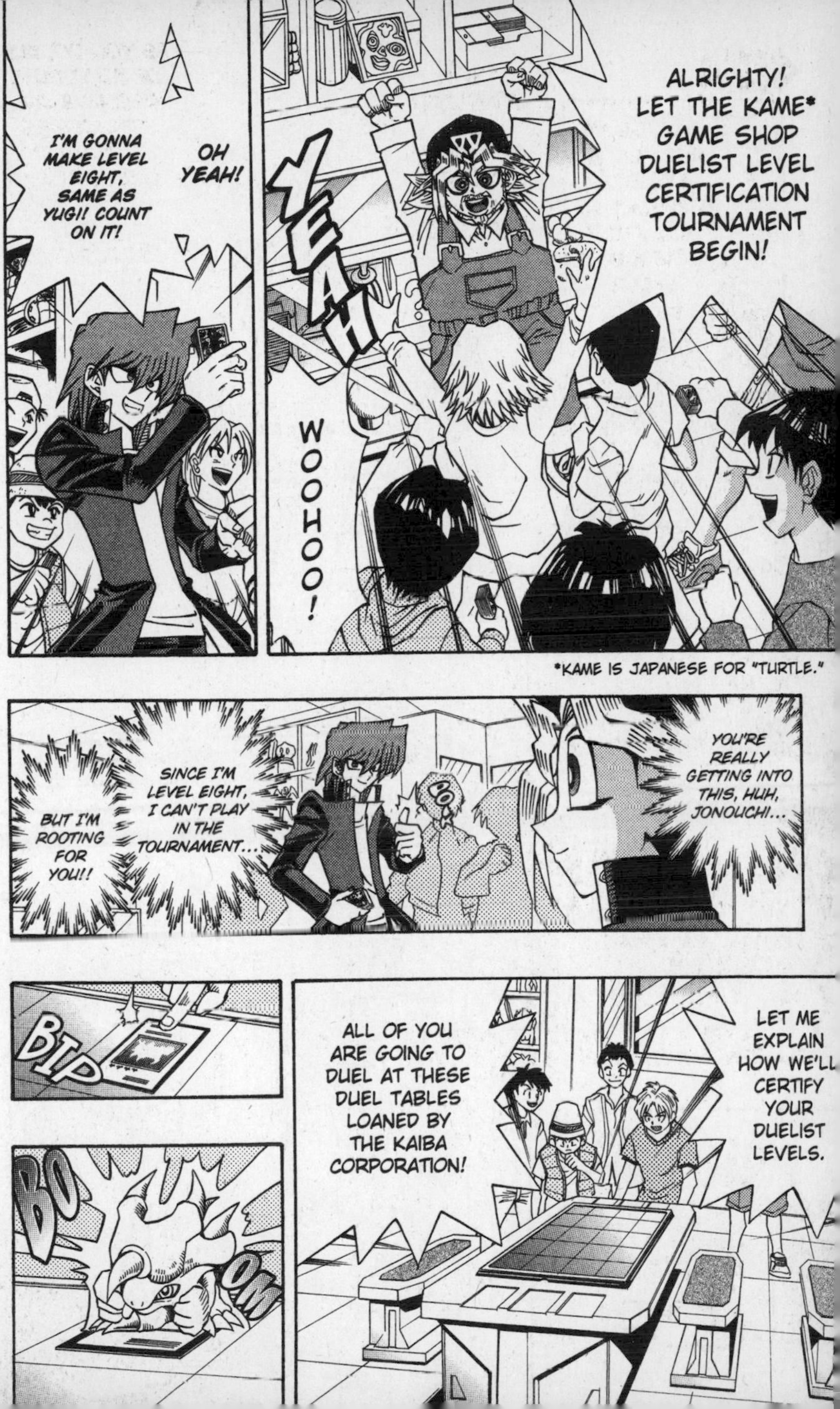
ALRIGHTY! LET THE KAME* GAME SHOP DUELIST LEVEL CERTIFICATION TOURNAMENT BEGIN!
YEAH
WOOHOO!
OH YEAH!
I'M GONNA MAKE LEVEL EIGHT, SAME AS YUGI!! COUNT ON IT!
YOU'RE REALLY GETTING INTO THIS, HUH, JONOUCHI...
BO
SINCE I'M LEVEL EIGHT, I CAN'T PLAY IN THE TOURNAMENT...
BUT I'M ROOTING FOR YOU!!
LET ME EXPLAIN HOW WE'LL CERTIFY YOUR DUELIST LEVELS.
ALL OF YOU ARE GOING TO DUEL AT THESE DUEL TABLES LOANED BY THE KAIBA CORPORATION!
BIP
BOOM

*KAME IS JAPANESE FOR "TURTLE."

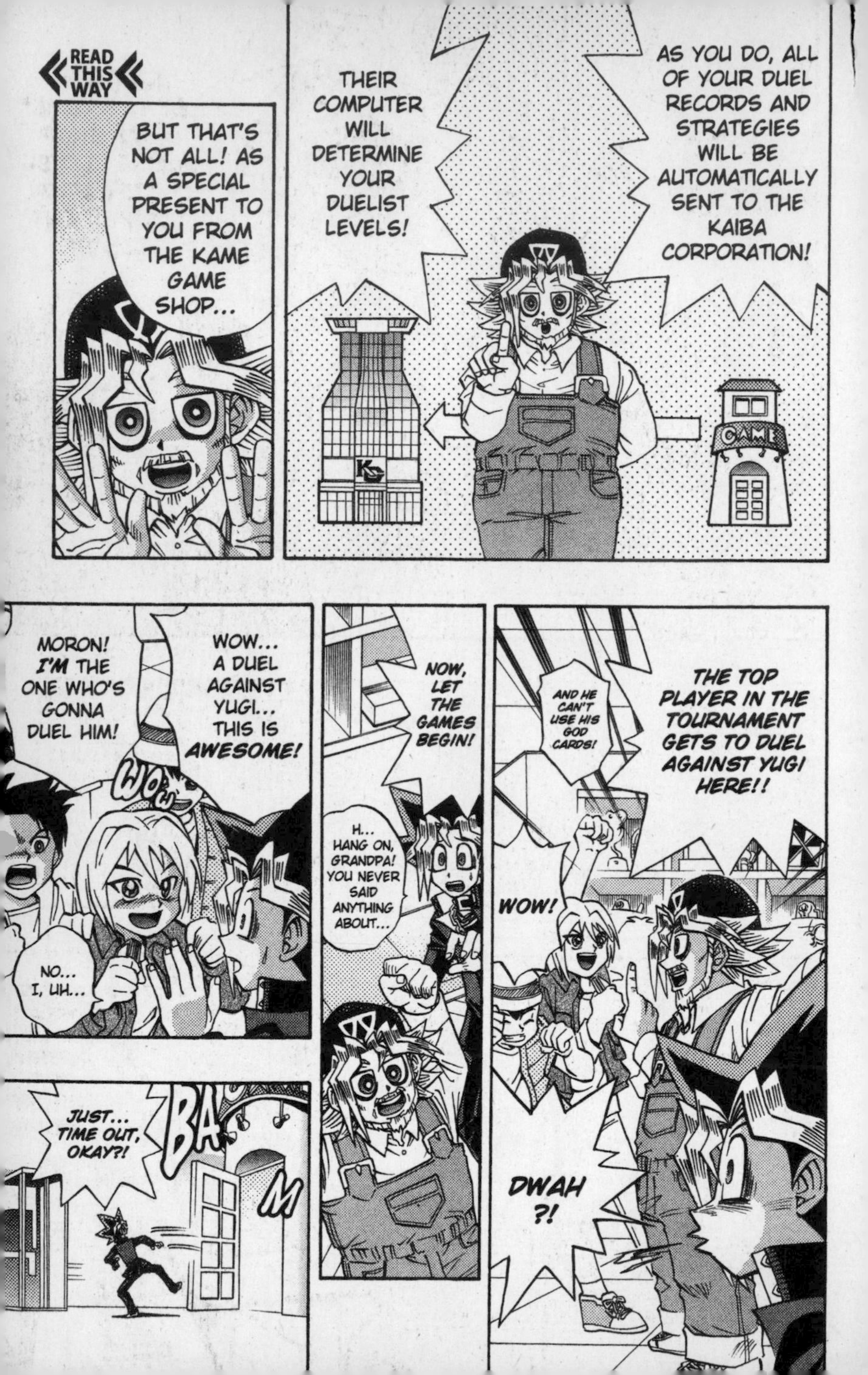
READ THIS WAY
AS YOU DO, ALL OF YOUR DUEL RECORDS AND STRATEGIES WILL BE AUTOMATICALLY SENT TO THE KAIBA CORPORATION!
THEIR COMPUTER WILL DETERMINE YOUR DUELIST LEVELS!
GAME
BUT THAT'S NOT ALL! AS A SPECIAL PRESENT TO YOU FROM THE KAME GAME SHOP...
THE TOP PLAYER IN THE TOURNAMENT GETS TO DUEL AGAINST YUGI HERE!!
AND HE CAN'T USE HIS GOD CARDS!
WOW!
DWAH ?!
NOW, LET THE GAMES BEGIN!
H... HANG ON, GRANDPA! YOU NEVER SAID ANYTHING ABOUT...
WOW... A DUEL AGAINST YUGI... THIS IS AWESOME!
MORON! I'M THE ONE WHO'S GONNA DUEL HIM!
NO... I, UH...
JUST... TIME OUT, OKAY?!
BA
M

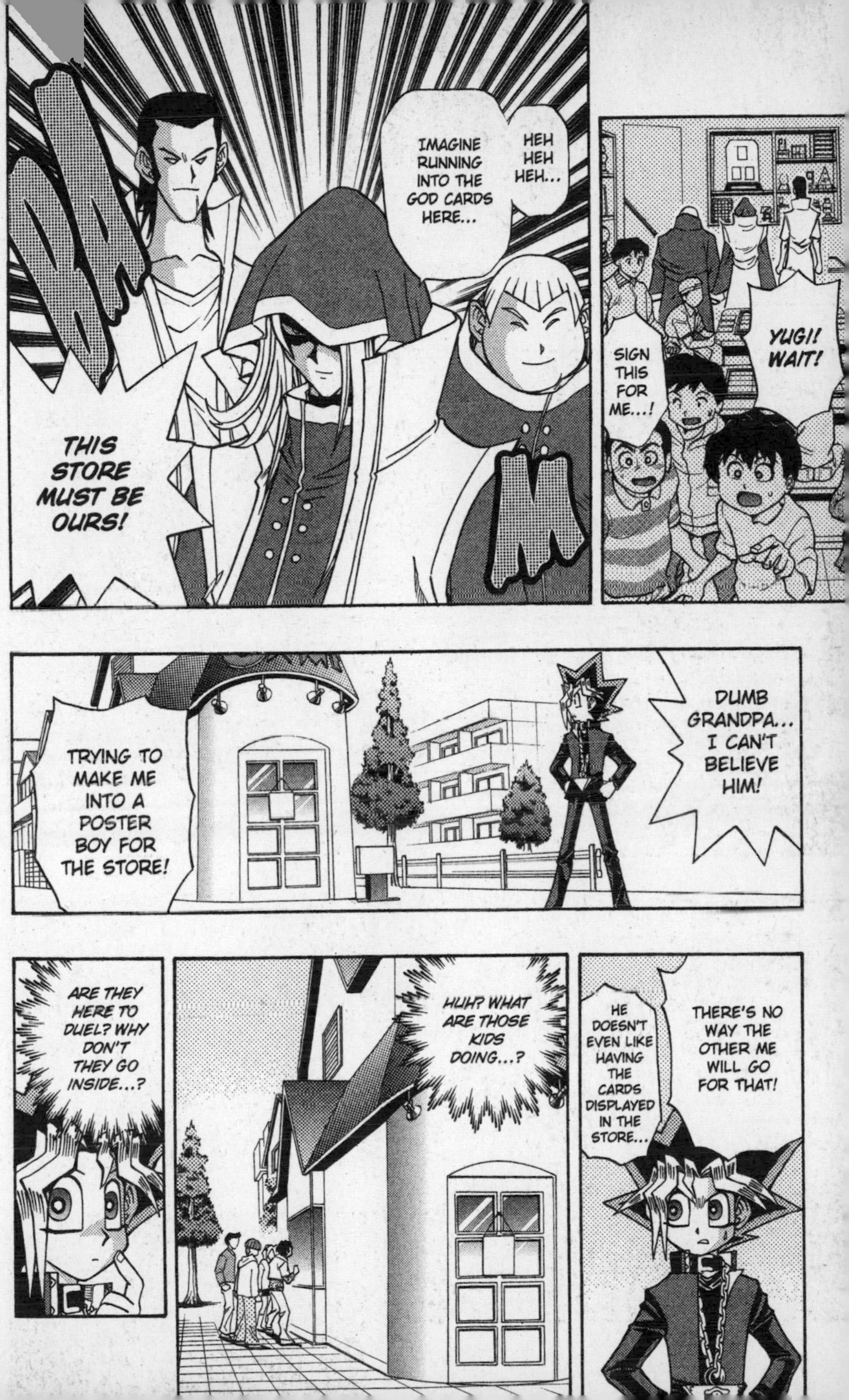
YUGI! WAIT!
SIGN THIS FOR ME...!
HEH HEH HEH...
IMAGINE RUNNING INTO THE GOD CARDS HERE...
THIS STORE MUST BE OURS!
DUMB GRANDPA... I CAN'T BELIEVE HIM!
TRYING TO MAKE ME INTO A POSTER BOY FOR THE STORE!
THERE'S NO WAY THE OTHER ME WILL GO FOR THAT!
HE DOESN'T EVEN LIKE HAVING THE CARDS DISPLAYED IN THE STORE...
HUH? WHAT ARE THOSE KIDS DOING...?
ARE THEY HERE TO DUEL? WHY DON'T THEY GO INSIDE...?

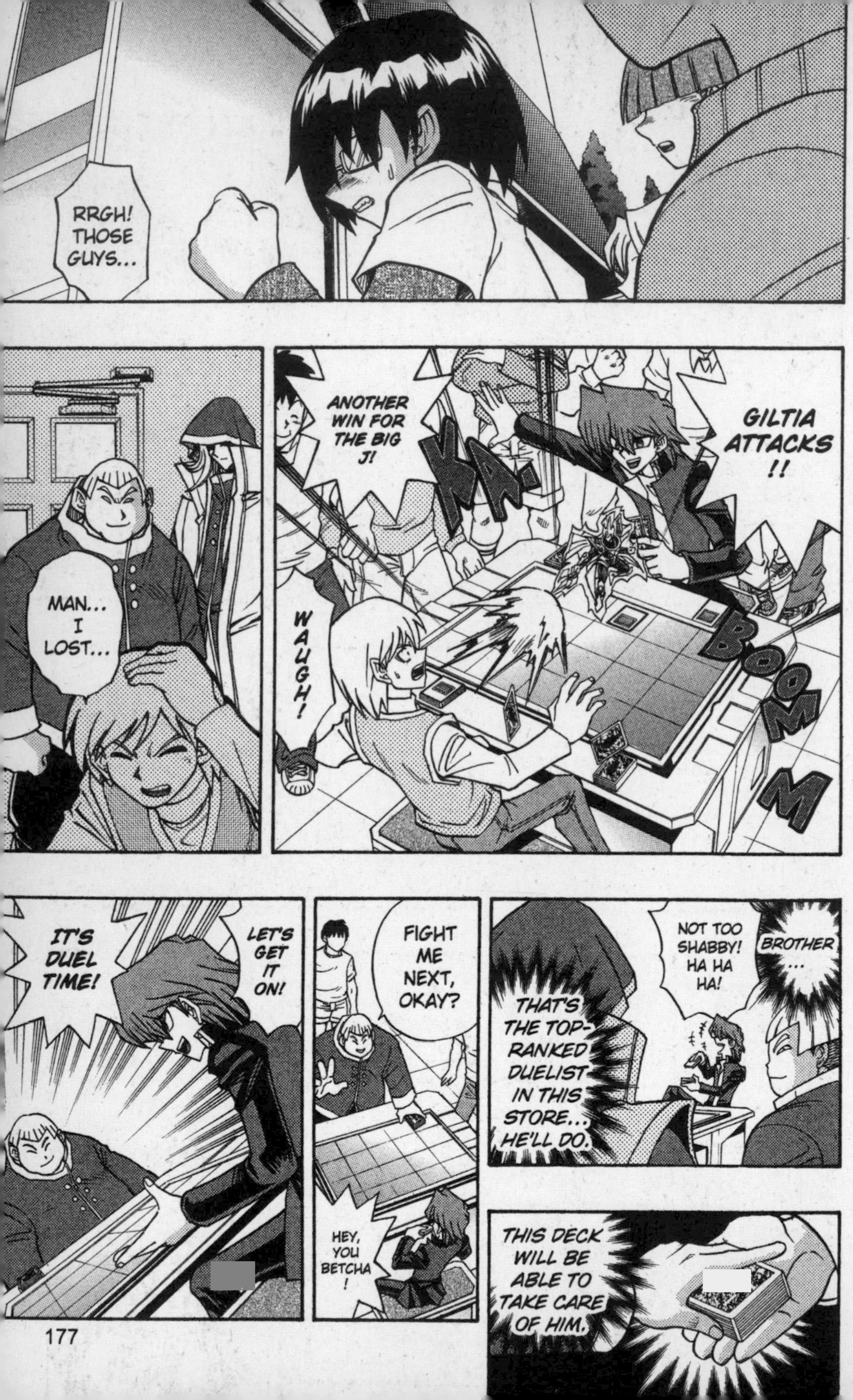
RRGH! THOSE GUYS...
GILTIA ATTACKS!!
KA-
ANOTHER WIN FOR THE BIG J!
BOOMM
WAUGH!
MAN... I LOST...
BROTHER...
NOT TOO SHABBY! HA HA HA!
THAT'S THE TOP-RANKED DUELIST IN THIS STORE... HE'LL DO.
THIS DECK WILL BE ABLE TO TAKE CARE OF HIM.
FIGHT ME NEXT, OKAY?
HEY, YOU BETCHA!
LET'S GET IT ON!
IT'S DUEL TIME!

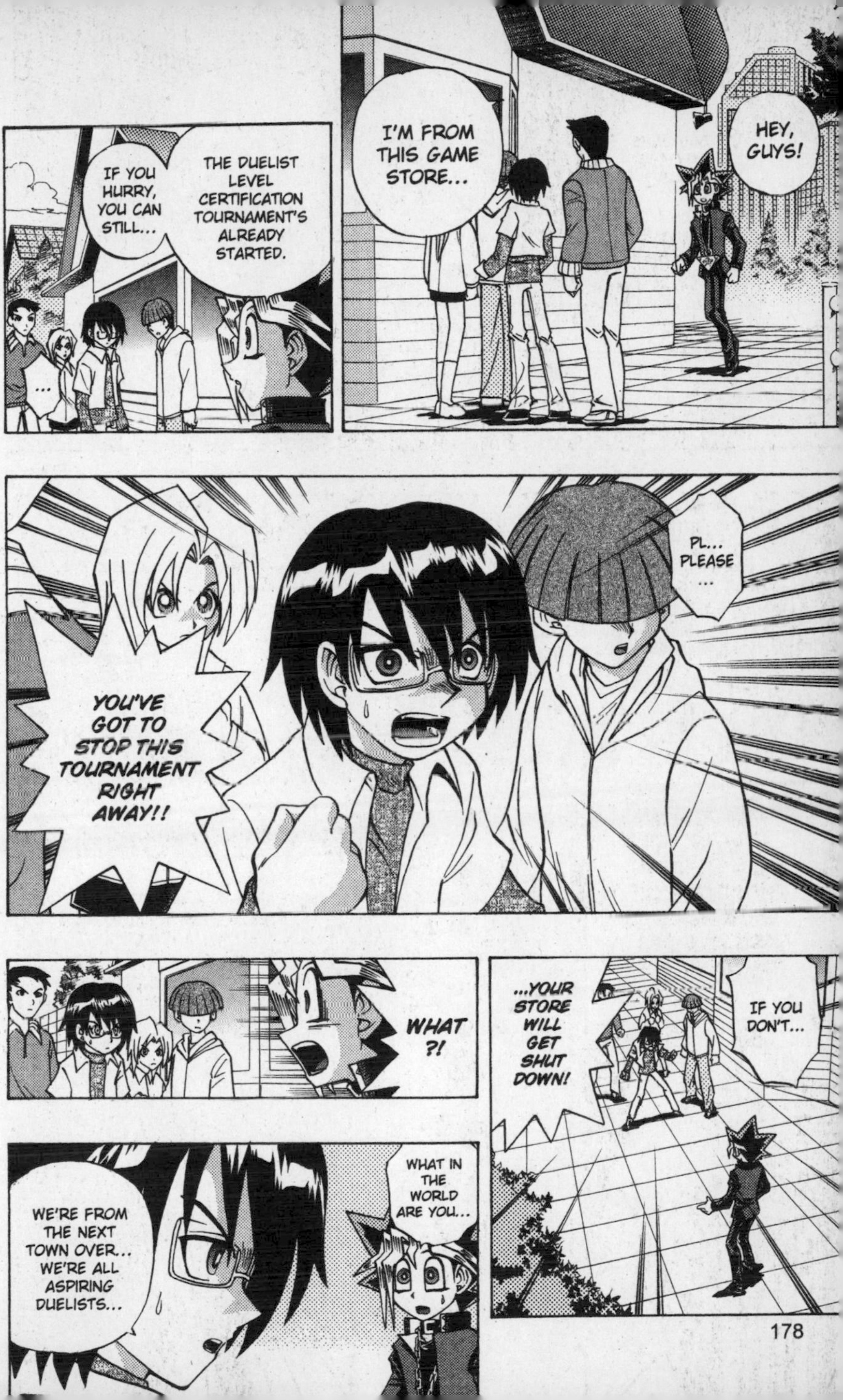
HEY, GUYS!
I'M FROM THIS GAME STORE...
THE DUELIST LEVEL CERTIFICATION TOURNAMENT'S ALREADY STARTED.
IF YOU HURRY, YOU CAN STILL...
...
PL... PLEASE ...
YOU'VE GOT TO STOP THIS TOURNAMENT RIGHT AWAY!!
IF YOU DON'T...
...YOUR STORE WILL GET SHUT DOWN!
WHAT ?!
WHAT IN THE WORLD ARE YOU...
WE'RE FROM THE NEXT TOWN OVER... WE'RE ALL ASPIRING DUELISTS...

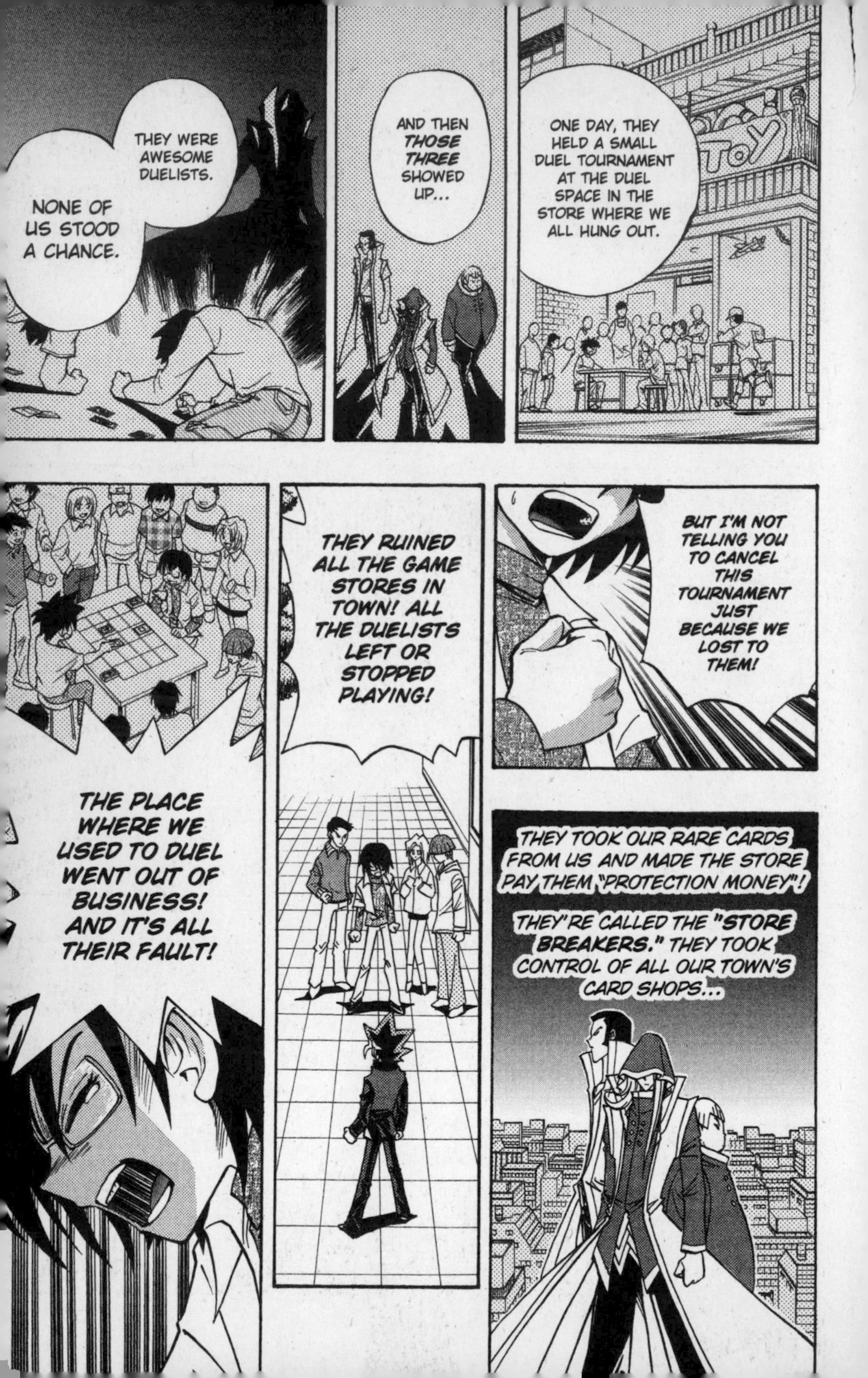
ONE DAY, THEY HELD A SMALL DUEL TOURNAMENT AT THE DUEL SPACE IN THE STORE WHERE WE ALL HUNG OUT.
TOY
AND THEN *THOSE THREE* SHOWED UP...
THEY WERE AWESOME DUELISTS.
NONE OF US STOOD A CHANCE.
BUT I'M NOT TELLING YOU TO CANCEL THIS TOURNAMENT JUST BECAUSE WE LOST TO THEM!
THEY TOOK OUR RARE CARDS FROM US AND MADE THE STORE PAY THEM "PROTECTION MONEY"!
THEY'RE CALLED THE "STORE BREAKERS." THEY TOOK CONTROL OF ALL OUR TOWN'S CARD SHOPS...
THEY RUINED ALL THE GAME STORES IN TOWN! ALL THE DUELISTS LEFT OR STOPPED PLAYING!
THE PLACE WHERE WE USED TO DUEL WENT OUT OF BUSINESS! AND IT'S ALL THEIR FAULT!

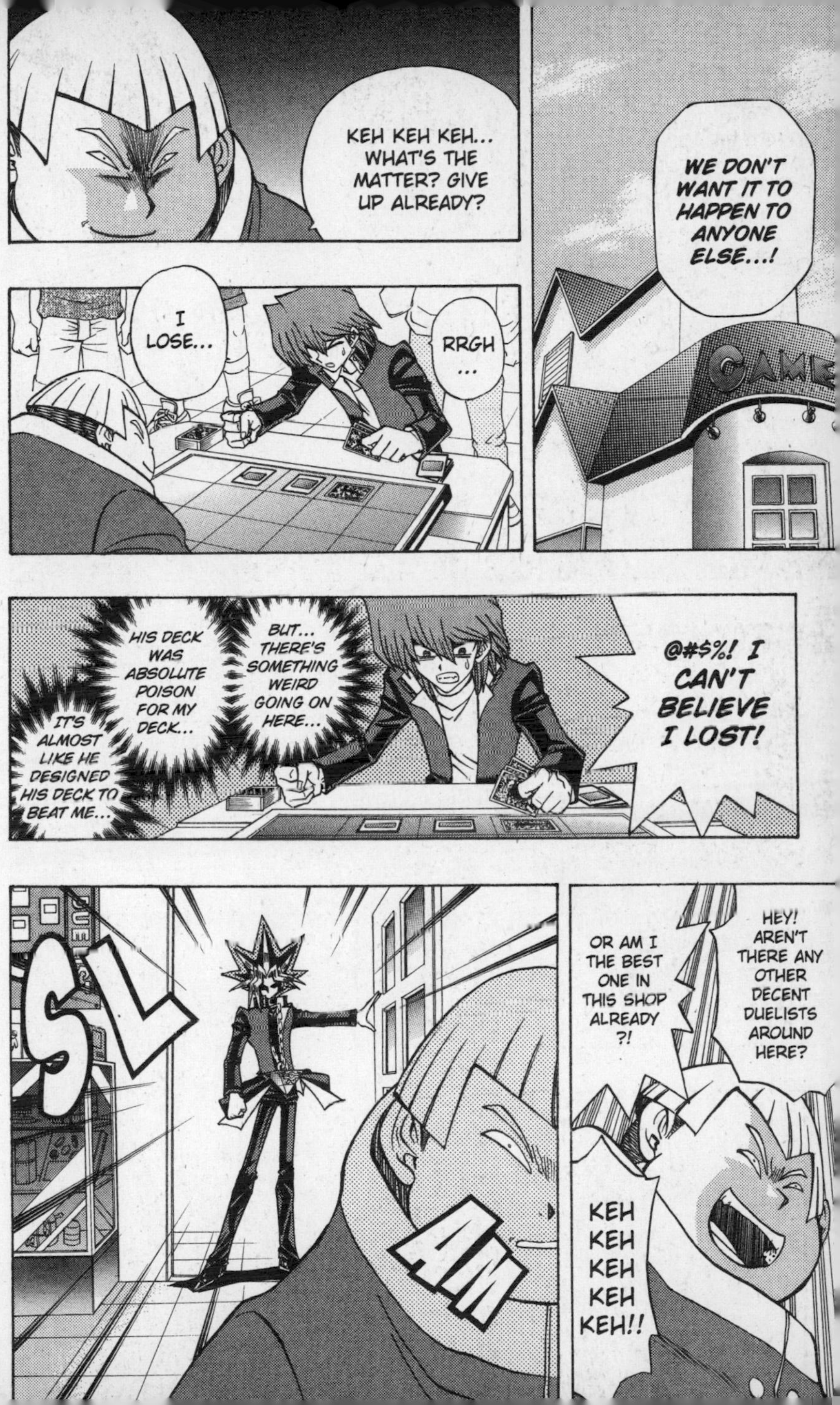
WE DON'T WANT IT TO HAPPEN TO ANYONE ELSE...!
KEH KEH KEH... WHAT'S THE MATTER? GIVE UP ALREADY?
RRGH ...
I LOSE...
@#$%! I CAN'T BELIEVE I LOST!
BUT... THERE'S SOMETHING WEIRD GOING ON HERE...
HIS DECK WAS ABSOLUTE POISON FOR MY DECK...
IT'S ALMOST LIKE HE DESIGNED HIS DECK TO BEAT ME...
HEY! AREN'T THERE ANY OTHER DECENT DUELISTS AROUND HERE?
OR AM I THE BEST ONE IN THIS SHOP ALREADY ?!
KEH KEH KEH KEH KEH!!
SL
AM

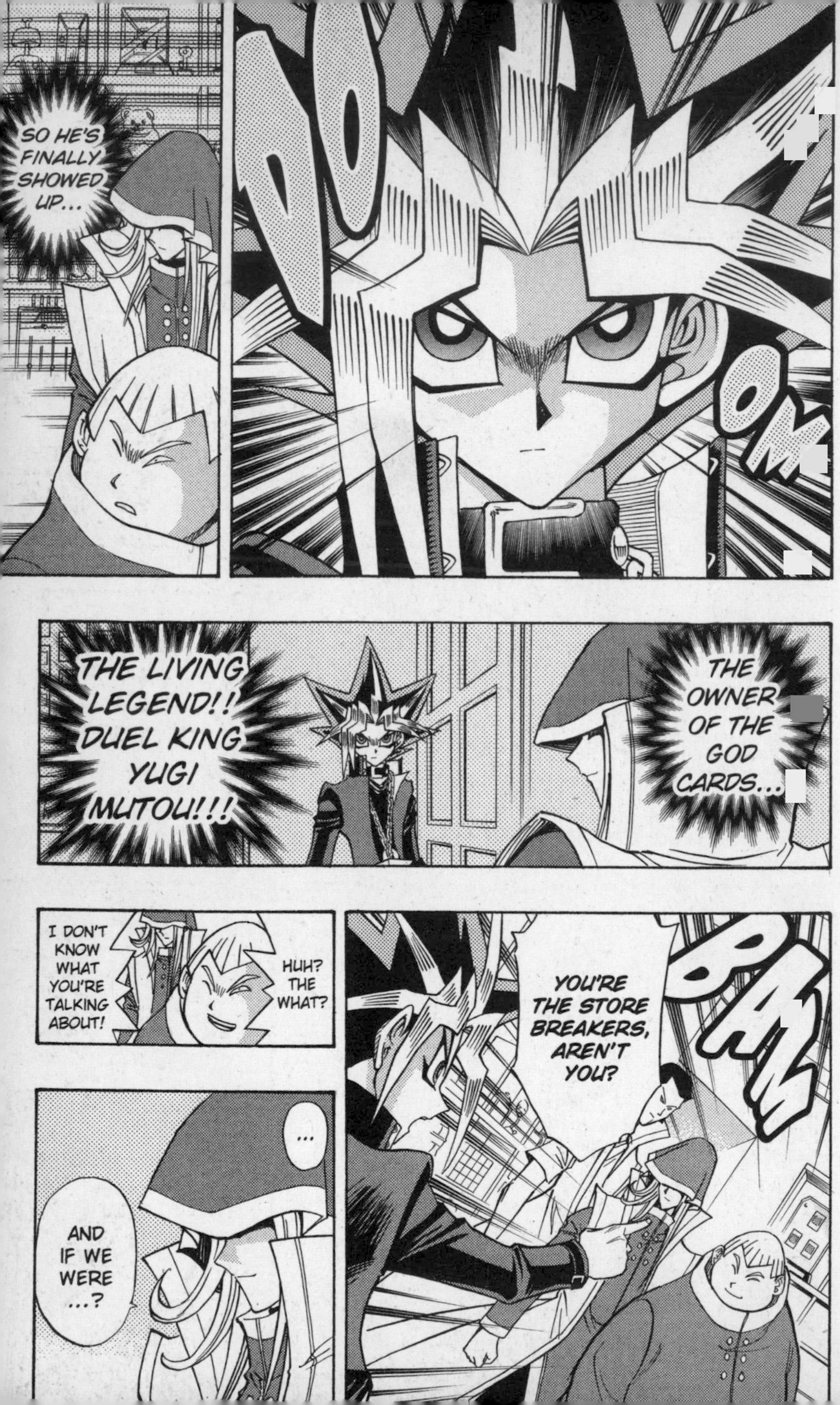

SO HE'S FINALLY SHOWED UP...
THE OWNER OF THE GOD CARDS...
THE LIVING LEGEND!! DUEL KING YUGI MUTOU!!!
BAM
YOU'RE THE STORE BREAKERS, AREN'T YOU?
HUH? THE WHAT?
I DON'T KNOW WHAT YOU'RE TALKING ABOUT!
...
AND IF WE WERE ...?

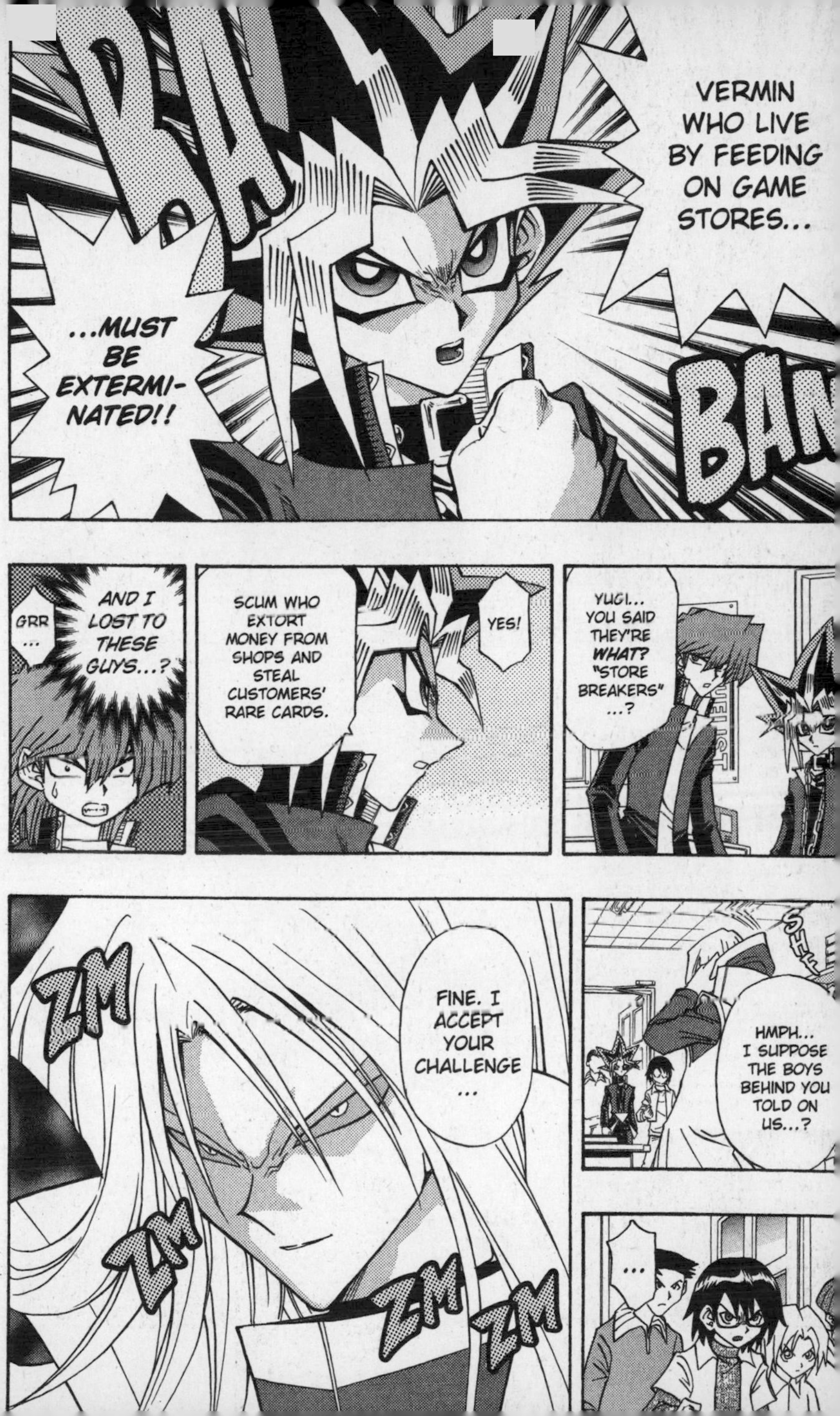
VERMIN WHO LIVE BY FEEDING ON GAME STORES...
BA
...MUST BE EXTERMINATED!!
YUGI... YOU SAID THEY'RE WHAT? "STORE BREAKERS"...?
YES!
SCUM WHO EXTORT MONEY FROM SHOPS AND STEAL CUSTOMERS' RARE CARDS.
AND I LOST TO THESE GUYS...?
GRR...
HMPH... I SUPPOSE THE BOYS BEHIND YOU TOLD ON US...?
...
FINE. I ACCEPT YOUR CHALLENGE...
ZM
ZM
ZM
ZM

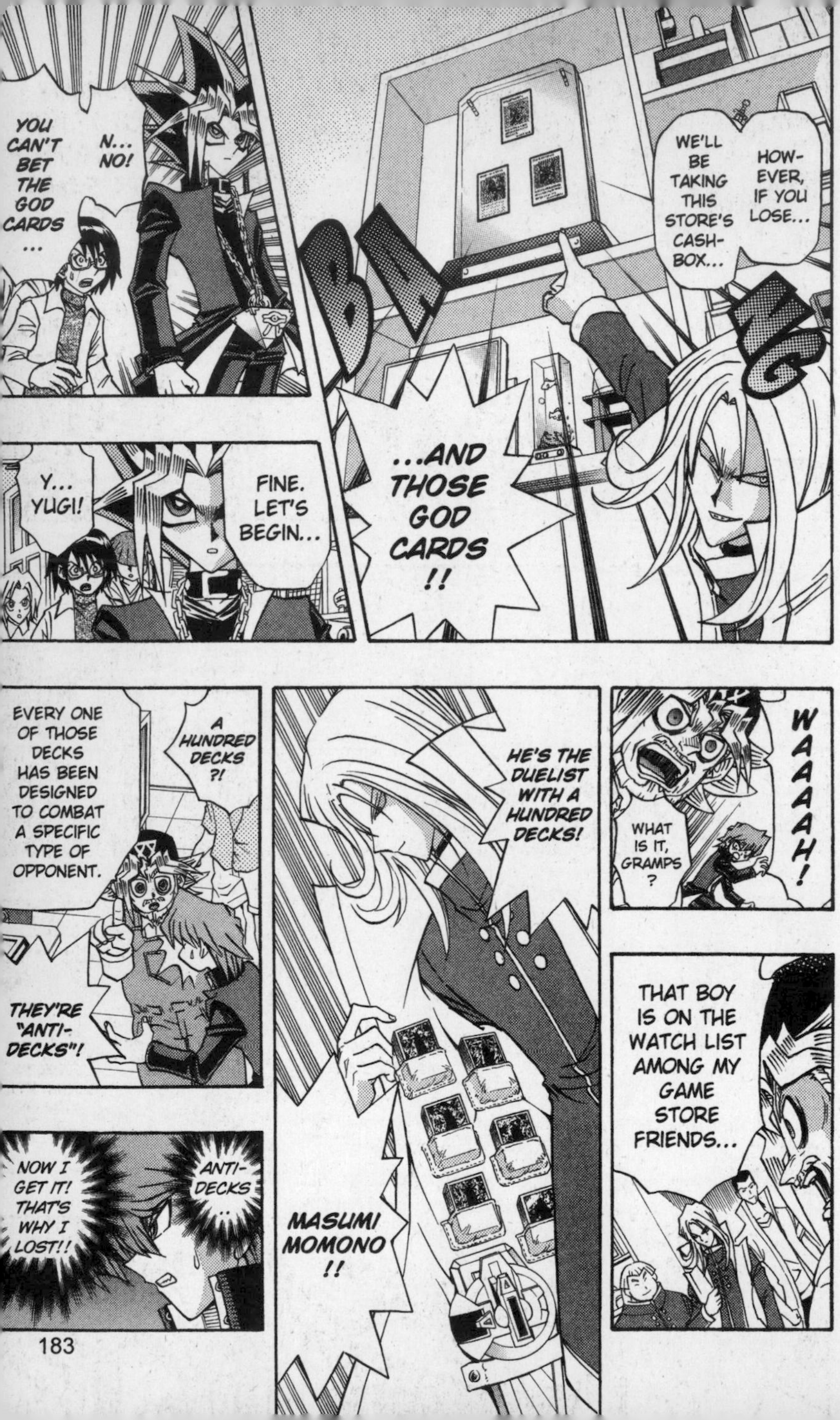
HOW-EVER, IF YOU LOSE...
WE'LL BE TAKING THIS STORE'S CASH-BOX...
BANG
...AND THOSE GOD CARDS!!
N... NO!
YOU CAN'T BET THE GOD CARDS...
FINE. LET'S BEGIN...
Y... YUGI!
WAAAAAH!
WHAT IS IT, GRAMPS?
THAT BOY IS ON THE WATCH LIST AMONG MY GAME STORE FRIENDS...
HE'S THE DUELIST WITH A HUNDRED DECKS!
MASUMI MOMONO!!
A HUNDRED DECKS?!
EVERY ONE OF THOSE DECKS HAS BEEN DESIGNED TO COMBAT A SPECIFIC TYPE OF OPPONENT.
THEY'RE "ANTI-DECKS"!
ANTI-DECKS...
NOW I GET IT! THAT'S WHY I LOST!!

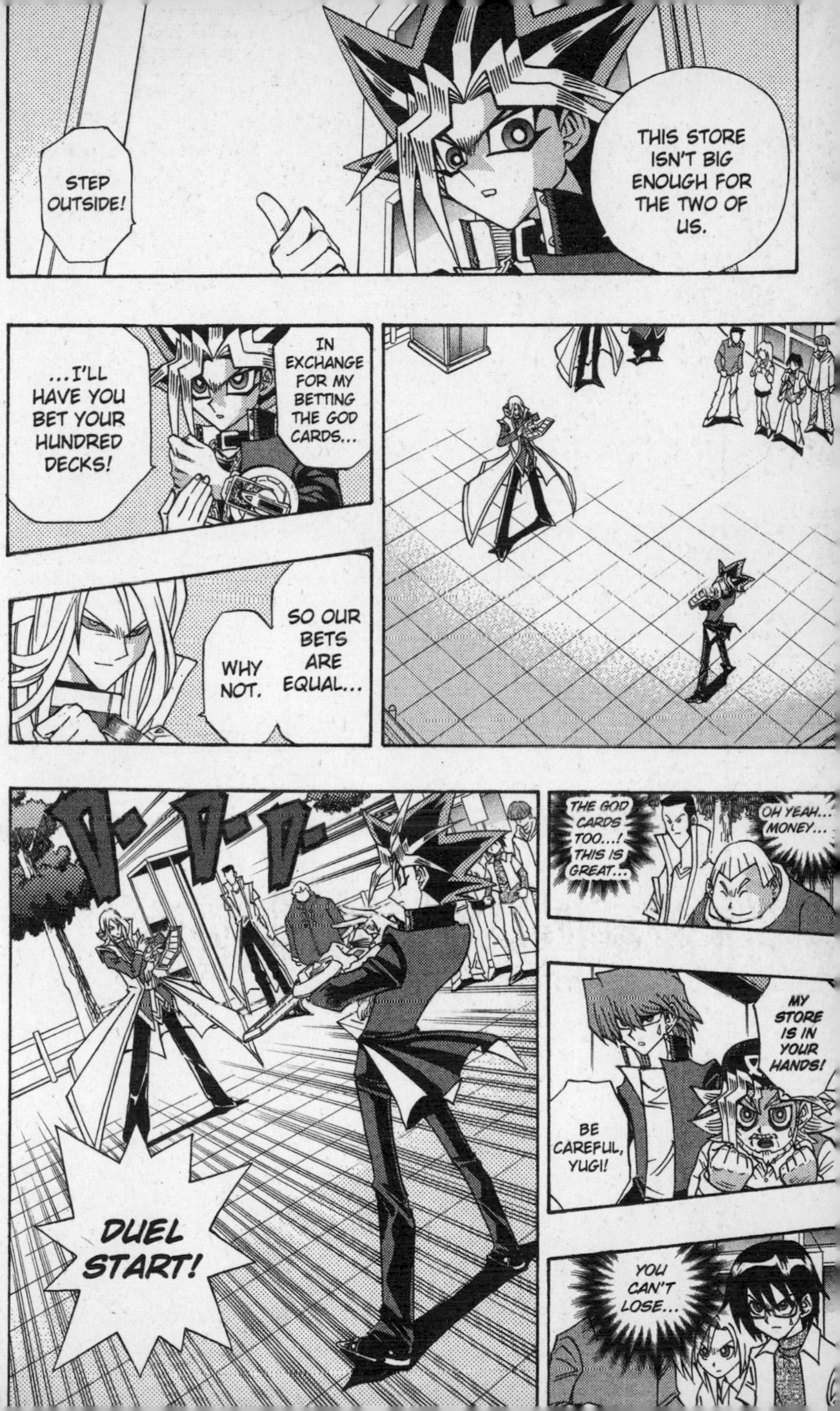
THIS STORE ISN'T BIG ENOUGH FOR THE TWO OF US.
STEP OUTSIDE!
IN EXCHANGE FOR MY BETTING THE GOD CARDS...
...I'LL HAVE YOU BET YOUR HUNDRED DECKS!
SO OUR BETS ARE EQUAL...
WHY NOT.
OH YEAH... MONEY...
THE GOD CARDS TOO...! THIS IS GREAT...
MY STORE IS IN YOUR HANDS!
BE CAREFUL, YUGI!
YOU CAN'T LOSE...
D- D- D-
DUEL START!

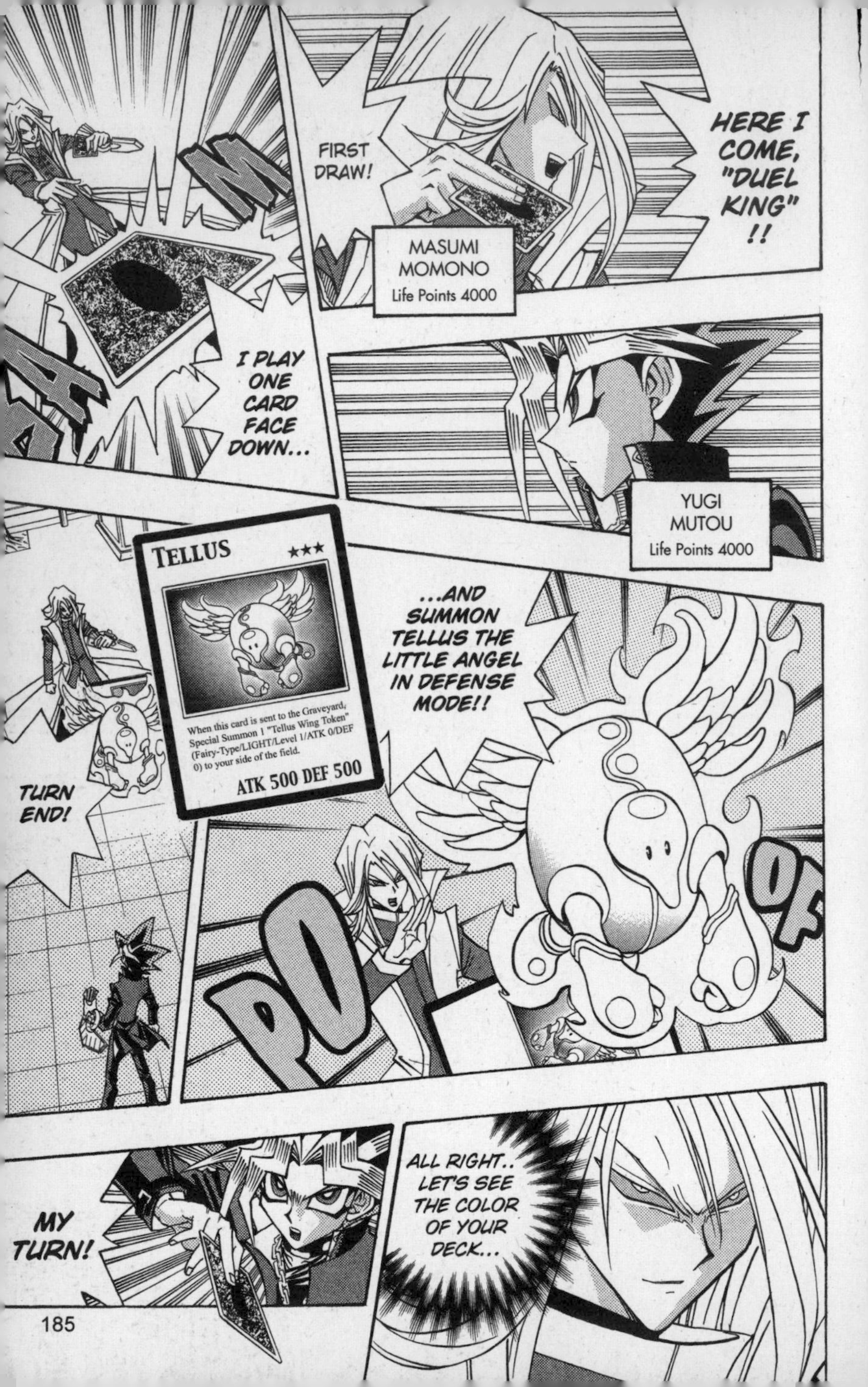
HERE I COME, "DUEL KING"!!
FIRST DRAW!
MASUMI MOMONO
Life Points 4000
YUGI MUTOU
Life Points 4000
I PLAY ONE CARD FACE DOWN...
...AND SUMMON TELLUS THE LITTLE ANGEL IN DEFENSE MODE!!
TELLUS ★★★
When this card is sent to the Graveyard, Special Summon 1 "Tellus Wing Token" (Fairy-Type/LIGHT/Level 1/ATK 0/DEF 0) to your side of the field.
ATK 500 DEF 500
PO
OF
TURN END!
ALL RIGHT.. LET'S SEE THE COLOR OF YOUR DECK...
MY TURN!

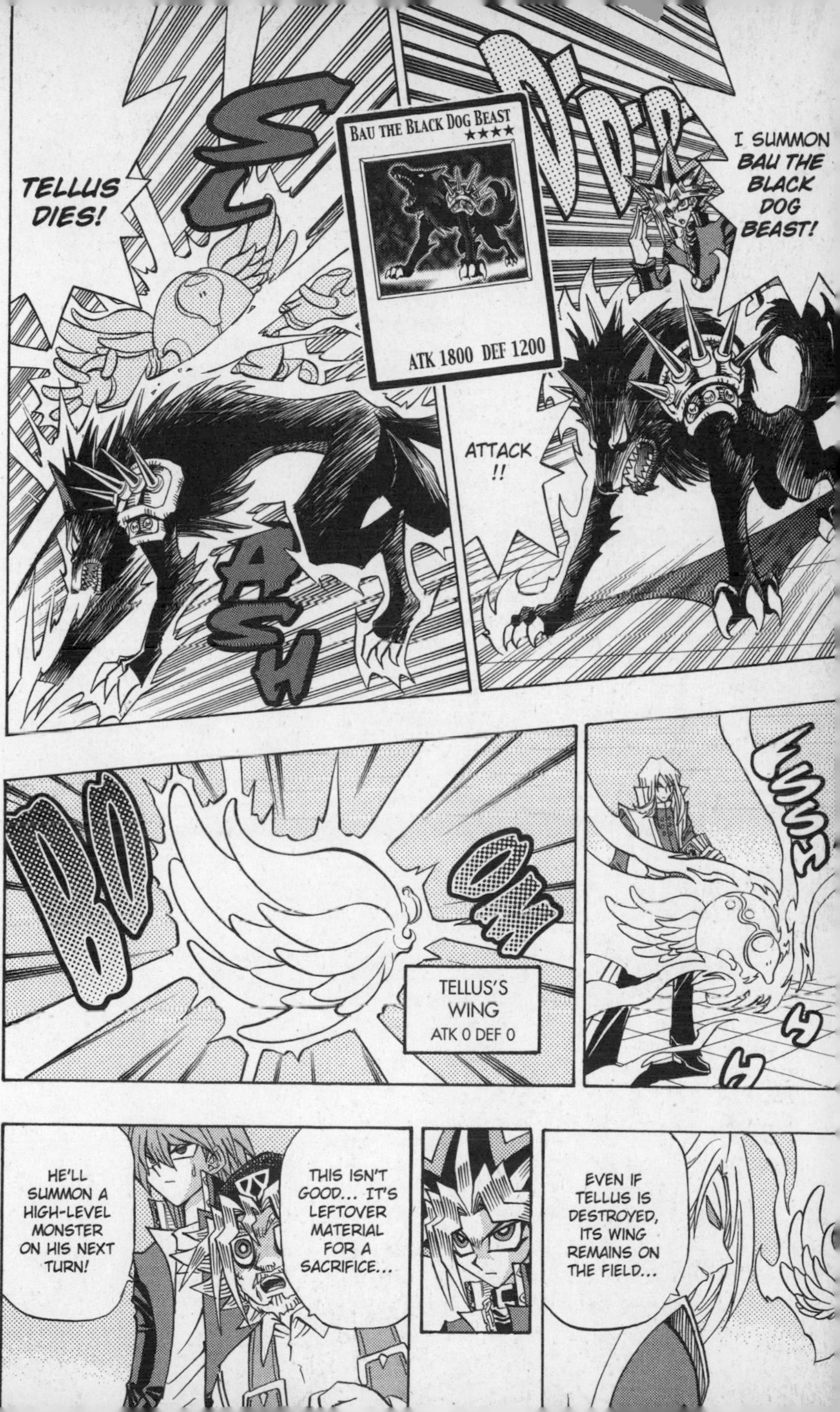
I SUMMON BAU THE BLACK DOG BEAST!
BAU THE BLACK DOG BEAST ★★★★
ATK 1800 DEF 1200
ATTACK!!
TELLUS DIES!
BOOM
TELLUS'S WING
ATK 0 DEF 0
EVEN IF TELLUS IS DESTROYED, ITS WING REMAINS ON THE FIELD...
THIS ISN'T GOOD... IT'S LEFTOVER MATERIAL FOR A SACRIFICE...
HE'LL SUMMON A HIGH-LEVEL MONSTER ON HIS NEXT TURN!

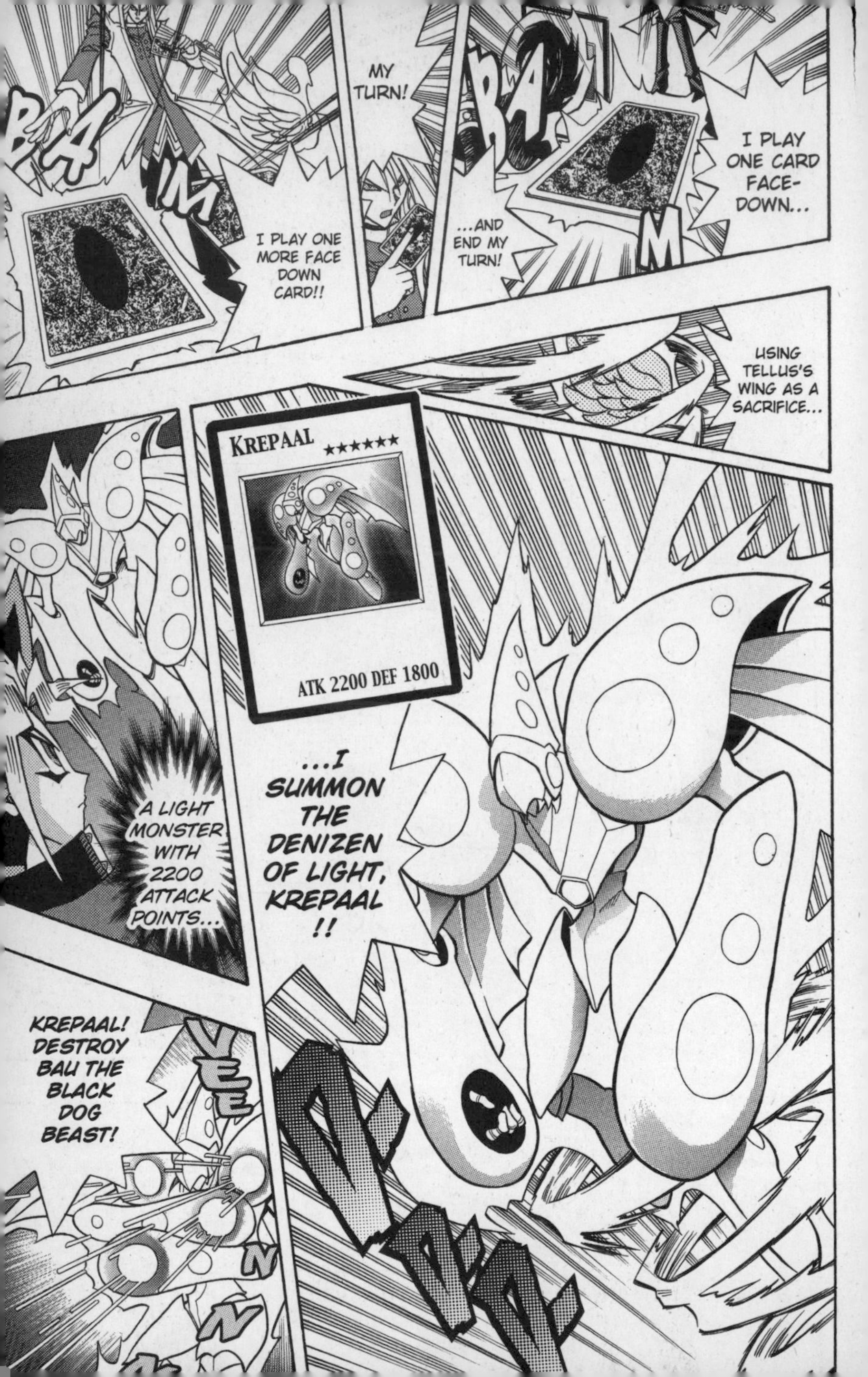

RA
M
I PLAY ONE CARD FACE-DOWN...
MY TURN!
...AND END MY TURN!
BA
IM
I PLAY ONE MORE FACE DOWN CARD!!
USING TELLUS'S WING AS A SACRIFICE...
KREPAAL ★★★★★★
ATK 2200 DEF 1800
...I SUMMON THE DENIZEN OF LIGHT, KREPAAL!!
A LIGHT MONSTER WITH 2200 ATTACK POINTS...
KREPAAL! DESTROY BAU THE BLACK DOG BEAST!
VEE
N
N

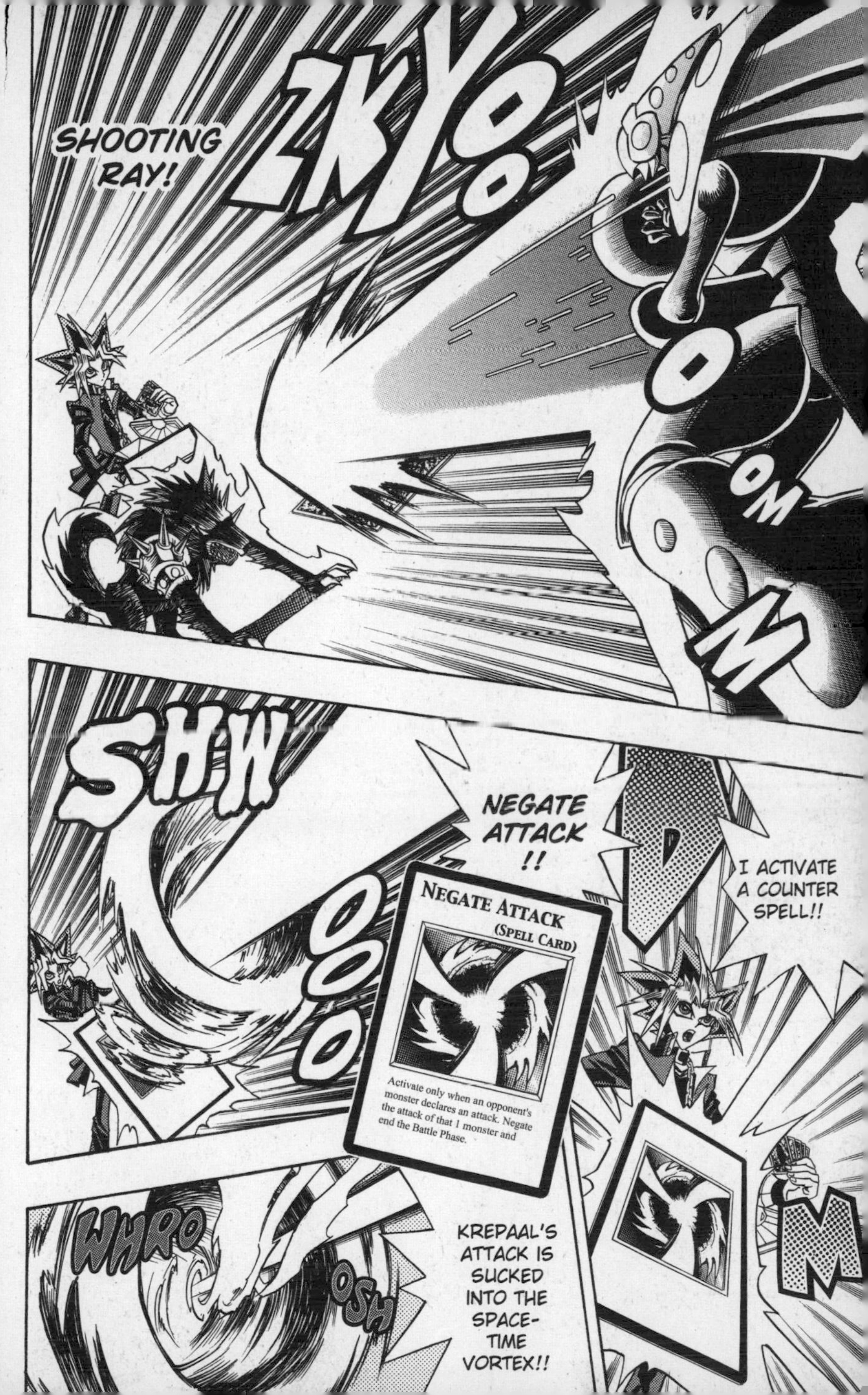
ZKYOOOOMM
SHOOTING RAY!
I ACTIVATE A COUNTER SPELL!!
NEGATE ATTACK !!
NEGATE ATTACK
(SPELL CARD)
Activate only when an opponent's monster declares an attack. Negate the attack of that 1 monster and end the Battle Phase.
SHWOOOO
M
KREPAAL'S ATTACK IS SUCKED INTO THE SPACE-TIME VORTEX!!
WHROOSH

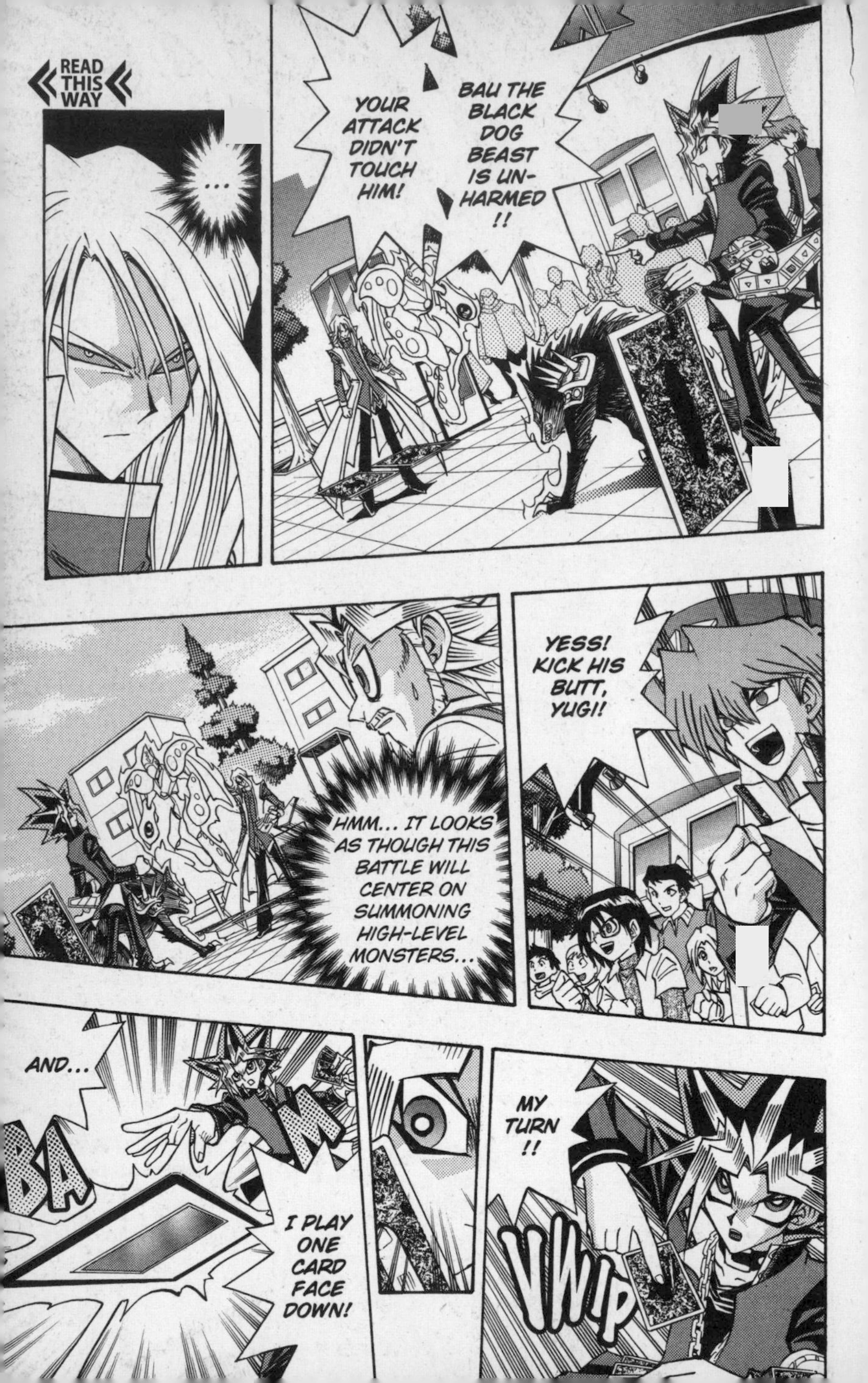
READ THIS WAY
BAU THE BLACK DOG BEAST IS UN-HARMED!!
YOUR ATTACK DIDN'T TOUCH HIM!
...
YESS! KICK HIS BUTT, YUGI!
HMM... IT LOOKS AS THOUGH THIS BATTLE WILL CENTER ON SUMMONING HIGH-LEVEL MONSTERS...
MY TURN!!
VWIP
AND...
BAM
I PLAY ONE CARD FACE DOWN!

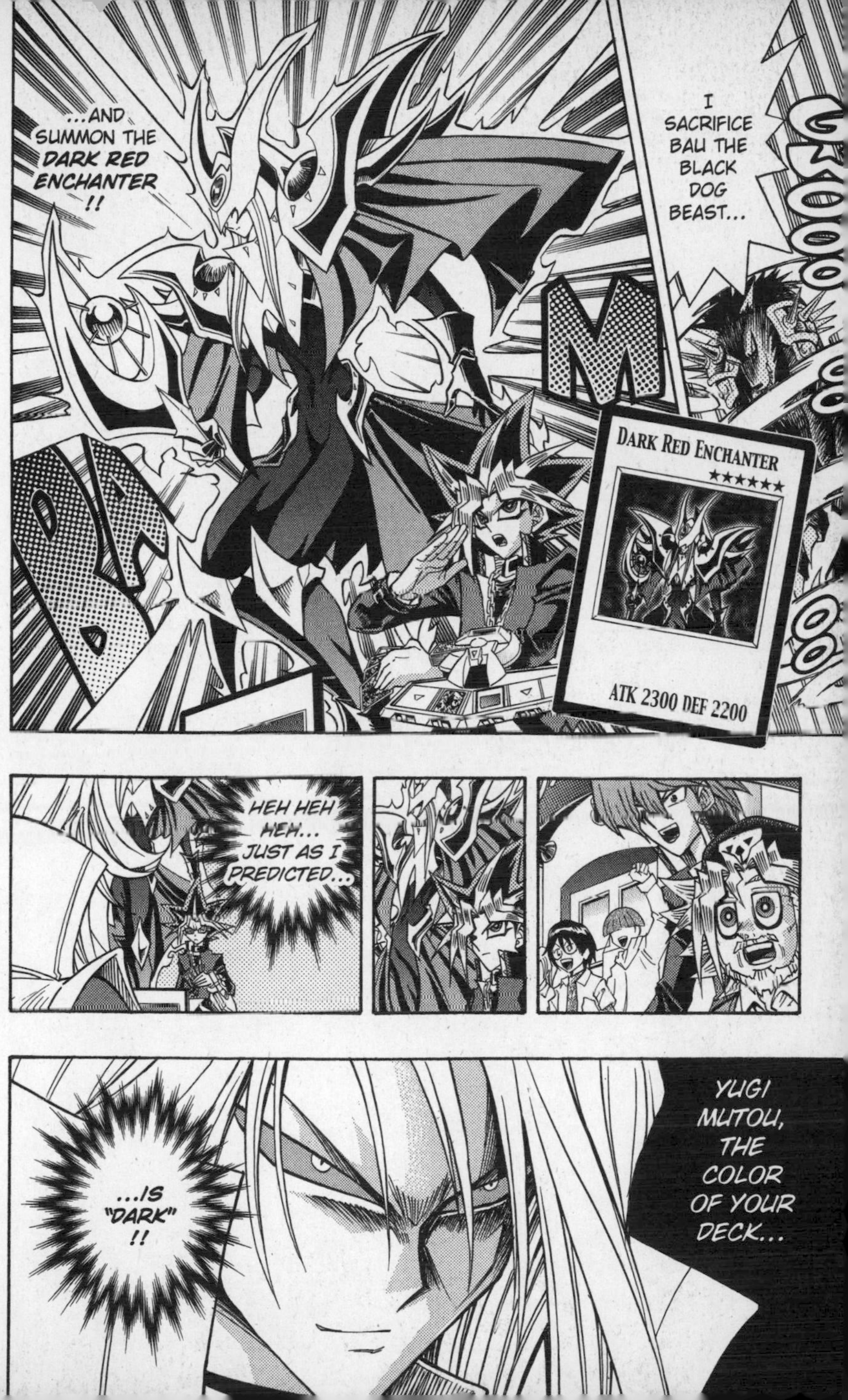
I SACRIFICE BAU THE BLACK DOG BEAST...
...AND SUMMON THE DARK RED ENCHANTER!!
DARK RED ENCHANTER
ATK 2300 DEF 2200
HEH HEH HEH... JUST AS I PREDICTED...
YUGI MUTOU, THE COLOR OF YOUR DECK...
...IS "DARK"!!

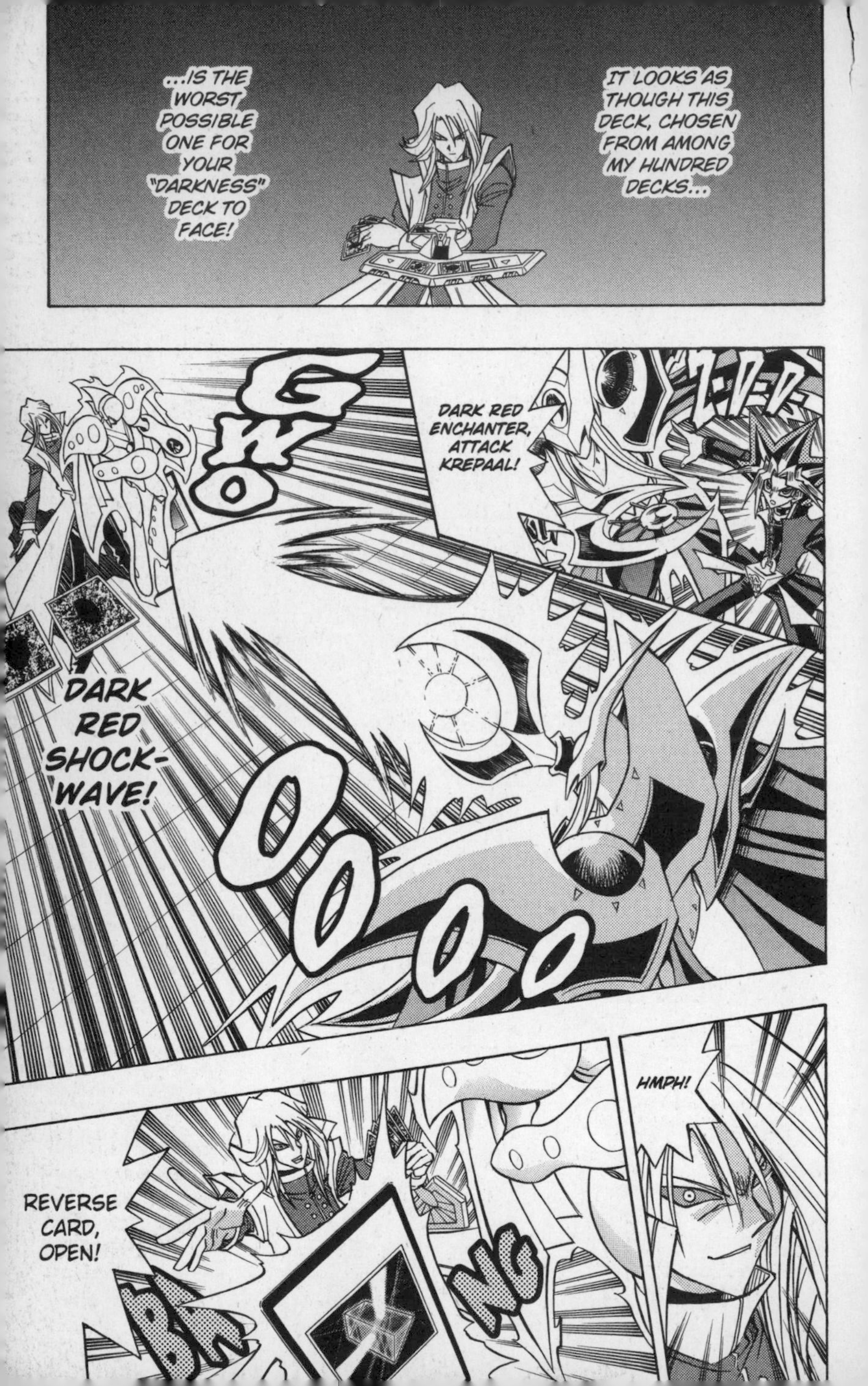
IT LOOKS AS THOUGH THIS DECK, CHOSEN FROM AMONG MY HUNDRED DECKS...
...IS THE WORST POSSIBLE ONE FOR YOUR "DARKNESS" DECK TO FACE!
DARK RED ENCHANTER, ATTACK KREPAAL!
GWO
DARK RED SHOCK-WAVE!
OOOOO
HMPH!
BANG
REVERSE CARD, OPEN!

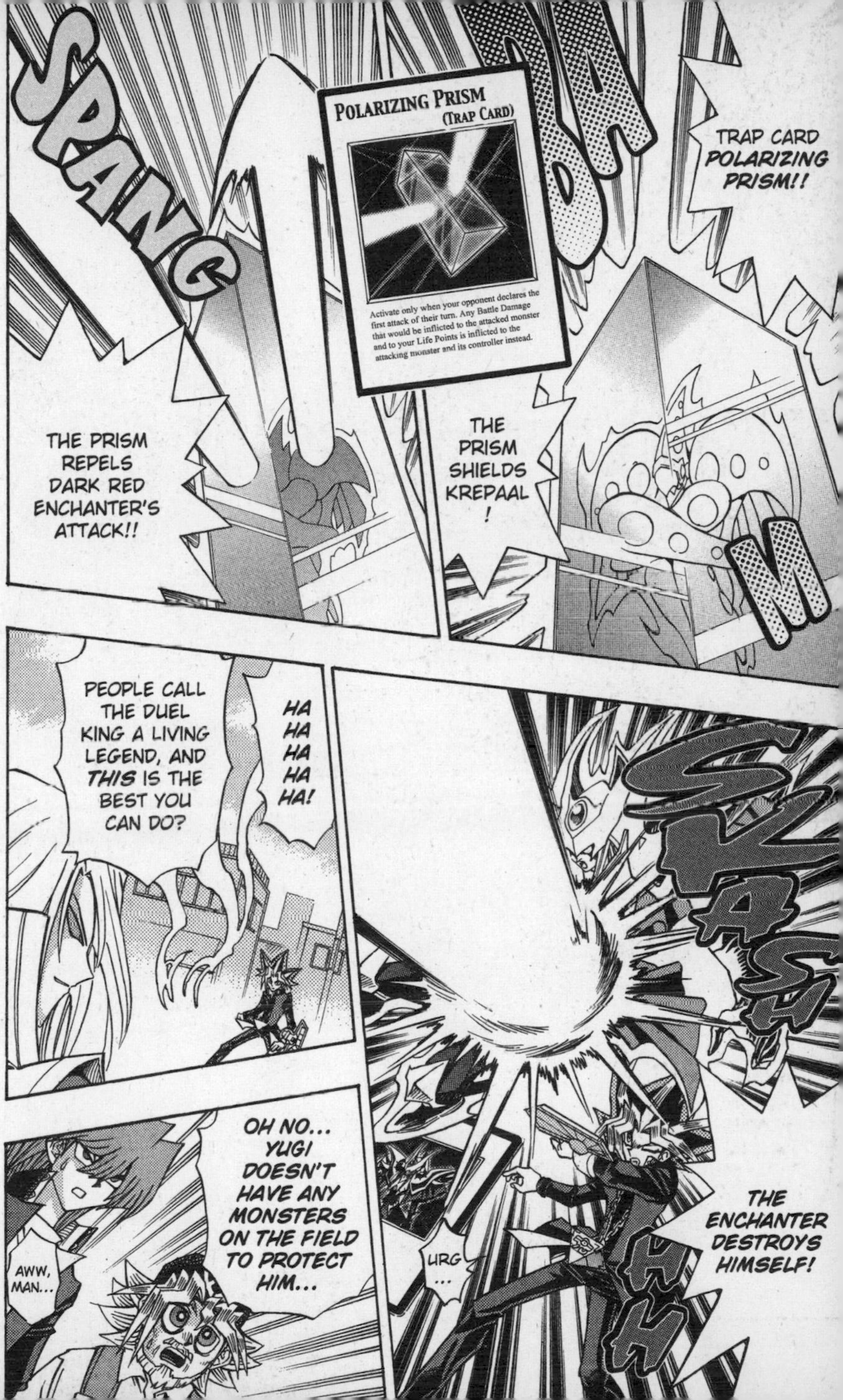
POLARIZING PRISM
(TRAP CARD)
Activate only when your opponent declares the first attack of their turn. Any Battle Damage that would be inflicted to the attacked monster and to your Life Points is inflicted to the attacking monster and its controller instead.
TRAP CARD POLARIZING PRISM!!
THE PRISM SHIELDS KREPAAL!
SPANG
THE PRISM REPELS DARK RED ENCHANTER'S ATTACK!!
SLASH
THE ENCHANTER DESTROYS HIMSELF!
URG...
PEOPLE CALL THE DUEL KING A LIVING LEGEND, AND *THIS* IS THE BEST YOU CAN DO?
HA HA HA HA HA!
OH NO... YUGI DOESN'T HAVE ANY MONSTERS ON THE FIELD TO PROTECT HIM...
AWW, MAN...

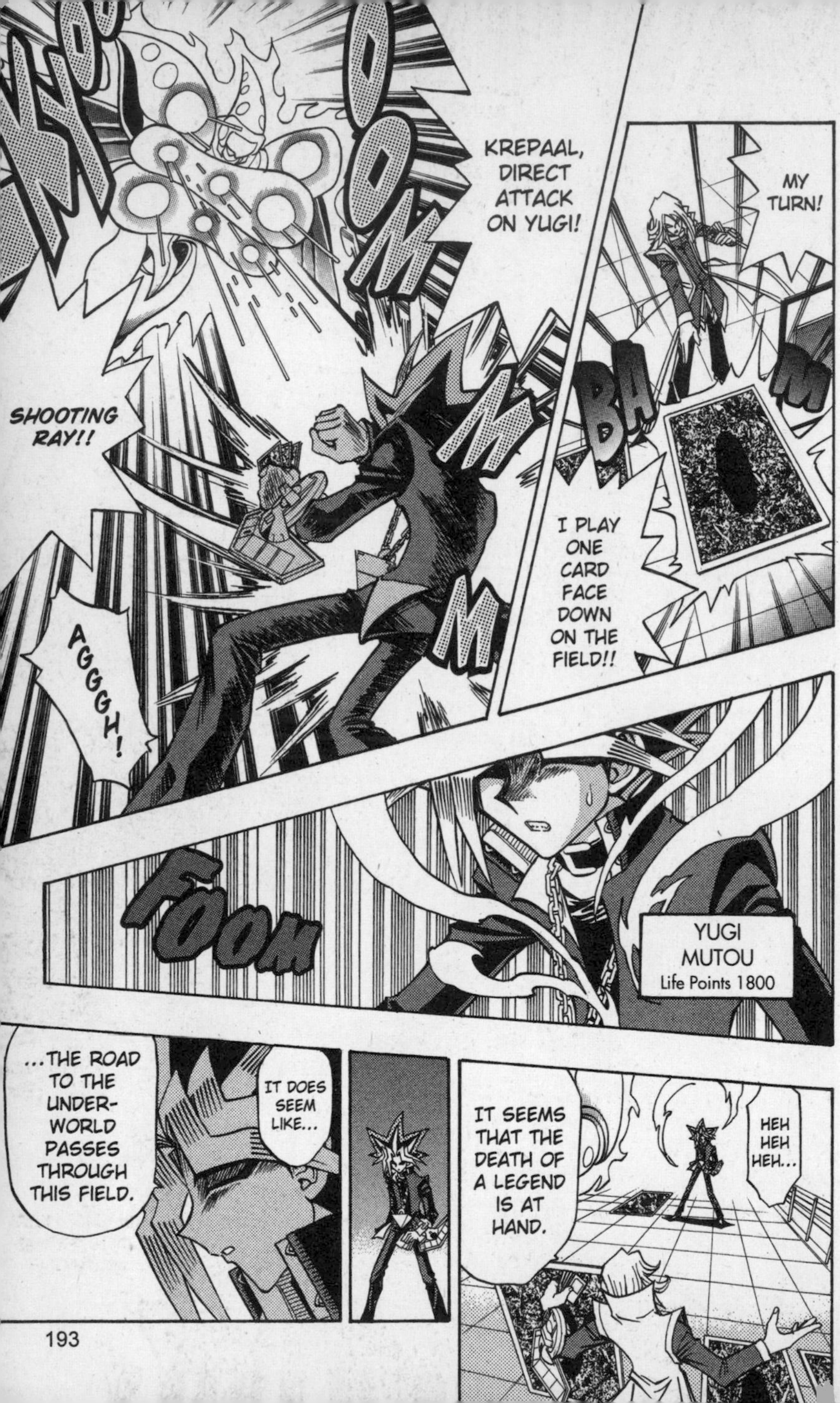
MY TURN!
BAMM
I PLAY ONE CARD FACE DOWN ON THE FIELD!!
KREPAAL, DIRECT ATTACK ON YUGI!
SHOOTING RAY!!
AGGGH!
FOOM
YUGI MUTOU
Life Points 1800
HEH HEH HEH...
IT SEEMS THAT THE DEATH OF A LEGEND IS AT HAND.
IT DOES SEEM LIKE...
...THE ROAD TO THE UNDER-WORLD PASSES THROUGH THIS FIELD.

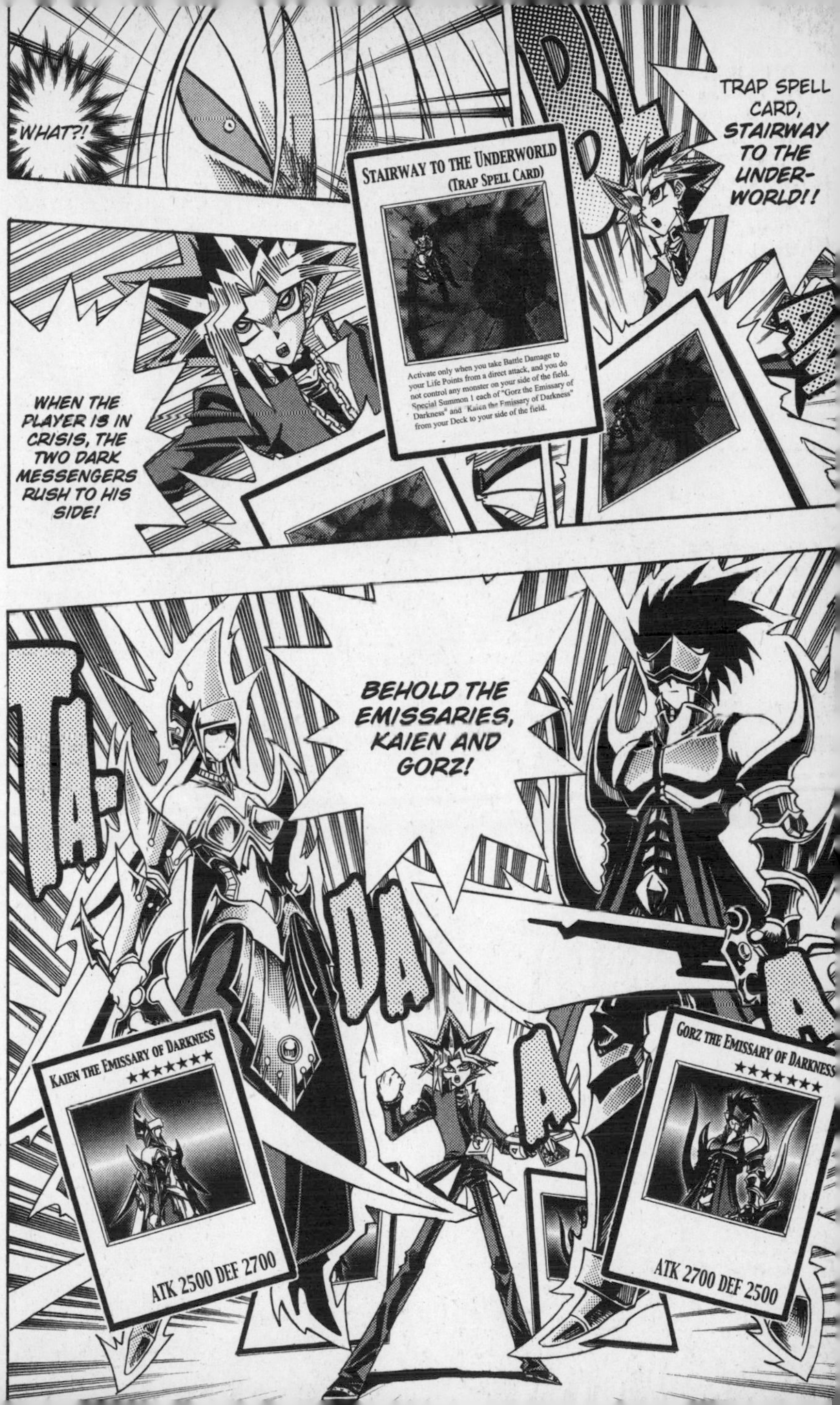

TRAP SPELL CARD, STAIRWAY TO THE UNDERWORLD!!
WHAT?!
STAIRWAY TO THE UNDERWORLD
(TRAP SPELL CARD)
Activate only when you take Battle Damage to your Life Points from a direct attack, and you do not control any monster on your side of the field. Special Summon 1 each of "Gorz the Emissary of Darkness" and "Kaien the Emissary of Darkness" from your Deck to your side of the field.
WHEN THE PLAYER IS IN CRISIS, THE TWO DARK MESSENGERS RUSH TO HIS SIDE!
BEHOLD THE EMISSARIES, KAIEN AND GORZ!
DA
TA
GORZ THE EMISSARY OF DARKNESS
ATK 2700 DEF 2500
KAIEN THE EMISSARY OF DARKNESS
ATK 2500 DEF 2700

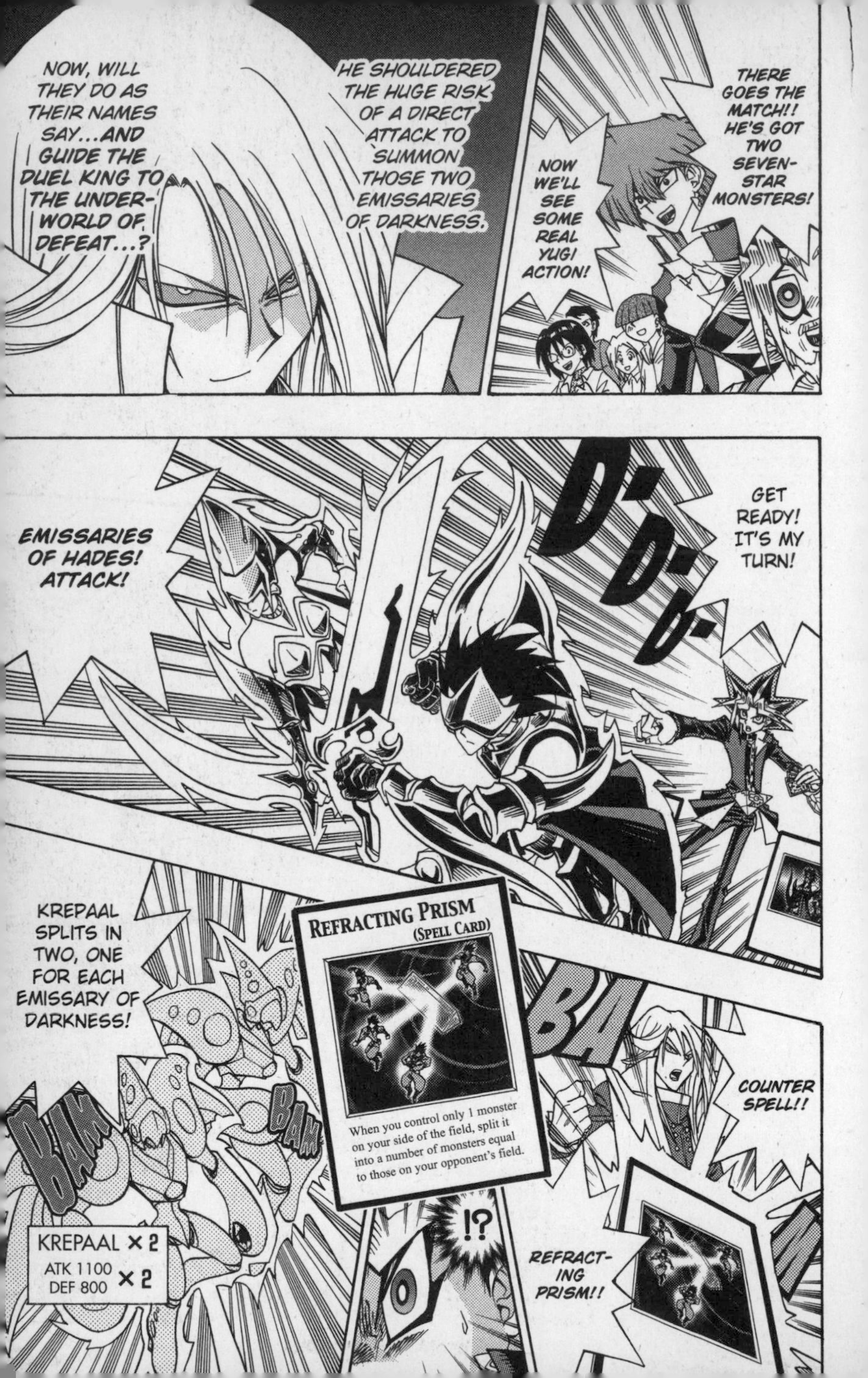
THERE GOES THE MATCH!! HE'S GOT TWO SEVEN-STAR MONSTERS!
NOW WE'LL SEE SOME REAL YUGI ACTION!
HE SHOULDERED THE HUGE RISK OF A DIRECT ATTACK TO SUMMON THOSE TWO EMISSARIES OF DARKNESS.
NOW, WILL THEY DO AS THEIR NAMES SAY...AND GUIDE THE DUEL KING TO THE UNDER-WORLD OF DEFEAT...?
GET READY! IT'S MY TURN!
D- D- D- D-
EMISSARIES OF HADES! ATTACK!
COUNTER SPELL!!
BA
REFRACT-ING PRISM!!
!?
REFRACTING PRISM
(SPELL CARD)
When you control only 1 monster on your side of the field, split it into a number of monsters equal to those on your opponent's field.
KREPAAL SPLITS IN TWO, ONE FOR EACH EMISSARY OF DARKNESS!
BAM
BAM
KREPAAL ×2
ATK 1100
DEF 800 ×2

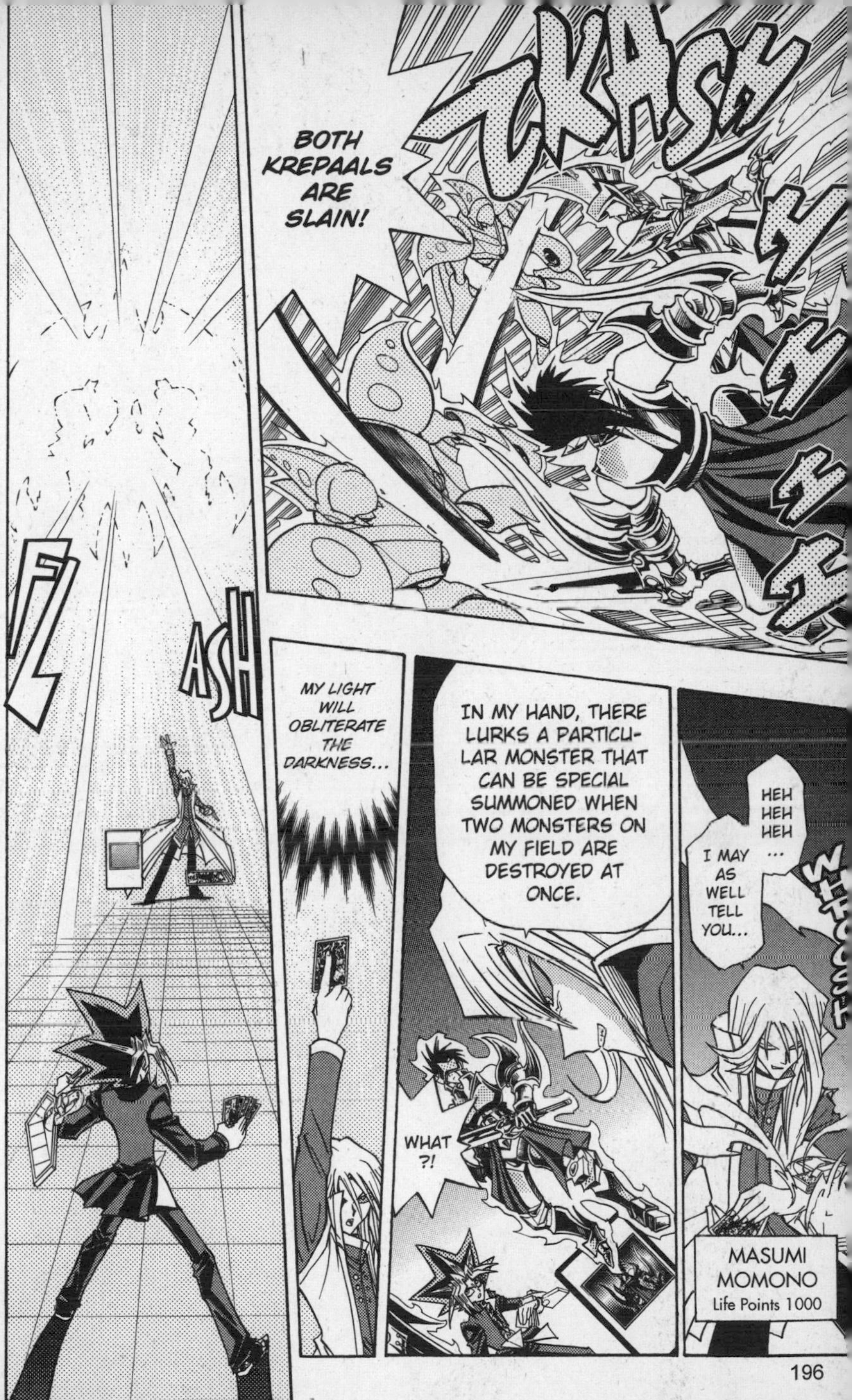
ZKASH
BOTH KREPAALS ARE SLAIN!
HEH HEH HEH...
I MAY AS WELL TELL YOU...
WHOOSH
MASUMI MOMONO
Life Points 1000
IN MY HAND, THERE LURKS A PARTICULAR MONSTER THAT CAN BE SPECIAL SUMMONED WHEN TWO MONSTERS ON MY FIELD ARE DESTROYED AT ONCE.
WHAT ?!
MY LIGHT WILL OBLITERATE THE DARKNESS...
FLASH

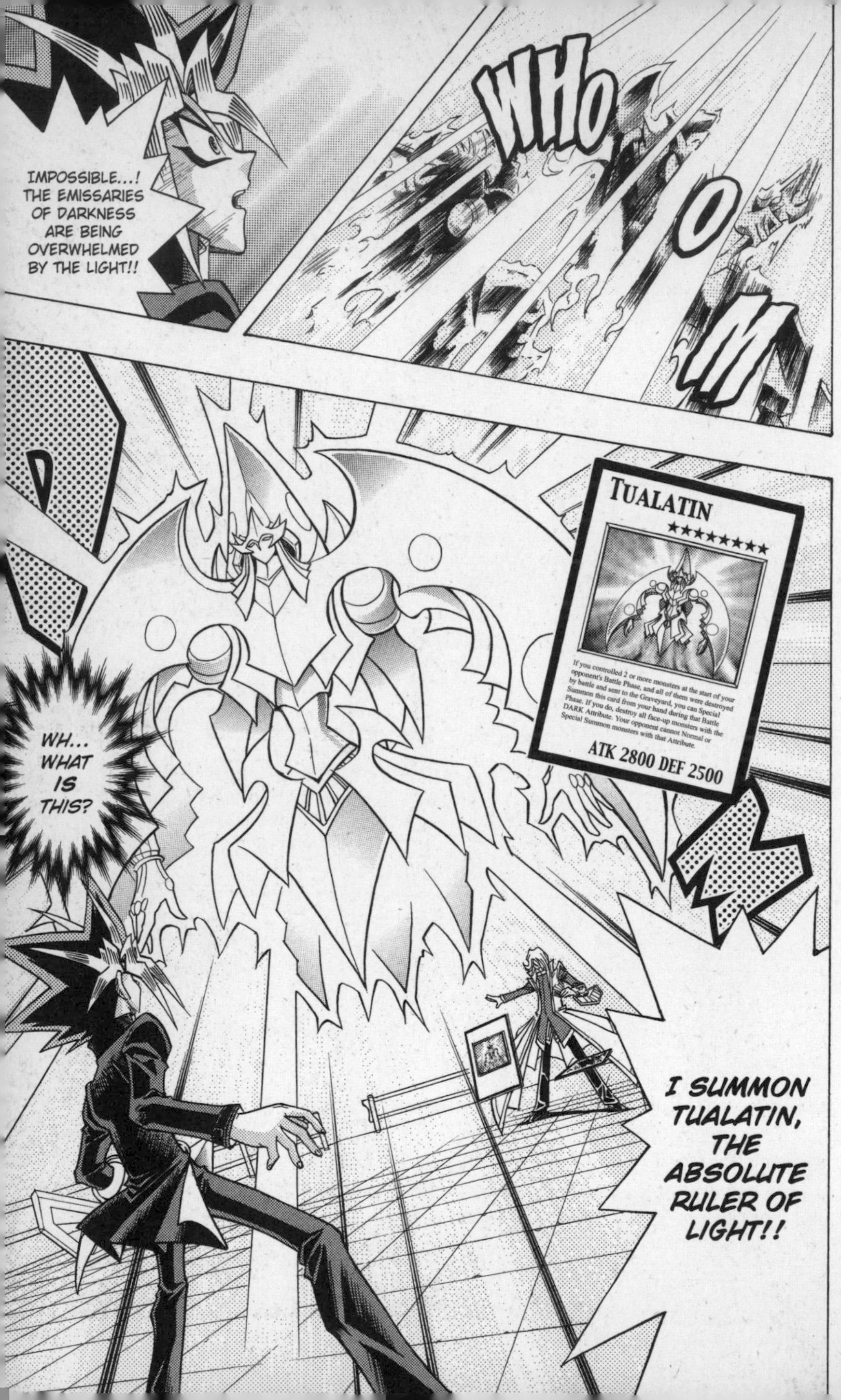
WHOOM
IMPOSSIBLE...! THE EMISSARIES OF DARKNESS ARE BEING OVERWHELMED BY THE LIGHT!!
TUALATIN
If you controlled 2 or more monsters at the start of your opponent's Battle Phase, and all of them were destroyed by battle and sent to the Graveyard, you can Special Summon this card from your hand during that Battle Phase. If you do, destroy all face-up monsters with the DARK Attribute. Your opponent cannot Normal or Special Summon monsters with that Attribute.
ATK 2800 DEF 2500
WH... WHAT IS THIS?
I SUMMON TUALATIN, THE ABSOLUTE RULER OF LIGHT!!

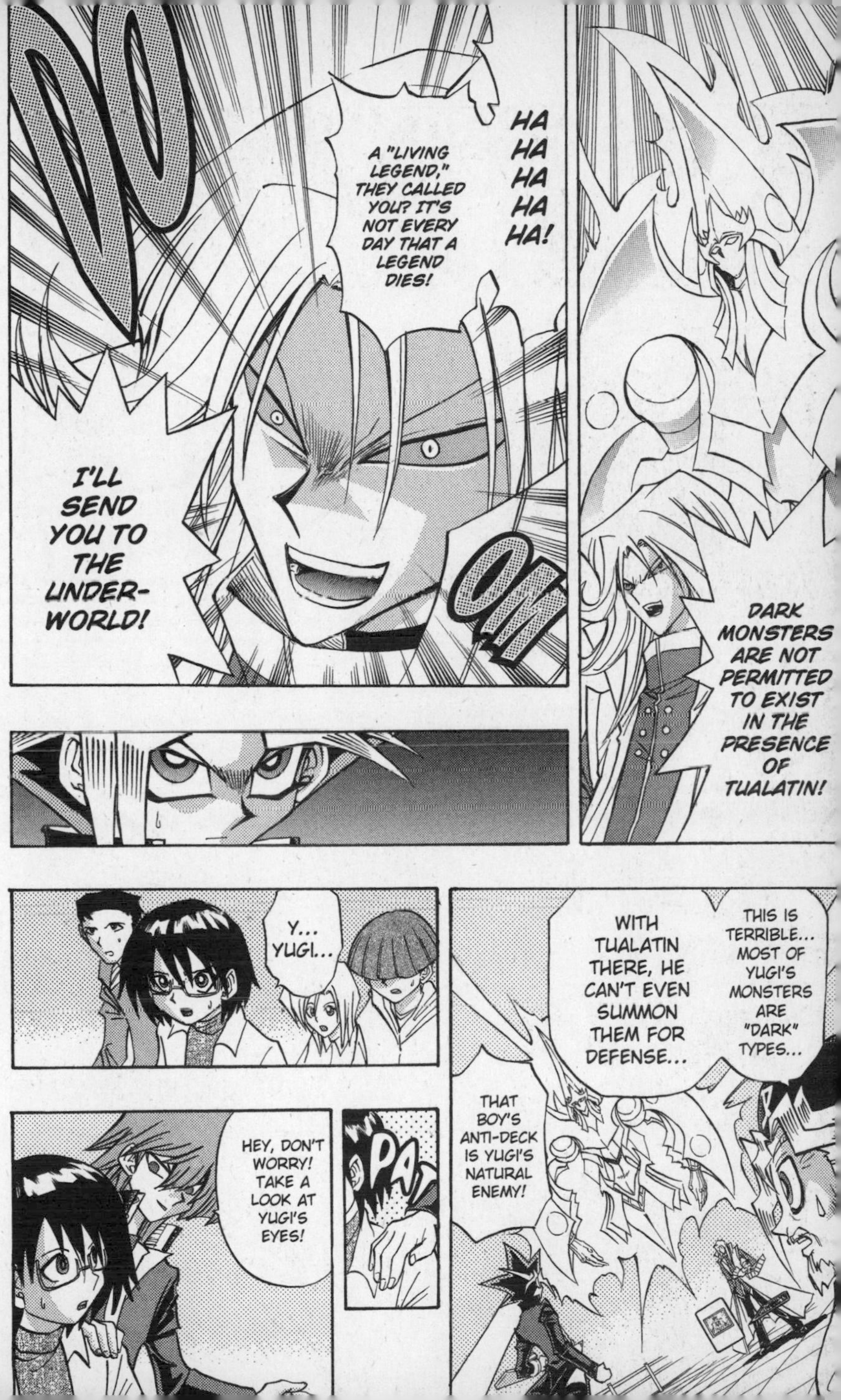

DARK MONSTERS ARE NOT PERMITTED TO EXIST IN THE PRESENCE OF TUALATIN!
HA HA HA HA HA!
A "LIVING LEGEND," THEY CALLED YOU? IT'S NOT EVERY DAY THAT A LEGEND DIES!
DO
OM
I'LL SEND YOU TO THE UNDER-WORLD!
THIS IS TERRIBLE... MOST OF YUGI'S MONSTERS ARE "DARK" TYPES...
WITH TUALATIN THERE, HE CAN'T EVEN SUMMON THEM FOR DEFENSE...
THAT BOY'S ANTI-DECK IS YUGI'S NATURAL ENEMY!
Y... YUGI...
PA
HEY, DON'T WORRY! TAKE A LOOK AT YUGI'S EYES!

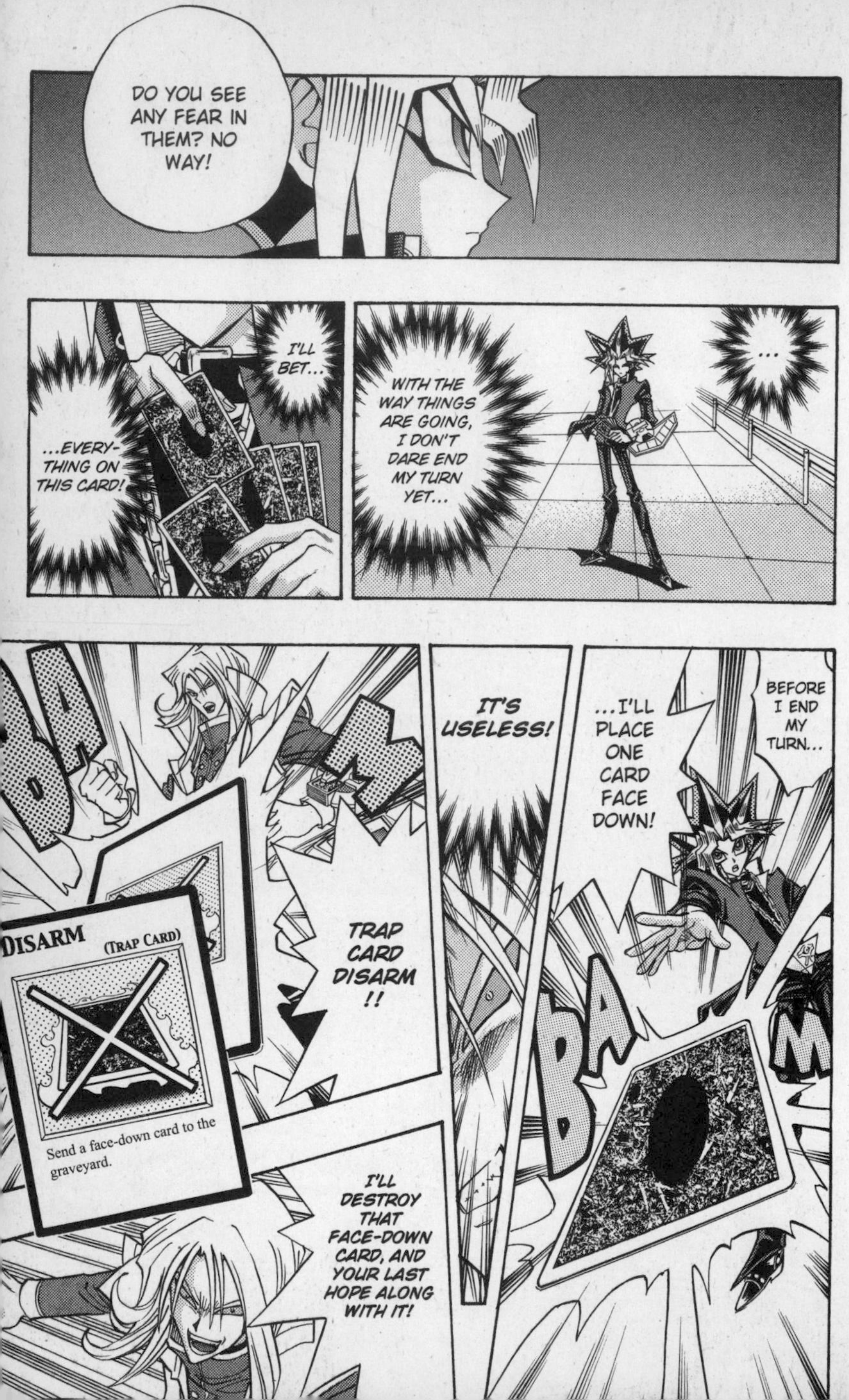
DO YOU SEE ANY FEAR IN THEM? NO WAY!
...
WITH THE WAY THINGS ARE GOING, I DON'T DARE END MY TURN YET...
I'LL BET...
...EVERYTHING ON THIS CARD!
BEFORE I END MY TURN...
...I'LL PLACE ONE CARD FACE DOWN!
BAM
IT'S USELESS!
BAM
DISARM (TRAP CARD)
Send a face-down card to the graveyard.
TRAP CARD DISARM !!
I'LL DESTROY THAT FACE-DOWN CARD, AND YOUR LAST HOPE ALONG WITH IT!

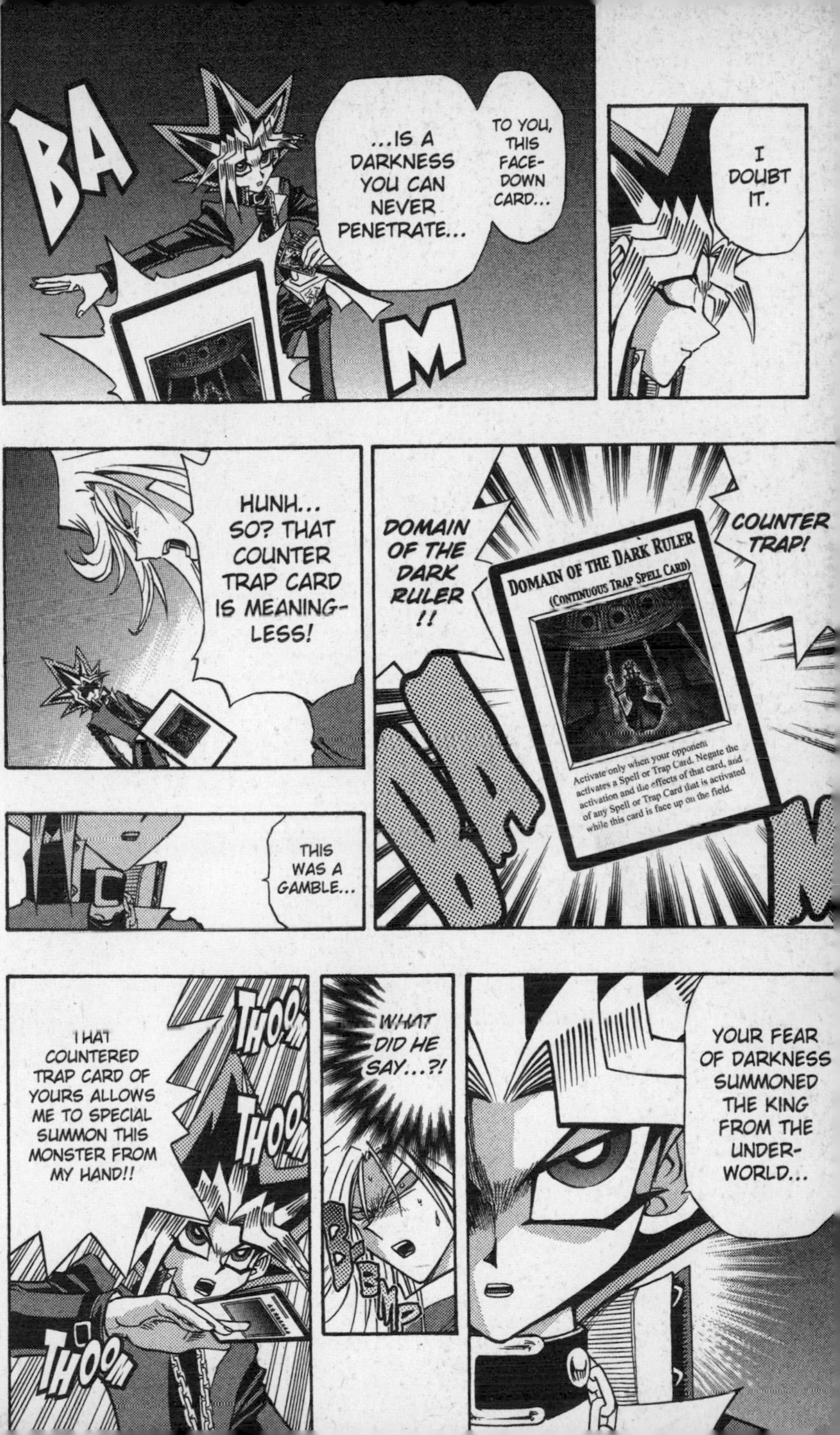
I DOUBT IT.
TO YOU, THIS FACE-DOWN CARD...
...IS A DARKNESS YOU CAN NEVER PENETRATE...
BA
M
COUNTER TRAP!
DOMAIN OF THE DARK RULER!!
DOMAIN OF THE DARK RULER
(CONTINUOUS TRAP SPELL CARD)
Activate only when your opponent activates a Spell or Trap Card. Negate the activation and the effects of that card, and of any Spell or Trap Card that is activated while this card is face up on the field.
BA
M
HUNH... SO? THAT COUNTER TRAP CARD IS MEANING-LESS!
THIS WAS A GAMBLE...
YOUR FEAR OF DARKNESS SUMMONED THE KING FROM THE UNDER-WORLD...
WHAT DID HE SAY...?!
THAT COUNTERED TRAP CARD OF YOURS ALLOWS ME TO SPECIAL SUMMON THIS MONSTER FROM MY HAND!!
THOOM
THOOM
THOOM

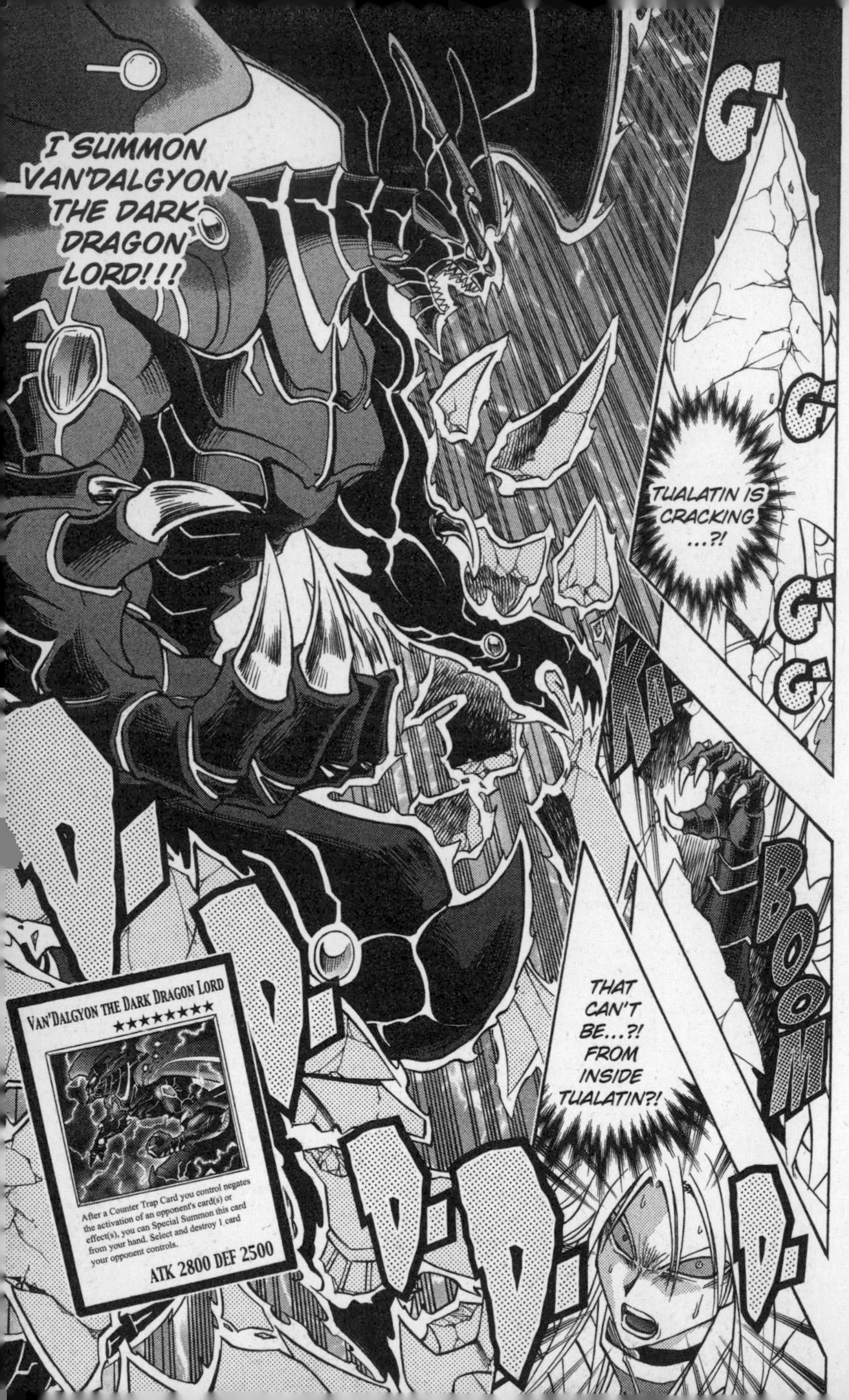

G
G
TUALATIN IS CRACKING ...?!
G
G
KA-
BOOM
THAT CAN'T BE...?! FROM INSIDE TUALATIN?!
I SUMMON VAN'DALGYON THE DARK DRAGON LORD!!!
VAN'DALGYON THE DARK DRAGON LORD
★★★★★★★★
After a Counter Trap Card you control negates the activation of an opponent's card(s) or effect(s), you can Special Summon this card from your hand. Select and destroy 1 card your opponent controls.
ATK 2800 DEF 2500

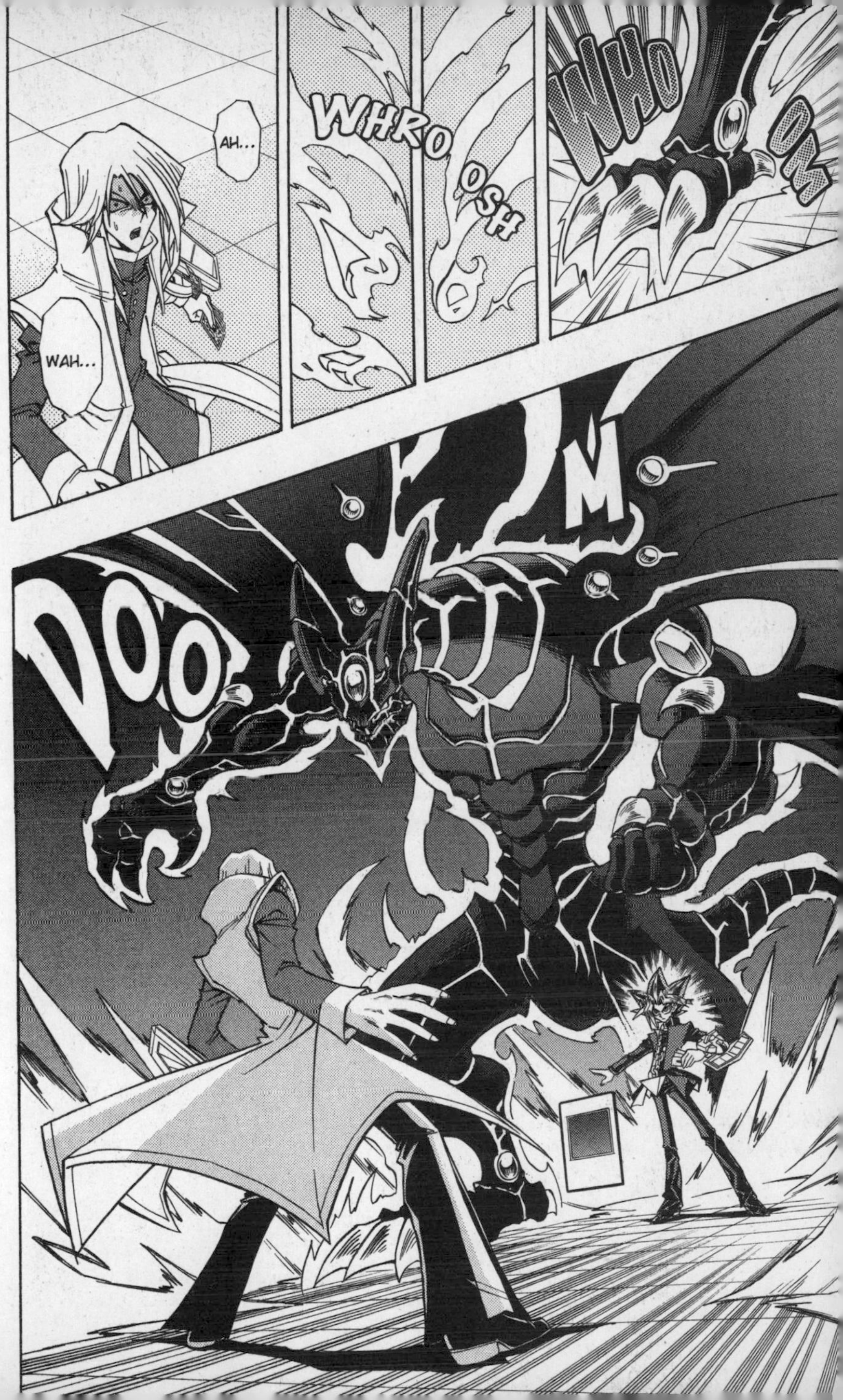
WHHO OM
WHRO OSH
AH...
WAH...
DOO M

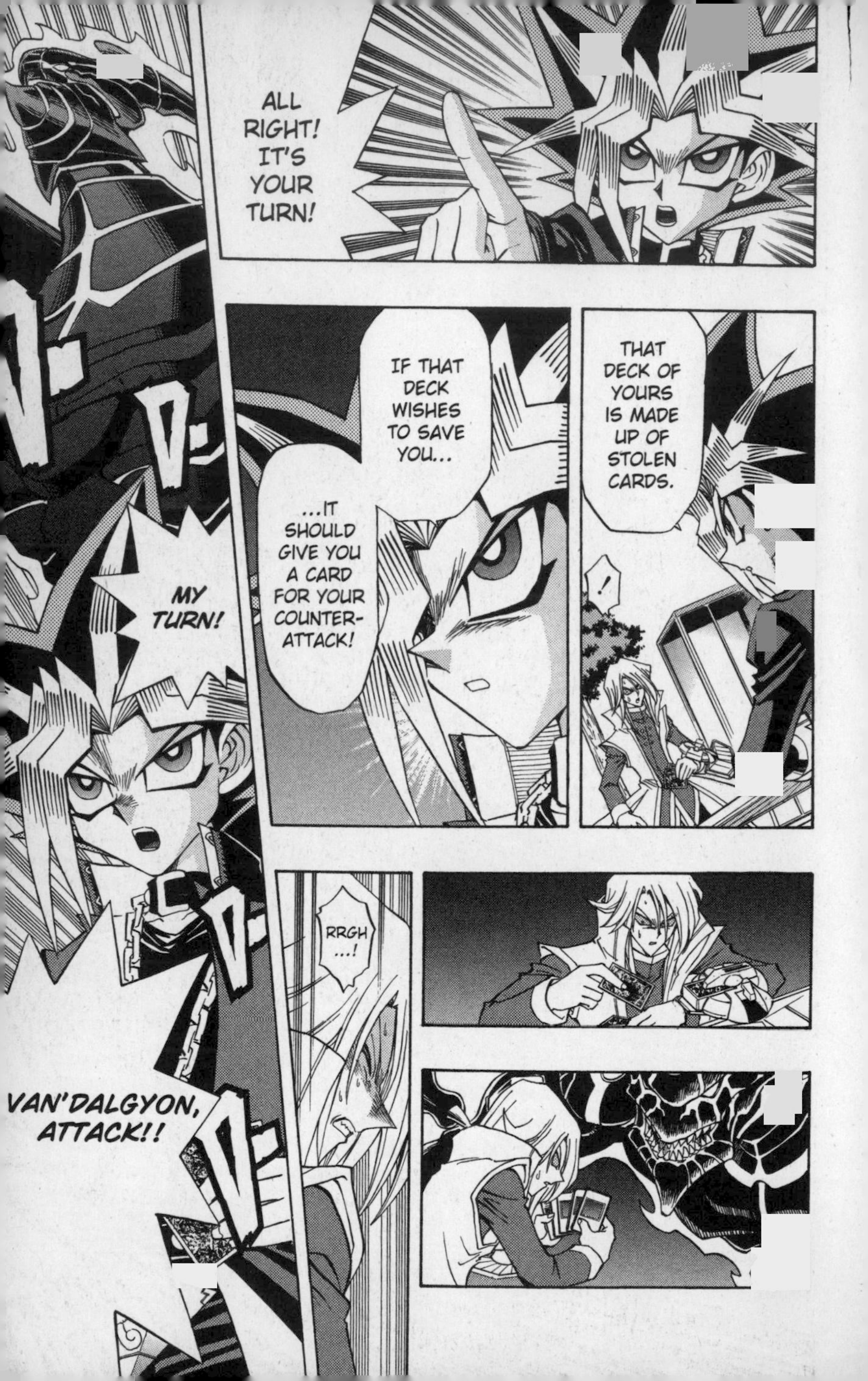
ALL RIGHT! IT'S YOUR TURN!
THAT DECK OF YOURS IS MADE UP OF STOLEN CARDS.
!
IF THAT DECK WISHES TO SAVE YOU...
...IT SHOULD GIVE YOU A CARD FOR YOUR COUNTER-ATTACK!
RRGH...!
MY TURN!
VAN'DALGYON, ATTACK!!

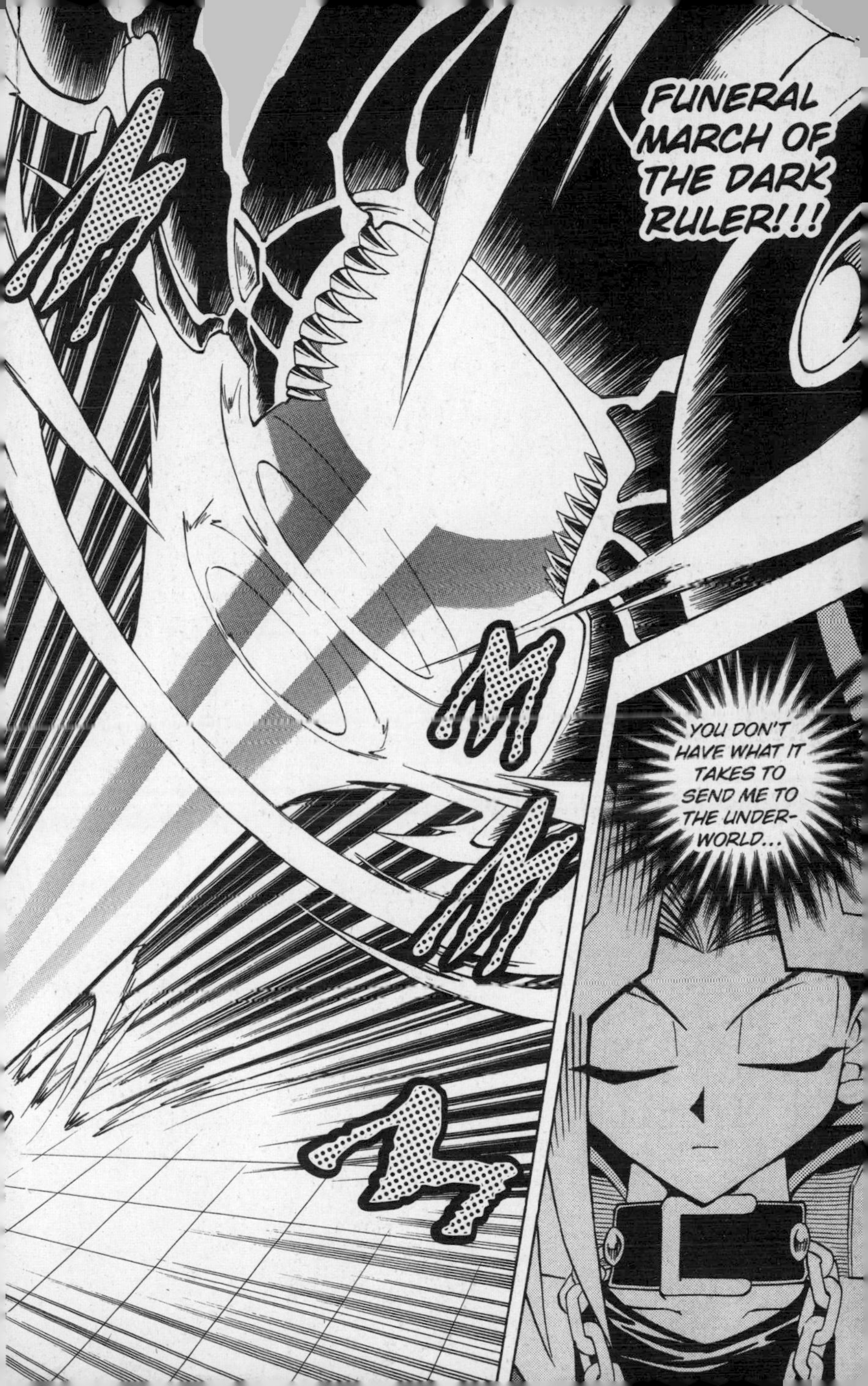
FUNERAL MARCH OF THE DARK RULER!!!
YOU DON'T HAVE WHAT IT TAKES TO SEND ME TO THE UNDER-WORLD...

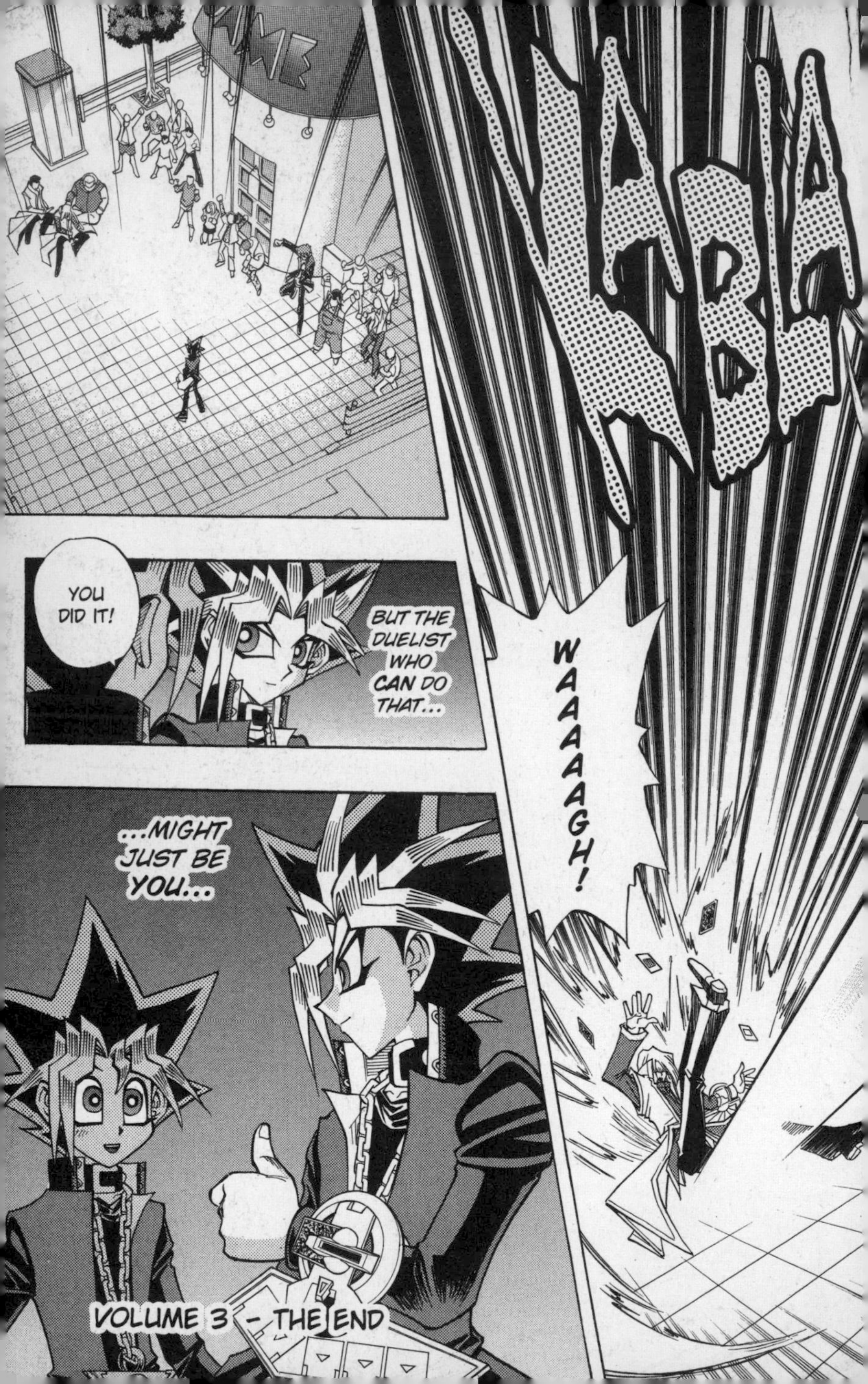

WAAAAAAGH!
YOU DID IT!
BUT THE DUELIST WHO CAN DO THAT...
...MIGHT JUST BE YOU...
VOLUME 3 - THE END

MASTER OF THE CARDS

Yu-Gi-Oh! R is an original story that takes place after *Yu-Gi-Oh!: Duelist* but before *Yu-Gi-Oh!: Millennium World*. It features many new cards never seen before in the manga or anime. As with all original *Yu-Gi-Oh!* cards, names can differ slightly between the Japanese and English versions, so we're showing you both for reference. Plus, we show you the card even if the card itself doesn't show up in the manga but the monster or trap does! And some cards you may have already seen in the original *Yu-Gi-Oh!*, but we still note them the first time they appear in this volume anyway!

EVERY CARD IN THIS VOLUME

First Appearance in This Volume	Japanese Card Name	English Card Name <<!>> = Not yet available in the TCG.
p.8	*Assault Lion* アサルト・リオン	Assault Lion <<!>>
p.13	*Busô Tensei* 武装転生	Armament Reincarnation <<!>>
p.14	*Mirror Barrier* ミラーバリア	Mirror Barrier <<!>>
p.14	*Spirit Slayer* スピリット・スレイヤー	Spirit Slayer <<!>>
p.14	*Jiai no Amulet* 慈愛のアミュレット	Amulet of Affection <<!>>
p.15	*Neon Laser Blaster* ネオンレーザーブラスター	Neon Laser Blaster <<!>>
p.15	*Luminate Armor* ラミネート・アーマー	Laminate Armor <<!>>
p.15	*Tenshi no Hodokoshi* 天使の施し	Graceful Charity
p.16	*Shubi Fûji* 守備封じ	Stop Defense
p.17	*Power Connection* パワーコネクション	Power Connection <<!>>
p.31	*Wyvern no Senshi* ワイバーンの戦士	Alligator's Sword <<!>>

p.31	*Little-Winguard* リトル・ウィンガード	Little-Winguard
p.33	*Kyûshutsugeki* 救出劇	Dramatic Rescue
p.34	*Puppet Pawn* パペット・クィーン	Puppet Pawn <<!>>
p.36	*Blue on Blue* ブルー・オン・ブルー	Blue on Blue <<!>>
p.38	*Senjô no Sangeki* 戦場の惨劇	Battlefield Tragedy <<!>>
p.39	*Promotion* プロモーション	Promotion <<!>>
p.39	*Puppet Queen* パペット・クィーン	Puppet Queen <<!>>
p.41	*Tetsu no Kishi Gear Fried* 鉄の騎士ギア・フリード	Gearfried the Iron Knight
p.42	*Shingari no Sentô* しんがりの戦闘	Rear-Guard Action <<!>>
p.45	*Puppet Rook* パペット・ルーク	Puppet Rook <<!>>
p.48	*Madôkishi Giltia* 魔導騎士ギルティア	Giltia the D. Knight
p.61	*Puppet King* パペット・キング	Puppet King
p.62	*Gilti-Gearfried* ギルティギア・フリード	Gilti-Gearfried the Magical Steel Knight
p.63	*Inochi no Tsuna* 命の綱	Rope of Life
p.65	*Extra Boost* エクストラ・ブースト	Extra Boost <<!>>
p.68	*Rengeki* 蓮撃	Repeating Attack <<!>>
p.112	*Toy Soldier* トイ・ソルジャー	Toy Soldier <<!>>
p.113	*Eva Abductor* イーバ・アブダクター	Eva Abductor <<!>>
p.115	*Suna no Toride* 砂の砦	Sand Fortress <<!>>

p.117	*Silent Swordsman Level 0* サイレント・ソードマンLV0	Silent Swordsman LV3
p.118	*Zeta Reticulant* ゼータ・レティキュラント	Zeta Reticulant
p.120	*Turn Jump (Toki no Hiyaku)* 時の飛躍	Turn Jump <<!>>
p.121	*Silent Swordsman LV3* サイレント・ソードマンLV3	Silent Swordsman LV5
p.121	*Akûkanbusshitsu Tensô Sôchi* 亜空間物質転送装置	Interdimensional Matter Transporter
p.123	*Cosmic Space* コスミック・スペース	Cosmic Space <<!>>
p.130	*Toy Magician* トイ・マジシャン	Toy Magician
p.131	*Lyra the Giver* リラ・ザ・ギバー	Lyra the Giver <<!>>
p.132	*Toy Box* トイ・ボックス	Toy Box <<!>>
p.135	*Yûgô* 融合	Polymerization
p.137	*Yamikure no Madôshi (Dark Red Enchanter)* 闇紅れの魔導師	Dark Red Enchanter
p.140	*Greed Quasar* グリード・クエーサー	Greed Quasar
p.155	*Strike Back* ストライク・バック	Strike Back <<!>>
p.157	*Eva Epsilon* イーバ・イプシロン	Eva Epsilon <<!>>
p.162	*Kanshakudama* 癇癪玉	Fit of Rage <<!>>
p.169	*The Devils Avatar*	The Wicked Avatar
p.173	*The Sun of God Dragon*	The Sun Dragon Ra
p.173	*The God of Obelisk*	The God of the Obelisk

p.173	*Saint Dragon—The God of Osiris*	Slifer the Sky Dragon
p.185	*Tellus* テルス	Tellus the Little Angel <<!>>
p.186	*Kokukenjû Bau* 黒犬獣バウ	Bau the Black Dog Beast <<!>>
p.186	*Tellus no Hane* テルスの羽	Tellus's Wing <<!>>
p.187	*Krepaal* クレパール	Krepaal <<!>>
p.188	*Kôgeki no Muryokuka* 攻撃の無力化	Negate Attack
p.191	*Henkô no Prism* 偏光プリズム	Polarizing Prism
p.194	*Meifu nisshuke Kaidan* 冥府につづく階段	Stairway to the Underworld <<!>>
p.194	*Meifu no Shisha Gorz* 冥府の使者ゴーズ	Gorz the Emissary of Darkness
p.194	*Meifu no Shisha Kaien* 冥府の使者カイエン	Kaien the Emissary of Darkness <<!>>
p.195	*Bunsan Prism* 分散プリズム	Refracting Prism <<!>>
p.197	*Tualatin* デュアラティン	Tualatin
p.199	*Disarm* ディスアーム	Disarm <<!>> (NOTE: This manga card has different effects from the actual "Disarm" game card)
p.200	*Meiô no Ma* 冥王の間	Domain of the Dark Ruler <<!>>
p.201	*Meiôryû Van'Dalgyon* 冥王竜ヴァンダルギオン	Van'Dalgyon the Dark Dragon Lord <<!>>

IN THE NEXT VOLUME...

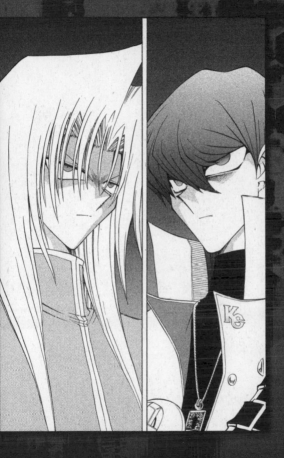

It's a battle for the heart of KaibaCorp—and the soul of Anzu! Gekko and Yugi fight against Richie and his gunslinger deck, while deeper within the building, Kaiba faces Yako—and Yako's evil gods! Will gods or dragons reign supreme? And will anyone be able to stop the "R.A. Project" as the spectre of Pegasus is summoned at last...?

COMING APRIL 2010!

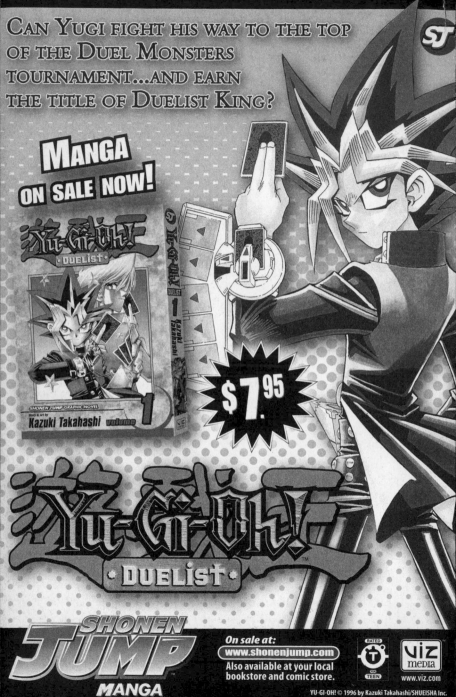

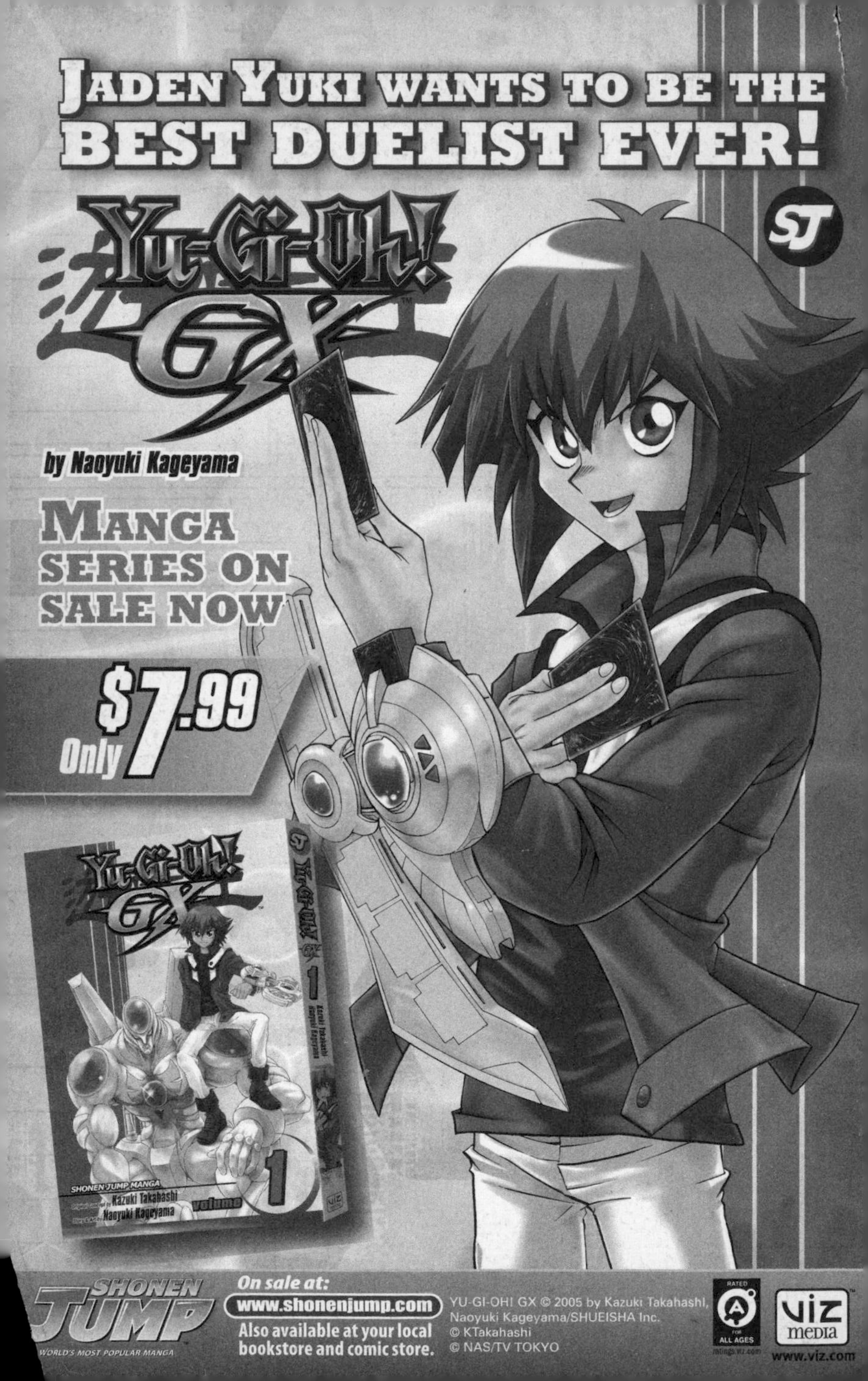
JADEN YUKI WANTS TO BE THE
BEST DUELIST EVER!
SJ
YU-GI-OH! GX™
by Naoyuki Kageyama
MANGA
SERIES ON
SALE NOW
Only $7.99
YU-GI-OH! GX
SHONEN JUMP MANGA
Kazuki Takahashi
Naoyuki Kageyama
volume 1
SHONEN JUMP
WORLD'S MOST POPULAR MANGA
On sale at:
www.shonenjump.com
Also available at your local bookstore and comic store.
YU-GI-OH! GX © 2005 by Kazuki Takahashi, Naoyuki Kageyama/SHUEISHA Inc.
© KTakahashi
© NAS/TV TOKYO
RATED A FOR ALL AGES
ratings.viz.com
VIZ media
www.viz.com

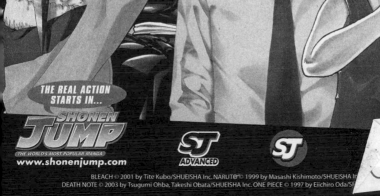

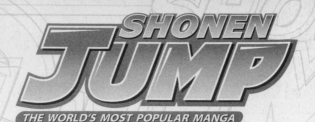
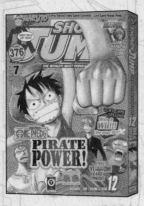
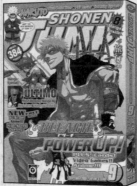
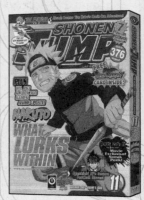

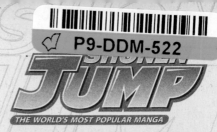

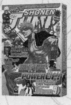